In the Name of God,

THE BIBLE: AN ISLAMIC PERSPECTIVE

MOSES

Jay R. Crook, Ph.D.

ABC International Group

Library of Congress Cataloging in Publication Data

Bibliographical references.

1. The Bible: An Islamic Perspective: Moses
I. Author. II. Title.
BP137.T331997 297'.1228 77-25941
ISBN 1-56744-742-2

Published by
ABC International Group

Distributed by
KAZI Publications, Inc.
3023 West Belmont Avenue
Chicago, IL 60618
(T) 773-267-7001; (F) 773-267-7002
email: info@kazi.org online: www.kazi.org

To
Dr. Sayyid Ja'far Shahidi,
Professor of Persian Literature
at Tehran University,
who set me on this journey into the ancient world
and without whose advice, counsel, wisdom, and knowledge
I should have lost my way;
and to
Dr. Laleh Bakhtiar
whose support and encouragement
enabled me to complete this journey
many long years after I had embarked upon it.

THE BIBLE: AN ISLAMIC PERSPECTIVE

Introduction to the Old Testament: Foreword to the Old Testament, Islamic Setting, Judaeo-Christian Literature in Hejaz at the Time of the Prophet, Origin of the Jews of Hejaz, Stories in the Quran, Oral Literature, Stories in Surabadi's *Commentary*, From Canaan to Palestine, the Bible, the Old Testament Text and Canon, Higher and Lower Criticism, Non-Canonical Writings, Other Sources; Maps, Glossary, Bibliographies (Coded and Alphabetical), Index.

From the Creation to the Flood: The Creation, the Mesopotamian *Genesis*, Adam and Eve, the Garden of Eden, the Fall, Cain and Abel, Enoch-Idris, Harut and Marut, Noah, the Flood, Noah's Son; Glossary, Coded Bibliography, Index.

Abraham: Abraham, the Idols and the Fire, Sarah, Isaac, Ishmael, the Sacrifice, Moriah, Lot, Sodom and Gomorrah, Nimrod, Hud, Saleh; Maps, Glossary, Coded Bibliography, Index.

Jacob and Joseph: Jacob and Esau, Jacob's Sons, Tribe of Benjamin, Joseph in Canaan and Egypt, Zulaykha, Potiphar, the Famine. Joseph and Jacob reunited, *Genesis* Afterword; Maps, Glossary, Coded Bibliography, Index.

Moses: Moses, Aaron, Pharaoh, Haman, the Tower of Babel, Esther, Jethro, the Theophany and Commission, the Mountain of God, the Kenite Hypothesis, the Plagues, the Exodus, the Ten Commandments, the Golden Calf, Al-Samiri, the Journey, Korah, Balaam, Joshua; Maps, Glossary, Coded Bibliography, Index.

From Judges to Monarchy: Job, Samson, Samuel, Saul, the Philistines, the Ark of the Covenant, the Rise of David, Goliath; Map, Glossary, Coded Bibliography, Index.

David and Solomon: The Rise of David, Goliath, David the King, the Psalms, Bathsheba, Solomon, the Temple and Palace, Solomon's Carpet, his Wisdom, the Ants, his Sedition, the Queen of Sheba, Asaph, Solomon's Death; Map, Glossary, Coded Bibliography, Index.

From Monarchy to Hellenism: Elijah, Jonah, Ezra, Nebuchadnezzar, Ezekiel, Habakkuk, Dhul-Qarnayn, Alexander the Great, Gog and Magog, Luqman, Afterword to the Old Testament, Glossary, Coded Bibliography, Index.

Introduction to the New Testament: Foreword to the New Testament, the Islamic Setting, Hejaz at the Rise of Islam, the Stories in the Quran and in Surabadi's *Commentary*, Oral Tradition, Palestine in New Testament Times, Societal Factions, New Testament Text and Canon, Extra-Biblical Writings, Gospel of Barnabas; Maps, Glossary, Bibliographies (Coded and Alphabetical), Index.

Jesus: Jesus, Son of God or Prophet? Biblical Life of Jesus, Titles, the Trinity, Mariolatry, Mary, Zechariah, John the Baptist, Birth and Infancy of Jesus, Mary's Scandal, Miracle Stories, Mary Magdalene, the Passion and Disappearance of Jesus, the Second Coming, the Paraclete, Millenarianism and Armageddon; Maps, Glossary, Coded Bibliography, Index.

Paul and Early Christianity: Paul in Christianity and Islam, Conversion, Stoning of Stephen, Paul and the Law, Circumcision, Immaculate Conception, Paul and the Apostles (Peter, James, John, and Barnabas), Paul's Death and Legacy, Doctrinal Disputes; Companions of the Cave, Companions of the Inscription, Barsisa, Companions of the Ditch, St. George, Afterword to the Bible; Map, Glossary, Coded Bibliography, Index.

Armageddon: The Second Coming, the Paraclete, Millenarianism and Armageddon (from *Jesus* above, published separately); Glossary, Coded Bibliography, Index.

TABLE OF CONTENTS

FOREWORD vii
ABBREVIATIONS AND SYMBOLS xiii
THE STORIES:
MOSES 1
A. Introductory Remarks 1
A Biblical Life of Moses 5
Who Was Moses? 13
The Levites 14
Moses' Name 16
Moses an Egyptian? 17
B. Pharaoh and Haman 21
The Tower of Babel 24
Pharaoh's Oppression of the Israelites 26
Haman, Esther, and Amun 31
C. The Birth and Infancy of Moses 38
D. The Flight to Midian 51
The Staff of Moses 62
Is Jethro Shu'ayb? 64
Midian and Mount Seir 66
The Tale of Sinuhe 68
E. The Revelation and the Commission 70
The First Theophany 74
The Mountain of God 76
The Kenite Hypothesis 82
The Staff 86
The White Hand 89
F. Moses and Pharaoh 92
The "Second" Theophany 94
The Ten Plagues 98
G. The Exodus 105
The Census 108
Crossing the Sea 113
H. In the Wilderness 121
The Twelve Springs 126
Manna 131

I. The Tables of Moses and the Golden Calf 134
The Yahwist's Account 138
The Elohist's Account 142
The Decalogue 144
The Seventy Elders 146
Another Theophany 148
The Golden Calf 150
Micah's golden Calf 158
Al-Samiri 167
J. Korah 177
K. The Israelites and the Cow 183
L. The Journey of Moses 188
M. Balaam 204
N. The Death of Aaron 215
O. The Death of Moses 219
Joshua 220

GLOSSARY 227
BIBLIOGRAPHY (CODED) 231
INDEX 237

Map: Routes of Exodus and Sites of the Holy Mountains 125
Map: Places Mentioned in the *Journey of Moses* 194

FOREWORD

This volume, the fifth in *The Bible: An Islamic Perspective* series, contains the complete text of Section I of Part Three, *The Era of Moses*, in the one-volume edition of *The Old Testament: An Islamic Perspective.* A special Foreword, Glossary, Coded Bibliography, and Index are included for each volume. The complete Glossary and the two Bibliographies (Coded and Alphabetical) for the one-volume Old Testament edition are included in *Introduction to the Old Testament*, the first of the eight volumes about the Old Testament and its contents. Together they contain the entire text of the one-volume edition.

The first volume, *Introduction to the Old Testament*, provides the reader with a survey of the literary, textual, and historical background for the examinations found in the subsequent seven volumes discussing the individual Biblical stories of the Old Testament prophets in detail. This is too extensive to be repeated here. However, because of the many references to them in our text, two points will be briefly noted.

The first is the cultural division of the Israelites into two camps, the North and the South. If one draws a line in a westerly direction from the northern end of the Dead Sea to the Mediterranean Sea, he will have drawn a kind of Mason-Dixon line, between the ten Northern tribes (led by the Josephic tribes) and their rivals, the two Southern tribes (led by Judah). Jerusalem lies just south of the line, inside the territory of Judah.

The origins of this rivalry are obscure (traditionally, they begin with the twelve sons of Jacob), but except for the reigns of David and Solomon, the relations between the two groups were more often than not characterized by one-upmanship, acrimony, hostility, and even war. This state of affairs lasted throughout most of the Old Testament era, its effects persisting even into New Testament times. The Northern tribes that formed the kingdom of Israel were eventually dispersed (they are represented today by the small Samaritan community of central Palestine), whilst the Southern kingdom of Judah survived to be ancestor of modern Jewry. The often unedifying squabbles of the two regions infuse much of what the reader will encounter in our study.

The second is the *Documentary Theory*. An understanding of the results of the higher criticism of the Biblical text is crucial to follow some of the arguments in our text.

Following certain textual clues in the Pentateuch (the first of which was the name used for God), over the past two and one-half centuries scholars have discovered different strains of narrative in the

Old Testament historical books. These account for many of the obvious contradictions, conflations, duplications, and textual seams that we shall be pointing out as we discuss the Stories. This discipline has reached the point where in much of the Pentateuch in particular, individual verses can be ascribed to one or another of the proposed sources. Scholars differ in details, but an overwhelming majority now accepts the general proposition. Out of a largely oral tradition, supplemented by some scraps of documentation and records, now irrecoverably lost, the early histories took shape. These are the principal strands thus far identified:

1. The Yahwist History, also called J, composed in the South (Judah) c. 1000 BCE with a Hebron orientation. For J, the name of God was always YHWH. This history underwent a redaction a century later. To distinguish them when necessary, the earlier redactor is referred to as J1; the later, J2. At Jerusalem, J2 endeavored to weave material appealing to the estranged North into his predominately Southern tradition.

2. The Elohist History of Israel, of Northern provenance, (also called E) was written about 700 BCE, perhaps after the fall of the Northern kingdom of Israel. Amid the ruins of the Northern monarchy, E wrote to preserve the Northern version of Israel's history. For E, the central event of Israelite history was the revelation of the Name of God (YHWH) to Moses at Sinai. He only uses YHWH after that moment. Before that, he had used *elohim* to signify God. Slightly later, the *Book of Law*, also of Northern provenance, was produced.

3. J and E were conflated by Southerners into JE, perhaps before the fall of Jerusalem in 586 BCE, perhaps after (in which case the work would have been performed in Babylon, not Palestine).

4. The Deuteronomist, also called D, wrote his history c, 610 BCE after the "discovery" of the *Book of the Law* (thought by many scholars to be the core of the *Deuteronomy*, the fifth book of the Pentateuch. D, of Southern origin in Jerusalem, accepted this as the basis of a vast history. D came to be combined with JE as JED, probably in Babylon in the second half of the 6th century BCE. There is much scholarly dispute about the exact sequence of events.

5. The last major contribution to the present shape of the Pentateuch was made by the Priestly Document (P). It is thought that P also incorporated the *Holiness Code* composed in Babylonia c. 570 BCE. It was probably written c. 500 BCE at Jerusalem, although there are many have differing opinions about this. In any event, the conflation of JED with P pretty much represents the completion of Pentateuch as we have it. This most likely was accomplished in the middle years of the 4th

century BCE, that is, only c. 350 BCE. These final redactions brought the books of *Genesis*, *Exodus*, *Leviticus*, *Numbers*, *Deuteronomy*, *Joshua*, *Judges*, *Samuel*, and *Kings* into a rough approximation of their present form. It will be seen that we are approaching the date of the earliest textual evidence (the Dead Sea Scrolls) and the date of the Egyptian Recension represented in the Greek translation of the *Septuagint* (LXX) of 250-100 BCE with its fragmentary manuscript evidence of the 2nd century BCE.

We are not yet done. There is still another major contributor to the historical books of the Old Testament:

6. He is the Chronicler (Ch). He probably composed his own history recapitulating the history of Israel with a great emphasis on the Temple of Jerusalem and its ritual between 300 and 250 BCE. In the Bible, his work is represented by the *Chronicles 1* and *2, Ezra*, and *Nehemiah.*

We cannot exaggerate the significance of the Documentary Theory or its impact on the world of Biblical scholarship. It has been as devastating to the idea of the Bible's being the literal Word of God as Darwin's Theory of Evolution has been to Creationism in the natural sciences. (We comment upon evolution in *From the Creation to the Flood.*) Few scholars now support the traditional view that Moses composed the Pentateuch under Divine Guidance. Instead, we find a patchwork quilt of pericopes stitched together over a period of some eight centuries for a variety of reasons, theological instruction being only one of them.

For the Muslim, the Documentary Theory validates the Quranic assertion that the Bible is not the pristine Word of God that the Christians and Jews had long claimed it to be. This will be pointed out in the course of our discussion of the individual Stories when appropriate. (The situation with the New Testament is rather different, although the results are similar. In this series, it is discussed in *Introduction to the New Testament.*)

As did much of the Story of Joseph, so too much of the Story of Moses focuses upon Egypt. Mesopotamia has receded into the distant background, except in the "Tower of Babel" and "Journey of Moses" where it comes to the fore again. The story of Moses moves from Egypt to desert regions south of the Dead Sea, and then on to the fringes of Canaan, the Promised Land, which he himself never entered.

Chronology: It is difficult to come by a uniform system of dating for Near Eastern events and rulers: some are "high," others are "low." We have used Laymon (by Gordon B. Duncan) for rulers of Judah and Israel, etc., (pp. 1271-1275), but occasionally other dating systems have crept in. One has only to compare chronologies in Laymon with those of the JB, and Albright's dates in RSV (pp. 1532-1534) which are somewhat earlier—the RSV also gives E.R. Thiele's dates—to get an idea of the extent of the problem. Approximation is the rule; exactitude is rare, especially in the earlier stages of the development of the Israelite nation. We are generally are firmer chronological ground in classical times, but many serious problems of dating remain. When they affect our discussion, they will be pointed out.

Our editorial comments or additions in direct quotations or summaries of the views of others are indicated by brackets: [ ]. Parentheses are used in the usual way. There are occasional references to material in other volumes, but this should not cause the reader any serious difficulty. Any clarifying material added to this edition is inserted between braces: { }. The location of cross-references may be checked by consulting the list of the volumes of the series on p. iv.

Pickthall's admirable work is used as the starting point and the basis for most of the Quranic translations. However, we have made one major change: substituting the English "God" for the Arabic "Allah" to avoid the invidious connotation that Jews, Christians, and Muslims are worshipping different Supreme Beings. We have also made other modifications based upon other versions, such as those of Allamah Yusuf Ali, Maulana Muhammad Ali, the English translation of Maududi, Arberry, and Sale, among others. We must take responsibility for the final wordings in this work. Quranic references are given in the following form: Q. 2:258, indicating that the quotation is the 258th verse of the second surah (chapter) of the Quran.

The (Persian) text of the *Quranic Stories of Surabadi* used in this survey is that prepared by Dr. Yahya Mahdavi and published by Tehran University in AHS1347. The elaborated medieval Islamic stories of the prophets in that volume have been used together with pertinent verses in the Quran for the expanded Islamic component of the comparison with the Biblical versions. The phrase "May the blessings and peace of God be upon him!" uttered following the Prophet's name and similar phrases honoring other Prophets and the Companions are not indicated in our text, but should be uttered by the Muslim reader either aloud or in his heart when they occur.

Italics are used in quotations from the Quran, for names of Biblical books and other writings when they occur in our text, especially where there is likely to be confusion between the name of the writer and his work as, for example: "The disciple Matthew is the putative author of *Matthew*." In Biblical citations, the name or abbreviation for the book is not put in italics when in conjunction with chapter and verse numbers. In translations from Persian, italics usually indicate a phrase or sentence originally in Arabic in the Persian text.

Biblical quotations are designated in the standard fashion, using the abbreviated name of the book, the chapter, colon, and verse or verses. The fourth verse of chapter one of *Genesis* = Gen. 1:4. The abbreviations used to designate the various books of the Bible will be found in the list following this Foreword.

We have used the *Revised Standard Version* of the Holy Bible (RSV) as the basis for Biblical quotations, with one important difference: we have restored the distinction between second-person singular and plural pronouns (with attendant changes in verbs), because we feel strongly that an important distinction is often lost by ignoring this difference. In addition to the RSV and *King James Version* (KJV) , we have consulted other translations of the Bible, principally the scholarly *Jerusalem Bible* (JB), for clarification and interpretation. The chief Biblical commentaries we have used are *The Interpreter's Bible* and *Broadman Bible Commentary* (BC), and we have made much use of Hastings' *Dictionary of the Bible* (DB) and the *Interpreter's Bible Dictionary* (IBD). The *Encyclopædia of Islam* (EI), the *Encyclopædia Judaica* (EJ), and the *Encyclopædia Britannica* (EB) have all been frequently consulted. Sources in the notes are indicated by a code for the sake of brevity. They are listed in the Bibliography alphabetically by code. All of the books we have quoted or cited in preparing this work are listed in the Coded Bibliography. A Glossary of technical and unfamiliar words and names is also appended.

Finally, we remind the reader that the words "an Islamic Perspective" in the title of this book mean just that: *one* of many possible Islamic views of the subject matter. Islam is not a monolithic religion and the views, opinions, and judgments found in this work are those of one Muslim, not of World Islam. Others may agree or disagree with our presentation, in part or in toto. We shall feel our time well spent if we have, for some, illuminated a few dusty corners of comparative religion and stimulated further enquiry.

The responsibility for the opinions expressed of this work and its deficiencies is my own. We would like to express my gratitude to Prof. Sayyid Ja‘far Shahidi for his guidance at the beginning of this project and to Laleh Bakhtiar, Ph.D., of Kazi Publications for her patient encouragement, support, and advice in bringing it to the public.

JRC (Muhammad Nur)
AH 1426/2005 CE

Abbreviations for the Books of the Bible and the Apocrypha

Old Testament	***OT***	***New Testament***	***NT***
Genesis	Gen.	Matthew	Mt.
Exodus	Ex.	Mark	Mk.
Leviticus	Lev.	Luke	Lk.
Numbers	Num.	John	Jn.
Deuteronomy	Deut.	Acts	Acts
Joshua	Josh.	Romans	Rom.
Judges	Jgs.	1 Corinthians	1 Cor.
Ruth	Ruth	2 Corinthians	2 Cor.
1 Samuel	1 Sam.	Galatians	Gal.
2 Samuel	2 Sam.	Ephesians	Eph.
1 Kings	1 K.	Philippians	Ph.
2 Kings	2 K.	Colossians	Col.
1 Chronicles	1 Ch.	1 Thessalonians	1 Th.
2 Chronicles	2 Ch.	2 Thessalonians	1 Th.
Ezra	Ezra	1 Timothy	1 Tim.
Nehemiah	Neh.	2 Timothy	2 Tim.
Esther	Est.	Titus	Titus
Job	Job	Philemon	Phlm.
Psalms	Ps.	Hebrews	Heb.
Proverbs	Prbs.	James	Jas.
Ecclesiastes	Ecc.	1 Peter	1 P.
Song of Solomon	Song	2 Peter	2 P.
Isaiah	Is.	1 John	1 Jn.
Jeremiah	Jer.	2 John	2 Jn.
Lamentations	Lam.	3 John	3 Jn.
Ezekiel	Ezek.	Jude	Jude
Daniel	Dan.	Revelation	Rev.
Hosea	Hos.		
Joel	Joel	***Apocrypha***	***Apo.***
Amos	Amos	1 Esdras	1 Esd.
Obadiah	Ob.	2 Esdras	2 Esd.
Jonah	Jonah	Tobit	Tob.
Micah	Mic.	Judith	Jud.
Nahum	Mic.	*Esther* Additions	EA
Habakkuk	Hab.	Wisdom of Solomon	Wis.
Zephaniah	Zeph.	Ecclesiasticus	Eccs.
Haggai	Hag.	Baruch	Bar.
Zechariah	Zech.	Letter of Jeremiah	JL
Malachi	Mal.	Prayer of Azariah	Azar.
		Susanna	Sus.
		Bel and the Dragon	Bel.
		Prayer of Manasseh	PM
		1 Maccabees	1 Mac.
		2 Maccabees	2 Mac.

Other Abbreviations

Besides the standard conventional and bibliographical abbreviations, a few less familiar ones have also been used in the text:

AH	= Hijri, Lunar
AHS	= Hijri, Solar
Ar.	= Arabic
BCE	= Before Common Era (= BC)
c.	= circa (about, approximately)
CE	= Common Era (= AD)
ch.	= chapter
chs.	= chapters
d.	= died
fl.	= flourished, active
Per.	= Persian
pl.	= plural
Pss.	= Psalms (plural)
rgd.	= reigned
sing.	= singular
v.	= verse
vv.	= verses

MOSES

No single figure in later Israel plays the many roles ascribed to Moses… (Moses, EJ, XII, 388)

A. INTRODUCTORY REMARKS

The most important personality of the Old Testament, the man who shaped Israel, was without doubt Moses. No other leader, no other prophet, no other lawgiver in the Old Testament can even approach the dominating, central position that Moses occupies in Judaism. He is the supreme hero of the Pentateuch, which is in fact the national epic of Israel.[1]

Traditionally, Moses is credited with promulgating, under divine guidance, the Torah containing the sacred Law to the rebellious, fractious Israelites. He gave them a national identity and a sense of oneness that has sustained them—despite their incessant quarreling, divisions, and disaster—to the present day. The Pentateuch is the written record of this transformation, as viewed retrospectively by men trying to preserve and glorify their national identity as God's Chosen People. Moses is the embodiment of this process. The traditional view is that the entire Pentateuch, except perhaps the last verses of *Deuteronomy* narrating his death and burial, is from the hand of Moses. Whilst the results of modern scholarship no longer support this view, insofar as the present text is concerned, authentic traditions of Moses surely stand behind many of the pericopes, and the text preserves some very ancient material indeed, mostly in songs and incantations.[2]

As a prophet, it is asserted, Moses spoke directly with God (without an intermediary as in the case of the Prophet of Islam), and in

---

[1] Moses is mentioned more often in the New Testament than any other Old Testament prophet (Moses, EJ, XII, 402).

[2] The view that Moses actually wrote all or most of the Pentateuch still has its defenders. "Moses had written Genesis out of previously existing documents… His own life and work comprise the subject matter of Exodus, Leviticus, Numbers, and Deuteronomy. He himself wrote these books." (Halley, p. 109) Though that is a popular rather than a scholarly opinion, the view of the Roman Catholic Church was stated in 1906, in a response that warned Catholic exegetes about the Documentary Theory and "required them to maintain the 'substantial' Mosaic authorship of the Pentateuch taken as a whole." In a later letter (1948) however, the Pontifical Biblical Commission took a more lenient view and admitted "a gradual growth of the Mosaic laws and of the historical narratives, a growth due to the social and religious conditions of later times." (JB, p. 7)

one tradition in *Exodus*, even saw Him.[3] He is considered the father of the prophets, even though a distinction is sometimes made between Moses and the others because he was in almost continuous communication with God, whilst other prophets received their revelations through dreams, trances, or in a state of religious ecstasy. He was also Israel's special intercessor, and he successfully interceded with God on several occasions to save Israel from total destruction by an irate Deity after their behavior had earned His wrath. Later Jewish tradition dwelt lovingly on the figure of Moses. It was said that he was born circumcised;[4] he surpassed all creation; indeed, he was half man and half God.[5] He entered Paradise alive;[6] he emitted a powerful light and his corpse never decayed.[7] With Aaron, he presides over the first division of Paradise.[8] As a culmination of this glorification, it was declared that the world had been created for Moses,[9] as it was created for the Prophet Muhammad in some Islamic traditions. Moreover, Moses, according to the 1st-century CE *Assumption of Moses* had been prepared to be Israel's mediator with God even before the foundation of the world![10]

Jewish tradition also depicted Moses as the king of Israel,[11] but the Pentateuch does not support the idea that he had the title or paraphernalia of royalty. Such exaltation would doubtless have been repugnant to the fugitives from the despotic government of royal Pharaonic Egypt. Nonetheless, he was a leader of men, as his ability to convince the people to follow him shows. He was able to rally them when they were marching through the harsh, hot aridity of Sinai and Midian. He overcame much murmuring against him, even open rebellion, as they recalled longingly the "comforts" of Egypt in that brutal landscape. He planned military expeditions and organized his people into a proto-nation. He gave the people laws and a kind of social constitution.

In some fashion, he was the instrument of the introduction of (or rededication to) YHWH-worship among the descendants of Jacob. The problem of Moses and YHWH-worship is perhaps the most discussed and disputed point of religious history to be raised about the

[3] A Muslim, of course, would consider such assertions and claims to be bordering upon blasphemy.
[4] Nathan, p. 23.
[5] LJ, III, 480-481. The assertion of demigodhood would be held blasphemous in Islam.
[6] LJ, V, 96; VI, 161, 162, 166.
[7] LJ, III, 93.
[8] LJ, I, 22.
[9] Moses, EJ, XII, 395.
[10] Moses, EJ, XII, 392.
[11] LJ, III, 153-154, etc.

Pentateuch.[12] However, there can be no question but that Moses is regarded as the traditional codifier of the formal aspect of YHWH-worship for Israel. It was often found necessary in later times to attribute virtually all legal and ritual innovations to Moses, in the same way that in the period of uncontrolled of Islamic religious literature, statements were attributed to the Prophet that he could not possibly have uttered. In Islam, these excesses fortunately brought about the scholarly compendia of Traditions edited by al-Bukhari, Muslim, and others, from which the spurious Traditions were excluded as much as possible.

Moshe Greenberg writes: "No single figure in later Israel plays the many roles ascribed to Moses... The best analogue to Moses in the history of religions, Muhammad, exhibits the very same multiplicity of roles: oracle, political-military leader, cult founder and lawgiver."[13] The parallel between the founder of the Israelite nationhood and the founder of Islam is indeed striking. The difference in the results is also striking. The YHWH-worship that Moses introduced or systematized among the Israelites led, in later interpretations at least, to a national religion with exclusivist tendencies based upon the tradition of being the Chosen of God; sentiments Judaism retains to the present day. Whilst the evidence, even in the Old Testament, is that YHWH-worship was not always a national club—and we hear of much intermarriage and conversion in the pre-Exilic period—during the later monarchy and especially after the Exile (invoking the authority of Moses once again), Judaism developed those features of separateness that still characterize it.

Admittedly, if the ancient Jews had not done so, the Jewish nation would have probably disappeared into the Middle Eastern racial melting pot as so many other nationalities had before and after them. It could be argued that during that period, this exclusivity was necessary so that monotheism would not perish from the earth. But with the rise of later monotheistic creeds such as those of some (non-Pauline) Christian sects and Islam, Judaism—no longer possessing a monopoly of this view of God—has had to rely increasingly upon racial criteria to maintain its cultural existence.[14] Even non-observing Jews often hark back to Moses when defending the Jewish experience.

---

[12] See Section E.

[13] Moses, EJ, XII, 388.

[14] Large-scale conversions to Judaism by non-Semites in later times, especially that of the Khazars in the 8th century CE who are the principal ancestors, many scholars believe, of the East European Jews and their descendants throughout the world, are minimized or disregarded altogether.

On the other hand, Islam, which considers itself the successor religion, or the logical result of Judaism and Christianity, though it espouses a religious Law (the Shari'ah), rejects any qualifications of birth for total admittance to its fold. Belief and deed are all that are required. It was thus in the beginning. The Arab nationalist reaction to this openness embodied by the Umayyads failed, and a multi-national, color-blind Islam in which race and origin should play no part remains the ideal, although compromised by the divisive ideology of nationalism in recent centuries. Only submission to the Will of God and right action are required to be a Muslim. The social and ritual demands of Islam are predicated upon those foundations.

The Quran attests to the importance of Moses in the prophetic history of Islam. Moses is mentioned twice as frequently as any other Biblical figure (136 times to 69 for Abraham, who is the second). The Moses of the Quran is essentially the Moses of the Old Testament, although there is no interest in the occasional outbursts of primitive anger and impatience attributed to him in the Bible. As the Quranic stories are predicated the traditions circulating in the Arabia of the Prophet and are not based directly upon the Bible, they afford us additional views of glimpses of Moses taken from other traditions that had become associated with Moses, especially in the accounts of Moses' journey (Q. 18:60-82) and Haman, the vizier of Pharaoh.[15] There are other differences of detail that will be pointed out and discussed in their appropriate contexts.

References to Moses occur in 34 of the 114 surahs of the Quran. Oddly enough, our basic text, Dr. Mahdavi's edition of the Quranic Stories of Surabadi's Commentary, does not have two of the most important sections, one concerning the Decalogue, the other the Journey of Moses. In view of their importance, we have taken the relative passages from *Tarikh-i Bal'ami* as the basis for our comparison of these stories.[16]

Although most of the principal events of the life of Moses are alluded to in the Quran, they are not in chronological order. It may be useful to give an overview of the Biblical version of the course of Moses' activities for comparison with the Islamic pericopes:

---

[15] See Section B.

[16] *Tarikh-i Bal'ami* (Bal'ami's History) is a Persian translation of the Arabic *Universal History* of Tabari (d. 923 CE). Bal'ami began his version 963 CE; it is one of the earliest examples extant of modern Persian prose and antedates Surabadi (d. 1101 CE) by more than a century.

Of the five "Books of Moses," the first, *Genesis*, tells us nothing of Moses. The era of Moses is recorded in the remaining four books: *Exodus*, *Leviticus*, *Numbers*, and *Deuteronomy*. Of these, *Leviticus* is almost entirely concerned with legal matter and offers practically no biographical material. *Deuteronomy* gives a recapitulation of many of the events recorded in *Exodus* and *Numbers*, as the Deuteronomist understood them, but he offers almost new material except the account of Moses' death in the last chapter (34), which itself is a conflation of material from J, E, and P. Thus, our main sources are to be found in *Exodus* and *Numbers*, though both books also contain large sections of a legal character. Virtually the entire Biblical story of Moses is to be found in those two books.

The material in *Exodus* and *Numbers* is from the same three primary sources, but much of it is in a very confused state. Scholars have proposed various reorganizations of verses in key passages in an endeavor to clarify and straighten out the text.[17] We shall discuss some of these textual problems when they impact upon our study. In order to prepare a foundation for our comparison, we shall need first an outline the Biblical story of Moses as it unfolds in the Pentateuch, starting with *Exodus*:

A BIBLICAL LIFE OF MOSES: Three hundred and twenty years after the death of Joseph, the condition of Jacob's descendants was greatly altered from the honorable state in which they were first held when they their ancestors entered Egypt. Now they were enslaved and impressed into forced labor on the construction projects of a different kind of Pharaoh (Ex. 1:8-22). It was thus when Moses was born in Egypt.

After the remarkable circumstances of his birth,[18] Moses was raised as an Egyptian in Pharaoh's court (Ex. 2:1-10). When he had grown up, he went to see how the Hebrews were faring and while going about, he saw an Egyptian beating a Hebrew. Not seeing anyone around, he killed the Egyptian. The next day, when he tried to intervene in quarrel between two Hebrews, one of them taunted him with the killing of the Egyptian, and Moses knew that his crime had been observed. Fearing retribution from Pharaoh, he fled to Midian (Ex. 2:11-15).[19]

---

[17] For example, one passage in *Exodus*
relating to the second delivery of the Tablets of the Law is reconstructed thus: Ex. 33:1-4a. 17, 12-13. 18-23; 34:6-9; 33: 14-16. (Moses, DB, p. 676.)

[18] See Section C.

[19] See Section D.

There he aided Reuel's (Jethro's)[20] daughters and married one of them, Zipporah.[21] He became a shepherd (Ex. 2:16-22). When Pharaoh died, God appeared to Moses in a burning bush at Horeb and commissioned him to go back to Egypt and lead the Hebrews out of their enslavement (Ex. 3-4:23). During this theophany, God also identified himself to Moses as YHWH, a name by which He had not been previously known.

Moses was awed by the magnitude of the task and felt inadequate to it. He complained that he was not eloquent, and succeeded in altering the conditions of the assignment to include the help of Aaron. Moses was given the signs of the white hand and the rod. On the way, YHWH tried to kill Moses, but He was foiled by Zipporah. (This extraordinary tradition in Ex. 4:24-26 still defies the efforts of exegetes. Many think it is out of place and should precede the theophany and not follow as it does in its present position in the text).[22]

In Egypt again, after securing the support of the Hebrew elders for their mission, Moses and Aaron went to Pharaoh. He rejected their request to lead the Hebrews out into the desert for a three-day festival. (They secretly planned to use the opportunity of the festival to flee Egypt). In answer, Pharaoh increased their labors (Ex. 4:27-5:21). The fickle Hebrews reproved Moses and Aaron for their interference that had only served to make their bondage more difficult. Moses retired for another theophany in which God ordered him to return to Egypt. He did so, and after the contests of the rod and the serpents, the plagues began. At first unyielding, but when faced with the destruction of his own children, Pharaoh agreed to permit the Hebrews to leave Egypt (Ex. 5:22-13:16).[23]

The Exodus proper began with God Himself going before Moses and his people, with Pharaoh, who had changed his mind, in hot pursuit.[24] The Hebrews crossed the sea that had miraculously parted for them, but when Pharaoh and his army tried to follow them, the waters returned, overwhelming them (Ex. 13:17-14:31).

Although much of the text up to this point is confused, the general sequence of events given above may be extracted from it. From the actual Exodus, that is, the departure from Egypt, the chronicler's task becomes more difficult. Apparently, the Hebrews made for Kadesh-Barnea, a well-watered oasis (scholars believe) on the border of Sinai

---

[20] See below for a discussion of the multiplicity of names for Moses' father-in-law.

[21] Zipporah: *Ṣafūrā* in Persian.

[22] See Section E. (Moses, DB, p. 675.)

[23] See Section F.

[24] See Section G.

and southern Palestine, but which is here called Horeb. On the way they were treated to the miracles of the water turned sweet, they rested at the twelve springs of Elim, and were fed with manna and quail, a gift of divine providence. This was followed by the provision of water at Massah and Meribah by Moses, who struck the rock with his rod (Ex. 15:22-17:7). The Hebrews defeated the Amalekites in a battle during this time, albeit with divine intervention (Ex. 17:8-16).

All of the above took place within a period of about three months from the departure from Egypt (Ex. 19:1). Now at Sinai, Moses went up the sacred mountain and received the Tablets of the Law, and remained there for forty days and nights without food or water (Ex.19, 24, 31:18). The people waiting for him below grew impatient and persuaded Aaron to fashion a golden calf for them, which they proceeded to worship (Ex. 22). When Moses returned, he broke the Tablets of the Law in anger and the people were punished terribly.[25] Moses then climbed up the mountain again and was given a second set of Tablets. After this event, Moses' face was so resplendent that he had to wear a veil (Ex. 33:7-34:35). At this point, the narrative of Moses' acts stops and the remainder of *Exodus* is concerned with Moses' instructions for the making of the Tabernacle in the Wilderness, which later became the prototype for the Temple in Jerusalem.[26] The next book, *Leviticus*, is a book of ceremonial and

[25] See Section H.

[26] The Tabernacle in which the Ark was housed was God's tent, or rather His moveable palace. After YHWH left the mountaintop, He commanded that the Tabernacle be erected as His residence, and the Ark was in some way His throne or footstool, the point of contact between Divinity and man, where Moses would converse with Him and the priests establish ceremonial worship, offering sacrifices to that Presence. As befits a migratory people, these symbols of the Divine Presence—the Ark and the Tabernacle—were portable and could be set up wherever the Israelites made camp. "So they set out from the mount of the Lord three days' journey; and the ark of the covenant of the Lord went before them three days' journey, to seek out a resting place for them. And the cloud of the Lord was over them by day, whenever they set out from the camp. And whenever the ark set out, Moses said, 'Arise, O Lord, and let Thy enemies be scattered; and let them that hate Thee flee before Thee.' And when it rested, he said, 'Return, O Lord, to the ten thousand thousands of Israel.'" (Num. 10:3-36)

From this passage—and it is not unique in the Bible in this respect—we see again that God is not omniscient and had to serve as a scout for the Hebrew horde, preceding them and seeking a place He must locate for them to alight. Primitive stuff indeed! God seems to be an invisible giant with supernatural but limited powers, not the Omnipotent Creator of the Universe. His interests are restricted to the welfare of Israel. There is no indication that any of His activities involve the rest of mankind except insomuch as they are Israel's enemies destined to be conquered, dispossessed, and reduced to servitude; or, occasionally, as a weapon to punish a disobedient or recalcitrant Israel. One gets the sense in much of the early portions of the Old Testament that God was totally preoccupied with the Children of Israel to the neglect of the rest of the world, religious laws, most of which is attributed to God Himself, with virtually no narrative, except to link passages.

When *Numbers* picks up the story of Moses again, two years and two months have elapsed since the Exodus. Now back at Kadesh-Barnea we have another account of manna and quails (Num. 11). Next, there was the sedition of Aaron and Miriam who spoke against Moses because of his Cushite wife. This resulted in God's punishing Miriam with leprosy, but Aaron escaped punishment. Fortunately for Miriam, at Aaron and Moses' request, God relented and changed her punishment to a week's confinement (Num. 12).

Spies were sent to Canaan and they returned with mixed reports of a fair land, but with powerful defenders. After an unauthorized battle with Amalekites in which the Israelites were defeated, many of them were disheartened and wished to return to Egypt. For this rebellion, God condemned them to wander in the wilderness for forty years (Num. 13-14). After the rebellion and the punishment of Korah (Num. 16),[27] and the trial of the twelve rods which asserted the primacy of Aaron (Num. 17:1-11) and, by implication, the later Jerusalem priesthood claiming descent from him, Miriam died and was buried at Kadesh-Barnea (Num. 20:1).

There was still another miracle of water from a rock, this time at Meribah (Num. 20:1-13). Moses sent messengers to the Edomites requesting permission to pass through their lands and thus circle around the Dead Sea to enter Canaan from the east, since they had found that they could not use the more direct northern route blocked by the Amalekites (Num. 20:14-21). The Edomites refused and the Hebrews were forced to make a long detour around their lands. On the way, at Mount Hor, Aaron died and was buried (Num. 20:22-29).[28] The people murmured again and were punished by a plague of serpents that Moses brought under control by setting up a copper serpent upon a staff (Num. 21:4-9).

---

even residing in their midst. This attitude on the part of God would be consonant with that of a tribal god, but His indifference to the welfare of the rest of mankind, not to mention the rest of the universe, is supremely incongruous for a Supreme Being.

Even after the Israelites had become established in Canaan, YHWH continued to reside in His tent. When David wanted to build a permanent Temple to replace the tent in which the Ark had been kept, God is reported to have come to the prophet Nathan in a dream, telling him: "'Go and tell my servant David, "Thus says the Lord: Wouldst thou build me a house to dwell in? I have not dwelt in a house since the day I brought up the people of Israel from Egypt to this day, but I have been moving about in a tent for my dwelling..."'" (2 Sam. 7:5-6)

[27] See Section I.

[28] See Section N.

Having made the detour around the Edomites, the Amorites refused passage to the Hebrews. In the ensuing battle, the Israelites were victorious and slew Sihon and Og (Num. 21:21-26, 32-35). The Israelites camped on the Plains of Moab opposite Jericho. Here are inserted the story and oracles of Balaam the seer which apparently do not belong to the Moses cycle, as Moses is not mentioned in them (Num. 22-24).[29]

There was still another of scene of Israelite apostasy at Beor which was the apparent cause of another plague sent by God (Num. 25). Then God called Moses to a mountain peak east of the Jordan and told him that because of his (Moses') rebellion, he would not be permitted to enter the Promised Land, but would only be allowed to see it. (This prohibition is usually attributed to the incident in which Moses struck the rock for water without first seeking divine permission in Num. 20:10-13.) God also instructed him to nominate Joshua as his successor (Num. 27:12-23).

After Moses returned to his people, there was a battle with the Midianites in which the Israelites were again victorious, and among others, Balaam was slain (Num. 31:1-12). Moses ordered a savage general massacre of the prisoners (the people with whom he had taken refuge when fleeing from Egypt), according to the Priestly text: "Now therefore, kill every male among the little ones, and kill every woman who has known man by lying with him. But all the young girls who have not known man by lying with him, keep alive for yourselves." (Num. 31:17-18)

The Reubenites and the Gadites asked for and received permission from Moses to settle east of the Jordan provided they continued to aid in the conquest on the other side of the Jordan (Num. 32). The biographical information in *Numbers* closes leaving Moses on the Plains of Moab opposite Jericho (Num. 33:50). To this, *Deuteronomy* adds the circumstances of the death and burial of Moses (Deut. 34:1-8).

There is no statement in the Pentateuch itself stating that Moses authored the five books which comprise it, although there are references to his writing of the Law.[30] The Quran confirms the gift of the Torah to Moses, as do Biblical tradition and the later writings in the Bible itself. However, the present Torah, after centuries of redaction and editing—as modern scholarship has shown—cannot be said to be the Law as Moses

[29] See Section L.

[30] "And Moses wrote this law, and gave it to the priests of the sons of Levi..." (Deut. 31:9) "When Moses had finished writing the words of this law in a book, to the very end..." (Deut. 31:24)

received it, as is pointed out in the Quran. Behind the Pentateuch we possess, the Torah of Moses undoubtedly lies, but most of the laws incorporated into the present text are demonstrably the product of much later times.[31]

There are many problems (other than the authorship of the Pentateuch) concerned with the above summary that broadly outlines most of what we know of the public life of Moses. The text in both *Exodus* and *Numbers* is extraordinarily confused and difficult, and we again find instances of the same kind of duplication we found in *Genesis*,[32] There are many ancient traditions inserted into the narrative.[33] In addition, the Balaam stories do not seem to belong to the story of Moses at all, but were included in *Numbers* by later editors finding their present positioning suitable.

Despite detailed itineraries such as that to be found in Num. 33:1-49, and the summary in the first three chapters of *Deuteronomy*, there is no agreement among scholars about the route of the Exodus and the wanderings of the Israelites in the deserts east of Egypt and south of Canaan. There are many unresolved questions:

Is Sinai/Horeb to be identified with Kadesh? Are Kadesh and Sinai/Horeb located east or west of the Aqabah depression? If Kadesh is to be identified with a site some 50 miles southwest of Beersheba, was that the original goal of the Israelites? Were the forty years of wandering really a settlement of the tribes in this region? Did the twelve tribes travel as a group, or were only the Josephic tribes (Ephraim and Manasseh) involved in the Exodus? Was YHWH already known to the Hebrews as the Yahwist seems to imply, or did He reveal Himself to Moses for the first time as the Elohist and Priestly collections state? If the latter is the case, does this account in fact conceal a conversion of Moses to a god already worshipped under the name YHWH by the Kenites into whom he had married? Is there any evidence of the name YHWH before the time of Moses?

At the appropriate places in our investigation of the sources of the Quranic stories of Surabadi's Commentary, we shall attempt to address these questions, but it should be observed that the formulation of such questions is viewed with disquiet by some Jewish and Christian

---

[31] For a discussion of the probable contents of the original Torah, see Silver, especially chapters 7 and 13.

[32] E.g., the water from the rock, told twice (Ex. 17:1-7 and Num. 20:2-13); the theophanies in Ex. 3-4 and 5-6.

[33] Zipporah uses a *flint* to circumcise her son, Ex. 4:25; the sympathetic magic of the copper serpent, Num. 21:4-9.

scholars. There is a tendency to accept the admittedly often tendentious accounts contained in the Bible as *prima facie* evidence in themselves, against any other interpretations which might give primacy in some theological matters to peoples other than the Hebrews, or permit interpretations substantially different from the received ones.

Buber, for example in his book *Moses*, an illuminating work in many respects, is essentially an apologist in the main questions. He rejects the possibility of any connection between the monotheism of Moses and that of Akhenaton, the Kenite theory, or any other proposition that would suggest that YHWH was not the monopoly of Moses and ancient Israel.[34] Buber may be quite right, but arguing from a text which clearly bears evidence of substantial alterations from its original version or sources to conform with later views of Israel's national and religious origins and current needs, is arguing from a flawed premise. It is just as useless as is the Muslim's arguing his case from the Quran with a person who does not believe that the Quran is God's word. The argument from the Quran becomes valid only after a person has accepted Islam.

As Watts says in discussing a similar question: "It is problematic that most scholars in this field are Jewish and Christian theologians who, liberal as they may try to be, have a special interest in giving temporal priority to the Hebrews in all matters of deep spiritual insight."[35] That said, the results of their scholarship are impressive and occasionally marked by reluctance, but rarely outright fraud. Overall, they are to be congratulated for their honesty and integrity in presenting the evidence we are now looking at from an Islamic perspective.

What is the extra-Biblical evidence of the events in *Exodus* and *Numbers*? First, let it be stated that there is not a single reference to any of the events of the story of Moses and the Exodus in any Egyptian inscription or document found thus far. No Egyptian monarch or army is reported to have been lost in the manner depicted in *Exodus*, or any circumstance remotely similar to it.[36] Although Buber would place the Exodus during the reign of Thutmose III (1490-1435 BCE)[37] and thus safely *before* Akhenaton, thereby eliminating any possibility of the dependence of Moses' monotheism upon that of Akhenaton, most scholars date the Exodus to the XIXth Dynasty (1308-1182 BCE), and therefore *after* Akhenaton.[38]

---

[34] See Buber in the Bibliographies.

[35] Watts-Hands, p. 132.

[36] Buber, p. 13

[37] Buber, p. 33.

[38] See Section G.

The first mention of Israel anywhere is on the stele of Mer-neptah (c. 1230 BCE) recording his conquests: "Israel is laid waste, his seed is not; Hurru is become a widow for Egypt!" The word Israel is accompanied by a hieroglyphic determinative indicating that Israel was a people, not a land; that is, that the Israelites had not yet become established in a definite territory with political institutions. This could also mean that there were already Israelite tribes in the Canaan area, probably east of the Jordan, with whom the tribes led by Joshua after the Exodus could have linked up for the Conquest.[39] There is increasing speculation that the Israelites whom Moses led out of Egypt were just the two Josephic tribes. Other tribes already in place on the outskirts of Canaan (such as Reuben and Gad?) were triggered into joining the enterprise that became the Conquest under the military leadership of Joshua. We shall return to this hypothesis later.

The Merneptah stele sheds light on the date of the Conquest, immediately after Moses, in the Biblical time frame. Archeological evidence also supports this period for the arrival of the Israelites in Canaan. Excavations at Bethel, Eglon, Kiriath-sepher (Deber), and Lachish show that these places were violently destroyed during the 13th century BCE, and Lachish more specifically between 1240 and 1230 BCE.[40] Based upon this evidence, the Conquest would appear to have taken place about the middle of the 13th century BCE. Going back a further forty years (the period of the "wandering") we arrive at a date of c. 1290 BCE for the Exodus. If this is approximately correct, then the Pharaoh of the birth story of Moses was Seti I, and the Pharaoh of the Exodus was none other than Rameses II, the Great, (rgd. 1301-1234 BCE), a king who had one of the longest reigns in all history, 67 years. His mummy is preserved in the Egyptian Museum at Cairo and shows no signs of the violent death ascribed to him in the Bible. We believe that the events depicted in *Exodus* and *Numbers* occurred against the

---

[39] ANE, I, p. 231. The relevant text: "Plundered is the Canaan with every evil; Carried off is Ashkelon; seized upon is Gezer; Yanoam is made as that which does not exist; Israel is laid waste, his seed is not; Hurru is become a widow for Egypt!" The stele boasts of the pharaoh's success in an expedition into the region of Canaan. Though it may be a scribal error, the determinative—if correct—would indicate that the Israelites were not yet a settled people, presumably moving about with flocks or trading caravans.

Bietak writes: "But Israel is mentioned along with Ashkelon, Gezer and Yinoam. These names follow a progression from the [Mediterranean] coast to the interior (Yinoam is southwest of the Sea of Galilee). The stele may indicate that the people of Israel were still east of the Jordan [River] at this time." (Manfred Bietak, *Israelites Found in Egypt*, BAR, Vol. 28, No. 5, Sep/Oct 2003, p. 82.)

[40] Israel, DB, p. 432.

background of the Egypt of the New Empire, and more specifically the XIXth Dynasty.[41]

It must also be noted that during this time Canaan was, as it had been for many centuries, under the control of Egypt. Sometimes this meant little more than that Canaan was acknowledged to be in Egypt's sphere of influence, whilst at other times there was stronger physical evidence of Egypt's power in the form of armies and officials. This in itself should not be viewed as a contradiction of the Biblical accounts that show little evidence of Egyptian control once the Hebrews had crossed the sea. So long as Egypt felt that her interests were not threatened, tribal movements and wars continued in outlying territories, and petty monarchs battled with each other over land and towns, but the power of Egypt always loomed in the distant background

We do not hear of Israelites treating with Mesopotamian powers at this stage of Israel's history. Such an act would have brought the wrath of Pharaoh upon their heads instantly. Thus, even though Moses and his Israelites had fled Egypt, all of their wandering and their final settlement were conducted in lands in which Egyptian suzerainty or influence prevailed.

We have no independent Egyptian notice of Moses and the events with which he is associated. While naturally the escape from bondage was of the greatest importance to the Israelites, it seems to have been a very minor defection from the Egyptian point of view. If the fleeing Israelites did inflict a defeat upon a pursuing Egyptian force, it was of such minor importance in the grand scheme of things that the Egyptians did not comment upon it in their records. In any event, the Egyptians, in common with other ancient powers, never dwelt upon their defeats or gave them permanence in inscriptions. Disasters were reinterpreted favorably. The glass was always half full. *Plus ça change, plus c'est la mÍme chose.*

WHO WAS MOSES? We dismiss arguments out of hand that he is a total fiction. With so much smoke, this time there must be a fire, and a large one at that! The Bible states that his (unnamed) father and mother were both from the tribe of Levi (Ex. 2:1). Gray allots this passage to E;[42] others admit the possibility of its belonging to J, as it is part of a conflation of J and E. Moses also had an (older) sister. However, the Priestly Document supplies these omissions, and tells in one place that

---

[41] See Section B for more about the problem of the Pharaoh of the Exodus.

[42] John Gray, writing in the commentary on *Exodus* in Laymon, p. 34.

his father was Amram, his mother Jochebed,[43] and his elder brother was Aaron—no brother is mentioned in the conflated JE story (Ex. 6:20). Miriam, the sister of Moses and Aaron, does not make an appearance by name until the jubilant scene following the Exodus where she is described as "Miriam, the prophetess, the sister of Aaron" (Ex. 15:20). The song attributed to her in the next verse is possibly the oldest poetry to be found in the Bible.[44]

Quite naturally, modern scholarship has challenged this picture of the sibling relationship Aaron, Moses, and Miriam by suggesting that it is a later device to link these important early figures together, especially Aaron and Moses, in the interests of the Levite and Jerusalem priesthood. Miriam's tomb at Kadesh may have at one time been an important cult center, losing its importance after the establishment of the Israelites in Canaan, but the putative relationship—if it indeed is putative—lingered on in text and tradition.

THE LEVITES: The tribe of Levi is another of the great problems of Biblical research. "How the ancient secular tribe became a priestly tribe is completely unknown."[45] Much of the Pentateuch is devoted to a delineation of the rights and duties of the priestly caste, the Levites. Not every Levite was a priest, but—in later times at least—to be a priest one had to be a Levite by descent.[46]

After the Conquest, the Levites were not given any territory, but a number of cities were assigned to them. A few daring scholars have suggested that the Levites were originally settled at Kadesh-Barnea, but were expelled by the Amalekites until the oasis was reconquered for them by Moses.[47] Regardless of the merit of that suggestion, Weber points out that "Levi" has no Hebrew etymology (the etymology given in Gen. 29:34[48] is of course folk etymology) and suggests Minaean

---

[43] The theophoric name of Moses' mother, with YHWH as an element, is undoubtedly anachronistic, as such names are not found until after the work of Moses, (Moses, EJ, XII, 38.)

[44] Albright-Ab to Ez, p. 21.

[45] Levi, DB, p. 578.

[46] "The Levites had a special relationship to the priestly office and the service of the sanctuary. In Deuteronomy, though the position is not entirely clear, priests and Levites seem to be equated (e.g. Deut. 18:1-5). In the Priestly Source, the specifically priestly functions are reserved for those Levites who are descended from Aaron, whereas the remaining Levites are responsible for other forms of service in the sanctuary (Num. 18:1-7)." (Anderson, p. 78.)

[47] Buber, p. 11. Buber rejects this hypothesis, probably correctly.

[48] "Again (Leah) conceived and bore a son, and said, 'Now this time my husband will be joined [Hebrew: *lawah*] to me, because I have borne him three sons'; therefore his name

associations,[49] but de Vaux rejects this theory and notes that the name Levi-El has been found in Mari texts.[50] Weber adds: "All indications point to their [the Levites'] origin in the southern steppe bordering the desert from the oasis of Kadesh to Seir.[51] A rather early tradition treats the Levites, first, as the quite personal following of Moses who enlisted their support against obstinate and disobedient opponents and secured his authority by a massacre among their near kin."[52] Weber also doubts that Moses was in fact a Levite.

Be that as it may, the Levites also seem to have had strong Egyptian associations. More than 250 years after the Exodus, we find that the Levite priest Eli has named his two sons Hophni and Phinehas, names of Egyptian origin.[53] The Bible has played down these Egyptian influences, but they can be detected in the names of many of the principals of the Exodus that have proven to be (or are suspected to be) Egyptian. This should not strike us as unusual. Joseph, we remember, was given an Egyptian name, Zaphenath-paneah (Gen. 41:45), and it is not unusual in the history of the world to see people of one nation, or a segment of them (usually those who consider themselves in some way an elite), adopt the clothes, habits, manners, and names of their conquerors; or—as they see it—their cultural superiors. We see the same process today in which much of the non-European world is clothed in European styles and ordering its daily life according to what is perceived to be the European fashion.[54] In any event, as we proceed we shall see this cultural

---

was called Levi." (Gen. 29:34) The two preceding sons were Reuben and Simeon; her fourth son was Judah.

[49] Weber, p. 170. The Minaeans were an Arabian people, sometimes connected with South Arabia (Yemen) and perhaps preceding the kingdom of Sheba. Other evidence shows them farther north, in north central and western Arabia. (Minaeans, DB, p. 660.)

[50] de Vaux, Vol. II, pp. 358-359. Mari was one of the most ancient cities in the world, founded by Sumerians on the banks of the upper Euphrates River at the beginning of the 3rd millennium BCE. It was destroyed by Hammurabi c. 1697 BCE. Its ruins lying in present-day Syria have yielded the famous Mari archives of more than 20,000 tablets that have been of immense importance in shedding light on the ancient Near East, and especially the age of the patriarchs.

[51] Seir: a mountainous region in modern southwestern Jordan.

[52] Weber, p. 170.

[53] Albright-Stone Age, p. 282.

[54] The term "European" here of course includes "American," as America is culturally European. Perhaps it should be considered a desire to achieve parity with the superior force through some sort of sympathetic magic. The Islamic world is not immune from this social and cultural phenomenon. Few Muslims realize that the necktie (cravat from "Croat") quite possibly originated in the 17th century CE as a stylized cross, used by the Christian Croats to distinguish themselves from the Muslim Turks with whom they were fighting.

emulation again in Israelite history, especially during the violent and bloody era of the Hellenization of the Near East, which is discussed at length in Vol. 2 dealing with the New Testament. {In series, see especially *Introduction to the New Testament* and *Paul.*}

MOSES' NAME: Putting aside the question of the literal truth of the birth story of Moses, there seems to a firm Israelite tradition that Moses grew up at the court of Pharaoh (or more probably, the local court of the representative of Pharaoh at Tanis).[55] Moses was educated as an Egyptian "and Moses was instructed in all the wisdom of the Egyptians" (Acts 7:22). Falling out of favor, Moses fled from Egypt, (an act which, as we shall see, has a close parallel in Egyptian literature).[56] Settled in a new life in the quite different pastoral desert landscape of Midian, Moses experienced a conversion, a religious experience so profound that he either recovered the ancient faith that had lingered in the traditions of his people and which he had half-learned as a child, or was confronted by a totally new realization of God. Whichever the case, he seems to have reacted violently against the way of life he had led amidst the high civilization of Egypt. Yet, there is no evidence that he took the step of changing his name, an act that frequently accompanies conversion, and one that signifies a new spiritual identity and new loyalties. This failure is strange, because he had ever reason to do so, as his name was most probably Egyptian.

Folk etymology, preserved in the text of *Exodus*, tells us that Moses was so called because Pharaoh's daughter "drew him out" of the water, equating "Moses" (*Mushe*) with the Hebrew verb *mashah*, "to draw out" (Ex. 2:10). This is patently absurd, because Pharaoh's daughter, an Egyptian, is credited with giving him a *Hebrew* name! In addition, as is well know, the form *Mushe*, could only mean "he who draws out" (active voice), not "he who is drawn out" (passive voice), as the situation would logically require. Scholars now generally agree that the name Moses is Egyptian in origin and means "child."[57]

Writes the historian Breasted: "It is important to notice that his name, Moses, was Egyptian. It is simply the Egyptian word 'mose' meaning 'child,' and is an abridgment of a fuller, probably theophoric, form of such names as 'Amenmose' meaning 'Amon-a-child' or 'Ptah-mose,' meaning 'Ptah-a-child'... The father of Moses without doubt prefixed to his son's name that of an Egyptian god like Amon or Ptah,

---

[55] See Sections A and B.

[56] See Section D.

[57] The Egyptian form is *mes, mesu.* (Moses, DB, p. 675.)

and his divine name was gradually lost in current usage, till the boy was 'Mose.'"[58] Perhaps it is possible to replace Breasted's suggestion that the theophoric portion of the name simply gradually fell into disuse by the proposition that it was deliberately suppressed, possibly on the authority of Moses himself, and this was his act of name-change. It may be further noted that the supposed Pharaoh of the Exodus himself possessed such a name: Rameses is the Greek form of *Ra-mose*, "Ra-(has given)-a-child.[59] *Mose* (Moses) by itself simply means "child."[60]

MOSES AN EGYPTIAN? Although admitting that an Egyptian name is not proof of Moses' being an Egyptian by race, the founder of psychoanalysis, Sigmund Freud, in the last years of his life constructed an ingenious theory that Moses was an Egyptian by race as well as culture; that he was a follower of the monotheistic Aton worship introduced by Akhenaton (rgd. 1370-1353 BCE). After the restoration of Amun-worship that followed the sad end of Akhenaton's reign, Moses fled the repressions of the restored Amun priesthood and sought to convert a group of Semites living on the eastern borders of Egypt to his religion, the Semites who later mixed with his people became the Israelites. At Kadesh, Moses was martyred (this is based upon a dubious interpretation of a passage in *Hosea* suggested by Sellin) and, of course, the whole series of events is given a psychoanalytic interpretation.[61] The proofs adduced for this theory are rather tenuous considering its larger implications, but nonetheless the suggestion that Moses was an Egyptian deserves more serious consideration than it has heretofore been given.[62]

Oddly enough, there is some evidence, admittedly capable of more than one interpretation, to support this thesis in the Bible itself. Newly arrived in Midian and having just saved Reuel/Jethro's daughters from the loutish shepherds and aided them in watering their flocks, the girls told their father: "'An Egyptian delivered us out of the hand of the shepherds...'" (Ex. 2:19) Assuredly Moses, in his Egyptian clothes and tonsured in the Egyptian fashion, would have appeared as an Egyptian to

---

[58] From *The Dawn of Conscience* by J.H. Breasted (New York: Charles Scribner's Sons, 1934, p. 350, cited by Freud in *Moses and Monotheism*. (Freud, p. 5.)

[59] Josephus seems to recognize the Egyptian origins of the name "Moses," although he gives us a false etymology based on the Greek form of the word (Moses). He says that it comes from *mou*, Egyptian for "water," and *eses*, "saved," thus, "saved from water." Neat, but incorrect. (Moses, EJ, XII, 379.)

[60] Ogden Goelet, *Moses' Egyptian Name*, BR, Vol. XIX, No. 3, June 2003, p. 14.

[61] Freud, esp. Part II.

[62] Such a disruptive, innovative idea is repugnant to most scholars, and especially those who wish to establish and maintain the spiritual precedence of the ancient Hebrews.

them, but the omission of any disclaimer or note of correction, or the establishment of kinship (the Israelites and Midianites were kinfolk) is strange.

There is still something else reported in the Bible that could also be interpreted to support the theory that Moses was an Egyptian, although again it is capable of more than one explanation. In the theophany of the Commission (Ex. 3:1-44:17), one of the principal reasons Moses cites for not being able to undertake God's command to return to Egypt and lead the Israelites out is: "'I am not eloquent, either heretofore or since Thou hast spoken to Thy servant; but I am slow of speech and of tongue.'" (Ex. 4:10) God then told Moses that He would teach him what to say, but Moses still protested, and finally God appointed Aaron to act as Moses' spokesman.

Now we can accept this at face value—that Moses was not facile with words or perhaps had some sort of speech impediment such as a stutter—or we can continue our enquiries into whether something else lies behind this passage. One very reasonable possibility is that Moses knew the language of the Semites (presumably a dialect of Canaanite) imperfectly as he had been raised in Egypt amongst Egyptians, and perhaps had only learned it after his flight to Midian. In this context, it must be remembered that Moses had a double mission. First, he had to convince the Israelites to follow him, and secondly he had to convince Pharaoh to let them go. Since he had been raised at the Egyptian court, he must have know Egyptian quite well, but how well did he know the Semitic language of his own people—if they were indeed his own people? His lack of Hebrew (or Canaanite) could be explained in two ways: raised at court away from his own people he had not been exposed to it, or... he simply was not a Semite to begin with.

There is still another possibility: we can also regard Moses' difficulty with language as a convenient literary device to associate with him his "brother" Aaron, who figured prominently in the later claims of the priesthood.[63]

This problem did not pass unremarked by the ancient Jews. They offered various explanations of Moses' speech defect, some of which have entered Islamic tradition. With respect to this question, we should remember that the highest authority in Islam, the Holy Quran, nowhere states that Moses was an Israelite; simply that he was sent to the Israelites. Because tradition (which, however, should not be dismissed lightly) and the religious predispositions of various groups to support one view, there is no reason why we should not consider another explanation.

---

[63] See Section E.

Because the most famous proponent of this theory was the controversial Freud—even worse, he was not a noted scholar in the "field"—the theory has unfortunately become bound up with the acceptance or rejection of some of his more extravagant theories in other fields, and it is not reviewed without some bias.

That Moses was an Egyptian is, of course, simply a working theory. It resolves some problems in the life of Moses and, of course, creates others. It has little support amongst modern Biblical scholars, although, given their conservatism in such matters, this in itself is no reason to reject the proposition outright. However, the burden of proof is on those who would make Moses an Egyptian, and such proof is not likely to be forthcoming at this late date.[64]

In this regard, we may argue that in many respects Mosaic Law does not correspond to what we know of Egyptian law. This argues for a Semitic provenance for the Mosaic code, the obvious problems created can be considerably reduced when we realize that most of the Law we now have in the Pentateuch was formulated centuries after Moses (see I below). We really do not what the Mosaic Torah contained or would have contained, as the Quran contends.

A direct relationship between Aton-worship and YHWH-worship is usually denied by emphasizing the differences, but there are some striking similarities that suggest some sort of a link, however remote. For example, Freud points out that the central feature of Egyptian religion was the cult of the dead and the belief in the afterlife. This was conspicuously absent from Akhenaton's Aton worship that concentrated only upon this life, an attitude it shared with ancient Judaism.[65]

However, Freud's conclusion that this is a proof of Moses' adherence to the cult of Aton-worship, or at least his being under its influence, can be countered with other equally tenuous explanations. One of these centers around the supposed Asiatic connections of Akhenaton's beautiful wife Nefertiti, who seems to have been the real driving force in the establishment of the monotheistic Aton-cult. As we have noted in other places, the prevailing view in the Fertile Crescent was that the

---

[64] However, many classical writers assumed that Moses was Egyptian by race (Gager, p. 19). Josephus quotes the Egyptian Manetho, who asserted that Moses was a rebellious prince. Manetho says that Moses was a scribe and that his name was originally Egyptian: Tisisthene (*Against Apion*, Josephus, p. 620). Though as quoted by Josephus, the passage does not actually state that Moses was an Egyptian, but this can possibly be inferred from the text. Manetho wrote in the 3rd century BCE. From this distance in time there is no way of knowing upon what traditions, if any, he based his material.

[65] Freud, p. 22.

afterlife was a dreary place for everyone, and was not dependent upon the quality or morality of one's earthly existence. It was assumed that wrongs and transgressions would be redressed by gods on earth in the shape of famines, blights, while good behavior would earn good harvests and many children. For the more thoughtful prophets, righteousness was its own reward and there was no expectation of a further transcendent accounting after death.

While we may we may speculate about the figure of the Egyptian noble fleeing to Midian where he married and adopted his in-laws' religion and way of life, finally returning to Egypt to lead some of the Semitic kinfolk of the Midianites out of Egypt, the degree of Egyptianization reflected in nomenclature is striking when set beside the relative absence of Egyptian influence in Jewish tradition. It would seem that the names were not altered in the general desire to expunge the Egyptian experience from the tribal memory simply because the origins of those names were forgotten in later times. How many English speakers today are aware that James is the Greek form of Jacob or that Jesus is the Greek form of Joshua?

In addition to the name of Moses, we find that the name "Miriam" is also Egyptian; probably a form compounded with *mer*, "love."[66] Aaron, too, is quite possibly of Egyptian origin, although its etymology is still unknown.[67] Thus, we find that the three principal characters of the Moses saga are likely to have borne Egyptian names. Furthermore, their Levite associations as well as their kinship with each other is also placed in a shadow by modern scholarship.

Although Moses appears to have always been highly regarded as the founder of the Hebrew nation and YHWH-worship, his present preeminence seems to date from the days of the declining monarchy (perhaps as an attempt to placate God) when greater emphasis was placed upon legal and ritual institutions, the foundations of which were ascribed to Moses. Before the crises of that era, Moses was more

---

[66] Miriam, EJ, XII, 82. The DB suggests another Egyptian derivation, from "beloved of Amun." Miriam is thought to have been older than her brothers Aaron and Moses. (Miriam, DB, p, 666.) Since all three siblings, if indeed they were siblings, probably have Egyptian names, the question of ethnicity arises again. *Micah* credits all three with leading the deliverance from Egypt: "For I brought you up from the land of Egypt, and redeemed you from the house of bondage; and I sent before you Moses, Aaron, and Miriam." (Mic. 6:4) She died and was buried at Kadesh. She too was denied entry into Canaan by God.

[67] Aaron, DB, p. 1.

important in the North than in the South.[68] With the collapse of the House of David and the transfer of the loyalty formerly given to it to the messianic restoration set in the future, exilic and post-exilic Judaism became even more dependent upon cohesive role of the Law. This, in turn, contributed to the enhancement of the role of Moses in Judaism.

Yet, Moses did not have to be rediscovered. He was too powerful, too potent a figure to be forgotten or dismissed. We can do no better here than to quote the last verses of the Pentateuch as his epitaph: "And there has not arisen a prophet since in Israel like Moses, whom the Lord knew face to face, none like him for all the signs and the wonders which the Lord sent him to do in the land of Egypt, to Pharaoh and to all his servants and to all his land, and for all the mighty power and all the great and terrible deeds which Moses wrought in the sight of all Israel." (Deut. 34:10-12)

B. PHARAOH AND HAMAN

(Haman) said to (Pharaoh): "Where art thou going?"
(Surabadi, p. 296)

Surabadi prefaces his account of the birth of Moses with a legendary history of Pharaoh: Pharaoh's name was originally Walid bin Rayyan (or more commonly Rayyan bin Walid). He lived for 400 years, and claimed to be God.[69] Before he made this claim he was of sound body, but afterwards seventy-two defects appeared in him. It is said that he was originally from Pushanj, a day's journey from Herat.[70] From there, accompanied by Haman, he traveled until he reached Egypt at the season of the melon harvest. Pharaoh and Haman stopped at a melon field and sought food; they were given a load of melons to take to the city to sell. The people bought them, but did not pay, so the pair returned empty-handed.[71]

---

[68] Silver, p. ix.

[69] Other Muslim authorities give different names such as al-Walīd bin Muṣᶜab, Muṣᶜab bin Rayyām, and Qābūs bin Muṣᶜab (the successor of Rayyān bin Walīd?). The Pharaoh at the time of Joseph was said to be Rayyān bin al-Walīd (or D ārim) al-ᶜAmlīqī. Some said that he lived 620 years. According to some, the Pharaoh of the time of Moses was al-Walīd bin Muṣᶜab. That he was supposed to have reigned the longest period of time is consistent with the assumption that Ramses II was the Pharaoh of Moses. (Pharaoh, Hughes, p. 452; Fir'awn, SEI, pp. 107-108.)

[70] This would appear to locate Pharaoh's origins in northwestern Afghanistan, a region familiar to Surabadi. Could this be a local tradition?

[71] Surabadi, pp. 297-298.

Pharaoh said that the people were lazy, so the two men went to the governor and requested work. They were given the Graveyard Gate to guard. Cholera struck and Pharaoh collected a dirham tax on each corpse that was brought out to the graveyard.[72] Thus, he acquired a large sum of money and by means of bribery gained control of the city. When the governor died, Pharaoh seized power.[73]

Next, he told Haman that he wanted to claim that he was God, and Haman advised him to do it little by little. The people at that time believed in the true religion. Haman advised him to prohibit their learned men from teaching; then the religion would gradually weaken and could be replaced. Any one who taught was to have his tongue cut out. Ultimately, the people accepted Pharaoh's claim of divinity.[74]

In this odd tale, Surabadi has introduced a number of elements, none of which—beyond the existence of Pharaoh and Haman—can be found in the Bible or the Quran. The account of the migration from Khorasan may be a very, very remote echo of the invasion by the Hyksos and the establishment of non-Egyptians upon the throne of Lower Egypt, told from an Iranian point of view. Though the bulk of the peoples who comprised the Hyksos were Semitic in origin, there were Indo-European elements among them as personal names used by them attest. However, that interpretation would be more appropriate to the time of Joseph than of Moses.

There is another possible source, even more remote from Moses: the Persian invasion in 525 BCE. (Egyptian historians considered the rulers of the Persian Empire the XXVIIth Egyptian Dynasty.) The first Persian ruler of Egypt, Cambyses (rgd. as Pharaoh 525-522 BCE), had origins in Fars in southern Iran rather than in Khorasan. The pharaohs of Egypt were accorded a kind of divinity, and they were identified with the Sun god.[75] Cambyses is said to have offended the Egyptians in a number of ways and to have ultimately gone mad, at least that is what Herodotus and other ancients tell us. Olmstead discounts such stories, saying they

---

[72] This tax on the dead was actually in the nature of an inheritance tax. Such taxes are attested in the records of Sumeria concerning the middle of the 3rd millennium BCE. "Even death brought no relief from levies and taxes. When a dead man was brought to the cemetery for burial, a number of officials and parasites made it their business to be on hand to relieve the bereaved family of quantities of barley, bread, and beer, and various furnishings." (Kramer-Sumer, p. 48) It would appear that this oppressive and heartless profession is the one Surabadi had envisioned for Pharaoh.

[73] Surabadi, p. 298.

[74] Surabadi, p. 298.

[75] Breasted-Religion, pp. 124-125.

have their origin in attempts to justify the "regime change" led by Darius the Great that occurred after Cambyses' death.[76]

The Bible does not speak of Pharaoh's pretensions of divinity in *Exodus*, but this additional detail is found in the Quran: *And Pharaoh said: O chiefs! I know not that ye have a god other than me*... (Q. 28:38) This is a reference to the divinity that the ancient Egyptians believed by to be inherent in their royalty. The claim was not an innovation by the Pharaoh of Moses, but rather based upon the most ancient traditions: "...(the Egyptians) believed that they were a divine nation, and that they were ruled by kings who were themselves god incarnate; their earliest kings, they asserted, were actually gods, who did not disdain to live upon earth, and to go up and down through it, and to mingle with men."[77] "The basic fact of Egyptian religions was the idea that the king was a god. The later ritual of daily service stresses the point that the priest in front of the god's image acted only as the substitute of the king. In festival rites the king represented the gods of his people with the same authority as he represented his people to the gods."[78]

In discussing the development of this belief, Fairservis writes: "...the gradual development of this concept, of Pharaoh as a god and the development of ceremony for, with, and by this god, is emblematic of the tendency to 'settle in.' The warlike prowess of an individual displayed in the conquering of human enemies seems replaced by the idea that the presence of Pharaoh was the reason for the fertility of the land. Accordingly, Pharaoh was to be worshipped as the 'bringer of good.'"[79] The stability and prosperity of the state of Egypt was based upon the premise of its ruler's assumed divinity and his special relationship with the gods.

Much has been made of the order by Pharaoh quoted in the Quran, given to Haman: *"So kindle for me (a fire), O Haman, to bake the mud; and set up for me a lofty tower in order that I may survey the god of Moses; and lo! I deem him* [Moses] *of the liars."* (Q. 28:38) And in another place: *And Pharaoh said: "O Haman! Build for me a tower that haply I may reach the roads, the roads of the heavens, and may look upon the God of Moses, though verily I think him* [Moses] *a liar." Thus was the evil that he did made fair-seeming unto Pharaoh, and he was barred from the (right) way. The plot of Pharaoh ended but in ruin.* (Q. 40:36-37)

---

[76] Herodotus, Bk. III, pp. 215-219, and elsewhere; Olmstead, p. 89.

[77] Budge-Gods, Vol. 1, p. 3.

[78] Rudolph Anthes, writing in Kramer-Myth, p. 33.

[79] Fairservis, p. 86.

Western scholars cite these as more instances of Quranic "confusion," asserting that the story is derived from the story of the Tower of Babel in *Genesis* and mistakenly intruded into the Islamic Moses traditions.

THE TOWER OF BABEL: In view of its importance to this controversy, let us first quote the Biblical story: "Now the whole earth had one language and few words. And as men migrated from the east, they found a plain in the land of Shinar [Lower Mesopotamia] and settled there. And they said to one another, 'Come, let us make bricks, and burn them thoroughly.' And they had brick for stone, and bitumen for mortar.[80] Then they said, 'Come, let us build ourselves a city, and a tower with its top in the heavens, and let us make a name for ourselves, lest we be scattered abroad upon the face of the whole earth.' (Gen. 11:1-4)

"And the Lord came down to see the city and the tower, which the sons of men had built. And the Lord said, 'Behold, they are one people and they have all one language; and nothing that they propose to do will now be impossible for them. Come, let us go down, and there confuse their language, that they may not understand one another's speech.' So the Lord scattered them abroad from there over the face of all the earth, and they left off building the city. Therefore its name was called Babel, because the Lord confused the language of all the earth; and from there the Lord scattered them abroad over the face of all the earth." (Gen. 11:5-9)

The modern reader will be struck by this diminished, anthropomorphic view of God. He is actually fearful of the power of mankind and their plots against them! They are potentially His equal! This is very primitive material indeed, material from a time when gods and men interacted in way which would be as repugnant to later Judaism as it is to Islam, although would not have raised eyebrows in ancient Greece or Rome.

The Tower of Babel pericope, possibly based upon Babylonian sources, is thought to have been added to the work of the First Yahwist by the Second Yahwist.[81] It seems to have been inspired by one of the

---

[80] This type of construction employing burnt bricks and bitumen as mortar is very ancient. We have inspected vaulted underground chambers, probably tombs, so constructed near the ancient ziggurat of Choga Zambil (in Khuzestan, Iran) of c. 1200 BCE, the largest ziggurat discovered so far in all of Mesopotamia. The temple and the remains of the city around it are roughly contemporaneous with the era of Moses.

[81] IB, I, 446.

great ziggurats of Mesopotamia, perhaps that of Babylon itself. Hooke points out that the story cannot be Mesopotamian in origin, because the tower is to be built to enable mankind to reach heaven. Mesopotamians would have known the real purpose of the tower, as being a kind of elevated landing place for the god descending to earth to reside in the temple for a special manifestation, and would not have invented such a story. An attempt to scale it would have been an impiety, and such a narrative an unthinkable blasphemy. Rather, it represents a speculation about such a tower that might be offered by nomads visiting Mesopotamia ignorant of its real purpose. Therefore, the origin of the tale, though it is about Mesopotamia, must be sought elsewhere.[82]

Furthermore, the story seems to have been suggested by the sight of some specific ruins, because not only is the tower unfinished, but also the city. Jewish tradition linked this story with Nimrod,[83] although in the Bible it stands by itself. Its main purpose appears to have been aetiological; to explain the origin of the different languages of mankind as a divine effort to block the power that a united mankind would wield. It also explains the invention of brick construction in terms of a people used to stone in construction (and therefore not from the stoneless alluvial plains of Mesopotamia). It also seems to explain the origin of some particularly spectacular ruins. In addition, the etymology of the name "Babel" is spurious; the real meaning would have been immediately apparent to any Semite: "Gate of God," or "Divine Gate."

If we assume that the Quranic references are to be ultimately traced to this story, the absence of its principal aetiological features is remarkable. There is no origin of mankind's diverse languages. There is no invention of fired brick construction. There is no name-origin of Babel. Only the building of a tower is shared. The mention in the Quran is an abbreviated reference that seems to imply that the listeners were familiar with the pericope, and its inclusion in the Moses story would suggest that it was already known as a part of the Moses-Pharaoh cycle. It is also not clear whether the order was carried out by Haman, or was simply a boast not intended to be implemented. Perhaps, it is simply a reference by Pharaoh to legends of the Mesopotamia ziggurats (which are thought to have been the pattern for the more famous Egyptian pyramids, some of which were also built of brick). Or it could be a reference to the many immense temples still to be found in Egypt that excite the wonder of even the jaded modern traveler. As we have emphasized in many places, there is no real evidence of new invention in

---

[82] Hooke, pp. 137-138.

[83] See "Nimrod" in Part III, E. {In this series, in *Abraham*.}

these stories in the Quran. They are references and excerpts from stories already in circulation in Arabia, turned to a new purpose.

In any case, there are other possibilities. Although Egypt is famous for its pyramids and temples of stone monuments, we tend to forget that stone was *only* used on a large scale for such religious structures such as temples and tombs, and for other public works for which nothing else would do. The bulk of Egyptian construction was in brick, most of it sun-dried, and thus has not survived. In the Delta region, where there were no handy sources of stone, even the great public buildings such as temples were built largely of brick.

Also, it is important to note that the Arabic word *ṣarḥ* used in the two Quranic verses quoted above and usually translated "tower" (perhaps under the influence of the superficial resemblance to the Tower of Babel pericope in *Genesis*) does not mean "tower" as we think of a tower in English at all. Wehr defines it as "castle, palace, lofty edifice, imposing structure,"[84] of which Egypt has a surfeit. Such a definition fits very well many of the structures erected by Rameses II, the greatest of all Egyptian builders, and the works of the much earlier Age of Pyramids as well. It is our belief that the similarity is accidental, and the story as it was circulated in the Hejaz was probably connected with tales of the pyramids of Middle Egypt, or the great temples erected throughout the land in which the gods resided, according to Egyptian belief.

In addition, the attitude attributed to Pharaoh in the Quran—his desire to confront the God of Moses—would have been quite plausible in that era. Gods were localized. Travelers from one country to another were at pains to placate the gods of whatever territory they passed through. The worshippers of the god Amun in Egypt did not deny the reality of the god Marduk in Babylonia, or of the gods of India had they known of them. Even today, Hindus accept the reality of the gods of other nations without denying their own gods. Gods were territorial. What probably surprised Pharaoh about the God of Moses was that (1) YHWH was out of His Own territory when invading Egypt, and (2) He was invisible and not to be worshipped in the form of an idol.

Pharaoh's Oppression of the Israelites: In the Quran the exact nature of Pharaoh's oppression is not stated, although we read of the *dreadful torment, slaying your sons and sparing your women...* (Q. 2:49)[85] Doubtless, the Arabs were familiar with the general context

---

[84] Wehr, p. 511.

[85] Curiously, Moses is credited with inflicting the same atrocities on the Midianites whom he defeated and in which Balaam was slain. (See sections A above and M below.)

already. The Bible is more specific. The Israelites, prospering by having been attached to the governing class at the time of Joseph, were now—four centuries later—enslaved by the restored native rule. From the Egyptian point of view, they were paying the hangers-on of the Hyksos back for their own oppression of the Egyptians during their rule.

So, the Hebrews had been put to work on vast public projects:[86] "therefore they set taskmasters over them to afflict them with heavy burdens; and they built for Pharaoh store-cities, Pithom and Raamses... So they made the people of Israel serve with rigor, and made their lives bitter with hard service, in mortar and brick, and in all kinds of work in the field..." (Ex. 1:11, 13-14) In another place, these tasks are specifically related to brickmaking: "Go now, and work: for no straw shall be given you, yet ye shall deliver the same number of bricks." (Ex. 5:18)

Despite the legendary character of the first chapters of *Exodus*, this accords well with what we know of the building activities of Rameses II, and is more evidence that he was one of the Pharaohs of Moses. The XIXth Dynasty, of which Rameses II was the most important monarch,[87] was marked by construction projects on a scale even surpassing those of the great Pyramids of the Fourth Dynasty. The dynasty was founded by a military leader descended from an old family of Upper Egypt upon the collapse of the glorious XVIIIth Dynasty—it had been wrecked by the religious innovations introduced by Akhenaton.

Under Rameses II, the center of power shifted from Thebes (modern Luxor) in the south to the north where he could be nearer his Asiatic conquests. "(Thebes) remained the religious capital of the state and at the greater feasts in its temple calendar the Pharaoh was often present, but his permanent residence was in the north. His constant presence here resulted in a development of the cities of the Delta, such as they had never before enjoyed. Tanis became a great and flourishing city, with a splendid temple... High above its massive pylons towered a monolithic granite colossus of Ramses, over ninety feet in height, weighing 900 tons, and visible across the level country of the surrounding Delta for many miles... (He built) a 'store-city which he called Pithom, or 'House of Atum'... Somewhere in the eastern Delta, he founded a residence city, Per-Ramses, or 'House of Ramses.' Its location

---

[86] Not including the pyramids, contrary to popular opinion. The Age of Pyramids had ended some *twelve* centuries earlier. The geographical location of the Israelites, as evidenced by the place names in the Biblical text, was still the northeastern regions of Egypt, that is, the eastern Delta, not the heartland of Egypt on the Nile.

[87] He reigned 67 of the dynasty's 145 years. (Breasted, p. 502.)

is not certain, although it has often been identified with Tanis; but it must have been close to the eastern frontier, for a poet of the time singing of its beauties refers to it as being between Egypt and Syria... Ramses himself was one of the gods of the city."[88]

This Per-Ramses is almost certainly the Raamses mentioned in *Exodus* in whose construction the Hebrews unwillingly participated, if we may trust the tradition recorded there. In corroboration of the traditions contained in *Exodus*, Egyptian records of the reign of Ramses II mention foreign slaves employed on the royal construction projects. Among them were the 'Apiru, that is Hebrews, a term which could easily have included the descendants of Jacob who still resided at that time in Goshen east of the Delta, a region that was the scene of much building activity inspired by the revived Egyptian Empire's military and strategic needs.[89]

Rameses II's building efforts went far beyond the normal works calculated to impress and awe his subjects and foreigners; the extent of his operations suggests a positive mania for the perpetuation of his name. He ruthlessly demolished older buildings up and down the Nile, including tombs and temples, in order to secure materials for his own works. The effects of such vast expenditures upon the economy of Egypt, as rich as it was, can scarcely be imagined.

What we know of Rameses II fits very well with the character of Pharaoh as presented in the Quran where his arrogance is stressed, and to a lesser extent the Pharaoh of the Bible. However, Rameses II was over 90 years old when he died, and he certainly did not perish in a military expedition in pursuit if the Hebrews. If we follow the text of *Exodus*, we must remember that there are *two* Pharaohs to be identified, not just one, because Ex. 2:23 states that while Moses was in Midian, Pharaoh died and was succeeded by a new Pharaoh, the Pharaoh of the Exodus. If we identify Rameses II with the Pharaoh of Moses' birth story, then the Pharaoh of the Exodus must be Merneptah, as he succeeded Rameses II.

There is a problem here because the stele of Merneptah that mentions Israel as being already in Canaan is dated from the fifth year of his reign (c.1231 BCE), hardly enough time for the Exodus and the forty

---

[88] Breasted, p. 371. Some of his other building projects still stud the face of Egypt from the four colossi at Abu Simbel that had to be moved from the waters backing up behind the High Dam above Aswan to numerous temples in thee region of Thebes. "...Surpassing in size all buildings of the ancient or modern world, his architects completed the colossal colonnaded hall of Karnak temple, already begun under the first Ramses, the Pharaoh's grandfather. Few of the great temples of Egypt have not some chamber, hall, colonnade or pylon which bears his name..." (Breasted, p. 372.)

[89] Exodus, EJ, VI, 1047.

years of wandering. Even if we do not take the period of 40 years to be literal truth, there is still ample evidence in the Biblical text that the Israelites spent a considerable time in the desert and semi-desert between Egypt and Syria before entering Israel in large numbers. Of course, it is possible, as has been suggested, that all of the tribes did not participate in the Exodus, and that there were already Israelite tribes settled in Canaan before the arrival of the group led by Moses and Joshua. This is a view to which we incline, as it would solve many more historical problems than it would create. This position is upsetting to conservative Biblical scholars who have been brought up to believe that the Exodus was of all twelve tribes of Israel, not just a few. The problem is complex and the final word has hardly been said, although the reign of Rameses II is increasingly favored for some role in the Exodus story.

If we assume that Rameses II is the Pharaoh of the Exodus, then his father Seti I would have been the Pharaoh of the birth narrative. Seti I was also a builder, but not on the scale of his son, though he is credited with the initiation of the building program.[90] Seti recovered Palestine for the Egyptian Empire and died (c. 1223 BCE) approximately 50 years of age. His mummy is among those on display in the Egyptian Museum at Cairo. Since the building of Per-Rameses, specifically associated with the birth narratives, would appear to be the work of Rameses, not Seti, it is difficult to see how Seti could have been the Pharaoh of the birth stories.

This difficulty in chronology is created by the assumption that there were two different Pharaohs. This problem does not exist in the Quranic narratives, where there is no mention of a succession having taken place during the time of Moses. Perhaps the mention of the two Pharaohs in the Bible is an attempt to reconcile the contradictory picture of the Pharaoh of the birth narrative with that of the Pharaoh of the Exodus. The very long reign of Rameses II would suit the Islamic traditions very well, except for the problem of his death.

At this point, it would do well to examine the word "pharaoh" itself. The word is derived from the Egyptian *per a'o* meaning "the Great House" and originally referred to the royal palace, not the person of the king himself. During the Eighteenth Dynasty (1575-1308 BCE) this term became applied as a deferential circumlocution for the king, although not officially. By the time of the Twenty-Second Dynasty (945-730 BCE), it

---

[90] IB, I, 836. See this reference also for a brief discussion of the arguments for and against Seti I-Rameses II or Rameses II-Merneptah as the pharaohs of the birth story and the Exodus.

was regularly added to the name of the monarch, but it never seems to have been an official title in Egypt.[91] Modern parallels to this usage are easily at hand. Americans refer to the president (or at least the institution of the presidency) as the "White House." The British speak of "Downing Street" when they mean the prime minister, and "Buckingham Palace" when they mean the Queen, at least in their official capacities. The Russian government is referred to as the Kremlin, and in Ottoman Turkey, the sultan and his officials were spoken of as the Sublime Porte.

Keeping in mind that in using such terms the institution described is more in our minds than the individuals holding the power, although both aspects are present, it is not improbable that the "pharaohs" of the Bible and the Quran are representatives of the power of those absolute monarchs rather than the monarchs themselves. That is, high-ranking government officials, governors, military commanders, and the like, attached to the court, rather than the god-king himself, who probably would not have been involved in such a minor affair as the application of a group of Semitic sojourners to leave Egypt and return to their homeland, not to speak of a trivial three-day festival. With this proviso, the era of Rameses II would accord very well with the Quranic story of Moses.

Surabadi's statement about the long life of Pharaoh seems to be based upon the tradition of the 430 years that separated the arrival of Jacob in Egypt from the Exodus of the Israelites from Egypt. Late Jewish tradition also attributes a remarkable life span to Pharaoh, making the Pharaoh of the oppression one with the Pharaoh of Joseph,[92] despite the notice of the death of the Joseph's Pharaoh in Ex. 1:8.

With regard to the seventy-two defects in Pharaoh's body mentioned by Surabadi, there is perhaps an echo here of the encounter of a different monarch with Abraham discussed earlier. However, in *Pirke de Rabbi Eliezer* we have: "But just as the leper is unclean and causes uncleanliness, likewise Pharaoh and his people were unclean, and they caused Israel to be unclean."[93] In the *Exodus Rabbah* this comparison becomes a definite statement that Pharaoh was a leper[94]: "the latter years of Israel's bondage in Egypt were the worst. To punish Pharaoh for his cruelty toward the children of Israel, God afflicted him a plague of leprosy, which covered his whole body… (Pharaoh) took counsel with his three advisers, Balaam, Jethro, and Job, how he might be healed of

---

[91] Pharaoh, EJ, XIII, 359; Pharaoh, DB, pp. 759-760.
[92] LJ, II, 78; V, 346.
[93] PRE, p. 316.
[94] Pharaoh, EJ, XIII, 360.

the awful malady that had seized upon him. Balaam spoke, saying, 'Thou canst regain thy health only if thou wilt slaughter Israelitish children and bathe in their blood'... In pursuance of the sanguinary advice given by Balaam, Pharaoh had his bailiffs snatch Israelitish babes from their mothers' breasts, and slaughtered them, and in the blood of these innocents, he bathed. His disease afflicted him for ten years, and every day an Israelitish child was killed for him... It was all in vain; indeed, at the end of the time his leprosy changed into boils, and he suffered more than before."[95]

Turning from this scene of bloody horror, it may be a relief to read how Moses gave the lie to Pharaoh's claims of divinity. According to the *Exodus Rabbah*: "(Pharaoh) called himself a god, and pretended that he felt no human needs. To keep up the illusion, he would repair to the edge of the river every morning, and ease nature there while alone and unobserved. At such a time it was that Moses appeared before him, and called out to him, 'Is there a god that hath human needs?' 'Verily, I am no god,' replied Pharaoh, 'I only pretend to be one before the Egyptians, who are such idiots, one should consider them asses rather than human beings.'"[96] This is obviously a little anti-Egyptian ethnic joke. Nonetheless, the anecdote is interesting for the impression created that Pharaoh did not consider himself an Egyptian. Is this an echo of the tradition in Surabadi of foreign origin of Pharaoh?

Incidentally, there seems to be some social criticism included by Surabadi related to his own day in the advice Haman gives for corrupting the people and leading them away from the worship of the true God by silencing the learned. The assumption that the people were originally believers, in the Islamic sense, and were later led into idolatry and king-worship is one frequently encountered in Islamic literature and in the Quran itself, where the function of the Prophet is seen as one of restoration rather than religious innovation.

HAMAN, ESTHER, AND AMUN: After our look at Pharaoh, we should now discuss the thorny question of Haman, whose introduction into the Pharaoh-Moses stories in the Quran has been the cause of so much head shaking by Jewish and Christian scholars. In the Quran, he is associated closely with Pharaoh as an opponent of Moses. Later tradition

---

[95] LJ, II, 296. Pharaoh's bathing in blood reminds us of the story of the infamous Hungarian Countess Elizabeth Bathory (d. 1614 CE) who is said to have slaughtered more than 600 virgins in order to renew her youth by bathing in their blood (Bathory, CE, p. 178).

[96] LJ, II, 347-348.

more explicitly makes him the chief henchman and advisor of Pharaoh and, with much elaboration, he is given this role by Surabadi. We have already cited verses of the Quran in which they are linked (see above). Here some others: *(We desired to) show Pharaoh and Haman and their hosts that which they feared from them.* (Q. 28:6); *Lo! Pharaoh and Haman and their hosts were ever sinning.* (Q. 28:8) *And Korah, Pharaoh, and Haman! Moses came unto them with clear proofs...* (Q. 29:39)

The only person bearing the name Haman in the Bible and Jewish tradition is a character in the *Book of Esther*, which shares with *Daniel* the honor of being the latest writing (2nd century BCE) incorporated into the canon of the Old Testament. *Esther*, in its Hebrew version, is unique in being the only book of the Bible in which God is not mentioned, nor indeed even directly referred to! It is an aetiological romance that relates the origin of the Jewish feast of Purim. Its canonicity was disputed by both the Jews and the Christians until the 2nd century CE, when it seems to have finally been admitted into the canon.[97]

---

[97] Esther, DB, p. 269; Trawick-NT, p. 328. For those unfamiliar with the story of Esther, we offer a brief summary here: In the third year of his reign (483 BCE) Ahasuerus (Xerxes) was in residence at his winter capital Susa situated in the Elamite plains [the modern Shush in southwestern Iran]. Giving a banquet that lasted a week, Ahasuerus summoned his wife Vashti, who was entertaining the ladies separately, to his court in order to display her beauty to the people. Her refusal to come when summoned angered the king and he put her away. [Early rabbinic commentators said that the cause of her anger was that she was to appear wearing nothing save her crown, Laymon, p. 233.] Maidens were to be brought before the king so that he might select Vashti's replacement.

It happened that there was a Jew in Susa, Mordecai of the tribe of Benjamin, who had been carried away from Jerusalem by Nebuchadnezzar. [This would make Mordecai about 120 years old.] He had brought up Esther, also called Hadassah, the orphaned daughter of his uncle and adopted her as his own daughter. After a year's beauty treatment (all the candidates were subjected to this ordeal), she was brought before the king who chose her and made her his queen, replacing Vashti. The king then chose Haman the Agagite as his vizier. [The Agagites and Benjaminites were enemies; see 1 Sam. 15:7-9.] When Haman passed Mordecai, Mordecai refused to bow to him. This enraged Haman who informed the king that certain people (the Jews) were plotting against him and Haman persuaded him to authorize a pogrom. When Esther heard of this, she decided to intercede. She arranged a dinner for the king to which Haman would be invited. Passing through the king's gate, Mordecai was waiting and did not rise in respect for the vizier as was customary. Haman ordered Mordecai be hanged on the morrow for the insult.

Meanwhile, the king learned that this Mordecai had saved his life (from assault by two of the king's disgruntled eunuchs), but had not been honored. He ordered that this be done. Haman arrived, thinking he was about to be honored, but discovered that the honoree was his enemy Mordecai. In a dramatic scene, Haman was exposed and hanged and Mordecai named vizier in his place. Shedding tears, Esther then persuaded the king to authorize the Jews, instead of being slaughtered, to slaughter their enemies. "In Susa

In this rather dubious book, the last of the "historical" books of the Old Testament and the least historical of them all, Haman is depicted as a court favorite of the Persian king Ahasuerus (usually identified with the Persian king Xerxes, rgd. 486-465 BCE). He is an enemy of the Jews and in particular Mordecai (who may be a cousin of Esther), and ultimately he meets the fate he had planned for Mordecai. Modern scholars are in general agreement—despite the existence of the supposed tombs of Esther and Mordecai in Hamadan, Iran—that there is absolutely no factual background for the story. Brockington refers to it as an "historical romance."[98] In other words, *Esther* is a total fiction.[99]

---

the capital itself the Jews slew and destroyed five hundred men... " (Est. 9:6) This massacre by the Jews was repeated in the other provinces of the Persian Empire, to a total slaughter of 75,000 of the king's subjects (Est. 9:16). To celebrate these bloody events, a joyous holiday on the 14th of Adar (Purim: the feast of the Lots) was established.

Modern feminists are rather uncomfortable with the story and tend to be more supportive of Vashti, who refused to be used as a sex object to titillate her husband's guests, than of the scheming sex toy Esther who used her beauty to advance herself and her causes.

[98] Esther, DB, p. 269. *Esther* is even less historical than the fabulous *Alexander Romance*, about which there will be more in this story (Section L), also in the story of Dhul-Qarnayn in the New Testament (Vol. 2, Stories, IV.I). {In this series, in *From Monarchy to Hellenism*.}

[99] Writes Philip L. Essley, Jr. of Tulsa, Oklahoma: "Those who claim the historical accuracy of Esther point to the book's familiarity with Persian customs, laws and the accurate description of the palace in Susa (essentially confirmed by archaeology). Those that deny it is based on history point out that 1) none of the individuals except Xerxes (Ahasuerus in the Bible) is named in secular Persian history, 2) Xerxes's queen's name was Amistris, not Vashti or Esther... 3) in the tenth month of the seventh year of Xerxes's reign, when he allegedly married Esther, the king was in fact fleeing from Greece after having watched the Greeks destroy most of his fleet in the battle of Salamis and defeat his army in the battle of Plataea, and 4) other than the Bible, there is no record of the decrees supposedly issued by Xerxes or a revolt or massacres on the 14th day of Adar in any year. Ancient Elam, whose capital was Susa, was a rival of Babylonia and Assyria for centuries. However, in 640 BC Ashurbanipal of Assyria destroyed Elam and Susa (the site of Esther)... In the process, the Babylonian god Marduk (*Merodach* in Persian) and goddess Ishtar (*Esther* in Persian) replaced the Elamic male and female gods Haman and Vashti. Are the similar names a coincidence or literary structure?"

Mr. Essley prefaces these comments with an impressive list of anachronisms found in *Judith*, a romance of the same period that did not make it into the Biblical canon, but is found in the Apocrypha included in many Bibles: "In the story we have seventh-century BC Assyria, under the rule of a sixth-century Chaldean (Babylonian) king, invading a fifth-century restored Judah, with an army led by a fourth-century Persian general (Holofernes was the Persian general under Artaxerxes III in the successful Persian campaign against Egypt in the fourth-century BC). In truth no major attacks were made on Jerusalem while under Persian rule in the fifth and fourth centuries (an unprecedented period of peace for war-weary Canaan)." (Philip L. Essley, Jr., Letter to BR, Vol. XVIII, No. 3, June 2002, p. 6)

The similarity in name and position of Haman in *Esther* and Haman in the Quran—they are both confidants and officials of powerful monarchs—has convinced European scholars that they are one and the same character, and that this is another instance of Quranic confusion.[100] Perhaps; but it is odd indeed that no other aspect of the extremely colorful tale of *Esther* is referred to in the Quran, and only the name of the villain Haman made the trip to the oral tradition of Arabia. In all other respects, the stories and situations are completely dissimilar. Eisenberg says: "...it is remarkable that neither the Quran nor commentary nor the Arab historians know anything of the true Haman of the book of Esther. It must be presumed nevertheless that the story of Haman was not quite unknown in Arabia."[101] (There is a certain amount of presumption in calling a fictional character in *Esther* the *true* Haman.)

The etymology of the name is Haman is unknown. Since other characters in *Esther* bear the names of deities (Esther = Ishtar,[102] Vashti = Mashti,[103] and Mordecai = Marduk[104]) it has been proposed that Haman stands in a similar relationship to the Elamite god Human, Humban, or Umman. It has also been related to the sacred drink *haoma* of ancient Aryan religion, and with the Persian name Humayun.[105] "Such similarity can hardly have come about by accident and may testify to an original Babylonian myth behind the Jewish story."[106] It has also been proposed that the struggle between Esther and Mordecai (the Semitic Babylonian

---

[100] Haman, SEI, p. 130.

[101] L. Eisenberg, writing in Haman, SEI, p. 130.

[102] It has been suggested that "Esther" is derived from the Persian for "star" (*sitārah*), but this may be a coincidence. More probably, it is one of the names of the ancient Near Eastern "Great Mother" worshipped in Phrygia and Lydia as Cybele, by the Mesopotamians as Ishtar, by the Syrians and Canaanites as Astarte, by the Egyptians as Isis, etc. Many of her attributes are to be found in the adoration of the Virgin Mary. (Great Mother of the Gods, CE, p. 863.) There is no historical record of a queen Esther for Xerxes, although some hopeful scholars have tried to squeeze "Esther" out of "Stateira," the name of the queen of Artaxerxes II (rgd. 404-358 BCE)

[103] Mashti, possibly an Elamite goddess. Historically, the queen of Xerxes was Amestris, not Vashti. Vashti may be a total fiction to introduce Esther into the story. (Harvey, writing in *Vashti*, IDB, Vol. 4, pp. 746-747.)

[104] Marduk, whose special cult center was in Babylon, was the omniscient king of the pantheon of Babylonian gods and the creator of mankind. (Marduk, CE, p. 1307.)

[105] Esther, DB, p. 269; Haman, EJ, VII, 1222. The Persian *humāyūn* means, "blessed, sacred, fortunate, august, royal, imperial" (Steingass, p. 1508). However, if the name is derived from the popular Elamite deity, the name would appear to mean "Hum is a creator" (Elamites, ERE, V, 252). See other explanations below in the text. It should be mentioned that the RSV (Note to Est. 1:10-2:4 on p. 603) considers the strange names "attempts to reproduce Persian names."

[106] Reidar B. Bjornard, writing in the Introduction to *Esther* in BC, Vol. 4, p. 2.

gods Ishtar and Marduk) on the one hand with Vashti and Haman (the possibly Indo-European Elamite deities Mashti and Human) on the other represents a struggle between Babylonian and Elamite deities.[107] Of course, all of these equivalencies are admittedly unproven, and since we are dealing with fancy, probably unprovable.

The absence of any reference to the story of Esther in the Quran and Islamic tradition (if we put aside the question of the identity of Haman for the moment) suggests that it may not have been in wide circulation among the Jews of the Hejaz. At first, this may seem remarkable for such a famous story, but it calls to mind an interesting fact about the Dead Sea Scrolls: "All the books of the Old Testament except Esther are represented."[108] Although this may be fortuitous, the absence of *Esther* among the finds has led some scholars to speculate that the book was rejected by the Qumran community. It could hardly have been unknown to them. This rejection was probably conscious and based upon the secular nature of the book. If this theory be true, and if there was a connection been the Jews of Hejaz and the Qumran Jews who sought sanctuary in Arabia after the catastrophes of the Jewish-Roman wars in Palestine, this curious lacuna in the Jewish lore current in western Arabia would become explicable. At the same time, it would tell us a little more about the kind of Judaism with which the Hejazi Jews had been in contact or had adhered to at some earlier stage in their history in Arabia. Already established Jewish communities in the Hejaz could have been proselytized by the Essenes fleeing from Qumran, after their centers in Palestine had been destroyed. [109]

While this might explain why there are no references to the colorful tale of Esther and Mordecai in the Quran, it does not explain how Haman came to be mentioned in the Quran. Modern Muslim commentators of course categorically deny the identity of the Haman of Egypt with the Haman of *Esther*, and most of them usually rely upon a homonymic coincidence for defense against the charges of confusion leveled by Western critics. Obviously, simple denial in this situation is not enough. Somewhere we have read the suggestion that the name Haman is connected with the Egyptian god Amun, rather than the Haman of *Esther*. This interesting idea is worth pursuing.

---

[107] H. Neil Richardson, writing in Laymon, p. 233; Elamites, ERE, V, 251.

[108] Dead Sea Scrolls, DB, p. 205.

[109] For a fuller discussion of this possibility, see the section about the Essenes in "Palestine in New Testament Times" in the Introduction to the companion volume dealing with the New Testament stories. {In this series, in *Introduction to the New Testament.*}

Amun was originally the local god of the city of Thebes (modern Luxor). When Thebes became the capital of Egypt during the Twelfth Dynasty, the god's role in the pantheon began to expand until at the beginning of the Empire period (the XVIIIth Dynasty) Amun's paramountcy was virtually unchallenged in Egypt.[110] During the Empire, Amun became assimilated with the sun god Ra, and was worshipped under the name Amun-Ra. The supremacy of the Amun-Ra among the Egyptian gods was complete. Except for the short period of heresy under Akhenaton, it remained so for the rest of the Empire period, including the period under our consideration, and a long time thereafter.

The Temple of Karnak at Thebes, by some calculations the largest building in the ancient world, was completed by Rameses II in honor of Amun. During the New Empire, the Temple of Amun became the largest landholder after Pharaoh, and its priesthood became correspondingly powerful. About a century after the period of Moses, during the reign of Rameses III, the temple lands of Amun amounted to 10% of the entire cultivated land of Egypt and employed 86,500 slaves (or serfs). All of the other temple establishments together shared another 5% of the land and some 30,000 slaves.[111] Inevitably, the High Priest of Amun was the second most powerful man in the land, and in the later Empire succeeded in making his office hereditary.[112] Finally, after the death of Rameses XII, in the logical culmination of the process, the High Priest of Amun, Hrihor, succeeded in making himself Pharaoh (1090 BCE).[113] Is the Haman of the Quran the High Priest of Amun?[114]

In this respect, it is interesting to quote the words of Jeremiah: "The Lord of hosts, the God of Israel, said: 'Behold, I am bringing punishment upon Amon of Thebes, and Pharaoh, Egypt and her gods and her kings, upon Pharaoh and those who trust in him." (Jer. 46:25) Jeremiah's usage of Amun and Pharaoh parallels that in the Quran. Of the six times the name Haman is used in the Quran, in four he is linked with Pharaoh as an opponent of Moses. In two of these four, the name Korah is added. Rather than confusion, this is exceptionally astute:

---

[110] Budge-Gods, Vol. 2, pp. 3-4.

[111] Breasted, pp. 414-415.

[112] Breasted, p. 384.

[113] Breasted, p. 437.

[114] The objection that Amun is the name of the god and not the high priest is not an obstacle. Literature offers many examples of individuals' being addressed rhetorically by a term related to their function rather than their proper name. For example, in Shakespeare's *Antony and Cleopatra*, Antony frequently addresses Cleopatra as "Egypt": "I am dying, Egypt, dying; only I here importune death awhile..." (Act IV, Scene 15)

Moses is being opposed in his task by the might of the state and priesthood of Egypt, personified as Pharaoh and Haman.[115]

The writings of the Roman historian Tacitus establish a link between Pharaoh and Hammon (Amun): "Most authors agree that during a plague in Egypt which disfigured bodies, King Bocchoris consulted the oracle of Hammon in search of a remedy and was instructed to purge the kingdom and to deport this race [the Hebrews], which was hateful to the gods, into other lands. Thus they were sought out, gathered and then abandoned in the desert. While most were overcome with tears, one of the exiles, Moses, exhorted them not to expect any help from gods or men, for they were deserted by both, but rather to rely on themselves and to consider as a heavenly guide whoever should first aid them in overcoming their present difficulties."[116]

Here we have the disfiguring plague, mentioned by Surabadi, but related to the plagues of Egypt. More importantly, we have the link between Pharaoh and the powerful priesthood of Amun, in this case represented by the famous oracle of Ammon (Amun) situated in the Libyan Desert west of the Nile at the oasis of Siwah, some 300 miles west of Cairo. This oracle was as influential in the ancient world as that of Delphi. Late in the 6th century BCE, the Persian emperor Cambyses lost in a sandstorm an army sent to destroy it. Alexander the Great visited it in 331 BCE to have his right to the throne of Egypt confirmed by his being declared a divinity and the son of Amun.[117] There would be nothing more natural than for Pharaoh to seek the aid of the High Priest of Amun.

How did news of Amun come to Arabia? It must be remembered that in addition to the land routes to Egypt via Midian and the Isthmus of Suez, there were also more direct sea routes across the Red Sea from Egypt in use in ancient times. The classical port of Berenice, accessible from Upper Egypt, lies opposite Yanbu' on the Hejaz littoral, and there were other ports as well, both in Egypt and Arabia. It is not at all

---

[115] The other usages of the name Haman in the Quran (Q. 28:38 and 40:36) are connected with the command, perhaps issued sarcastically, to build a tower to challenge the God of Moses. If this Pharaoh is the builder Ramses II, as seems likely, the reference here is singularly apropos: confronted by Moses and his invisible God, Pharaoh turned to the High Priest of Amun to challenge Him, as he had already challenged his own mortality with his frenetic and colossal construction projects. Perhaps this exchange was sharpened by the memory of the chaos and civil strife caused by Akhenaton's failed attempt to convert Egypt to monotheism a century earlier.

[116] Tacitus, *Histories*, 5.3, quoted by Gager, p. 127.

[117] See Dhul-Qarnayn in Vol. 2, the New Testament Stories, IV.I. {In this series, in *From Monarchy to Hellenism.*}

unlikely that the trading Arabs circulated traditions that linked Pharaoh and Amun, the most powerful figures of Egypt at its apogee of power, and also the stupendous buildings linked with both names."

There are still another possibilities. There was a Horite clan, located around Mount Seir (now in southwestern Jordan and close to the caravan routes from Makkah to Syria) called Hemanite from an eponymous ancestor Heman (*Hīmān*) (Gen. 36:22). The Chronicler spells his name Homan (*Hūmān*) (1 Ch. 1:39). Jewish tradition mentions an angel Ḥemah, slain by Moses in Midian.[118] There is also one Heman, a legendary wise man, whose wisdom was excelled by that of Solomon (1 K. 4:31). Nothing other than his name has been preserved. Heman may have been associated with music, and it has been suggested that he was an Edomite.[119] It is just possible that this is the Haman of the Quran. At one time, he must have been a well-known figure, though now even Jewish tradition offers us little but his name. Perhaps he played some role in the administration of the area where the Semites were settled in Egypt. Being an Edomite would be sufficient reason for later Jews to ignore his story, but his memory may have been preserved in northwestern Arabia.[120]

In the absence of definite documentary links (although the citation from Tacitus strengthens the already strong hypothesis Haman is High Priest of Amun), the above should suffice to demonstrate that other explanations could be offered other than confusion with the Haman of *Esther* (of whose history all of the sensational details are forgotten) favored by Western critics. It is our belief that Haman is most likely the High Priest of Amun, quite appropriate in the context of the story of Pharaoh and Moses. *And God knows best.*

C. THE BIRTH AND INFANCY OF MOSES

Shall I show you one who will nurse him? (Q. 20:40)

In Surabadi's account of the birth of Moses, we are first told that Pharaoh's astrologers and priests had predicted that his kingdom would be destroyed by the Israelites. Or, according to another tradition, Pharaoh

[118] LJ, II, 328.
[119] BC, III, 170-171.
[120] Edom and Midian were neighbors, and to some extent, co-extensive. However, in this case, the disappearance of the strong fricative *ḥ* is difficult to explain. The softer *h* disappears easily in many languages, including English, but not the strong fricative among Semites.

himself saw a dream in which a fire arose from Jericho and Dar'a[121] that destroyed his kingdom. The Israelites had been brought to Egypt from Jericho and Dar'a. Pharaoh asked his astrologers and priests who among the Israelites would bring about the downfall of his kingdom. They replied that that person had not yet been born. Pharaoh then ordered that all of their male children should be killed and the females taken into slavery.[122]

However, the Egyptians were frivolous and only good for war. They discovered that they needed the Israelites for their skills and labor. Consequently, the order was revised so that the slaughter should be carried out every other year. Aaron was born in a year in which there was no slaughter of the male newborn, but Moses was not.[123]

The above is a considerably embroidered commentary on this verse: *Lo! Pharaoh exalted himself in the land and made its people into factions. A tribe among them he oppressed, killing their sons and sparing their women. Lo! He was of those who work corruption.* (Q. 28:4) In the context of the passage, this is almost certainly a reference to the slaughter of the male children of the Israelites. Except for the matter of male infanticide, none of the other details in Surabadi's account are found in the Quran.

Surabadi does not seem to connect the presence of the Israelites in Egypt with the descendants of those who had come to Egypt in the time of Joseph—the Biblical view. Hence, Surabadi has them brought from Palestine and southern Syria, a region historically within the sphere of Egyptian influence of that era.

The first chapter of *Exodus* sets out the circumstances of the descendants of Jacob in Egypt: "Then Joseph died, and all his brothers, and all that generation. But the descendants of Israel were fruitful and increased greatly; they multiplied and grew exceedingly strong; so that the land was filled with them." (Ex. 1:6-7) How much had they multiplied? If we are to accept the traditional interpretation of the census figures given in Num. 1:46, they would have grown to about two millions. In Roman times, the population of Egypt was about 7,000,000, according to Breasted's estimate,[124] and it must have been considerably

---

[121] Jericho (*Arīḥā*) and Dar'a (*Adhriᶜā*). Jericho is located about fifteen miles NW of Jerusalem in the valley of the Jordan in eastern Palestine; Dar'a is located about thirty miles ESE of the Sea of Galilee in southwestern Syria.

[122] Surabadi, p. 298. In another place (p. 9) Surabadi calls the astrologers and priests Copts. In Islamic times, up to the present, Egyptian Christians have been referred to as Copts, as opposed to the majority Muslim population.

[123] Surabadi, p. 298.

[124] Breasted, p. 6.

less some twelve centuries earlier. If we suggest the not unreasonable figure of 4,000,000 for that earlier period, then the Israelites would have made up half of the population of Egypt![125]

Of course, we know that that could not have been the case. As we shall see, there are excellent reasons for assuming an Exodus of only 20,000 souls. However, in the region of the eastern Delta, with a local concentration, the number of Israelites (and other Semites) had developed to the point where they had become locally conspicuous and cause for concern on the part of the Egyptian authorities.[126]

"Now there arose a new king over Egypt, who did not know Joseph. And he said to his people, 'Behold, the people of Israel are too many and too mighty for us. Come, let us deal shrewdly with them, lest they multiply, and, if war befall us, they join our enemies and fight against us and escape from the land.'" (Ex. 1:8-10) The Israelites were enslaved and set to hard tasks (Ex. 1:11-14), probably on the construction projects of Rameses II in the eastern Delta.[127]

The Biblical phrase quoted above "now there arose a new king over Egypt," can readily be interpreted to mean the direct successor of the Pharaoh of Joseph. Since elsewhere it is stated that about four centuries had elapsed between the time of Joseph and the time of Moses, this ambiguity is probably responsible, in part, for the traditions of Pharaoh's extraordinarily long life.[128]

The Biblical story quoted above is principally from J, with some glosses by P. The Elohist history is the source of the story of Pharaoh's slaughter of infants and the circumstances of the birth of Moses: "Then the king of Egypt said to the Hebrew midwives, one of whom was named Shiprah and the other Puah,[129] 'When ye serve as midwife to the Hebrew women, and see them upon the birthstool, if it is a son, ye shall kill him; but if it is a daughter, she shall live.' ...Then Pharaoh commanded all his people, 'Every son that is born to the Hebrews ye shall cast into the Nile, but ye shall let every daughter live'" (Ex. 1:15-16, 22) The statement in

---

[125] McEvedy and Jones propose more conservative estimates of the population of Egypt: about 4,000,000 for the beginning of the Common Era (1 CE) and about 3,000,000 at the time of the New Empire of which the era of Moses is a part. (McEvedy, pp. 226-227.)

[126] See Section G below for a more detailed discussion of this problem.

[127] See previous Section, B.

[128] See above. As noted, Rameses II had one of the longest reigns of any monarch in history.

[129] The text seems to suggest that these two midwives sufficed for the entire population of the Israelites. If that was the case, they could not possibly have provided midwifery services to all of the pregnant women of a population of 2,000,000, as they would have had to deal with some 50 to 60,000 births per year, or 1000 to 1200 per week! Based upon this passage, the Israelites could have numbered only a few thousands.

the Quran obviously follows this tradition of E. The circumstances of Pharaoh's dream or the predictions of the astrologers and priests of Surabadi are not found in *Exodus*, nor are they in the Quran.

It has been pointed out that these accounts by J and E are mutually contradictory. If the Israelites were enslaved and used as labor in Egyptian construction schemes, then it would not have been to the Egyptians' advantage to destroy their own labor supply by killing the male children.[130]

Jewish tradition amplifies the oppression and the slaughter of the male infants considerably.[131] Although Surabadi speaks of Pharaoh's edict to kill the males as though it continued for a number of years, Jewish tradition gives it a more limited period. The Talmudic tractate *Sotah* mentions one day, the *Book of Jubilees* seven months.[132] Both of these sources are pre-Islamic. The *Pirke de Rabbi Eliezer* states that three years elapsed between the edict and the birth of Moses.[133] In Jewish tradition, there is a story that on the day of the birth of Moses, the astrologers came to Pharaoh saying that they had seen something that they did not understand, but seemed to imply that a danger had been averted. Furthermore, it was said that "on account of the merits of Moses, the 600,000 men children of the Hebrews begotten in the same night with him, and thrown into the water on the same day, were rescued miraculously together with him[134]..." The numbers here are inflated fantastically. In this pericope, the astrologers appear to call an end to the slaughter rather than precipitating it, as in Surabadi.

In some Jewish traditions, fearing the power of Israel, Pharaoh called his three counselors, Jethro, Job, and Balaam, and asked their advice. (These were same three who had advised Pharaoh to bathe in the blood of the Israelite infants in another tradition related above.) In this story, too, Balaam plays the role of the adversary of Israel and advises the king that nothing would work save: "if it please the king, let him order all the male children that shall be born in Israel from this day forward to be thrown into the water. Thereby canst thou wipe out their name, for neither any of them nor any of their fathers was tried this

---

[130] Contrary to popular opinion, slaves were a fairly expensive commodity, except when there was a glut of prisoners from wars, as slave prices from ancient times to the end of slavery in the 19th century show. Killing a slave for a trivial reason would have been a bit like running and expensive car off a cliff because the radio would not work.

[131] One use of the theme, Pharaoh's bathing in their blood, has been cited in the previous section.

[132] LJ, V, 399-400.

[133] PRE, p. 378.

[134] LJ, II, 268-269.

way."[135] The purpose of this advice is not given in order to prevent the survival of Moses especially.

Josephus tells us of a warning given to Pharaoh by a sacred scribe that is very similar to that of the astrologers and priests in Surabadi. "One of those sacred scribes, who are very sagacious in foretelling future events truly, told the king that about this time there would be a child born to the Israelites, who, if he were reared, would bring the Egyptian dominion low and would raise the Israelites... Which thing was so feared by the king, that, according to this man's opinion, he commanded that they should cast every male child, which was born to the Israelites, into the river, and destroy it... That if any parents should disobey him, and venture to save their male children alive, they and their families should be destroyed."[136] In this story, we see that not only were the children threatened, but also their families if they disobeyed, and this was the punishment feared by Moses' mother when she threw him into the oven in Surabadi's account (see below). The tradition reflected in Josephus surely is the same as that which has come to the Muslim commentators.

The Biblical parallel to and a probable source of Surabadi's material about the prophesies of the astrologers and priests may be the birth narrative of Jesus found in *Matthew*: "Now when Jesus was born in Bethlehem of Judaea in the days of Herod the king, behold, wise men from the East came to Jerusalem, saying, 'Where is he who has been born king of the Jews? For we have seen his star in the East, and have come to worship him.' When Herod the king heard this, he was troubled, and all Jerusalem with him; and assembling all the chief priests and scribes of the people, he inquired of them where the Christ was to be born..." (Mt. 2:1-4)

Herod asked the wise men to report the finding of the child to him, but instead, after finding him and having been apprised of Herod's intentions in a dream, they returned to their own country by a different route. Joseph, also warned in a dream, took his wife and child to safety in Egypt. "Then Herod, when he saw that he had been tricked by the wise men, was in a furious rage, and he sent and killed all the male children in Bethlehem and in all that region who were two years or under, according to the time which he had ascertained from the wise men." (Mt. 2:16)

A closer extra-Biblical parallel has doubtless already occurred to the reader, that with Abraham. His birth had been foretold to Nimrod and was followed by the slaughter of infants, from which Abraham was

---

[135] LJ, II, 254-256.

[136] Josephus, Antiquities, II.9.2, pp. 55-56.

miraculously spared.[137] The story in *Matthew* is itself doubtless dependent upon Moses' birth story, with whom Christians liked to compare Jesus.[138] The 11th-century CE *Book of Yashar* gives us an account of Nimrod's dream of warning which we may compare with Surabadi's tradition of Pharaoh's dream: One of Nimrod's wise men, Anoqo, interpreted it to mean that the king would lose his life at the hands of a descendant of Abraham, and he was advised to kill Abraham.[139] However, the most famous royal dream warning of destruction to a kingdom at the hands of an infant is the well-known story concerning Cyrus the Great of Persia, as found in the 5th-century BCE *Histories* of Herodotus.[140] In the Bible, *Daniel* uses the same literary device: Nebuchadnezzar is said to have had two dreams, both successfully interpreted by Daniel, in the first of which the destruction of worldly kingdoms is predicted, heralding the Messianic era, and in the second, the king's insanity (Dan. 2,4).

Returning to Surabadi's story, after listing the twelve marvels of Moses (birth, nursing, upbringing, exile, marriage, shepherding, afflictions, revelation and messengership, proof and miracles, polemic

---

[137] See Part Two, III.B.

[138] The parallels and sources of the Jesus birth story are discussed at greater length in the companion volume devoted to the New Testament stories (II.A of the Stories). {In this series, in *Jesus*.}

[139] LJ, I, 204-205.

[140] "(The last Median king) Astyages had a daughter called Mandane, and he dreamed one night that she made water in such enormous quantities that it filled his city and swamped the whole of Asia. He told his dream to the Magi... and was much alarmed by what they said it meant. Consequently, when Mandane was old enough to marry, he did not give her to some Mede of suitable rank, but was induced by his fear of the dream's significance to marry her to a Persian named Cambyses though he considered him much below a Mede even of middle rank. Before Mandane and Cambyses had been married a year, Astyages had another dream. This time it was that a vine grew from his daughter's private parts and spread over Asia. As before, he told the interpreters about this dream, and then sent for his daughter, who was now pregnant.

"When she arrived, he kept her under strict watch, intending to make away with the child; for the fact was that the Magi had interpreted the dream to mean that his daughter's son would usurp his throne. To guard against this, Astyages, when Cyrus was born, sent for his kinsman Harpagus, the steward of his property, whom he trusted more than anyone..." Astyages told Harpagus to take the child away and kill it. But when he saw the child, his heart softened and he sent the infant away to a herdsman Mitradates who raised the boy as his own. The boy, of course, was Cyrus, destined to become Cyrus the Great, the founder of history's first world empire. He did indeed drive Astyages from the throne, but he "treated him with consideration and kept him at the court until he died." (Herodotus, Bk. I, pp. 85-96.) The same plot device, popular in ancient times, will also be familiar to those who have seen the animated film *Snow White and the Seven Dwarfs*.

and debate, victory, and prayer and nearness to God) Surabadi proceeds to his version of the birth story: At the time of the birth of Moses all pregnant women gave birth without pain, prisoners were freed, the unfortunate were relieved, a star appeared over Egypt, light shone from Egypt, the palace of Pharaoh shook and his throne fell down and was broken,[141] and Haman heard a loud sound in his heart.[142]

Though none of this material is found in the birth narratives of Moses in the Bible or the Quran, some of it may be traced to other writings. Josephus mentions the ease of Moses' birth: "However, the mother's labour was such as afforded a confirmation to what was foretold by God; for it was not known to those that watched her, by the easiness of her pains, and because the throes of delivery did not fall upon her with violence."[143] The star over Egypt is strikingly reminiscent of the star of Bethlehem that appeared, according to Matthew, at the birth of Jesus (Mt. 2:2,7,9,10).[144] The Talmud (*Sotah*) and Jewish traditions speak of the light that appeared at the time of Moses' birth: "At the moment of the child's appearance, the whole house was filled with radiance equal to the splendor of the sun and the moon.[145]

After Moses was born, according to Surabadi, when the police came to kill him, his mother threw him into an oven, exclaiming: "Letting him burn in the oven is better than his being killed upon my belly by the police of Pharaoh!" The men searched the house but did not find the child. It never occurred to them he could be in the roaring oven. When they left, his mother opened the oven saw Moses playing with the embers. She knew that this prodigy would not remain a secret in Egypt. After giving him milk, she made a casket waterproof with pitch and,

---

[141] Kisa'i tells of Moses' breaking Pharaoh's throne at a later time: "When Moses was nine, he kicked the legs of the chair Pharaoh was sitting on and it broke. Pharaoh fell and broke his nose, and the blood flowed over his beard. He wanted to kill Moses, but Asiyah said, 'Sire, it would do you no harm to have a son of such strength who could drive away your enemies.'" (Kisa'i, pp. 218-219]

[142] Surabadi, pp. 298-299.

[143] Josephus, Antiquities, II.9.4, p. 56.

[144] See quotation from *Matthew* above.

[145] LJ, II, 264. This light lasted three months, being withdrawn when Moses entered the household of Pharaoh (LJ, V, 397). The 2nd-century Christian apocryphal work, the *Protevangelium*, relates: "And (Joseph and the midwife) stood in the place of the cave: and behold, a bright cloud overshadowing the cave. And the midwife said: My soul is magnified this day, because mine eyes have seen marvellous things; for salvation is born unto Israel. And immediately the cloud withdrew itself out of the cave, and a great light appeared in the cave so that our eyes could not endure it. And by little and little that light withdrew itself until the young child appeared: and it went and to the breast of its mother Mary." (James, pp. 44,46.) Compare also the light that appears in the birth narrative of Abraham. (See Part Two above, III.B) {In this series, in *Abraham*.}

telling herself that the Lord would protect him as He had in the fire, she gave the casket to her daughter Miriam to put in a canal, instructing her to watch what happened to it.

Miriam did this, and she followed the casket until it entered a canal that passed through Pharaoh's garden. Seventy maidens were playing there. They saw the little ark, but were unable to catch it and bring it ashore until one of them pronounced "In the Name of God" (*bismillah*). The casket was brought to Isiyah[146] who opened it and was captivated by the beauty of the child's smile.[147]

Laqitah, the adopted daughter of Pharaoh, was also present. It is said that Pharaoh had claimed to have created Laqitah when she was born, and thereafter seventy-two defects had appeared in the infant. When the casket was opened, Moses looked at Isiyah with one eye and Laqitah with the other. Instantly Isiyah gained wisdom and Latiqah shed her defects. All who looked upon him were taken by his grace except Pharaoh, who refused to look and said that the infant was an enemy Israelite child and should be killed. This threat was removed when, one day, the infant Moses said "Baba" to him. After that, Pharaoh became fond of him. That one word had ten rewards: Moses escaped the slaughter, the killing of infants became unlawful and ceased, the king held him to his breast, kissed him, and adopted him, Moses was wrapped in silk by the king, a crown was placed upon his head, the sun's eye (a flower) was adorned on his behalf, and the court prostrated themselves before him.[148]

Forty wet nurses were brought, but Moses would not take their milk. Finally, his sister brought his mother, who found Moses the center of attention at the court including Pharaoh and Haman. Moses took his mother's breast and began to suck. When Haman saw this, his suspicions apparently aroused, he asked the woman, whose name was Nukhai'dh,[149] if she were the child's mother in fact. She replied evasively that she wished she were. Thereafter, Moses lived like a prince with 400 servants, etc.[150]

The incident of Moses' being thrown into the oven by his mother is not found in the Bible or the Quran, nor does it seem to be associated with Moses in Jewish tradition. In the latter, King Manasseh (rgd. 687-642 BCE) was punished by being put in an oven in Babylonia, but the

---

[146] Surabadi writes Isiyah, but Āsiyah is the more common form in Islamic literature.
[147] Surabadi, pp. 249-250, 299.
[148] Laqitah: Laqīṭah. Surabadi, pp. 299-300.
[149] Nukha'idh: Nūkhāʾīdh.
[150] Surabadi, pp. 250-251, 300.

similarity ends there.[151] The name of Moses' mother, given by Surabadi as Nukha'idh, is doubtless a garbling of the Biblical Jochebed, caused by a misreading of the dots on the letters. (It appears more correctly in other Muslim writings as Yukhabid.) Isiyah is an alternative form of the more usual Asiyah, as Pharaoh's wife is called in Islamic tradition. Pharaoh's wife (or daughter) is not named in the Bible, nor is she in the Quran, contrary to the impression created by Prof. Hirschberg, perhaps inadvertently, in the relevant article in *Encyclopædia Judaica.*[152]

Two passages in the Quran refer to the story of Moses' birth, both focusing on the mother: *And when We inspired in thy mother (O Moses) that which is inspired. Saying: Throw him into the ark and throw it into the river,*[153] *then the river shall throw it onto the bank, and there an enemy to Me and an enemy to him shall take him. And I endued thee with love from Me that thou might be trained according to My will. When thy sister went and said: Shall I show you one who will nurse him? And We restored thee unto thy mother that her eyes might be refreshed and might not sorrow.* (Q. 20:38-40) In this passage, we have the casting into the river, the intervention of his sister, and his reunion with his mother.

In another place, a fuller version is given: *And We inspired the mother of Moses, saying: Suckle him and, when thou fearest for him, then cast him into the river and do not fear or grieve. Lo! We shall bring him back unto thee and shall make him (one) of Our messengers. And the family of Pharaoh took him up, that he might become for them an enemy*

---

[151] LJ, IV, 279-280. In the *Pirke de Rabbi Eliezer*, there is a tradition that the Egyptians burnt the children of the Israelites in the furnace of fire, and later writings make this an act of sacrifice to the Egyptian gods (PRE, p. 381). It is possible some such tradition influenced the episode found in Surabadi. It should be pointed out that there is no record that the Egyptians practiced human sacrifice in historical times, although it was practiced in Canaan even into the period of the Israelite monarchy.

[152] Moses, EJ, XII, 403; Pharaoh, EJ, XIII, 362. In the latter reference, Prof. Hirschberg writes: "Pharaoh of the Koran is the king who oppressed the people of Israel in Egypt; Musa (Moses) and Harun (Aaron) negotiated with him. In accordance with the counsel of his advisors, among them Haman, Pharaoh ordered that all male children be killed (Sura 2:46; 7:137). Asiya, the wife of Pharaoh, adopted Moses, who had been found in an ark (28:9)." The Quranic verse cited does not mention her by name: *And the wife of Pharaoh said: (He will be) a consolation for me and for thee...* (Q. 28:9) Many commentators think that a verse in Surah al-Tahrim refers to her: *And God cites an example for those who believe: the wife of Pharaoh when she said: My Lord! Build for me a home with thee in Paradise, and deliver me from Pharaoh and his work, and deliver me from the tyrannical people.* (Q. 66:11)

[153] "river": In this and the following quotation, the word used in the Quran is *yamm*, usually translated as "sea" or "open sea" and not "river." However, the Nile, the largest river in the Near East, is still called in Arabic *Baḥr ul-Nīl*, the "Nile Sea" because of its size and importance.

and a sorrow. Lo! Pharaoh and Haman and their hosts were ever sinning. And the wife of Pharaoh said: (He will be) a consolation for me and for thee. Kill him not. Perhaps he may be of use to us, or we may choose him for a son. And they perceived not. (Q. 28:7-9)

And the heart of the mother of Moses became void, and she would have betrayed him if We had not fortified her heart, that she might be of the believers. And she said unto his sister: Trace him. So she observed him from afar, and they perceived not. And We had before forbidden foster-mothers for him, so she said: Shall I show you a household who will rear him for you and take care of him? So We restored him to his mother that she might be comforted and not grieve, and that she might know that the promise of God is true. But most of them know not. (Q. 28:10-13)

These accounts follow the Biblical account remarkably closely, except in a few details: No personal names occur in the Biblical version (Ex. 2:1-10)[154] save that of Moses at the end: "Now a man from the house of Levi went and took to wife a daughter of Levi. The woman conceived and bore a son; and when she saw that he was a goodly child, she hid him three months." (Ex. 2:1-2) (This implies that Moses was their *first* child.) This period is referred to in the Quran when it speaks of Moses' mother nursing her child. "And when she could hide him no longer she took for him a basket made of bulrushes, and daubed it with bitumen and pitch; and she put the child in it and placed it among the reeds at the river's brink. And his sister stood a distance, to know what would be done to him." (Ex. 2:3-4) (Now we learn that Moses had an older sister.)

Up to this point the narratives are virtually the same, except for the greater attention to the workings of Providence and the anguished thoughts of the mother in the Quran, whilst the Elohist's account in *Exodus*, gives more details about the construction of the ark. Then:

"Now the daughter of Pharaoh came down to bathe at the river, and her maidens walked beside the river; she saw the basket among the reeds and set her maid to fetch it. When she opened it she saw the child; and lo, the babe was crying. She took pity on him and said, 'This is one of the Hebrews' children.'" (Ex. 2:5-6) In this passage, the differences become stronger. The Elohist states that it was the daughter of Pharaoh who discovered him, while the Quran only mentions the "family of Pharaoh" who rescued the infant Moses from the water. In Surabadi, it was the smile of the child rather than his crying which excited the

[154] Gray assigns this pericope to the Elohist (Laymon, p. 34). It is remarkable how often the Quran uses the traditions of the Elohist as opposed to those of the Yahwist.

Egyptian woman's compassion for his plight. At this point Surabadi introduced Laqitah, Pharaoh's daughter who had the seventy-two defects cured by Moses' smile. In Talmudic tradition, Pharaoh's daughter was cured of leprosy as she extended her arm to retrieve the casket.[155] Josephus calls her Thermuthis;[156] rabbinic tradition speaks of her as Bithiah, a daughter of Pharaoh who married Mered of the tribe of Judah in another context (1 Ch. 4:17). The Arabic "Asiyah" and Surabadi's "Isiyah" are probably related to this name.

"Then his sister said to Pharaoh's daughter, 'Shall I go and call to thee a nurse from the Hebrew women to nurse the child for thee?' And Pharaoh's daughter said to her, Go.' So the girl went and called the child's mother. And Pharaoh's daughter said to her, 'Take this child away, and nurse him for me, and I will give thee thy wages.' So the woman took the child and nursed him. And the child grew, and she brought him to Pharaoh's daughter, and he became her son; and she named him Moses, for she said, 'Because I drew him out of the water.'" (Ex. 2:7-10)

There are no significant divergences between this and the Quranic version save in the matter of the folk etymology of the name Moses[157] omitted by the Quran and the relationship of Moses' foster mother to Pharaoh. However, in the Biblical account, Moses' nationality is apparently evident to the people of Pharaoh, but no comment is made about sparing him from the threat of death that presumably hung over him, or the suspension of the order to kill the Hebrew children. Surabadi's tradition, recognizing this difficulty, makes Moses' nationality a secret, unknown to or only guessed at by Pharaoh and Haman. Pharaoh at least is won over to him, and Moses' real mother responds in a way not to lie about Moses' relationship to her (and therefore his race) without divulging it.

Neither does the Bible mention the infant Moses' refusal to take any of the breasts offered him for nursing until his mother was brought to him. His sister simply appears on the spot and offers a wet nurse who is accepted immediately without question. However, Talmudic tradition also contributes this detail of the child's refusal of the milk of the wet nurses. In the Quran, it simply brings about the reunion of mother and child, but in Jewish tradition it is given racial overtones: "(Pharaoh's daughter) ordered an Egyptian woman to be brought, to nurse the child, but the little one refused to take milk from her breasts, as he refused to

---

[155] LJ, II, 267.
[156] Josephus, Antiquities, II.9.5, p. 56.
[157] See Section A above.

take it from one after another of the Egyptian women fetched thither. Thus it had been ordained by God, that none of them might boast later on, and say, 'I suckled him that now holds converse with the Shekinah.' Nor was the mouth destined to speak with God to draw nourishment from the unclean body of an Egyptian woman."[158]

Another tradition, from the much-edited *Deuteronomy Rabbah*, contradicts the Quranic statement that his mother nursed him before he was placed in the ark on the water, but the purpose of this assertion is to show Moses' maturity at birth: "The infant was not yet a day old when he began to walk and speak with his parents, and as though he were an adult, he refused to drink milk from his mother's breast."[159] This pericope rather obviates the whole point of the reunion of mother and child in the Bible and the Quran.

In sum, the principal difference remaining between the Biblical and Quranic accounts of this story is the identity of the woman who adopted Moses. In the Bible, she is explicitly called Pharaoh's daughter, and the figure of Laqitah, introduced by Surabadi, seems to be a response to Judaeo-Christian insistence on the correctness of this view. Jewish tradition knows of the cure of the foster mother (Pharaoh's daughter) upon finding Moses. In Surabadi, the person is also Pharaoh's daughter, certainly this is influenced by the Jewish accounts on this point, but the foster mother is Pharaoh' "wife," and therefore a different person.

In respect to this point, it is important to note that the Quranic phrase *imraʾatu firᶜawn* is somewhat ambiguous. Such an expression could mean "a/the woman of Pharaoh" or "a/the wife of Pharaoh. If we are to regard the Biblical "daughter of Pharaoh" as the definitive version because of its antiquity, the meaning of the Arabic might conceivably include such a relationship, although only in the general sense that Pharaoh's daughter is a woman of his court.

Jewish tradition naturally follows the lead of the Bible here and speaks of Pharaoh's daughter rather than his wife. However, Josephus, though he explicitly states that Thermuthis is Pharaoh's daughter, may also preserve an alternative tradition that corresponds more closely with the Quranic usage. In his version of the arrival of Moses' sister (here called Miriam) and the summoning of his mother to act as wet nurse, he writes: "Now Miriam was by when this happened, not to appear to be there on purpose, but only as staying to see the child; and she said, 'It is in vain that thou, O queen, callest for these women for the nourishing of the child, who are no way of kin to it; but still, if thou wilt order one of

[158] LJ, II, 267.
[159] LJ, II, 264.

the Hebrew women to be brought, perhaps it may admit the breast of one its own nation.' Now since she seemed to speak well, Thermuthis bid her procure such a one, and to bring one of those Hebrew women that gave suck. So when she had such authority given her, she came back and brought the mother, who was known to nobody there. And now the child gladly admitted the breast, and seemed to stick close to it; and so it was, that at the queen's desire, the nursing child was entirely intrusted to the mother."[160]

It may be notice that in this passage "queen" is not simply an honorific. If it had only occurred in Miriam's statement, it might have been so, but Josephus himself, as narrator, also calls her a queen. In addition to this, the refusal to nurse, also mentioned in the Quran, is found here. Does this tradition in Josephus stand in some sort of relationship to the Arabian tradition found in the Quran? It is our belief that it does.

The Biblical and Quranic versions, if we accept the interpretation that in the Quran the wife of Pharaoh is actually meant, may be reconciled in another somewhat astonishing way. Rameses II, who seems to be the Pharaoh under discussion, like many other of his Egyptian predecessors and successors, married his own daughters.[161] Thus, both the Biblical statements and the Quranic verse could be reconciled, and this could be the situation also reflected in Josephus.

Finally, we may return to the world of Mesopotamia for a legend that may stand behind part of the birth narrative of Moses. A tablet found in the royal library of Nineveh of the 7th Century BCE contains a copy of a much older legend about Sargon of Akkad, the first Semitic king to reign in Mesopotamia, c. 2350-2300 BCE and the founder of the first "world" empire (most of the Fertile Crescent). As we shall see, it has many of the elements of the Moses story:[162]

> "Sargon, the mighty king, king of Agade, am I.
> My mother was a nun (?); my father I knew not.
> My father's kinsmen lived in the hills.
> My city was Azupiranu, on the banks of the Euphrates.
> When my mother, the nun (?), had conceived me, she bore me
> in secret.
> She put me in a basket of rushes, with bitumen sealed me in.
> Then she cast me into the river, but the river did not

---

[160] Josephus, Antiquities, II.9.5, p. 57.
[161] Halley, p. 113.
[162] Gaster, Vol. I, p. 225; AAWH, Vol. 1, pp. 27, 31.

overwhelm me.
The river bore me up, and carried me to a drawer of water, one Akki.
As he dipped his ewer, Akki hauled me out.
He (adopted me and) reared me as his own son.
He set me to tending his garden.
While I was so engaged, the goddess Ishtar granted me her love.
I came to reign over the kingdom for four and ... years.
The black-headed people I ruled and gov(erned)."[163]

In this fragment we can see many parallels with the career of Moses: the basket of rushes sealed with bitumen, being set adrift and then rescued, the mean occupation (Moses worked as a shepherd), the theophany, the attainment of power over a great civilization (Egypt for Moses, Sumeria for Sargon). Many of these parallels are perhaps fortuitous, but the incident of the basket cast into the river is suggestive. Even closer to the scene of the Moses story, there is an Egyptian legend about the infant god Horus who was concealed among the marsh reeds in order to protect him from the god Seth who sought to destroy him.[164]

Did either or both of these stories play a part in the formation of the ancient traditions surrounding the birth of Moses? Did one or the other of these legends travel from Mesopotamia or Egypt, as had so many others already noted in *Genesis*, and find a new use in Palestine enhancing the wonder of the story of Moses? Once the story had been absorbed into the Mosaic cycle, it could have easily passed to Arabia where it is used in the Quran as a parable of God's providence.

D. THE FLIGHT TO MIDIAN

And thou didst kill a man and We delivered thee from great distress, and tried thee with a heavy trial. And thou didst tarry some years among the folk of Midian. (Q. 20:40)

The significance of the flight to Midian by Moses and his residence there is undoubtedly of far greater importance that the present text of *Exodus* and *Numbers* suggests. The theological influences to

[163] Quoted by Gaster (Gaster, Vol. I, pp. 225-226. The black-headed people are the non-Semitic Sumerians who were the first inhabitants of Mesopotamia in historical times. The meaning of the word translated as "nun" is not certain, hence the question marks.
[164] Moses, EJ, XII, 379.

which Moses may have been exposed while in Midian, and their consequences still affect a large portion of mankind. That will be discussed in the following section (E).

The Biblical version of the events leading to the flight are to be found in *Exodus*: "One day, when Moses had grown up, he went out to his people and looked on their burdens; and he saw an Egyptian beating a Hebrew, one of his people. He looked this way and that, and seeing no one, he killed the Egyptian and hid him in the sand. When he went out the next day, behold, two Hebrews were struggling together; and he said to the man that did the wrong, 'Why dost thou strike thy fellow?' He answered, 'Who made thee a prince and judge over us? Dost thou mean to kill me as thou didst kill the Egyptian?' Then Moses was afraid, and thought, 'Surely the thing is known.' When Pharaoh heard of it, he sought to kill Moses." (Ex. 2:11-15a)

The principal account of this episode in the Quran is to be found in Surah Qasas (Q. 28). The differences with the Bible are minor: *And when he reached his full strength and was mature, We gave him wisdom and knowledge. Thus do We reward the good. And he entered the city at a time of carelessness of its folk, and he found therein two men fighting, one of his own party* [a Hebrew], *and the other of his enemies* [an Egyptian]*; and he who was of his party asked him to help against him who was of his enemies. So Moses struck him with his fist and killed him. He said: This is the work of Satan! Lo! He* [Satan] *is an enemy and a plain misleader.* (Q. 28:14-15) The Quran adds the time of day, presumably in the afternoon when people are resting away from the midday heat. (This is Surabadi's understanding; see below.)

Two details about the killing are added: the oppressed Hebrew called for Moses to aid him. This could imply that Moses' national identity was known to him. Secondly, the cause of death was stated: a blow of the fist. In the Bible, the death of the Egyptian was premeditated —Moses looked around to see if anyone were watching before killing the Egyptian—but in the Quran it is understood to be accidental (killing was not the intended object of the blow; more likely Moses simply wanted to disable the Egyptian or knock him unconscious). The crime was manslaughter, not murder. Moses himself seemed to be astonished at this result of his quick action when he said: *This is the work of Satan!* This is followed by a prayer: *(Moses) said: My Lord! Lo! I have wronged my soul, so forgive me. Then He forgave him. Lo! He is the Forgiving, the Merciful. (Moses) said: My Lord! Forasmuch as Thou hast favored me, I will nevermore be a supporter of the guilty.* (Q. 28:16-17)

Instead of a premeditated murder, the Quran offers an impetuous act by a powerful, but untried, young man who did not yet know his own strength. He was immediately repentant because of the unforeseen death of the Egyptian, and turned to God for forgiveness. God's ready forgiveness would also suggest that the killing was accidental, not intentional. In the Biblical version, Moses expressed no remorse for the death of the Egyptian he had deliberately caused. From the nuances of this Quranic story, we learn that even the killing of one's enemy demands contrition and the acknowledgment of responsibility. Though sanctioned by the state, nevertheless God Himself must be satisfied as to the justice of both the intention and the deed.

The Bible does not tell us how the murder became known. We may surmise that even if there were no spectators to the deed, the Hebrew victim whom Moses had delivered from the Egyptian's cruelty had noised it about. This is the conclusion that later Jewish commentators came to. And though the Bible made no connection between the Hebrew saved by Moses and the two Hebrews fighting the next day, later Jewish tradition does; as does the Quran: *And morning found him in the city, fearing, vigilant, when behold! He who had appealed to him the day before cried out to him for help. Moses said unto him: 'Lo, thou art indeed a plain hothead.' And when he would have fallen upon the man who was an enemy unto them both, he said: 'O Moses! Wouldst thou kill me as thou didst kill a person yesterday? Thou wouldst be nothing but a tyrant in the land, thou wouldst not be of the reformers.'* (Q. 28:18-19)

Since it was the opponent of the man whom he had helped the previous day so addressing him, it was clear to him that the secret had not been kept. The addition of these details is logical and psychologically sound. The man he had helped could not keep the matter to himself, and had talked about it among his family and friends, with the result that when Moses came upon the man quarreling again, he was so taunted by the opponent. (It is possible to interpret this verse to mean that it was a repetition of the incident of the day before, the Hebrew's opponent once again possibly an Egyptian. This is Surabadi's view, see below.) To this the Quran adds another circumstance not found in the Biblical story, although again a natural development of the story: *And a man came from the uttermost part of the city, running. He said: O Moses, Lo, the chiefs take counsel against thee to slay thee; therefore, escape. Lo! I am of those who give thee good advice.' So he departed from that place, fearing, vigilant. He said: 'My Lord! Deliver me from the wrongdoing folk.'* (Q. 28:20-21)

The news of the death of the Egyptian had reached the magistrates of the city. A friend of Moses, perhaps from the council or associated with it, rushed to warn Moses to flee the wrath of the Egyptians, his arrival following immediately upon the scene with the two Hebrews.

Surabadi's account seems to strike a balance between the Bible and the Quran: Moses used to go out in the heat of the day in disguise (this seems to be an Islamic addition), when the people were resting, and he would contemplate the people in their error. One day he saw an Egyptian officer, Rīqā, trying to force an Israelite to carry some straw to a stable. A fight started and when the Israelite sought aid, Moses struck the Egyptian with his fist so forcefully that he died upon the spot, while the Israelite fled. The next day Moses entered the market apprehensively and came upon the same Israelite fighting with another Egyptian officer. Once again he sought Moses' aid, and when Moses reproved him because of his quarrelsomeness, the Israelite asked sharply whether Moses intended to kill him the way he had killed the Egyptian the previous day. The Egyptian then realized that it was Moses who had killed his comrade on the previous day. Releasing the Israelite, he ran off to tell Pharaoh.[165]

This deviates from both the Bible and the Quran. The Bible implies that the two strugglers of the second incident were both Hebrews, not a Hebrew and an Egyptian. Of course, we do not know (from the text of *Exodus*) whether either of the two was the Hebrew of the previous day. On this point, the Quranic text is ambiguous and capable of different interpretations (although the Arabs first hearing it probably knew which was which). Who taunted Moses with the crime, the Hebrew Moses had saved the day before, or the man's opponent? We have given Surabadi's interpretation, and this is also Maulana Muhammad Ali's view.[166]

Our own inclination is to read the text as does Yusuf Ali[167] to mean that after this reproof Moses made common cause with the man he had saved in a similar situation the day before; that it was the opponent, having heard of the killing, who taunted Moses with it. Although some time could have intervened between the second fight and the arrival of the warning message, the Quranic text seems to read that one followed almost immediately upon the other. In other words, there would have been no need for the device introduced by Surabadi of having the

---

[165] Surabadi, pp. 300-301.
[166] Quran-MMA, p. 745.
[167] Quran-Yusuf Ali, p. 1006.

opponent learn who was responsible for the crime of the previous day and rushing off to report the news to Pharaoh.

This would have taken some time, and still more time for the council to convene and discuss the case before arriving at its decision, and then for Moses' friend to warn him. If we assume that the story was already about and the council had already met when Moses came upon the quarreling pair, then the arrival of the messenger upon the scene of the quarrel is not only explicable but also dramatically effective.

In Surabadi's version, after the initial killing, Pharaoh convened a council. One of those present, Kharbīl, was a believer, and it was he who rushed to inform Moses of the decision to execute him and who warned him to flee.[168] Apparently, the enhancement of the figure of the "*man who came running*," or the believer from Pharaoh's people (Q. 40:28), in Islamic tradition is related to the presence of Jethro on Pharaoh's council. He is supposed to have participated in the councils that recommended Pharaoh cure himself of leprosy by washing in the blood of Israelite infants (see above) and recommended the slaughter of the infants to break the might of the Israelites (see above). In both of these traditions, Jethro is depicted in opposition to the decisions. We shall have more to say about Jethro below.

Jewish tradition gives a different account of the circumstances leading up to the quarrel with the Egyptian: "While Moses abode in Goshen, an incident of great importance occurred. To superintend the service of the children of Israel, an officer from among them was set over every ten, and ten such officers were under the surveillance of an Egyptian taskmaster. One of these Hebrew officers, Dathan by name, had a wife, Shelomith, the daughter of Dibri, of the tribe of Dan, who was of extraordinary beauty, but inclined to be very loquacious. Whenever the Egyptian taskmaster set over her husband came to their house on business connected with his office, she would approach him pleasantly and enter into conversation with him.

"The beautiful Israelitish woman enkindled a mad passion in his breast, and he sought and found a cunning way of satisfying his lustful desire. One day, he appeared at break of dawn at the house of Dathan, roused him from his sleep, and ordered him to hurry his detachment of men to their work. The husband scarcely out of sight, he executed the villainy he had planned, and dishonored the woman, and the fruit of this illicit relation was the blasphemer of the Name [of God; the blasphemer was one Zelophedad] whom Moses ordered to execution on the march through the Desert."

---

[168] Surabadi, p. 301.

A very neat tie-in. The story continues: "At the moment when the Egyptian slipped out of Shelomith's chamber, Dathan returned home. Vexed that his crime had come to the knowledge of the injured husband, the taskmaster goaded him on to work with excessive vigor, and dealt him blow after blow with the intention to kill him. Young Moses happened to visit the place at which the much-abused and tortured Hebrew was at work. Dathan hastened toward him, and complained of all the wrong and suffering the Egyptian had inflicted upon him. Full of wrath, Moses, whom the holy spirit had acquainted with the injury done the Hebrew officer by the Egyptian taskmaster, cried out to the latter, saying: 'Not enough that thou hast dishonored this man's wife, thou aimest to kill him, too'

"Neither physical strength nor a weapon was needed to carry to carry out his purpose. He merely pronounced the Name of God, and the Egyptian was a corpse."[169]

Jewish tradition also makes the betrayal of the situation to Pharaoh the deliberate act of two Hebrews, Dathan and Abiram.[170] Betrayed by the man whom he had saved, Moses was condemned to death but saved by the angel Michael who enabled Moses to flee.[171]

Another parallel to some of the details in which the Quran differs from the Bible may be found in the Hellenistic writer Artapanus (c. 100 CE). He writes that jealousy of Moses by the king, prompted by the success of Moses in an expedition to Ethiopia (see section L below), caused the king to plot against the life of Moses. "Having alienated the Egyptians from Moses, Chenephres [the king] induced Chanethothes to undertake to slay Moses. The plot conspired against him was reported to Moses [as in the Quran], and on the advice of Aaron he sailed across the Nile from Memphis, intending to take refuge in Arabia. Chanethothes, informed of Moses' proposed flight, placed himself in ambush with the intention to kill him. When he saw Moses approach, he drew his sword against him. But Moses seized his hand and slew him with his own hand."[172] Thus Chanethothes would be the name of the Egyptian slain, the Riqa of Surabadi.

---

[169] LJ, II, 279-280.

[170] Dathan and Abiram were later involved with Korah in the insurrection against the leadership of Moses related in *Numbers* (Num. 16:1ff); see Section I below. Making them the two Hebrews who exposed Moses is typical of the Talmudic tendency to tie independent incidents together through exegesis and the identification of unnamed characters (and even, sometimes, named characters) with others in another part of the Bible, often creating a tangled web of relationships.

[171] LJ, II, 281-282.

[172] Quoted in LJ, V, 407-408.

And when he turned his face toward Midian, he said: Perhaps my Lord will guide me in the right road. (Q. 28:22) Surabadi continues his story with the flight of Moses to Midian. In Midian, Moses came upon a well, covered with a stone that required the strength of forty men to lift it. It was supplied with a bucket that required forty men to haul it up. He saw a crowd of men at the well and two girls sitting with their sheep off to one side. Moses asked them about their condition, and they replied that they were the daughters of Shu'ayb,[173] and that if there were water left after the other shepherds had watered their flocks, they would be allowed to water theirs. Their father was very old. Moses asked the other shepherds why they would not help the girls, but they replied rudely: "If thou art more of a man, draw it thyself!" Thereupon, Moses pushed aside the heavy stone by himself and drew water by himself, giving it to the girls' flocks. Then he continued on his way. He became tired and hungry, and complained to God of being poor and a stranger in this land; that he was ill, sad, and perplexed. God replied that only people without God are so.[174]

This is a much amplified account based upon the two verses in the Quran: *And when he came to the waters of Midian he found a company of the people there drawing water, and he found, apart from them, two women holding back their flocks. He said, 'What is your business?' They said, 'We may not draw water until the shepherds drive off, and our father is passing old.' So he drew water for them; then he turned away to the shade, and he said, 'O my Lord, surely I have need of whatever good Thou shalt have sent down upon me.'* (Q. 28:23-24)

The Biblical version of these events is part of the conflation of J and E. Gray assigns these verses[175] to the Yahwist (J): "But Moses fled from Pharaoh, and stayed in the land of Midian; and he sat down by a well. Now the priest of Midian had seven daughters, and they came and drew water, and filled the troughs to water their father's flock. The shepherds came and drove them away; but Moses stood up and helped them, and watered their flock." (Ex. 2:15b-17)

This account differs significantly from the Quran only in the number of daughters (see below) and the addition of Moses' supplication. A somewhat different sequence of events at the well may be seen, but it does not affect the main flow of the story. Western critics

---

[173] Shu'ayb: This identification of the father of the girls with the Midianite prophet Shu'ayb mentioned in Q. 7:83-91, though common in the commentaries, is not universally accepted by Muslim scholars. See below in this section.

[174] Surabadi, pp. 301-302.

[175] Laymon, p. 34.

charge that in the story of Moses at the well in Midian there is still another instance of the confusion in the Quranic account when compared with that of the "true" Biblical account.

In the Bible, there are no less than three stories of a prospective bride being discovered at a well (for that is what was happening above). The first is Rebekah, who was drawing water when the servant of Abraham, sent to bring a wife from among Abraham's kin for Isaac, reached her city. In that incident, she gave him water and watered his camels. Impressed, the servant enquired of her family and eventually she was married to Isaac (Gen. 24).

The second is that concerning Jacob and Rachel, also in *Genesis*, and it is the story which, the critics say, is confused in the Quran with the story of Moses and well in Midian. This is story from *Genesis*: "(Jacob) saw a well in the field, and lo, three flocks of sheep lying beside it; for out of that well the flocks were watered. The stone on the well's mouth was large, and when all the flocks were gathered there, the shepherds would roll the stone from the mouth of the well, and water the sheep, and put the stone back in its place upon the well.

"Jacob said to them, 'My brothers, where do ye come from?' They said, 'We are from Haran,' He said to them, 'Do ye know Laban the son of Nahor?' They said, 'We know him.' He said to them, 'Is it well with him?' They, 'It is well; and see Rachel his daughter is coming with the sheep!' He said, 'Behold, it is still high day, it is not time for the animals to be gathered together; water the sheep, and go, pasture them.' But they said, 'We cannot until all the flocks are gathered together, and the stone is rolled from the mouth of the well; then we water the sheep.'

"While he was still speaking with them, Rachel came with her father's sheep; for she kept them. Now when Jacob saw Rachel the daughter of Laban his mother's brother, Jacob went up and rolled the stone from the well's mouth, and watered the flock of Laban his mother's brother." (Gen. 29:2-10)

As can be seen, the pericope of Jacob meeting Rachel at the well has clearly influenced Surabadi's story in one point, the matter of the heavy stone covering the mouth of the well. This detail, its most conspicuous feature, is *absent* from the Quranic account. It would surely have been there had it been the basis for the episode of the Quranic story of Moses under consideration. In other respects, the stories are quite different. The shepherds have gathered together with no animosity towards Rachel—indeed they respect her father. (In the Moses story, the shepherds appear to be contemptuous of the women's old, weak father. They would not have behaved so rudely had he been a man of power and influence; the note that he was a priest makes their attitude somewhat perplexing.)

In *Genesis*, they are awaiting the gathering of the flocks to be watered together at a customary time. They appear to be waiting for the others to come, including at the beginning, Rachel. Jacob's rolling aside of the stone seems to be a kind of bravura gesture to impress the beautiful (and rich) Rachel with his physical strength. There is no element of defiance of the other shepherds. None of them had begun watering his flocks.

Because two women are mentioned in the Quranic account of Moses at the well, Western critics assume that Rachel and Leah are meant; yet, it must be noted that there is only one young woman at the well in the Jacob pericope. In fact, the only similarities are the fact of the well, the gathering of the shepherds to water their flocks, a hero (Jacob in one, Moses in the other), and the woman or women. All of these elements are common to both the Biblical and the Quranic versions of the story of Moses at the well in Midian. There is no need to look farther afield for its source. The principal difference is the number of girls at the well: the Bible mentions seven, the Quran two. It is a difference, but not a confusion. However, Surabadi and other commentators must be considered guilty of strengthening the Western critics' hands, as *they* have seemed to confuse the story of Moses with that of Jacob. The Quranic text continues:

Then there came unto him one of the two women, walking shyly. She said: 'Lo! My father biddeth thee, that he may reward thee with a payment for that thou didst water (the flock) for us. Then, when he came unto him and told him the (whole) story, (Shu'ayb) said: 'Fear not! Thou hast escaped from the wrongdoing folk.' One of the two women said: 'O my father! Hire him! For the best (man) that thou canst hire is the strong, the trustworthy.' He said: 'Lo! I desire to marry thee to one of these two daughters of mine on condition that thou hirest thyself to me for (the term of) eight pilgrimages. Then if thou completest ten it will be of thine own accord, for I would not make it hard for thee. God willing, thou wilt find me of the righteous.' (Moses) said: 'That (is settled) between thee and me. Whichever of the two terms I fulfill, there will be no injustice to me, and God is Surety over what we say.' (Q. 28:25-28)

Surabadi amplifies the text of the Quran here, relating that the girls returned to their father with their flocks and reported what Moses had done to help them. One of them suggested that he be hired. Shu'ayb proposed instead that Moses marry one of the girls and the dowry (or bride-payment) would be that he would work for him for 8 years, or 10 years should Moses be gracious. An agreement was reached and Moses became the shepherd for Shu'ayb's flocks.

There is no mention of hire in the Biblical account: "When (the daughters) came to their father Reuel, he said, 'How is it that ye have come so soon today?' They said, 'An Egyptian[176] delivered us out of the hand of the shepherds, and even drew water for us and watered the flock.' He said to his daughters, 'And where is he? Why have ye left the man? Call him, that he may eat bread.' And Moses was content to dwell with the man, and he gave Moses his daughter Zipporah." (Ex. 2:18-21)

Whilst the dependence of the Quranic scene at the well on that of the Jacob story is more imagined and coincidental than real, there is one real parallel between the Quranic version of Moses' marriage and the Biblical account of Jacob's marriage (See above Part Two, V.B). {In this series, in *Jacob and Joseph.*} The mention of the hire has caught the attention of Western critics and caused them to charge that here is another example of Quranic confusion between the circumstances of Moses' marriage and those of Jacob.

It must be noted that except for the matter of the hire, in every other particular the stories are different. In *Genesis,* Jacob proposes the terms of the contract; whilst in the Quran the father does. In *Genesis,* the wedding is consummated after the contract has been fulfilled; in the Quran, it is at the beginning. In *Genesis* the term specified is seven years, "a week of years," surely a significant detail that would likely to have been repeated because of the importance of that number to ancient peoples; but in the Quran we read of a vague, eight, possibly ten, years. In *Genesis,* Jacob marries both daughters; in the Quran Moses marries only one. Indeed the "contract" in the Quran is hardly a contract at all,[177] whilst in *Genesis* the terms of the contract are very rigid, as Jacob finds out to his cost.

The amicable ambiance of the Quran is quite different from the hard bargaining of *Genesis.* The father was impressed by Moses and apparently had no son. He wished to have Moses in his family—and Moses had already proved himself at the well. The father offered to make Moses one of the family, if he would stay and work for him. Furthermore, if he would agree to stay for a considerable period of time, he would make the tie even stronger, by giving one of his daughters to him in marriage. The agreement is informal, and is of a type common to the present day throughout much of the world. As we have seen, the differences between the Quranic episode and the story of Jacob in

---

[176] See Introduction, Section A, above.

[177] In a real contract, either 8 or 10 years would have been specified.

Genesis are far greater than the similarities (aside from the unremarkable existence of a well from which shepherds draw water for their flocks), which can be reduced to two points: the mention of aiding the daughters and the mention of "hire." In all else, these two pericopes differ.

However, this has not prevented Surabadi from falling into the same trap as the critics of the Quran, and he borrows heavily from the Jacob story to fill out his narrative of the years Moses spent in Midian, as we have already seen above, and of which we shall see more below.

The import of the Quranic text is that after the period of eight or ten years had expired, Moses' obligation to the Midianites would be considered fulfilled. It is not stated how long he actually lived in Midian. In Jewish tradition, this is usually said to be 40 years,[178] although Artapanus makes it 30 years.[179] In this respect Maulana Muhammad Ali writes: "According to rabbinical accounts, Moses lived with Jethro [Shu'ayb] for ten years, which corroborates the Quranic story in substance..." and then he proceeds to give an interesting interpretation of the "eight or ten" years: "But what is stated here has really a deeper significance beneath it. In Moses' stay at Midian for ten years, there is a prophetic reference to the ten years of the Prophet's life at Madinah. The mention of eight years has another underlying significance, for it was after eight years that the Prophet came back to Makkah as a conqueror, a clear reference to which is contained further on v. 85: *He Who has made the Quran binding on thee will surely bring thee back to the place of return*. This occurred exactly eight years after his Flight [*Hijrah*]."[180]

However, according to Surabadi, Moses worked for Shu'ayb eight years and after that, Shu'ayb gave him every lamb that was the same color as its mother (or, in another tradition, every female lamb). Moses touched the staff Shu'ayb had given him to the water the sheep drank, and that year they gave birth only to females. The next year the agreement was changed to males, and Moses did the same thing; as a result, only males were born. The flocks of Moses became greater than those of Shu'ayb.[181]

This unworthy bit of chicanery and misuse of divine power for personal gain attributed to Moses is another of Surabadi's (that is, his

---

[178] LJ, II, 301.

[179] LJ, V, 406. This figure is, of course, artificial and is based upon a rabbinical penchant for symmetry. Thus Moses is supposed to have lived 40 years in Egypt, 40 years in Midian, and 40 years as the leader of the Israelites (Asimov-OT, pp. 129-130), a total of 120 years (Deut. 34:7). Moses was more likely nearer 20 than 40 when he fled to Midian. The *Book of Jubilees* says that he was 21 (LJ, V, 406).

[180] Quran-MMA, p. 748.

[181] Surabadi, p. 304.

source's) borrowing from the Jacob cycle of *Genesis*, and has absolutely no support in the Quran. The parallel story, found in Gen. 30:25-43, has been summarized in elsewhere.[182] The criteria for distinguishing the lambs belonging to one or the other are different, but the basic theme is the same and the dependence is obvious. Its inclusion by the commentators in the story of Moses, or that of any other prophet, is to be deplored, as it lends the appearance of divine sanction to such trickery.

THE STAFF OF MOSES: According to Surabadi, the staff mentioned in the pericope being employed for such an unworthy purpose is the one of myrtle that Adam had carried with him from Paradise. When Shu'ayb hired him, he wanted to give him a staff, but not that one. He sent his daughter to bring a staff, and she brought the one of myrtle. He told her to take it back and bring another. She did so, but it turned out to be the same one again. This was repeated seven times, until finally Shu'ayb realized that it was destined to be possessed by Moses. He surrendered it to him, saying: "Keep this well and hold it dear so that thou may see wonders."[183] (We have already seen one in its improper use by Moses in Surabadi's story above.)

This story of the origin of Moses' staff is not found in the Bible or in the Quran; however, it is in Jewish tradition. For example, in the *Pirke de Rabbi Eliezer*: "Rabbi Levi said: That rod which was created in the twilight was delivered to the first man out of the garden of Eden. Adam delivered it to Enoch, and Enoch delivered it to Noah, and Noah (handed it on) to Shem. Shem passed it on to Abraham, Abraham (transmitted it) to Isaac, and Isaac (gave it over) to Jacob, and Jacob brought it down into Egypt and passed in on to his son Joseph, and when Joseph died and they pillaged his household goods, it was placed in the palace of Pharaoh. And Jethro was one of the magicians of Egypt, and he saw the rod and the letters which were upon it, and he desired in his heart (to have it), and he took it and brought it, and planted it in the midst of the garden of his house. No one was able to approach it any more.

"When Moses came to his house he went into the garden of Jethro's house, and saw the rod and read the letters which were upon it, and he put forth his hand and took it. Jethro watched Moses and said: This one in the future will redeem Israel from Egypt. Therefore he gave him Zipporah his daughter to wife..."[184] In another version, wresting the rod from the garden was a kind of test to which Jethro put Moses before

---

[182] See Part Two, V, B. {In this series, see "Jacob" in *Jacob and Joseph.*}
[183] Surabadi, p. 303.
[184] PRE, pp. 312-313.

he would allow him to marry Zipporah.[185] Surabadi mentions that Shu'ayb was blind,[186] but this does not seem to be supported by any Biblical or traditional text about Jethro.

In connection with the wondrous rod, Surabadi relates to us a story of Moses' killing the dragon that lived in a fertile valley that had been left uninhabited because of the people's fear of the monster. Moses led his flocks into the valley, and when the dragon came forward, he killed it with a blow of his staff.[187] This particular prodigy has no basis in the Quran or the Bible, and is not mentioned in *Legends of the Jews*. The slaying of the dragon is a popular theme in the mythology legends of the world; numerous parallels are available that require no further comment here: Perseus in Greek mythology, St. George in Christian legend, Daniel in Jewish tradition, Marduk in Mesopotamian mythology, and Baal against the Prince of the Sea in Ugartic mythology. In central Afghanistan a rock formation is pointed out west of Bamyan that is reputedly the petrified remains of a dragon slain by Ali, the son-in-law of the Prophet.[188]

The ascription of such a feat to Moses is perhaps suggested by the story that at the court of Pharaoh, the staff itself became a dragon (see below). Other possibilities suggest themselves: in the Bible, a beast, usually depicted as a kind of monstrous crocodile, is used to personify Egypt.[189] Influenced by this imagery, Moses' defeat of a dragon in Midian would prefigure his defeat of Egypt. Another reptilian parallel that exists in the Biblical story of Moses may be connected with the Surabadi pericope: The incident occurred during the 40 years of wandering. The people were complaining once again against the leadership of Moses (the Israelites do a great of whining in the Exodus): "Then the Lord sent fiery serpents among the people, and they bit the people, so that many of the people of Israel died. And the people came to Moses, and said, 'We have sinned, for we have spoken against the Lord and against thee; pray to the Lord, that He take away the serpents from us.' So Moses prayed for the people. And the Lord said to Moses, 'Make a fiery serpent, and set it on a pole; and every one who is bitten, when he sees it, shall live.' So Moses made a bronze serpent and set it on a pole;

---

[185] LJ, II, 291-295.

[186] Surabadi, p. 303.

[187] Surabadi, pp. 303-304.

[188] See the story of St. George in Vol. 2, IV.G for more about the dragon. {In this series, in *Paul and Early Christianity*.}

[189] Dragon, DB, p. 221.

and if a serpent bit any man, he would look at the bronze serpent and live." (Num. 21:6-9)

This appears to be an aetiological story to explain the presence of a bronze serpent (by ascribing it to Moses) that was venerated by the Judaeans in YHWH-worship. Called the Nehushtan, it was destroyed by the Judaean king Hezekiah (rgd. 715-687 BCE) as part of his religious reforms (2 K. 18:4).[190] It is not impossible that a report of this tradition lies behind Surabadi's story.

Surabadi next tells us that after Moses had had two sons by Zipporah, he felt a desire to see his family in Egypt once again. When he left Midian, Zipporah was again pregnant. The Quran has none of these details. In Surabadi's commentary, this data is in the nature of an appendix and omits the real reason for Moses' return to Egypt: the command of God to return and liberate the Israelites.[191] Surabadi attributes to Moses a genuine, natural desire to see his relatives again, but the Bible offers no support for such feelings in Moses. "And Moses was content to dwell with the man [Reuel/Jethro], and he gave Moses his daughter Zipporah. She bore a son, and he called his name Gershom; for he said, 'I have been a sojourner in a foreign land.'" (Ex. 2:21-22)

After the theophany and the divine command to lead Israel out of Egypt to be discussed in the following section: "Moses went back to Jethro his father-in-law and said to him, 'Let me go back, I pray, to my kinsmen in Egypt and see whether they are still alive.' And Jethro said to Moses, 'Go in peace.'... So Moses took his wife and sons and set them on an ass, and went back to the land of Egypt, and in his hand Moses took the rod of God." (Ex. 4:18,20) Moses is using the desire to see his family as a pretext to execute God's command to liberate the Hebrews. In another place, we learn the name of the other son, Eliezer (Ex. 18:4). The Bible speaks only of two sons. If Zipporah were pregnant again, as in Surabadi, the issue was either a girl (the girls are only mentioned irregularly in Biblical genealogies), or did not survive. The Chronicler also knows only of two sons: "The sons of Moses: Gershom and Eliezer." (1 Ch. 23:15)

IS JETHRO SHU'AYB? The reader not familiar with the vagaries of Biblical text may be a little perplexed by the name of Moses' father-in-law. One time he is called Reuel, and another time Jethro (and many Muslims call him Shu'ayb, if that identification be correct). Many scholars share the reader's perplexity. Apparently in the Northern E

---

[190] Laymon, p. 204; Ark, ERE, Vol. I, 792.

[191] See next Section.

tradition he was uniformly referred to as Jethro.[192] In *Exodus*, the Southern J calls him Reuel (Ex. 2:18). Both sources refer to him as a "priest of Midian,"[193] which clearly hints at Jethro's (we shall call him Jethro for the sake of simplicity) possessing a religious or possibly a prophetic function.[194]

However, the question of Jethro's name is further confused by yet another name: Hobab. In *Numbers* we read: "And Moses said to Hobab the son of Reuel the Midianite, Moses' father-in-law..." (Num. 10:29) Depending upon punctuation, this verse can be read to mean that Hobab, the son of Reuel, is Moses' father-in-law, or that Hobab is the son of Moses' father-in-law Reuel, thereby making him his brother-in-law. If this had been the only evidence, then we could safely interpret the passage to mean Moses' brother-in-law. Yet, in *Judges* we find: "Now Heber [not the patriarch Eber of *Genesis*] the Kenite had separated from the Kenites, the descendants of Hobab the father-in-law of Moses..." (Jgs. 4:11)[195] From this it is clear that there was a third tradition about the name of Moses' father-in-law, and—incidentally—we learn that he was a Kenite, a member of one of the Midianite clans. This may have serious implications, as we shall see in the next section.

Thus we see that Moses' father-in-law, from the Biblical evidence, is known by three different and phonologically unrelated names: Jethro, Reuel, and Hobab. No wonder the Muslim commentators felt free to add a fourth to the list and identify him with Shu'ayb, [196] although not without reservation, as even Surabadi shows: "He stayed,

---

[192] Ex. 3:1; 4:18; 18:1; etc.

[193] Ex. 2:16; 3:1; etc.

[194] This will be discussed in the following Section.

[195] The problem created by Num. 10:29, which states that Hobab is the son of Reuel, still defies all attempts at rationalization. To make matters worse, that verse is assigned to the Yahwist (J), and—were it not for the statement in *Judges*—probably would be interpreted to mean that Hobab was Moses' brother-in-law. This would make J internally consistent. The passage in *Judges* might be dependent upon an error in the transmission of oral tradition, but it is odd that redactor of J did not see the contradiction. After the conflation with E and P, this no longer stood out and so was left in the text as one of the many lesser and greater inconsistencies of the Bible. For his part, the Elohist was firmly and consistently behind the Jethro tradition.

[196] The Elohist (E) knows the father-in-law of Moses as Jethro. The Yahwist (J) calls him Reuel in *Exodus* but refers to him as Hobab in *Numbers* (Num. 10:29). McNeile, writing in the article on "Hobab" (Heb: Ḥobāb) in the DB (p. 387), speculates that the Arabic Shu'ayb (who in Islamic tradition is the father-in-law of Moses) is in some manner related to Hobab, but the extreme shift from the Hebrew hard guttural *H* to Arabic *Sh* and the middle consonant from Hebrew *B* to Arabic *'Ayn* would be unusual between the sister Semitic languages. The form Shu'ayb is an Arabic diminutive from the root *sh-'-b*, which has a range of meanings: among them are "people, branch, and dividing."

ten years, among the people of Midian with Shu'ayb; or, they have related, with Jethro[197] the nephew of Shu'ayb..."[198] This introduces still another schema of the relationship of Moses with his in-laws and Shu'ayb. The Quran mentions Moses' father-in-law without naming him. The absence of such an identification should give us pause from rashly assuming that Shu'ayb and Moses' father-in-law are the same person. In the Quran, Shu'ayb was not old and feeble as was Jethro, and he was sent to Midian (Q. 7:85; 11: 84), in particular to a section of them called the "people of thicket" (Q. 26:176). Ignoring Shu'ayb's warning to reform their lives, they were destroyed, presumably be an earthquake (Q. 11:94).

Although the religious character of Jethro has been established by both the Biblical text and Jewish tradition, which generally show him a righteous man, no mission of warning seems to have been associated with his name. "In the city of Midian, named thus for a son of Abraham by Keturah, the man Jethro had lived for many years doing a priest's service before the idols. As time went on, he grew more and more convinced of the vanity of idol worship. His priesthood became repugnant to him, and he resolved to give up his charge."[199] Although the tradition speaks of a city, Midian was a largely pastoral region principally east of the Gulf of Aqabah.

Whereas the impression created in the Bible makes Midian rather remote from Egyptian power (it was 200 miles to the east of the Nile over difficult arid and mountainous territory), Jewish tradition depicts it as more closely attached to Egypt and involves Jethro himself in the councils of Pharaoh. In the absence of any more explicit confirmation in the Quran in places where it might be expected, we can only regard the identification of Shu'ayb with Jethro as highly speculative. The tradition of the prophet Shu'ayb in Midian seems to be another of those that passed down into Arabia without entering the mainstream of Biblical and Jewish tradition. A clue doubtless lies in the phrase "people of the thicket," but it has not been deciphered as of yet, though it must have been understood by Arabs of the Prophet's time.

MIDIAN AND MOUNT SEIR: As our focus is now upon Midian, it may be appropriate to look at the area for a moment. The Midianites were, in the Biblical paradigm of racial relationships, descendants of Abraham by Keturah (Gen. 25:1-2), who is probably also Hagar,[200] and

---

[197] Surabadi uses the form Yathrun or Yathrawn.

[198] Surabadi, p. 251.

[199] LJ, II, 289.

[200] See III, G in Part Two. {In this series, in *Abraham*.}

therefore close kin of the Ishmaelites. Indeed the terms, when used in a general sense, were probably roughly co-extensive.[201] The extent of their territory seems to have varied, depending upon their own prosperity and the amount of pressure their neighbors were able to bear upon them. However, the core of their lands was east of the line of the Gulf of Aqabah and the Arabah valley, the southwestern region of modern Jordan and the northwestern corner of Saudi Arabia. The names of the five sons of Midian (Ephah, Epher, Hanoch, Abida, and Eldaah) given in a genealogical table (Gen. 25:4) aid us in fixing their territory more precisely, at least at the time of the Yahwist (c. 1000 BCE) who is responsible for the passage. The "sons" were doubtless eponymous ancestors of Midianite clans.

Ephah has been associated with the modern oasis town of Tabuk in northwestern Arabia.[202] A Hanoch is also listed as a son of Reuben (Gen. 46:9), and while it may be simply a case of two individuals bearing the same name, it could also represent an adoption of the Midianite clan by the Reubenites. (Hanoch the Midianite is from J; Hanoch the Reubenite is from the later P. The tribe of Reuben was settled east of the Jordan north of Midian.) This might indicate a distribution of Midianites from east of the Dead Sea to the northern Hejaz, a distance of some 250 miles. A conspicuous absence from the list of clans is mention of the Kenites who are definitely stated to be Midianites,[203] and to which clan Moses' father-in-law belonged. Therefore, the Kenites were detached (except in the passages cited above) from the Midianites of whom the Israelites disapproved. The possible significance of this will be discussed in the next Section.

The Midianites appear to have been an originally semi-nomadic people who gradually became nomadic, perhaps as the result of desertification. In addition to their herding, they seem to have also been traders and raiders. In the absence of a firm basis of archeological work in the region, we have little extra-Biblical evidence about their history.[204] They seem to have entered the land of Midian roughly during the period in which the Abrahamites moved into Canaan and were an intermittent power in the lands south and east of Palestine until they received a crushing defeat at the hands of Gideon and the Israelites about the 12th

---

[201] Asimov-OT, p. 92.

[202] OBA, p. 67. The author of this work spent several years as a teacher in Tabuk, an important agricultural region.

[203] Jgs. 1:16; 4:11; Num. 10:29. See also "Jethro, EJ, X, 18-19.

[204] How slow Muslims are to explore their own historical and archeological roots before the evidence is bulldozed away in "development" and "modernization"!

century BCE. After this, they were no longer a political or military factor in the region.[205] In general, the territory of the Midianites was semi-desert and desert. There are a number water holes and oases and some small districts that could be called "thickets."

One of the most conspicuous features of this region is Mount Seir, or as it is sometimes known, Mount Esau. It is a mountainous chain that stretches about 100 miles from north to south, lying east of the Arabah-Aqabah rift valley. It seems to have been shared by Edom (in the north) and Midian (in the south. This is presumably the region to which Moses fled. Even today, the memory of Moses is preserved in the small town of Wadi Musa (Valley of Moses) about midway in the length of the mountain, and this tradition is not unreasonable, as we shall see.

"(Mount Seir) attains a general elevation of 4,000 to 5,000 feet above sea level, far higher than the heights of Hauran, the Gilead, or Moab..." It is actually the highest elevation along the Great Rift Valley between Mt. Hermon west of Damascus (9,232 ft.) and Shifa in northwestern Saudi Arabia (8,461 ft.)... "which gives it in parts a different climate and aspect... Almost treeless on its slopes to the desert the mount bears on its back and west flanks plentiful timber, groves of the evergreen oak and the *butm* or terebinth, and stretches of juniper, a conifer with a trunk often a foot in diameter, which fetches a good price in Kerak or Ma'an. Poplar and willow are frequent along Wady Hesa and found elsewhere on the limestone. Below 3,000 feet flourish laurels, oleanders and tamarisks, tarfa. Pasture abounds—'the greatest sheep flocks which I have seen of the Arabs were in the rocky coomb-land between Shobek and Petra'"[206]

This should convince the most reluctant reader that the conditions associated in the Quran with the "people of the thicket" who dwelt in Midian do indeed exist in that region. Even though Shu'ayb may not be the Jethro of Moses, he was probably a prophet in the same region in which the Biblical Jethro lived. This will be seen to be of considerable importance when we come to consider the Kenite Hypothesis in the next Section.

The Tale of Sinuhe: Finally, it is interesting to compare the story of the flight of Moses with still another parallel to the Bible to be found in ancient literature, this time Egyptian. It is the *Story of Sinuhe*; the earliest manuscripts of this tale (which may be based upon fact) date from about 1800 BCE. Clearing antedating Moses by at least 500 years,

---

[205] Midian, EJ, XI, 1505-1506; Midian, DB, p. 658.

[206] Geo HL, p. 362, 363, 364. The quotation is from Doughty.

and manuscript evidence of Moses' flight to and residence in Midian by several hundred years more.[207] Sinuhe writes that he was a court official and he styles himself "the hereditary prince and count, judge and District Overseer of the domains of the Sovereign in the land of the Asiatics, real acquaintance of the king, his beloved, the Attendant Sinuhe..." these seem to be his titles after his restoration to favor; originally he "was an attendant who followed his lord, a servant of the royal harem (and of) the hereditary Princess, the great of favor, the wife of King Sen-Usert in (the pyramid town) Khenem-sut, the daughter of King Amen-em-het in (the pyramid town Qa-nefru, Nefru, the lady of reverence."[208] Here we see that Sinuhe was an attendant of the king's daughter Nefru; compare this with Moses and the daughter of Pharaoh in *Exodus*.

The XIIth Dynasty king Amen-em-het died c. 1960 BCE, and for some reason which the text does not give, Sinuhe fell out of favor with the new king Sen-Usert I (rgd. 1971-1928 BCE)—the old king shared his reign with his son in his last years—and he (Sinuhe) apparently overheard a royal conversation in which his death or severe punishment was discussed. "While I was standing (near by) I heard his voice as he was speaking and I was distraught, my arms spread out (in dismay), trembling fell upon my limbs. I removed myself by leaps and bounds to seek a hiding place for myself. I placed myself between two bushes, in order to cut (myself) off from the road and its travel."[209]

Sinuhe then fled past the "Mistress of the Red Mountain" (still called "Red Mountain" today in Arabic, Jabal al-Ahmar, east of Cairo) and then crossed the line of defenses, "the Wall of the Ruler," across the Isthmus of Suez "made to oppose the Asiatics and to crush the Sand-crossers. I took a crouching position in a bush, for fear lest the watchmen upon the wall where their day's (duty) was might see me." Then he speaks of his trek across the waterless wastes of Sinai: "I set out at evening time, and when day broke, I reached Peten. I halted at the Island of Kem-wer. An attack of thirst overtook me. I was parched, and my throat was dusty. I said: 'This is the taste of death!' (But then) I lifted up my heart and collected myself, for I heard the sound of the lowing of cattle, and I spied Asiatics. The shaikh among them, who had been in Egypt, recognized me. Then he gave me water while he boiled milk for me. I went with him to his tribe. What they did (for me) was good."[210]

---

[207] ANE, I, p. 5.
[208] ANE, I, p. 5.
[209] ANE, I, p. 6.
[210] ANE, I, p. 7.

He seems to have settled in the pasturage on the western side of the Syrian desert. About his life there he writes: "He set me at the head of his children. He married me to his eldest daughter. He let me choose for myself of his country, of the choicest of that which was with him on his frontier with another country... He made me ruler of a tribe of the choicest of his country. Bread was made for me as daily fare, wine as daily provision, cooked meat and roast fowl, beside the wild beasts of the desert, for they hunted for me and laid before me, beside the catch of my (own) hound...

"I spent many years, and my children grew up to be strong men, each man as the restrainer of his (own) tribe. The messenger who went north or who went south to the Residence City [that is, the residence of Pharaoh in Egypt] stopped over with me, (for) I used to make everybody stop over. I gave water to the thirsty. I put him who had strayed (back) on the road. I rescued him who had been robbed..."[211] Sinuhe became very prosperous in his adopted land. Eventually he was cleared of the charges against him in Egypt, whatever they were, and returned to Egypt in triumph.

This story, as the numerous manuscripts of it show, was an extremely popular one in ancient Egypt, and therefore was most likely known to the Semites (the Asiatics) dwelling on the steppes of Goshen east of the Delta. Whether it played any role in the development of the Moses story can only be speculated upon; all there are some potentially embarrassing parallels. There are indications in the text that Sinuhe's flight was not unique (he appears to speak of other Egyptian exiles living in the regions beyond Egypt's frontiers).[212] The tradition of Moses' taking refuge in Midian, which was about the nearest habitable region not directly under Egyptian control during that period, need not be dependent upon Sinuhe's fascinating glimpse of life in Egypt 3700 years ago. It could reflect a fairly common circumstance in ancient Egypt.

E. THE REVELATION AND THE COMMISSION

"I AM WHO I AM" (Ex. 3:14)

In the preceding material, we have frequently mentioned the difference between the Yahwist and the Elohist (with the Priestly Document following the Elohist in this respect) concerning the use of the divine name YHWH. After the events to be discussed in this section that

---

[211] ANE, I. P. 7-8.

[212] ANE, I, p. 7, note 2.

particular Biblical distinction will disappear, but a difference in theological approach remains that helps scholars to separate the different strands of the text.

To recapitulate, the Southern (Judahite) Yahwist (J) tradition seems to assume that YHWH-worship existed from the very beginning of history. Though other titles for God may have been used by the patriarchs, He was also known to them as YHWH. This position has its parallel in Islam, which holds that God had revealed Himself to the prophets and messengers from the very beginning of human history, beginning with Adam. Though the commonalty of mankind have often ignored or retreated from this basic truth of the unseen, ineffable, one Supreme Being, lapsing into the easier worship of idols, natural objects, animals, and even mortal humans, the central fact of the Most High One looming behind everything was known or suspected. This crucial and eternal truth has been preached in a continuing tradition of prophets, from Adam to the time of last, Muhammad, peace be upon them all.

For the Yahwist, the significance of the theophany, the central event of this section, lies in the commission given to Moses to lead Israel out of Egypt; that is, it is an act of salvation. For the Yahwist it did not represent the commencement of the special relationship between YHWH and Israel, but rather was a crucial sign of His favor.

The Northern (Josephic) Elohist (E) tradition takes quite a different view. Whilst the patriarchs may have been granted a special knowledge of God intuitively, they had not received the benefit of the revelation of His true nature, as represented by His personal name YHWH. The knowledge of this name established the people who knew it, the Israelites, in a special relationship with God as His Chosen People. The significance of the knowledge of one's personal name, be it of man or god, is a well-known feature of Semitic religion.[213]

Thus, in the Elohist view (and P follows E in this), the name (and true nature) of YHWH was unknown to the ancient Hebrews (and, by implication, the rest of mankind) until its revelation to Moses in a scene of supernatural terror and awe on the Holy Mountain. Until that moment, E always referred to the Deity as *Elohim*, a word plural in form but almost always used in a singular sense in the Bible when referring to God.[214] It is only with the revelation of the Divine Name to Moses that E

---

[213] Anderson, p. 32; de Vaux, p. 327.

[214] *Elohim*: the singular would be *Eloh*, a cognate of the Arabic *Ilāh* "god" (the Arabic plural is *ālihah* "gods"), seems to be a vestige of a time when the plurality of gods was accepted. In later times, probably with the growth of monotheism in ancient Israel, the meaning shifted and came to mean the one god of Israel, although it still retained its

begins to use that name in his text to refer to God. For him, the real religious history of Israel begins at this moment.[215] It is important to keep these distinctions between the Yahwist and the Elohist-Priestly views in mind when examining the traditions of Moses, and especially the material of this section.

It is at this point that the figure of Aaron is introduced into the Biblical story for the first time. The first two chapters of *Exodus* make no mention of a brother, although a sister (to be later identified with the prophetess Miriam) was mentioned. Aaron is brought into the narrative

---

plural meaning when referring to the polytheistic beliefs of other peoples. (In Persian, the literary word *yazdān* meaning God is also a plural derived from the singular *yazd.* See note in Burhan, Vol. 4, p. 2432.) Phipps opines: "Elohim, the name that is used for deity some twenty-five hundred times in the Hebrew Bible, may have developed via the merging of the names of the two primordial deities and the addition of the plural *-im* ending. Walter Eichrodt explains that the plural Elohim was used 'to express the higher unity subsuming the individual gods and combining in one concept the whole pantheon.'" [Walter Eichrodt, *Theology of the Old Testament* (Philadelphia: Westminster, 1961) p. 185.] (Phipps, p. 20.)

Originally, each Israelite shrine seems to have possessed its own god. With the introduction of YHWH-worship, YHWH absorbed, assimilated, or displaced, these local deities. (Albright-Ab to Ez, p. 18) Probably at the same time, He absorbed the usage to Himself of the term *elohim* when referring to the totality of the gods (of Canaan), and thus the word came to be uniformly construed as a grammatical singular. This odd usage of a plural noun with a singular verb probably did not originate with the Hebrews. Akkadian records of the 14th century BCE found in Egypt have *ilani*, "gods," also construed as a singular when referring to a single Deity. (God, DB, p. 334) *Elohim*, when meant to indicate the pantheon of gods, would be a grammatical plural, but when used to designate the abstract aspect of their divinity, which all the gods shared in common, it became a singular. It was this usage which passed into Hebrew. There are parallels in British English in the usage of collective words such as "government," "cabinet," and "team" that can be singular or plural depending upon whether the group as a unit or the individuals who constitute it is intended.

It should also be noted that though YHWH-worship was monotheistic, it originally did not deny the reality of other gods worshipped by other peoples, as we shall see. Israel's special god was One, and therefore Israel worshipped one God and was monotheistic; furthermore He was invisible and not to be depicted. In these respects Israel's monotheism differed from the polytheism of their more civilized neighbors, all of whom worshipped national pantheons. But originally Israel' monotheism was not a denial of the reality of the gods of Egypt, Canaan, Babylonia, etc. (Anderson, p. 34) That development, universal monotheism, came much later in Israel's religious history. The monotheism of Moses, according to the Biblical record, was a national monotheism. Evidence in support of this proposition will be cited in the relevant contexts when appropriate.

[215] As we have observed, the lapse of this distinction in usage between the Elohist and the Yahwist makes the task of separating the two sources more difficult henceforth. See the Introduction, III. {In this series, see the Foreword to this volume, and also *Introduction to the Old Testament* for a more detailed discussion.}

ostensibly to serve as Moses' spokesman because of some problem with Moses' speech (Ex. 4:10-16). The appearance of Aaron in the story of Moses presents problems. His Biblical role seems to have been moulded by the rival claims of various clans of hereditary priests in the periods of the monarchy and the post-Exile religious establishment. The reconstruction of these events is difficult, but in monarchical times, the priesthood at Jerusalem was in the hands of the Zadokites of Levite descent, while the Aaronites were associated with other sanctuaries in Palestine. Apparently, their strongest connections were with the Northern sanctuaries. There are compelling reasons to believe that the Aaronites were not originally considered Levites,[216] as Moses was probably not, notwithstanding E's assertions at the beginning of ch. 2 of *Exodus*.

With the destruction of the Solomon's Temple at Jerusalem 586 BCE by the Babylonian Nebuchadnezzar, the Zadokite priesthood seems to have lapsed, or had been carried off to Babylon during the Exile. During this traumatic period for the Jews, the Aaronites became the primary priesthood of YHWH worship in Palestine. It is thought that the destruction of Jerusalem allowed the Northern shrines to revive or increase their influence. As these were probably already in the hands of the Aaronites, the rebuilding of the Jerusalem Temple and the re-institution of the Zadokite priesthood as its functionaries by Nehemiah and Ezra must have precipitated an inter-priestly crisis. This crisis seems to have been resolved by ascribing Aaronite descent to the Zadokites and Levite descent to the Aaronites![217]

---

[216] Aaron, EJ, II, 19.

[217] Aaron, DB, pp. 1-2; Aaron, EJ, II, 18-20. The situation was considerably more complex than the above remarks might indicate, but this summary will suffice for our purposes to show the broad outlines of the problem. It should be remembered that priesthood in Judaism was hereditary and dependent upon lineage. Descendants of other tribes could officiate in other capacities, but the all-important sacrifices had to be carried out by the priestly caste.

Jerusalem was the latest of the shrines of YHWH-worship to be founded in Palestine. It was originally a Jebusite city that contained a shrine dedicated to El-'Elyon, a Canaanite deity who is known from other ancient sources. When David conquered Jerusalem, he brought the Ark there and established YHWH-worship with some thought towards making the city his new capital and a national center as well since it was his personal conquest and had no particular association with the Israelite tribes. Accordingly, one Zadok was established as high priest of the new YHWH-worship. (Although this office appears to have been initially shared, Solomon seems to have made it hereditary in the Zadokite clan.)

Because the local El-'Elyon was absorbed by YHWH and El-'Elyon become one of His titles, it has been suggested that the Zadokite priesthood were originally in the service of the Canaanite deity, and that David invited Zadok to lead the new YHWH-worship. Zadok is not heard of before the conquest of Jerusalem. The meeting between

With this in mind, the minor role (or as some scholars suppose, total absence) of Aaron in the J account is understandable; J's was the view of the non-Aaronite Zadokite priesthood. Aaron's more prominent role in E's material is thus explicable by the influence of the Aaronites in the Northern sanctuaries and among the laity. In a later layer, great concern is shown by the Priestly Writer (P) to trace the privileges of the Levite priesthood, and especially the Jerusalem (Zadokite) priesthood, to Aaron. The great enhancement of his role in the narrative portions of *Exodus* speaks of a period in which the compromise had been achieved: the priesthood at Jerusalem was now associated with all the Aaronite priests in Palestine, though in a paramount position, echoing the paramountcy of Jerusalem as the royal city. All now traced their ancestry to Aaron, who had become a Levite. Finally, during the same period, with its concentration upon the Law, the authority of Moses was called upon to sanctify all the minutiae of Jewish religious law. The anomaly of the towering figure of Moses as the founder of Israel's religious institutions lacking any prominent role in the priesthood, who were now Aaronite Levites, was resolved by stressing that Aaron was Moses' elder brother (and therefore the presumed inheritor of priestly functions), even though *Exodus* makes Moses his parents' firstborn (male). Of course, Moses himself became a Levite in the process.[218]

The First Theophany: Surabadi's account of the theophany begins with Moses and his family, together with their flocks, lost in the desert on a cold winter night while returning from a visit to Shu'ayb. They were all miserable and Moses tried to make a fire, but the spark

---

Abraham and the king-priest of Salem (Jerusalem), Melchizedek, recorded in Gen. 14:18-20 is thought to attempt to further sanctity both the shrine at Jerusalem and the Zadokite priesthood by associating it with Abraham.

Note the element *zedek* in the priest's name; the only other king-priest of pre-Davidic Jerusalem whose name remains to us is also compounded with *zedek*: Adonizedek. (Jgs. 19:1). It is thought that the use of *zedek* may have been part of the title of the Jerusalem king-priest of which Zedek may have the last example before converting to YHWH-worship. The theory of the Canaanite origin of the Jerusalem priesthood, though attractive, cannot be considered proven, though it has gained fairly wide acceptance among some circles of scholars. (See de Vaux, pp. 311, 372-374; Melchizedek, DB, p. 642; Zadok, DB, p. 1050; rebuttal of Canaanite theory in Priests and Levites, DB, p. 794; God, Names of, EJ, VII, 675.)

[218] There was an hereditary priesthood at the sanctuary of Dan in northern Israel claiming descent from Moses, but it was regarded with the most profound disapproval by the redactors of the Bible with their Aaronite associations. The most scurrilous tales were told about its founding in an effort to combat the popularity it retained up to the Assyrian conquest of 721 BCE. (See below for the story.) (De Vaux, p. 308; also Jgs. 17-18; 1 K. 12:29-30.)

would not catch. In anger, Moses struck the flint, and it broke into speech: "'O Moses! Give not rein to thy anger; for, not only I, but no other iron and flint has permission to give forth fire this night.' Moses was astonished. He asked: 'Why not?' It replied: 'Because the light of prophethood and messengerhood has been brought to a shepherd.'" Then Moses saw a fire in the distance. He told his people to wait while he went to get some embers and directions from the persons who, he presumed, had lit the fire.[219]

This is an elaboration of the circumstances implied in the Quran: *When (Moses) saw a fire and said unto the people of his household: 'Wait! Lo, I see a fire afar off. Perhaps I may bring you a brand therefrom or may find guidance at the fire.* (Q. 20:10)[220]

The comparable Biblical passage narrating what is called the First Theophany,[221] mentions neither the need for fire nor the accompanying family: "Now Moses was keeping the flock of his father-in-law, Jethro, the priest of Midian; and he led his flock to the west side of the wilderness, and came to Horeb, the mountain of God. And the angel of the Lord appeared to him in a flame of fire..." (Ex. 3:1-2a) Thus begins the much-edited account of the first theophany, combining elements from J and E. The Biblical narrative continues: "And the angel of the Lord appeared to him in a flame of fire out of the midst of a bush; and he looked, and lo, the bush was burning, yet it was not consumed. And Moses said, 'I will turn aside and see this great sight, why the bush is not burnt.'" (Ex. 3:2-3)

Mention of the angel here is a later redactor's[222] attempt to increase the distance between man and God by interposing one of the heavenly court, as we have see in the case of the theophany vouchsafed to Abraham.[223] As the passage shows, it is quite clear that no angel is

---

[219] Surabadi, p. 243.

[220] Q. 27:7 and 28:29 have substantially the same account: Q. 27:7: *When Moses said unto the people of his household: 'Lo, I spy afar off a fire; I will bring you tidings thence, or bring to you a borrowed flame that ye may warm yourselves.* Q. 28:29: *Then, when Moses had fulfilled the term, and was travelling with the people of his household, he saw in the distance a fire and said unto his people: 'Bide ye (here)! Lo, I see in the distance a fire; perhaps I shall bring you tidings thence, or a brand from the fire that ye may warm yourselves.* The attentive reader will surely have noticed the minor differences among the three passages, further evidence that the thrust of the story was being adapted to the point of its repetition rather than the recounting of rehearsed historical chronicles. The point of the stories of the prophets alluded to in the Quran is illustrative and inspiring, not a recitation of historical data.

[221] The Second Theophany will be discussed in the succeeding Section (F).

[222] Probably the Second Yahwist.

[223] See Part Two, III, G. {In this series, in *Abraham: An Islamic Perspective.*}

speaking on God's behalf; it is He Himself addressing Moses from the burning bush. *Exodus* makes no mention of any others with Moses in this incident, but Jewish tradition, in the *Exodus Rabbah*,[224] describes Moses with other shepherds. The vision of the burning bush is vouchsafed to Moses alone, remaining unseen by the others, as in the Quran. In both the Quran and the Bible, Moses is attracted to the fire by curiosity, but the causes appear to be different: in the Quran, Moses seems to need fire and directions, whereas in the Bible, it is solely curiosity. Jewish tradition prefaces this incident with an account emphasizing Moses' trustworthiness as a shepherd, influenced of course by the parallel of Moses and the Israelites with the shepherd and his sheep. It is an image that Christians later used with Christ.[225]

THE MOUNTAIN OF GOD: In the Biblical passage quoted above, the Mountain of God is identified with the mountain called Horeb, thus marking the verse as from the Northern Elohist. The mountain is more famous under its other name Sinai (if, indeed, the two traditions speak of the same mountain), now usually thought to be Jabal Musa (Ar., *Mountain of Moses*) in the triangular peninsula between the Gulfs of Suez and Aqabah. This tradition of the location of the mountain is of Christian origin and cannot be attested earlier than the 4th century CE. Aside from the extraordinary difficulty of the country—what good shepherd would lead his flocks from the rich pastures of Mount Seir to the wastes of Jabal Musa?—we last saw Moses in Midian which lies *east* of that conspicuous gash in the earth's surface, the Wadi Arabah. The western side of the wilderness probably means the western side of Seir. In addition, as we shall see later, "... in spite of efforts to disprove it, the phenomena connected with the theophany at Sinai/Horeb are clearly volcanic, and geological evidence has shown that there are no signs of volcanic activity in the southwest corner of the [Sinai] peninsula, but there is abundant evidence of such activity in the region to the south of Edom"[226]

The Biblical directions for locating Mount Sinai/Horeb are not very helpful. Elijah took 40 days and 40 nights to reach Horeb from Beersheba (1 K. 19:8). (He could have reached Makkah in that time.) The Deuteronomist (who also, with E, calls the mountain Horeb) writes: "It is eleven days journey from Horeb by the way of Mount Seir to

---

[224] LJ, II, 304-305.

[225] Cf. Jn. 10:11, in which Jesus is depicted as saying, "I am the good shepherd. The good shepherd lays down his life for his sheep."

[226] Sinai, DB, p. 923; see also Anderson, p. 24.

Kadesh-Barnea." (Deut. 1:2) This appears to make Mount Seir between Kadesh and Horeb, which would eliminate a location in the Egyptian Sinai, and would suggest Midian once again, perhaps one of the peaks such as Jabal al-Lawz in northwestern Saudi Arabia, an idea once scoffed at but now gaining more advocates. However, some peak of Mount Seir may be meant, and perhaps we should not take the "eleven days" too literally. The specific coupling of Seir and Horeb is noteworthy. The very ancient "Song of Deborah" (before c. 1000 BCE) also associated YHWH with Seir: "Lord, when Thou didst go forth from Seir, when Thou didst march from the region of Edom..." (Jgs. 5:4) Also, in 10th-century BCE "Blessing of Moses": "The Lord came from Sinai, and dawned from Seir upon us..." (Deut. 33:2)

Once again, there is no unanimity of opinion on this problem, but the Seir identification is gaining supporters, particularly when coupled with another theory also attracting scholars: that the traditions of the Exodus and the Holy Mountain were originally separate. Sites in the Sinai Peninsula are largely determined upon the fact that the Biblical text, as it stands today, links the two traditions, so that the Holy Mount must, of necessity, have lain on a possible route from Egypt to Kadesh. This makes the identification with Seir awkward. Gray, writing Laymon, acknowledges the volcanic activity in the Seir region in historical times, but objects to locating the Mountain of God there.[227] However, separating the two traditions eliminates the necessity for locating Sinai/Horeb in Sinai. This theory also appears to be gaining acceptance.[228] More will be said about the question below.

Surabadi continues: Moses came to a tree that appeared to be on fire, but its branches were green. Moses placed some brush at the end of his staff to get fire, but the fire went to another side. Though he could not see anyone, he heard a voice, saying: "O Moses, I am thy Lord. Remove thy shoes." Surabadi observes that the shoes were made of the hide of a dead ass, or some say a camel. Moses had been barefoot when he left Shu'ayb and had made slippers from the skin of the dead animal along the way. Moses was told to remove his shoes so that the blessedness of that earth upon which the prophets had walked would be received by him. In another tradition, the reason was that he should not concern himself with his family for God would take care of them. He should prepare himself for revelation. It is also said that as soon as Moses left

---

[227] Laymon, p. 39.
[228] Sinai, DB, p. 923; Mount Sinai, EJ, XIV, 1599.

his family, a son was born who grew instantly into manhood and took charge of the family's flocks, leading them back to Midian.

Surabadi also informs us that when departing, Moses was told by Zipporah that he should not go at that time because of the snakes and scorpions in the wilderness of Tuwa (Ar. *Ṭūwā*). Moses replied that he could protect himself with his staff against the snakes and against the scorpions with the shoes. Since he had relied upon them rather than God, he was told take the shoes off. They immediately became scorpions and the staff became a snake, a precursor of the miracle that would occur later in the course of the theophany.

As usual, Surabadi has gone considerably beyond the Quranic text, and most of his additions do not seem to be found in the earlier Jewish traditions, although some were used by later Jewish writers. The Quran appears to name the site of the burning bush the blessed valley of Tuwa, although some commentators have taken the word to mean "Twice": *And when he reached it, he was called by name: 'O Moses! Lo! I, even I, am thy Lord. So take off thy shoes, for lo, thou art in the holy valley of Tuwa.* (Q. 20:11-12)

In another place a more vivid description is given of the scene of the fire: *And when he reached it, he was called from the right side of the valley in the blessed field, from the [burning] tree: 'O Moses! Draw near and fear not. Lo, I, even, I am God, the Lord of the Worlds.'* (Q. 28:30) This description is so particularized, it suggests that a strong tradition is reflected in the text of the Quran, some place or shrine which had been pointed out to the Hejazi caravaneers on their way to and from Syria, on a route which would have taken by Mount Seir. Is this too a fragment of evidence in support of the identification of one of the peaks of Mount Seir or Jabal al-Lawz with Horeb?

The Bible, too, mentions the command to remove the shoes: "When the Lord saw that turned aside to see, God called unto him out of the bush,[229] 'Moses! Moses!' And he said, 'Here am I.' Then He said, 'Do not come near' put off thy shoes from thy feet, for the place upon which thou are standing is holy ground.' And He said, 'I am the God of thy father, the God of Abraham, the God of Isaac, and the God of Jacob.' And Moses hid his face, for he was afraid to look at God." (Ex. 3:4-6)

In both the Quran and the Bible God is manifesting himself to Moses in the fire. Both the Quran and the Bible seem to imply that the site of the burning bush was already sacred.[230] Indeed, we probably have

---

[229] Note that in this version God is the speaker, not an angel.

[230] In support of this, we may cite the epithet of God "(He) that dwelt in the bush" found in the 10th century BCE "Blessing of Moses." (Deut. 33:16, Moses, EJ, XII, 380.)

here another example of a shrine associated with a tree.[231] In this respect, the evidence of the Quran is extremely important, as it supports the Biblical text and even adds details that seem to be based upon observation or the reports of a local tradition otherwise lost.

There is a greater distance between man and God in the Quranic version than in the Biblical account, in which Moses hides his face, seemingly able to view the form of God that is some manner disclosed in the fire. That is why the Second Yahwist (J2) thought it necessary to create the impression that it was not God Himself in the bush; rather it was an angel of God. It is also why such a device was not necessary in the Quran where God is not localized in the fire, itself merely a device to draw Moses to the sacred spot, and also to put him into the appropriate state in which to receive his first divine revelation. Noteworthy, too, is God's identification of Himself. In the Bible, He says that He is the God of the Israelites and their patriarchal ancestors, Abraham, Isaac, and Jacob—a relatively small portion of mankind. However, in the Quran, God is the Lord of everything that is: *Lo, I, even I, am God, the Lord of the Worlds.'* (Q. 28:30)

In the Quran, this is followed by the commissioning of Moses as a messenger: *Verily I Myself have chosen thee, so hearken unto that which is inspired. Lo! I, even I, am God. There is no God save Me. So serve Me and establish worship for My remembrance. Lo, the Hour is surely coming. But I shall keep it hidden, that every soul may be rewarded for that which it strives (to accomplish). Therefore, let not him turn thee aside from it who believes not therein, but follows his own desire, lest thou perish.'* (Q. 20:13-16) At this point Surabadi abandons artifice and lets an unadorned translation of these magnificent verses into Persian resound grandly.

The address of God to Moses in the Bible is quite different and restricted to the Israelites. "Then the Lord said, 'I have seen the affliction of My people who are in Egypt, and have heard their cry because of their

---

[231] Cf. the Oak of Shechem (Gen. 35:4; the Palm of Deborah (Jgs. 4:5); the Oak of Mamre (Gen. 13:19) etc. See de Vaux, pp. 278-279; Smith, pp. 185, 191-195. This miraculous appearance of the Divinity in the burning bush is not without ancient parallels. "At Aphaca at the annual feast the goddess appeared in the form of a fiery meteor, which descended from the mountain-top and plunged into the water, while according to another account fire played about the temple, presumably... in the tree-tops of the sacred grove. Similarly is was believed that fire played about the branches of the sacred olive tree between the Ambrosian rocks at Tyre, without scorching its leaves... The same phenomenon, according to Africanus and Eustathius, was seen at the terebinth of Mamre; the whole tree seemed to be aflame, but when the fire sank again remained unharmed..." (Smith, p. 193.)

taskmasters; I know their sufferings, and I have come down to deliver them out of the hand of the Egyptians, and to bring them up out of that land to a good and broad land, a land flowing with milk and honey [Canaan]...'" (Ex. 3:7-8)

Moses protested: "'Who am I that I should go to Pharaoh, and bring the sons of Israel out of Egypt?' (God) said, 'But I will be with thee; and this shall be the sign for thee, that I have sent thee: when thou hast brought forth the people out of Egypt, thou shalt serve God on this mountain.'" (Ex. 3:11-12) The first quotation is from J and the second is from E. Already we can see what appears to be a difference in destination. For J, Canaan (Palestine) is the object of the Israelites after they are liberated; but E seems to plan a future in which the Israelites will be led to the Holy Mountain where Moses (and his descendants) will serve as priests.

The next two verses of *Exodus* describe the event that is, for E and P, the most important event in the history of Israel: the revelation of the divine name to Moses. "Then Moses said to God, 'If I come to the people of Israel and say to them, "The God of your fathers has sent me to you," and they ask me, "What is His name?" what shall I say unto them?' God said to Moses, 'I AM WHO I AM.' And He said, 'Say this to the people of Israel, "I AM has sent me to you."'" (Ex. 3:13-14) Thus, YHWH disclosed His Name to man for the first time, as He would later be known to His chosen people, Israel.[232]

YHWH, the name of God, has caused much discussion in the world of Biblical scholarship and a considerable literature has grown up concerning its etymology, meaning, correct pronunciation, and ritual use. The etymology given in the verse quoted above is considered folk etymology. Yahweh would mean "he is." The vowelization of the word has been preserved by Greek transliterations,[233] so we know that the correct form is *Yahweh*, even though in later times the Jews regarded the name with such awe that while writing the consonants YHWH, they substituted the vowels of *Adonai* ("my Lord"), thereby creating the written form *Yehowah*, but reading this hybrid as *Adonai*. This practice

---

[232] However, in the Yahwist/Deuteronomist view, and the Islamic view paralleling it, God had made His true identity known to mankind from the very beginning, but people were continually being diverted from His pure worship and His law through indifference, laziness, the machinations of evil, lust, greed, etc., necessitating the periodic renewal and reminder of the message throughout history.

[233] The pronunciation of Hebrew short vowels was not indicated in the Old Testament until the invention of the diacritics possibly in the 8th century CE, centuries after the consonantal texts had been stabilized. See "The Text of the Old Testament" in Introduction, III.D. {In this series, in *Introduction to the Old Testament.*}

led to the regular, though erroneous, usage in Europe (among Gentiles) of *Jehovah*, still current in English. In time, it seems the actual voweling of YHWH was forgotten and had to be recovered from the Greeks. Prof. Meek believes that the name YHWH was foreign to the Hebrews and was in fact of *Arabic* origin, "from the Arabic root *hwy*, 'to blow'"[234]

Although there is still hardly unanimity on the etymology of the word, the view of Albright and others seems to be prevailing, that *Yahweh* is the third person singular of a causative form of the verb *H-W-Y* meaning "to fall, become, or come into existence." Perhaps it was originally part of a sentence formula, as some ancient names were: *Yahweh asher yihweh* "he brings into existence whatever exists."[235]

Did the patriarchs before the time of Moses worship a god named YHWH? We do not know and opinion is divided. It is quite possible that the Northern (Josephic) tribes did not know of YHWH until He was introduced to them by Moses. The Elohist text certainly indicates that Moses did not know this name of God (and hence this God) until the theophany, and he did not expect that the Israelites living in Egypt (the Josephites?) would recognize it. The editor apparently also felt this way, and the verse of the revelation of the Divine Name was followed immediately by an explanation drawn from the Yahwist, telling us who this YHWH was: "God also said unto Moses, 'Say this to the people of Israel, 'The Lord, the God of your fathers, the God of Abraham, the God of Isaac, and God of Jacob, has sent me to you': this is My Name for ever, and thus I am to be remembered throughout all generations.'" (Ex. 3:15) Is this a declaration of the assimilation of three separate deities?

In the next verse, also ascribed to the Yahwist, the same triple formula is repeated: "'Go and gather the elders of Israel together, and say to them, 'The Lord, the God of your fathers, the God of Abraham, the God of Isaac, the God of Jacob, has appeared to me...'" (Ex. 3:16) The tradition of the Southern Yahwist suggests that YHWH was not new to him and his people, but we cannot be sure that the ancestors of the

---

[234] God, DB, p. 334; Names of God, EJ, VII, 680.

[235] Albright-Stone Age, pp. 15-16; Names of God, EJ, VII, 680. Another form of Yahweh is attested in names formed with a theophoric element: *Yahu*. It has been suggested that this has a parallel in the Arabic usage *Ya Huwa!* in religious, especially ecstatic liturgy. It is now believed the *yahu* is a jussive form of *yahwiyu*, *YHW*. Of course, the form *huwa* and the verb *HWY* are quite probably related cognately anyway. (Albright-Stone Age, p. 16; God, EB, p. 334.) Joseph Campbell quotes Meek's argument that the confusion about the meaning of the name indicates that the stem HWY was foreign to the Hebrews; however, it is still represented in modern Arabic which is a close relative or development of the language spoken by the Kenite/Midianites. "The most probable [origin of the name] in our opinion is... from the Arabic root *hwy*, 'to blow.'" (Campbell, III, 132-133.)

Southerners worshipped God under that name. However, they may have learned of YHWH from their despised neighbors to the south, the Midianites.[236]

THE KENITE HYPOTHESIS: This brings us to the Kenite Hypothesis (some call it "Midianite"): "The fact that J and E locate Moses' first encounter with Yhwh during his residence among his Midianite in-laws, and the fact that J speaks of Yahwism long before Moses, while E and P claim the name Yhwh was first revealed at Sinai (Horeb), spawned a thesis in the 19th century that Yhwh was a Kenite or Midianite deity."[237] In 1862, F.W. Ghillany (using a pseudonym at the time) first suggested that Moses not only learned the name of YHWH from the Kenite clan to which his Midianite father-in-law, Jethro, belonged, but many aspects of the cult and social institutions associated with YHWH-worship as well.[238] In other words, YHWH had revealed Himself to the Midianites *before* He had revealed Himself to the Israelites! The implications of this thesis are stunning. It would make a section of the close kin of the Arabs, the Midianites—whom the later Israelites strove to vilify and obliterate, perhaps because of this secret knowledge—the earliest receivers of the primitive revelation of the invisible One God Who would gradually disclose Himself to mankind as the sole Lord of the Universe. For the Muslim, this process culminates in the revelation of the Quran.

We have already noted that the Kenites were on friendly terms with Israel (in distinction to the bulk of the Midianites who appear as Israel's implacable enemies in the Bible). The Kenites appear to have ultimately been absorbed by the Judahites, as apparently were many other Canaanite clans. It has been suggested that these Kenites were a nomadic tribe of smiths, and this is reinforced by their association with Midian where there were copper mines.[239] It has been proposed that their god was YHWH, probably worshipped without an idol, and that he was particularly associated with a mountain in Midian[240] that had exhibited

---

[236] Anderson, p. 39.

[237] Baruch Halpern, Kenites, ABD, Vol. IV, p. 20.

[238] Baruch Halpern, Kenites, ABD, Vol. IV, p. 20; Kenites, EJ, X, 906-907. The EJ article minimizes this possibility.

[239] Kenites, DB, p. 548.

[240] Further evidence of the mountain origin of YHWH may be adduced from one of His epithets, *El Shaddai* (Almighty), which was "most likely directly related to the Assyrian 'shadu' (mountain) and the original connotation was 'God of the mountain' rather than 'God Almighty.'" (BC, I, 342; also see God, DB, p. 335; also Gray, writing in Laymon, p. 41.) This ties in well with what we know of worship at "high places" in Canaan and

volcanic activity at some time within the period of the residence of the Kenites in that region. For example: "And Mount Sinai was wrapped in smoke, because the Lord descended upon it in fire; and the smoke of it went up like the smoke of a kiln, and the whole mountain quaked greatly." (Ex. 19:18) The Yahwist is clearly describing the phenomena of a volcanic eruption.

Jethro, the Kenite/Midianite father-in-law of Moses, was also a priest. Was he the priest of YHWH? The events related in Exodus 18 seem to suggest so. After the successful escape from Egypt, Moses and the Israelites camped by the Mountain of God. There Jethro, bringing Moses' family, came to visit him. Moses described the escape to Jethro who rejoiced "for all the good that the Lord had done to Israel." (Ex. 18:9) Jethro's God is the God of Moses.

"And Jethro said, 'Blessed be the Lord, who has delivered you out of the hand of the Egyptians and out of the hand of Pharaoh. Now I know that the Lord is greater than all gods, because He delivered the people from under the hand of the Egyptians, when they dealt arrogantly with them. [This is from the Yahwist. Note that the reality of other gods is not denied; only the Lord's being stronger than they is asserted.] And Jethro, Moses' father-in-law, offered a burnt offering and sacrifices to God; and Aaron came with all the elders of Israel to eat bread with Moses' father-in-law before God." (Ex. 18:10-12; the last sentence is from E.)

Thus, in this conflated account, Jethro is associated with YHWH, and in the last (Elohist) verse, he is shown conducting the ritual sacrifice to Him. The absence of Moses from the feast has been interpreted to show that since Moses had already been received into YHWH-worship formally during his earlier stay with Jethro, his participation was unnecessary. The ceremony was the initiation of Aaron and the elders into the cult of YHWH-worship. Furthermore, in the following verses Jethro gave administrative and organizational advice to Moses and taught him judicial procedure: all of which were aspects of the cult in ancient times (Ex. 18:13-26).[241]

Naturally, this hypothesis has not been very attractive to those who wish to support the primacy of Israel in all things monotheistic and the uniqueness of Israel's religious experience. Nevertheless, the ascription of the founding of these institutions to a clan of the hated Midianites argues for the authenticity of the tradition. It was too well

---

Israel before their suppression in favor of the centralized cult at Jerusalem under David and Solomon.

[241] See IB, I, 13-26.

known to be denied. We also see that the monotheism of the Pentateuch is not absolute; it is in fact henotheism. Monotheism was the way YHWH was worshipped—He ruled alone, without a pantheon of lesser gods to assist Him, but His worship was not yet considered incumbent upon other peoples who were not of the elect. As the story of Moses proceeds, we shall increasingly see how anthropomorphic and territorial was the concept of God in the Pentateuch. Already we have seen that God has told Moses that He will accompany him to Egypt. This should be read quite literally, as subsequent events will show. YHWH is invading Egypt and challenging His peers, the gods of Egypt. This alone would justify questioning whether Moses' revelation was fully understood by his contemporaries and their early descendants.

Is there any extra-Biblical evidence to support the Kenite Hypothesis? As a matter of fact, there is. Two Egyptian texts of about 1400 BCE, thus antedating the period of Moses by more than a century, mention a "land of Yahweh Bedouins." The region referred to lay east of Egypt, the very region of Midian.[242] There is also archeological evidence: "The excavations at biblical Timna, just (north) of Eilat, uncovered a 12th-century BCE temple. This temple was characterized by what archaeologists call 'Midianite' pottery. And, it was apparently a tent-shrine, much like the tabernacle in the biblical tradition. Inside it, the excavators uncovered a copper snake...

"Curiously, the only zoomorphic icon associated with Moses in any source earlier than P is a copper snake called Nehushtan (2 K. 18:4; Num. 21:9). The tent-shrine, if that indeed is what it is was, is not altogether unexpected on the desert fringe, but it may be that Israel's notions of its early cult were in part shaped by Midian-Kenite models. Snakes, too, were common icons in the Mediterranean basin..."[243] There is also the more tenuous evidence that the Exodus and the Israelite Conquest from the east followed Midian trading routes.

This is, of course, circumstantial evidence, but it lends support to the Kenite Hypothesis if one does not assume that God restricted His revelation to just one people. If one can suspend one's preconceived certainties inherited from centuries of assumptions based upon flawed documents and flawed history, one may glimpse a completely different picture of the emergence of monotheism. There is no reason we must assume the late Biblical genealogies absorbing Moses and Aaron into the

---

[242] Wolff, pp. 17-18; Moses, EJ, XII, 381.

[243] Baruch Halpern, *Kenites*, ABD, Vol. IV, 20. For Nehushtan, see "The Staff of Moses" in the preceding section D.

Hebrews are any more historically accurate than much else of what we have been examining.

All of this strengthens the theory that the area in which Moses took refuge already knew of YHWH and that he learned of YHWH and His worship during his sojourn there. In other words, Egyptian, Israelite, or a mixture of both, Moses may have been a convert to YHWHism. It should not shock our sensibilities to entertain the *possibility* that God revealed himself to a messenger or messengers in Arab Midian before He did so in Israel, and that Moses embraced the truth at the hands of Jethro, his Midianite father-in-law.

The tradition of Shu'ayb, the prophet of Midian, to be found in Arabia and in the Quran can also be enlisted in support of this theory. We have already discussed the tentative identification of Jethro with Shu'ayb, and the reasons for its probable rejection.[244] In our opinion, Shu'ayb may well antedate the era of Moses by a period of unknown length. The circumstances of Shu'ayb could be involved with some development of the tradition of YHWH-worship in Midian, which Moses found already there (if the Kenite Hypothesis be correct). The prophet Shu'ayb of Midian, whose existence was forgotten or suppressed by the ancient Israelites (it is also possible that he was never known to them), was remembered by the Midianites and their successors the Ishmaelites in that region. The tradition like others, moved south down the Hejaz until it was enshrined in the text of the Quran. Today, we might enlist that memory in support of the theory that monotheism, perhaps not yet the absolute monotheism of later Judaism, but a localized monotheism, existed in Midian before it was adopted or co-opted by Israel.

It may, therefore, be one of the supreme ironies of history that the sacred name of God amongst the Israelites, YHWH, is of Midianite (Arab) origin, and they may very well have learned of Him from the desert Arabs. The basis of the national identity of this people, that is YHWH-worship, would thus become a borrowing from Arabia. The God of Israel was not the God of Isaac and Jacob at all, but rather the God of Ishmael and Esau. As Joseph Campbell reluctantly expresses it: "Hence we are forced, to some extent, to agree with Mohammad's startling claim that the people of his own Semitic stock were the first worshippers of the God proclaimed in the Bible."[245]

The course of events in the story of the Exodus and the sojourn in the wilderness may shed more light on the problem.

---

[244] See in preceding Section above.

[245] Campbell, III, pp. 430-431.

The Staff: *"And what is that in thy right hand, O Moses?" He said: "This is my staff whereon I lean, and wherewith I beat down branches for my sheep, and wherein I find other uses."* (Q. 20:17-18) To this, Surabadi adds that Moses was asked this in the way a child is asked, to bluff him, or to have him certify that it was a staff before it was turned into a snake.

He said: "Cast it down, O Moses!" So he cast it down, and lo, it was a serpent, gliding. He said: "Grasp it and fear not. We shall return it to its former state." Q. 20:19-20) Surabadi interpreted these verses to mean that God had told Moses to cast down the staff because he relied too much upon it, or more obviously, so that God might show His power by turning it into a snake, and to teach Moses not be frightened when the miracle was performed before Pharaoh. After it had become a snake, he had been told to seize it again, which he did with trepidation. It became a staff again in his hand.[246]

The Quranic version is less elaborate than Surabadi's commentary. In another place, there is a longer version of the speech, delivered by God after Moses has approached the fire: *"O Moses! Lo, it is I, God, the Mighty, the Wise: And throw down thy staff!" But when he saw it writhing as it were a demon, he turned to flee headlong: (but God said:) "O Moses! Fear not! Lo, the emissaries fear not in My presence, save him who has done wrong and afterward has changed evil for good. And lo! I am Forgiving, Merciful."* (Q. 27:9-11)[247] Comforting words for the imperfect believer; he has nothing to fear before his compassionate Creator. The "evil" referred to in the verse is taken to be a reference to Moses' crime of manslaughter in Egypt, later redeemed by his good behavior in Midian.

In the Bible, the miracle of the staff is preceded by a speech attributed to God in which He gives directions how to act when delivering the message. It also gives a precognition of the miracles and plagues that will occur in Egypt. And finally God is depicted (by E) as instructing Moses to have the Israelites loot the defeated Egyptians: "'And I will give this people favor in the sight of the Egyptians; and when ye go, ye shall not go empty, but each woman shall ask of her neighbor, and of her who sojourns in her house, jewelry of silver and

---

[246] Surabadi, pp. 245-246.

[247] These internal differences within passages touching upon the same incident or person suggest to us that the speeches are not to be taken as the literal words of the speaker (after all Moses, did not speak classical Arabic), but as types and gists. The point is the message itself, not the words in which it is couched. The verse gives hope to an imperfect man, Moses, and by extension, gives hope to all of us with all of our imperfections that we may enjoy God's mercy and forgiveness, *inshāllāh*.

gold, and clothing, and ye shall put them on your sons and on your daughters; thus ye shall despoil the Egyptians.'" (Ex. 3:21-22)

Rather unexpected instructions from the Creator of the Universe.

Then, we arrive at the Biblical passage (from the Yahwist) paralleling the Islamic versions quoted above: "then Moses answered, But behold, they will not believe me or listen to my voice, for they will say, "The Lord did not appear to thee,"' The Lord said to him, 'What is that in thy hand?' He said, 'A rod.' And he said, 'Cast it on the ground.' So he cast it on the ground, and it became a serpent; and Moses fled from it. But the Lord said to Moses, 'Put out thy hand, and take it by the tail'—so he put out his hand and caught it, and it became a rod in his hand—'that they may believe that the Lord, the God of their fathers, the God of Abraham, the God of Isaac, and the God of Jacob, has appeared unto thee.'" (Ex. 4:1-5)[248]

The difference between this passage from *Exodus* and the verse quoted above from the Quran is negligible: only Moses' explanation of his use of his staff is added to the Quranic version. However, both Jewish and Islamic traditions have developed the theme of the Rod of Moses with competing imaginings. We have already met it as the rod which Adam carried with him from Paradise and passed on to his sons, and then handed down the ages from generation to generation until it came to Jethro, who surrendered it to Moses. More will be said its properties below.[249]

In the Biblical account, Moses keeps putting forth objections to the mission God has set before him. This has led to some rabbinic criticism of Moses' behavior. For example in the medieval (11th century CE) *Abkir Midrash*, quoted in *Yalkut*, we have: "And the Lord said unto him, 'What is that in thine hand?' And (Moses) said, 'A rod." And the Lord said: 'Thou deservest to be castigated with it. If thou didst not intend to take My mission upon thyself, thou shouldst have said so in the beginning. Instead, thou didst hold back with thy refusal, until I revealed to thee the great secret of the Ineffable Name, that thou mightest know it if the children of Israel should ask thee concerning it. And now thou sayest, I will not go. Now, therefore, if thou wilt not execute My charge

---

[248] Note that in these formulae God does not use the inclusive "your fathers" instead of "their fathers." Does it mean, as it appears to, that He is not the god of Moses' fathers? Another indication that Moses was an Egyptian whose fathers worshipped idols?

[249] It is interesting that these traditions put the rod in the custody of a Midianite, notwithstanding the device of his obtaining it from the household of Pharaoh. More support for Midianites being in the main stream of YHWH-worship?

to thee, it will be executed by this rod. It was My wish to distinguish thee and make thee My instrument for doing many miracles.'"[250] Though the tradition is a late, its hectoring tone owes nothing to Islamic tradition.

After the miracle of the staff at the theophany, Surabadi tells us that there was another sign. Moses was told to draw his hand from under the other and it shone with a white light brighter than the sun. Then he was told to go to Pharaoh and call him to God. Moses then requested that God open his breast to prophethood and messengership and banish the rashness and haste in it, for messengership was difficult, and bringing the message to Pharaoh and disputing with him was difficult. "And untie my tongue so that they understand my speech."

In an explanation of this problem with Moses' speech, Surabadi offers the following story: When Moses was a two-year old, while he was being held by Pharaoh, he tugged at Pharaoh's bejeweled beard. Pharaoh became angry and said that the child was an enemy, but Isiyah asked, what could a child know? To test him, two trays were brought in, one of coals, and the other of oleaster. Moses wanted to reach for the oleaster,[251] but Gabriel directed him to the coals. He seized a handful and put them in his mouth, thereby burning his tongue. This was the cause of Moses' speech defect. The reason his hand was not burned was because it had been toughened on the beard of Pharaoh. But his tongue had flattered him by calling him "baba," and therefore it was susceptible to being burnt. He cites another (contradictory) tradition, in which it was said that the hand did not burn because it was the source of light, and fire could not affect it, as it could not affect the heart of a believer.[252] The Quran does not attribute luminosity to Moses' hand.

Moses then asked God to make his brother Aaron his counsellor and aide. This petition was granted. Moses was forty when he received the revelation and was sent with his brother to call Pharaoh to God.[253] Finally, in a typical medieval Islamic development of the story, Surabadi adds: When Moses was sent to Pharaoh, the angels protested that Moses was not adequately fitted out. In response, he was given the clothing of purity, the steed of divine grace, the sword of proof, the aid of continence, and the army of God's help.[254]

---

[250] Quoted in LJ, II, pp. 320-321.
[251] "oleaster": the wild olive.
[252] Surabadi, pp. 247-248.
[253] Surabadi, pp. 248-249, 251.
[254] Surabadi, 251-252.

THE WHITE HAND: The miracle of the white hand of Moses is mentioned in both the Quran and the Bible. *"And thrust thy hand within thine armpit, it will come forth white without harm. Another sign that We show thee from Our great signs."* (Q. 20:22-23) And in the Bible, the Yahwist tells us: "Again, the Lord said to him, 'put thy hand into thy bosom'; and he put his hand into his bosom; and when he took it out, behold! his hand was leprous, as white as snow. Then God said, 'Put thy hand back into thy bosom.' So he put his hand back into his bosom; and when he took it out, behold! it was restored like the rest of his flesh. 'If they will not believe thee,' God said, 'or heed the first sign, they may believe the latter sign...'" (Ex. 4:6-8)

In this, God Himself does not seem to know whether the Israelites (for they are the object of this passage, not Pharaoh, as in the Quran) will be impressed by these miracles to the point of believing in Moses' mission and following him. In the event that they are not, God proposes still a third sign, turning the water from the Nile into blood (Ex. 4:90).

The miracle of the white hand of Moses is not specifically mentioned again in the Biblical text although presumably it was included among the signs shown to the Israelites when Moses and Aaron successfully enlisted their support in the project to leave Egypt (Ex. 4:30). It must be emphasized that there is a fundamental difference between the approach of the Quran and that of the Bible in the nature of Moses' mission. In the Bible, Moses is sent to the Israelites only, to lead them out of bondage in Egypt into Canaan and to establish their rituals and institutions, that is, the Law. There is no Biblical record of Moses' inviting Pharaoh to worship the One Universal God, or even the more limited God of the Israelites, YHWH. The Biblical mission of Moses is national.

But in the Quran it has become universal. It does not refer to the necessity of his convincing the Israelites to accept his leadership. That is assumed. Moses' mission was to invite the Egyptians, as represented by Pharaoh and his court, to the true religion of the One Invisible God, Whom he calls the Lord of the Worlds; and secondly, to lead the Israelites out of Egypt in a bid for the free worship of the One God.[255] Another difference is the addition in the Quran of the phrase "without harm" to God's command to Moses to withdraw his hand from his armpit, which could be taken as a denial of the Biblical statement that Moses' hand had become leprous. Jewish rabbinical tradition has offered many explanations about the hand: "The Lord now bade Moses put his

---

[255] Q. 7:104-105; 20:46-48; 26:15-17; 44:18.

hand into his bosom and take it out again, and when he took it out, behold, his hand was leprous, as white as snow. And God bade him put his hand into his bosom again, and it turned again as his other flesh. Beside being a chastisement for his hasty words, the plague on his hand was to teach him that as the leper defiles, so the Egyptians defiled Israel, and as Moses was healed of his uncleanness, so God would cleanse the children of Israel of the pollution the Egyptians had brought upon them."[256]

However, Josephus refrains from using the term "leprous" in describing Moses' hand in his account: "After this God bid Moses to put his right hand into his bosom; he obeyed, and when he took it out it was white, and in color like to chalk, but afterwards it returned to its wonted color again."[257]

The Quran also notes Moses' reservation about his ability to speak eloquently: *(Moses) said: "My Lord! Relieve my mind and ease my task for me; and loose a knot from my tongue, that they may understand my speech. Appoint for me an aide from my folk, Aaron, my brother. Confirm my strength with him and let him share my task, that we may glorify Thee much..."* (Q. 20:25-33) *(Moses) said: "My Lord! Lo, I fear that they will deny me. And I shall be embarrassed, and my tongue will not speak plainly, therefore send for Aaron..."* (Q. 26:12-13) And Moses expresses another fear: *"And they have a crime (counted) against me, so I fear they will kill me."* (Q. 26:14) This was a reference to the manslaughter Moses had committed and which had prompted him to flee from Egypt.[258]

In the above, though we see Moses pleading for more assistance, both divine and human, the underlying assumption is that he has tacitly accepted the task God has given to him. However, the parallel Biblical passage has a quite different tone: "But Moses said to the Lord, 'Oh, my Lord, I am not eloquent, either heretofore or since Thou hast spoken to Thy servant; but I am slow of speech and of tongue.' Then the Lord said to him, 'Who has made man's mouth? Who makes him dumb, or deaf, or seeing, or blind? Is it not I, the Lord? Now therefore go, and I will be with thy mouth and teach thee what thou shalt speak.' But he said, 'Oh,

---

[256] LJ, II, 321. Lepers were ritually unclean. No less than two whole chapters of *Leviticus* (13 and 14) are devoted to the regulations concerning the treatment and cleansing of lepers.

[257] Josephus, Antiquities, II.12.3, p. 59.

[258] That in the Quran Aaron is called Moses' brother is not necessarily an obstacle to an absence of a blood kinship, as it is quite common to address a comrade or close friend as "brother," especially in the Middle East.

my Lord, send, I pray, some other person.' Then the anger of the Lord was kindled against Moses and he said, 'Is there not Aaron, thy brother, the Levite? I know that he can speak well; and behold, he is coming out to meet thee, and when he sees thee he will be glad in his heart. And thou shalt speak to him and put the words in his mouth; and I will be with thy mouth and his mouth, and will teach thee what thou shalt do. He shall speak for thee to the people; and he shall be a mouth for thee, and thou shalt be to him as God. And thou shalt take in thy hand this rod, with which thou shalt do the signs.'" (Ex. 4:10-17)

Moses then returned to Jethro and, dissimulating somewhat as described above in section D, told him that he wanted to go back to Egypt to see his kinsfolk. Jethro told him: "'Go in peace.' And the Lord said to Moses in Midian, 'Go back to Egypt; for all the men who were seeking thy life are dead.' So Moses took his wife and his sons and set on an ass, and went back to the land of Egypt; and in his hand Moses took the rod of God." (Ex. 4:19-20)

We have already noted above the problem of Moses' language difficulties as a possible indication that he did not know the Semitic language of the Israelites adequately for the purposes of his mission (see above, section A); the assumption is that Moses was fluent in Egyptian, but not the Hebrew dialect of Canaanite. In this respect, Jewish tradition, as represented in the *Tanhuma*, also associates Moses' objection about his speech with his lack of Hebrew. God granted him the knowledge of seventy languages to remove this objection of his.[259] In another Jewish tradition, it is said that Moses prophesied in seventy-one languages.[260]

One of the possible explanations of the problem (discussed above) would be that Moses was actually an Egyptian who had taken refuge with the Semitic Midianites, married among them, learned their language in an imperfect manner, and had become a convert to their unique religion of single invisible God. The residence of God was conceived to be on a mountain with which volcanic phenomena were associated, and whose worship included sacrifices, but no idols. To our way of thinking, this would not diminish him in the least, as his race is of no concern, but Jews would be understandably upset, just as many Englishmen would be if it were asserted that Shakespeare was actually a Russian.

Of course, this is speculation, and could be entirely or partly incorrect. Nevertheless, the circumstantial evidence for such a chain of events is both strong and plausible. In the Bible Moses' problem with

---

[259] LJ, II, 322-323.
[260] LJ, II, 322; VI, 225.

speech may be simply a device to introduce Aaron into the narrative, and perhaps the tradition has no more significance than that, except for the stubborn insistence upon the point. The Quran also recognizes the connection between Moses' lack of eloquence and the appointment of Aaron, but the phrases "knot upon my tongue" and "that they may understand my words" suggest problems of communication greater than simple ineloquence.

In any event, Surabadi's pericope about Moses and the coals is also found in the *Exodus Rabbah* (9th and 10th centuries CE) in virtually the same form, possibly under Islamic influence.[261] The *Exodus Rabbah* makes the test the suggestion of Jethro and instead of oleaster, the other tray has gold (in another version, onyx), but the results are the same thanks to the intervention of Gabriel, as in the Islamic story.[262] Tabari also mentions the story, substituting pearls for Surabadi's oleaster.[263] *Pirke de Rabbi Eliezer* does not refer to the story, nor does Josephus.

Surabadi notes that Moses was forty years old when he received his first revelation, obviously influenced by the strong tradition of the Prophet's receiving his first revelation at that age. Jewish tradition, cited earlier, makes Moses eighty years old.

Finally, it may be noted that at the point where Moses, in the Quran, asks God to "open his breast," medieval Jewish tradition inserts an account of the ascension of Moses, which is very similar to Muslim accounts of the Night Journey of the Prophet.[264] There is no justification for this insertion in the Biblical text, but perhaps here Jewish tradition was influenced by the Islamic development of the story and the mystical interpretations given to the phrase used several times in the Quran.

F. MOSES AND PHARAOH

Here is a dramatic story... (Trawick-NT, p. 65)

Then, after them, We sent Moses with out signs unto Pharaoh and his council, but they abused them. Now, see the nature of the consequence for the workers of corruption! Moses said: "O Pharaoh!

---

[261] Compare also the vision of Isaiah in which he sees the heavenly court and bewails his unclean lips. "Then flew one of the seraphim to me, having in his hand a burning coal which he had taken with tongs from the altar. And he touched my mouth and said: 'Behold, this has touched thy lips; thy guilt is taken away, and thy sin forgiven.'" (Is. 6:6-7.)

[262] LJ, II, 174; V, 402.

[263] Tabari, I, 303.

[264] LJ, II, 309-316.

Lo, I am messenger from the Lord of the Worlds [not just the God of the Patriarchs], *approved upon the condition that I speak nothing but the truth concerning God. I come unto you (lords of Egypt) with a clear proof from your Lord* [not *our* Lord]. *So let the Children of Israel go with me." (Pharaoh) said: "If Thou comest with a sign, then produce it, if thou art of those who speak the truth." Then (Moses) flung down his staff and, behold! it was a serpent manifest! And he drew forth his hand, and lo! it was white for the beholders! The elders of Pharaoh's people said: "Lo! This is some knowledgeable sorcerer who would expel you from your land. Now what do ye advise?" They said (unto Pharaoh): Put him off—him and his brother—and send summoners into the cities to bring every knowledgeable sorcerer unto thee."* (Q. 7:103-112)

In Surah Ta Ha, to which Surabadi is linking his commentary in this section, there is also an address to Pharaoh calling him to God in obedience to the command: *"And speak unto him a gentle word, that mayhap he may heed or fear."* (Q. 20:50-55) Pharaoh must accept God of his own free will. He may accept or refuse Islam (Submission to God); his is the choice. Note also that the day of the festival is to be appointed for the trial with the Egyptian sorcerers: *(Moses) said: "Your rendezvous shall be the day of the festival, and let the people assemble when the sun has risen high."* (Q. 20:59)

Surabadi amplifies his account by including the figure of Haman:[265] Pharaoh had been convinced by Moses' speech, but Haman dissuaded him, pointing out that he (Pharaoh) was a king and a god, and could not agree to serve another god. Then Pharaoh accused Moses of trying to force him from his kingdom through magic and said that he would have his magicians challenge him. The date for the contest was set, as in the Quran. Thus we have the following sequence of events: the audience in which Moses, with Aaron, shows Pharaoh the signs (the rod and the white hand); the call to Pharaoh to submit to God; a delay while the Egyptians summon their sorcerers for a public contest to be held on a festival day; and the contest itself.[266]

In the Biblical account, Aaron had come out of Egypt to meet Moses by the Mountain of God. They then traveled first to the Israelites in Egypt, to whom Moses showed the signs and convinced the people to accept his leadership. Then: "Moses and Aaron went to Pharaoh and said, 'Thus says the Lord, the God of Israel, "Let My people go, that they

---

[265] The *Proverbs Midrash* introduces Balaam in much the same role as Surabadi's Haman, counseling Pharaoh against Moses and Aaron, and suggesting the contest with the magicians.

[266] Surabadi, pp. 252-253.

may hold a feast to Me in the wilderness.'" But Pharaoh said, 'Who is the Lord, that I should heed His voice and let Israel go? I did not know the Lord, and moreover I will not let Israel go.' Then they said, 'The God of the Hebrews has met with us; let us go, we pray, a three days' journey into the wilderness, and sacrifice to the Lord out God, lest He fall upon us with pestilence or with the sword.' But the king of Egypt said to them, 'Moses and Aaron, why do ye take the people away from their work? Get to your burdens.'" (Ex. 5:1-4) Then Pharaoh commanded that the labor of the Israelites be increased.

In this first encounter (from JE), there is no record of Moses' showing his signs to Pharaoh, as he had already done to the Israelites. Instead, in its aftermath, the Israelites, their burden of labor now increased, repudiated Moses and Aaron (Ex. 5:20-21). Note also that the Lord (YHWH) is not known in Egypt and that He seems to be restricted to being the God of the Israelites. Furthermore, He is neither omnipotent nor omniscient, for He resorts to a deception (the pretext of the feast in the wilderness) to get His people out of Egypt. This is not the Lord of the Worlds, Who merely utters "Be!" and it is. Instead, we are at an early stage of the evolution of the monotheistic idea from a tribal god to the One God, the Creator of all that is in the universe.

THE "SECOND" THEOPHANY: As the text of the *Exodus* stands today, this encounter is followed by the so-called Second Theophany (Ex. 5:22-7:7). In it, Moses is first once again instructed in His Name: "And God said to Moses, 'I am the Lord. I appeared to Abraham, to Isaac, and to Jacob, as God Almighty,[267] but by My name the Lord I did not make Myself known to them. I also established My covenant with them, to give them the land of Canaan, the land in which they dwelt as sojourners." God tells Moses to expound upon His concern for the Israelites and seems to be almost pleading to be accepted as their God. After promising to deliver them out of Egypt, He is represented as telling Moses to say on His behalf: "I will redeem you with an outstretched arm and with great acts of judgment, and I will take you for my people, and I will be your God; and ye shall know that I am the Lord your God, who has brought you out from under the burdens of the Egyptians. And I will bring you into the land which I swore to give to Abraham, to Isaac, and to Jacob; I will give it to you for a possession. I am the Lord.'" (Ex. 6:6b-8)

The people did not heed this declaration by YHWH, so Moses complained to Him when He ordered him to go to Pharaoh to obtain the

---

[267] Or: God of the Mountain; see Note 1682 above.

release the unwilling Israelites: "But Moses said to the Lord, 'Behold, the people of Israel have not listened to me; how then shall Pharaoh listen to me, who am a man of uncircumcised lips?' But the Lord spoke to Aaron, and gave them a charge to the people of Israel and to Pharaoh king of Egypt to bring the people of Israel out of the land of Egypt." (Ex. 6:12-13) Note that Aaron has also been included in this version of the theophany, a circumstance unreported in the earlier text. P (5th century BCE or later) is at work exalting his priestly caste among the post-Exilic Israelites.

This exaltation of Aaron continues when P summarizes: "These are the Aaron and Moses to whom the Lord said: 'Bring out the people of Israel from the land of Egypt by their hosts.' It was they who spoke to Pharaoh king of Egypt about bringing out the people of Israel from Egypt, this Moses and this Aaron. On the day when the Lord spoke to Moses in the land of Egypt, the Lord said to Moses, 'I am the Lord; tell Pharaoh king of Egypt all that I say unto thee.' But Moses said to the Lord, 'Behold, I am of uncircumcised lips; how then shall Pharaoh listen to me?' and the Lord said to Moses, 'See, I make thee as God to Pharaoh; and Aaron thy brother shall be thy prophet [*naby*]. Thou shalt speak all that I command thee; And Aaron thy brother shall tell Pharaoh to let the people of Israel go out of his land...' Now Moses was eighty years old, and Aaron eighty-three years old, when they spoke to Pharaoh." (Ex. 6:26-7:2,7)

Aaron is now the equal of Moses in position (in the Priestly Writer's account) and his elder brother to boot! The implications of this have been discussed above. Once more, the problem of Moses' difficulty with language is the prime cause of Aaron's role as Moses' interpreter. Did Moses stutter? Was it a language problem?[268]

Scholars now realize that this Second Theophany is the really the 5th-century BCE or later Priestly (P) version of the First Theophany on the Holy Mountain which we discussed in the previous section. P had the conflated account of J and E to draw upon in Ex.3 and 4. In the light of modern scholarship, the Quran correctly refers to only one theophany, that is, the call symbolized by the fire. In the older JE version the pericope of the plagues directly followed the complaints of the overburdened Israelites against Moses.

---

[268] Gray notes that "uncircumcised lips" may signify "defective lips." A harelip comes to mind. He also dismisses P's remarks about the ages of Moses and Aaron as "artificial." (Laymon, pp. 41-42.)

In Surabadi's story, on the day of the contest, amid a scene of great splendor, Moses and Aaron appeared in simple dress, provoking laughter from the Egyptians. The sorcerers said that if Moses were victorious, it would be because of his God and faith, but if they themselves were, it would be because of Pharaoh's great wealth. *And the sorcerers came to Pharaoh, saying: "Surely there will be a reward for us if we are victors."* (Q. 7:113)

Surabadi records that it was said that there were 70,000 sorcerers with a like number of staffs, (in another tradition) that they had 70 assloads of staffs and ropes, and they were 70 chosen from among the 70,000. The sorcerers made their staffs in the form of snakes, and filled them with mercury. They painted them and leather ropes in the same manner. They were on a height. When they cast down their "staffs," they all made for Moses. Moses was frightened, but then cast down his own staff. It became a dragon and consumed all the sorcerers' snakes, and then made for the pavilion of Pharaoh to consume him as well. Pharaoh pleaded for a respite, and Moses seized the tail of the dragon and it immediately changed back into a wooden staff. The Egyptian sorcerers prostrated themselves and said that they were convinced. Pharaoh was furious [despite just having been rescued from the dragon] and threatened them for believing in Moses and his God without his permission. But Moses and Aaron persisted, and Pharaoh told Moses to take the slaves out of Egypt.[269]

This contest is narrated in the Quran in several places. Taking the narrative from Surah Ta Ha, which is the basis of Surabadi's commentary in this section, we read: *(The sorcerers) said: "O Moses! Wilt thou throw first, or let us be the first to throw?" He said: "Nay, do ye throw! Then lo, their cords and their staves, by their magic appeared to him as though they ran. And Moses conceived a fear in his mind. We said: "Fear not! Lo, thou art the higher. Throw that which is in thy right hand! It will eat up that which they have made. Verily, that which they have made is but a sorcerer's artifice, and a sorcerer shall not be successful to whatever point (of skill) he may attain." Then the sorcerers were flung down prostrate, crying: "We believe in the Lord of Aaron and Moses."* (Q. 20:65-70) This is followed by Pharaoh's anger against his sorcerers as in Surabadi.

At this point, the Egyptians appear to have judged the God invoked by Moses superior to their own gods. They had not yet realized that the God of Moses was the One God, the only God. Incidentally, the Quranic text regards the tricks of the Egyptians as illusions and unreal,

---

[269] Surabadi, pp. 252-255.

just as their gods were unreal. In the Biblical text, the snakes brought to life by the Egyptian magicians are depicted as quite real, as we shall see. Even the relatively late Priestly Writer who tells the story in *Exodus* is either as yet untouched by God's universality, did not notice the inconsistency, or is simply recounting a well-established primitive tradition.

Let us turn to the Biblical version of the contest. In it, the gods of Egypt are real. They had powers of magic and could work miracles, but the miracles wrought by YHWH were more powerful. In the Quran, there is no provisional acceptance of the divinity of the gods of ancient Egypt. Above, we have seen how the Quran speaks of God as the God of Pharaoh as well. There is no parallel to this in *Exodus*, where Moses consistently refers to the Lord as the God of the Hebrews.

"So Moses and Aaron went to Pharaoh and did as the Lord commanded; Aaron cast down his rod before Pharaoh and his servants, and it became a serpent. Then Pharaoh summoned the wise men and the sorcerers; and they also, the magicians of Egypt, did the same by their secret arts. For every man cast down his rod, and they became serpents. But Aaron's rod swallowed up their rods. Still Pharaoh's heart was hardened, and he would not listen to them; as the Lord had said." (Ex. 7:10-13)

All of this is usually thought of as having occurred at one audience, although it would be logical to assume that it would have taken some time to summon the wise men and the sorcerers, as in the Quran. The reader will have noticed that in this account by P, the rod has become Aaron's instead of Moses'. In the earlier sources the rod clearly belongs to Moses, but in the Priestly concern for the enhancement of the role of Aaron and the Aaronid priesthood in the foundation-story of Israel's religion and national identity, the rod has now been placed in the hands of Aaron.

As in the Quran (Q. 7:127-129), so in the Bible this contest did not settle the issue and Pharaoh was not persuaded to release the Israelites. Further signs were necessary before Pharaoh would finally give his permission.

The *Tanhuma* (perhaps under Islamic influence) also makes the occasion of the contest some kind of festival day, in this case the birthday of Pharaoh.[270] Later Jewish tradition, too, paints a scene of great magnificence: Pharaoh's palace was surrounded by an army. It had 400 entrances, each one guarded by 60,000 troops; all this to enhance the feat of Moses and Aaron in securing an audience at all, for they finally had to

[270] LJ, II, 331.

enter Pharaoh's presence by miraculous means.[271] And in the *Exodus Rabbah*, Balaam dismissed the marvel of Aaron's rod-turned-snake's devouring those created by the magicians with superb cheek, saying: "There is nothing marvelous or astonishing in this feat. Your serpent has but devoured our serpents, which is in accordance with a law of nature, one living being devours another. If thou wishest us to acknowledge that the spirit of God worketh in thee, then cast thy rod to the earth, and if, being wood, it swallows up our rods of wood, then we shall acknowledge that the spirit of God is in thee." This was done, causing Pharaoh to fear whether this wonderful rod of Aaron might not swallow up him and his throne also.[272]

THE TEN PLAGUES: *And they said: "Whatever portent thou (O Moses) bringest wherewith to bewitch us, we shall not put faith in thee. So We sent them widespread death*[273] *and the locusts and the vermin and the frogs and the blood—a succession of clear signs. But they were arrogant and became guilty.* (Q. 7:133)

Our edition of the *Stories of the Prophets* drawn from Surabadi's Commentary does not include the material paralleling the Ten Plagues that were sent upon Egypt to convince the Pharaoh to let Israel go after the miracle of the rod had failed to secure the Hebrews their freedom. Surabadi refers to the last plague, that of the death of the firstborn, when he relates how Moses led the people out of Egypt on the pretext of a celebration, an echo of the device used in *Exodus* commented upon above. As it happened, the eldest born of each house died and so the Egyptians were all in mourning for three days and three nights; the opportunity seized by Moses to flee Egypt.[274]

In two places in the Quran the number of signs given to Moses is said to be nine, and this indicates there must have been a strong tradition about that particular number: *And We gave unto Moses nine signs, clear proofs.* (Q. 17:101) *And put thy hand into the bosom of thy robe, it will*

---

[271] LJ, II, 331-332.

[272] LJ, II, 335-336.

[273] *"widespread death"* (Ar. *ṭūfān*): The Arabic word is used more commonly to mean a "destructive storm." Noah's Flood is referred to as Noah's *ṭūfān*. However, it is used metaphorically to describe a widespread calamity, usually with considerable death, such as an epidemic. Both Yusuf Ali and Maulana Muhammad Ali take it in that sense. The Arabic root implies circular motion (Quran-Yusuf Ali, p. 378; Quran-MMA, p. 345; Wehr, pp. 573-574). Arberry and Pickthall translate the word as "flood" (Quran-Arberry, p. 158; Quran-Pickthall, p. 158). If the word is taken to mean death, it would refer to the last of the Biblical plagues, but if it refers to a storm, it could be the ninth: darkness.

[274] Surabadi, pp. 9-10.

come forth white but unhurt, (a sign) among nine signs unto Pharaoh and his people. Verily, they were ever an ever-evil folk. (Q. 27:12)

This figure probably includes the rod and certainly the white hand, as well as those listed above in Q. 7:133. The full list of nine, according to Yusuf Ali, is: the rod, the radiant hand, years of drought (Q. 7:130); failed crops (Q. 7:130); epidemics; locusts, lice, frogs, and water turning to blood.[275] How this compares with the Biblical list we shall see below. But before beginning, we should note that the Quran speaks of "signs" (*āyāt*), not plagues. That said; let us look at the Biblical plagues:

The story of the plagues is given at rather great length in *Exodus*, from Ex. 7:14 to 12:32. It is also a composite of material from J, E, and P, plus glosses by the Deuteronomist, together with other editorial additions. This is not the place to go into a detailed study of the plagues themselves, but several points about the narrative should be made. For the most part, they are amplified natural phenomena: unusual numbers and concentrations of pests, animals, diseases, and storms. The darkness is probably meant to suggest some sort of sandstorm. Only the first (the turning of the water of the Nile into blood) and the last (the death of the firstborn) require a more elaborate explanation, or greater reliance upon the miraculous, that is, the supernatural. For all of the others, the miracle lies in the timing and size of its occurrence.

Though most scholars are reluctant to put it so, the plagues represent the battles between YHWH, Who has invaded Egypt for the purpose of bringing out His chosen people, and the ancient Egyptian gods. Their opposing human proxies are Moses and Aaron on one side and the Egyptian magicians on the other.[276] The power of these gods of Egypt is real, as it was in the contest with the rods, but the point of the narrative is that YHWH was victorious over them on their own terrain. After two more contests, the gods of Egypt seem to retreat from the field and leave it entirely to YHWH, Who continues afflicting the Egyptians until finally Pharaoh agrees to let the Israelites go. (Why he was ready to endure such a series of catastrophes and humiliations to keep his slaves may be something of a mystery to the modern mind.) However, Pharaoh was not so overwhelmed by these miracles not to change his mind and take off in pursuit of Moses and his followers shortly after the last one.

---

[275] Quran-Yusuf Ali, p. 378.

[276] One must not underestimate the power of Egyptian magic. It was famous in the ancient world, and it was even suggested by the pagan critics of Christianity that Jesus had come to Egypt and learned to perform his miracles from Egyptian sorcerers. See companion volume on the New Testament Stories. {In this series, in *Jesus.*}

In the Bible, the first of the ten plagues is that of blood. "Moses and Aaron did as the Lord commanded; in the sight of Pharaoh and in the sight of his servants, he lifted up the rod and struck the water that was in the Nile, and all the water that was in the Nile turned to blood. And the fish in the Nile died; and the Nile became foul, so that the Egyptians could not drink water from the Nile; and there was blood throughout all the land of Egypt. But the magicians of Egypt did the same by their secret arts; so Pharaoh's heart remained hardened..." (Ex. 7:20-22a)

This involves an obvious impossibility. If the river had already been turned into blood, how could the magicians have done the same thing? Perhaps originally the miracle was more local and involved canals or different branches of the river in the Delta rather than the whole river. In this contest, we see that YHWH and the gods of Egypt are tied.

Apropos of this plague there is an even more ancient parallel: In Sumerian texts, we read of the goddess Inanna who, having been taken advantage of by a mortal male while asleep in a garden, sent three plagues upon Sumer. In the first, all the wells of the land became filled with blood, so that the palm groves and vineyards were all saturated with blood. The second plague was destructive winds and storms (the darkness of *Exodus*?). The nature of the third is unknown, as the text is fragmentary.[277]

The second plague, that of the frogs, ended in the same way, with the Egyptians equaling the feats of Moses and Aaron (Ex. 8:1-15). It is only at the third plague, that of the gnats, that the gods of Egypt prove themselves impotent: "The magicians tried by their secret arts to bring forth gnats, but they could not... And the magicians said to Pharaoh, 'This is the finger of God.' But Pharaoh's heart was hardened, and he would not listen to them; as the Lord had said." (Ex. 8:18-19) And the Egyptian sorcerers remained just as helpless in the subsequent seven plagues.

The exact nature of the some of the plagues is in doubt, as in the case of the third plague. The Quran refers to it as *qummal* or "lice." The Hebrew word used is *ken*, the exact meaning of which is unknown, but supposed to be "gnat." The LXX translated the Hebrew word with the Greek *skniphes*, a small insect which pierced the skin and set up itching. This would be more suggestive of mosquitoes or lice than of gnats. The King James translators call them lice, the New English Bible maggots, the Jerusalem Bible gadflies, and the RSV gnats. Since these insects infested man and beast, their activities are more suggestive of lice than any of the other possibilities.

---

[277] Kramer-Sumer, p. 71.

The agents of the fourth plague, not mentioned in the Quran, are even more doubtful. The Hebrew word is *'arob*, meaning "mixture" or "swarm." The RSV calls them "flies," and suggests in a note that the fourth plague is simply a variant of the third plague.[278] Some rabbinic commentators have also thought that the word refers to wild beasts, especially lions and leopards. However, advocates of a plague of flying insects appear to have a stronger case.[279]

The Quran refers to drought and famine. These events are not specifically mentioned in the Biblical narrative, although they would be a natural consequence in whole or part of some of the Biblical plagues, especially those of the blood (in Jewish tradition this is depicted as causing a severe water shortage, thirst, and drought), the pestilence that afflicted the animals, the hail (destructive of standing crops), and the locusts (which consume them).[280] It may be useful to compare the Biblical and Quranic plagues in a table:

Biblical Plague and Textual Reference	***Biblical Source***	***Quranic Order (Q. 7:133)***
1. Blood (Ex. 7:14-24)	JEP	5
2. Frogs (Ex. 7:25-8:15)	JP	4
3. Lice (Ex. 8:16-19)	J	3
4. Flies (Ex. 8:20-32)	J	-
5. Murrain (Ex. 9:1-7)	J	-
6. Boils (Ex. 9:8-12)	P	-
7. Hail (Ex. 10:1-20)	JE	-
8. Locusts (Ex. 10:1-20)	JE	2
9. Darkness (Ex. 10:21-23)	E	-
10. Death (Ex. 11:1-12:32)	JEP	1

Thus Yahwist material is found in seven, possibly eight, of the plagues; Elohist material in only five, and Priestly in five. This does not

[278] RSV, p. 76. The JB calls them "gadflies." (JB, p. 87.) Roy Honeycutt, Jr., writing in the Broadman Commentary, notes an ingenious "rational" explanation of the plagues: "Some suggest that there was a direct causal relationship between each of the plagues. Finegan, for example, indicates that the pollution of the Nile [plague 1] killed great numbers of fish... which in turn drove the frogs [plague 2] ashore. The masses of dead fish were points of origination for the spread of... (anthrax), which is carried by insects [plague 3]. The insects, especially the files of the fourth plague spread the disease, spread the disease from the dead frogs, causing the plague of cattle and the boils of plagues 5 and 6." (BC, Vol. 1, p. 355.)

[279] Rendsburg, Gary A. "Beasts or Bugs?" BR, Vol. XIX, No. 2; April 2003; pp. 18-23.

[280] At the time of Moses' abandonment by his mother, Jewish tradition says that Egypt was afflicted with scorching heat, leprosy, and boils. (LJ, II, 266.)

mean that the original forms of these sources were limited to the numbers given above, but rather that the conflated material has come down to us in this form. In these accounts, later editors could have selected one version over another or eliminated passages of extensive duplication. The selection of the plagues (as opposed to the signs) listed in Quran seems to follow the Yahwist, however, in reverse order. This may be a coincidence. Although the present text of *Exodus* gives us ten plagues, the nine signs in the Quran may be an allusion to another tradition of nine signs, perhaps roughly corresponding to the Yahwist's list. The only sign specifically included among the nine in the Quran is, however, that of the white hand, which is not one of the plagues.

Perhaps we should examine the question from another angle. If we accept the proposition that the rod and the white hand are two of the nine signs mentioned in the Quran, then we should look for a list of seven more signs, probably including the five mentioned in Q. 7:133. These would be among the plagues, although there are possibilities such as the crossing of the sea, water from the rock, etc. Returning to the plagues, is there evidence of such a list of seven plagues?

Actually there is, once again remarkably corroborating the Quran. Scholars have suggested a first version of the plagues in which there were six items: blood, frogs, lice, boils (?), darkness, and the death of the firstborn. It is thought that the second version of the plagues extended the number to seven: blood, frogs, insects, animal murrain, hail with fire, locusts, and finally the death of the firstborn. This would appear to be the original Yahwist-Elohist (JE) conflated version.[281] All of the plagues in Q. 7:133 are to be found on this list. It should also be remembered that Quranic verse does not claim to be exhaustive, but is rather in the nature of giving examples of a genre.

Furthermore, there are other references to the plagues to be found in the Bible. Two psalms each give a list of seven items. In Psalm 78 from the time of David[282] we read:

> "He (God) turned their rivers to blood,
> so that they could not drink of their streams. (1)
> He sent among them swarms of flies, which devoured them,
> and frogs, which destroyed them. (2)
> He gave their crops to the caterpillar,
> and the fruit of their labor to the locust. (3)
> He destroyed their vines with hail,

[281] Plagues of Egypt, EJ, XIII, 610-611.

[282] Lawrence E. Toombs, writing in Laymon, p. 284. This psalm would appear to be a century earlier than the work of the Yahwist and two centuries earlier than the Elohist.

and their sycamores with frost. (4)
He gave their cattle to the hail,
and their flocks to the thunderbolts (5)
He let loose on them his fierce anger,
wrath, indignation, and distress,
a company of destroying angels. (6)
He made a path for his anger;
but he did not spare them from death,
but gave their lives over to the plague.
He smote all the firstborn of Egypt,
the first issue of their strength in the tents of Ham. (7)
(Ps. 78:44-51)

In this hymn we have seven items, some arranged in parallels, a favorite device of Hebrew poetry: (1) blood, (2) flies/frogs, (3) caterpillars/locusts, (4) hail/frost, (5) hail/lightning, (6) death by pestilence, and (7) the death of the firstborn. The doublets are different aspects of the plagues; thus, the flies and frogs assaulted Egypt together and were counted as one by the psalmist.

In Psalm 105 there is still another list of seven plagues: (1) darkness, (2) blood causing the fish to die, (3) frogs, (4) flies and gnats, (5) hail and lightning, (6) locusts, and (7) the death of the firstborn (Ps. 105:28-36). The items mentioned in the Quranic verse appear on both of these lists. Incidentally, neither of these two sources (nor the Quran) mentions the plague of boils that seems to have originated with the Priestly Document.

Therefore, in all likelihood the original tradition was of seven plagues and, with the rod and the white hand, we arrive at the Quranic figure of nine signs (not plagues). The differences between the two lists suggest that an "official" version had not yet coalesced during the early monarchic period. The expansion to ten separate plagues is doubtless a later development achieved by dividing some of the plagues (that is, flies from the frogs, or gnats, etc.) and probably by the addition of the plague of boils by a later redactor from the Priestly circle.[283]

---

[283] Like 7 and 12, 10 was also a favorite schematic number of ancient and later Jewish writers. In addition to the ten plagues and the ten commandments, we have the ten temptations of Abraham, the ten curses, the ten pious ones, the ten cosmocrators, the ten words of Creation, the ten punishments, the ten revelations, the wages of Jacob charged ten times, the ten classes of angels, the ten candlesticks, the ten mysteries, the ten attributes of God, a schema of the ten heavens, etc. (See LJ, VII, 467-468.)

The most decisive of the plagues was the last one, and it is the only one to which Surabadi gives much space. In the Bible, after the plague of darkness that lasted three days, Pharaoh agreed to let the people go, but their flocks and herds would have to remain behind in Egypt. Moses would not agree to these terms, so once again Pharaoh's heart was hardened and he refused to allow the people to go. From the Elohist:

"The Lord said unto Moses, 'Yet one plague more I will bring upon Pharaoh and upon Egypt; afterwards he will let you go hence; when he lets you go, he will drive you away completely.'" (Ex. 11:1) Then the Yahwist takes up the tale: "And Moses said, 'Thus says the Lord: About midnight I will go forth in the midst of Egypt; and all the firstborn in the land of Egypt shall die, from the firstborn of Pharaoh who sits upon his throne, even to the firstborn of the maidservant who is behind the mill; and the firstborn of the cattle. And there shall be a great cry throughout all the land of Egypt, such as there has never been, nor ever shall be again. But against any of the people of Israel, either man or beast, not a dog shall growl; that ye may know that the Lord makes a distinction between the Egyptians and Israel...'" (Ex. 11:4-7)

Then God, almost in the character of a night-demon, is reputed to have said, "'For I will pass through the land of Egypt that night, and I will smite all the firstborn in the land of Egypt, both man and beast; and on all the gods of Egypt I will execute judgments: I am the Lord. The blood shall be a sign for you, upon the houses where you are; and when I see the blood, I will pass over you, and no plague shall fall upon you to destroy you, when I smite the land of Egypt.'" (Ex. 12:12-13)

While perhaps delighting the hearts of the Israelites, these primitive verses depict a God—certainly not the Universal God of Mercy—who discriminates between races, favoring one over another. Innocent animals are also to suffer, as are the other slaves and captives held by the Egyptians in Egypt. Not only that, He is not omniscient and requires the sign of the blood to inform Him of the presence of His favored folk. Even worse, from the point of view of absolute monotheism, He even takes vengeance on the defeated gods of Egypt. If they were non-existent, why would He waste words upon them?

Let us return to the Biblical story: The Israelites followed these instructions. "At midnight the Lord smote all the firstborn in the land of Egypt, from the firstborn of Pharaoh who sat on his throne to the firstborn of the captive who was in the dungeon, and all the firstborn of the cattle. And Pharaoh rose up in the night, he, and all his servants, and all the Egyptians; and there was a great cry in Egypt, for there was not a house where one was not dead. And he summoned Moses and Aaron by night, and said, 'Rise up, go forth from among my people, both ye and the people of Israel; and go, serve the Lord, as ye have said. Take your flocks and your herds, as ye have said, and be gone, and bless me also.'" (Ex. 12:29-32)

While for the Muslim this episode is a demonstration of the power of God, the final disaster which He had let loose upon the Egyptians, prompting them to let the Hebrews free in accordance with God's plan; for the Jew this plague has an even greater importance. Jews from ancient times to the present find the origins of their Paschal Feast, or the Passover in this story. Many modern scholars, however, no longer believe that the feast originated with this plague, as the Biblical text would have it. More likely than not, they believe, it originated among pasturing folk who offered the firstborn of their flocks in the springtime to whatever deity or spirit they worshipped and then consumed the animal ritually in one night, so that nothing of it remained in the morning. The blood was smeared on tent posts to ward off demons. Among the settled Jews this pastoral origin of the Paschal Feast seems to have been forgotten or suppressed in favor of a later association with Moses and the Exodus from Egypt.[284] *And God knows best.*

G. THE EXODUS

The Moses led Israel onward from the Red Sea. (Ex. 15:22)

Although the selection from Surabadi describing the Exodus comes from his commentary of Surah Baqarah (Q. 2), the Quranic reports are fuller in other places, and we shall turn to one of them: *And We revealed to Moses, "Go with My servants by night; surely ye will be pursued." Then Pharaoh sent into the cities summoners, (saying), "Lo, these indeed are but a little troop, and indeed they are offenders against us. And lo, we are a host on guard." So We expelled them from gardens and fountains, and treasures, and a noble state. Thus they followed (the Israelites) at sunrise; and when the two hosts saw each other, those with Moses said, "Lo, we are indeed overtaken!" Said he, "Nay, for lo, my Lord is with me. He will guide me." Then We revealed to Moses, "Strike the sea with thy staff." And it parted, and each part was as a great mountain. And there We brought near the others to that place, and We saved Moses and those with him, everyone; then We drowned the others.* (Q. 26:52-66)

---

[284] Schauss, pp. 38-40; Buber, p. 70.

In his narrative of these events, Surabadi explains that Moses led the Israelites out of Egypt on the pretext of holding a festival. They sought ornaments and robes, put them on, and departed towards the sea. As it happened, from each Egyptian household a dear one had died and the Egyptians were in mourning for three days. At the end of the period, Pharaoh collected an immense army, while Moses had only 300,000 fighting men [this despite the fact that the Quran in the above quotation refers to the small number of the Israelites; see below]. The vanguard of Pharaoh's army had 1,000,000 horsemen and a right wing, a left wing, a van, and a center with like numbers. There were 12,000 piebald horses at the front of the army.[285]

The departure of the Israelites by night alluded to in the Quran is confirmed by events as depicted in the Bible. After the full horror of the tenth and final plague had become apparent, during that same night Pharaoh, defeated, summoned Moses and Aaron and told them to leave Egypt with their people and their flocks (Ex. 12:31-32; quoted in the previous section). Then: "And the Egyptians were urgent with the people, to send them out of the land in haste; for they said, 'We are all dead men.' So the people took their dough before it was leavened, their kneading bowls being bound up in their mantles on their shoulders." (Ex. 12:33-34) This passage from the Yahwist, a picture of haste and forcible expulsion, contrasts with the looting of the defeated and mourning Egyptians described with evident approval by the Elohist immediately thereafter: "The people of Israel had also done as Moses told them, for they had asked of the Egyptians jewelry of silver and gold, and clothing; and the Lord had given the people favor in the sight of the Egyptians, so that they let them have what they asked. Thus they despoiled the Egyptians." (Ex. 12:35-36)

This is a completely different picture. The passage harks back to Ex. 3:21-22 (quoted above in section E) and is perhaps a continuation or consequence of it. The Israelites had (treacherously as it turns out) ingratiated themselves with the Egyptians to borrow their finery and then flee Egypt with it. For the Yahwist, the Israelites were being terrorized as the Egyptians responded to the death that YHWH through Moses had brought upon them. Instead of looting, they were forced into a hasty departure; that is, they were in full flight. For the Elohist, this is another opportunity for an Israelite leader to turn the tables on his perceived oppressors by means of trickery. With YHWH's approval—for though He had defeated the gods of Egypt they are not yet dead—the Israelites left Egypt after borrowing everything of value they could convince the

---

[285] Surabadi, p. 10.

generous Egyptians to lend them on the excuse that they were going to hold a festival of YHWH-worship in the desert. Once again, the Biblical text appears parochial and morally dubious, tainting the episode with deception and lying. The Israelites are depicted as decamping in the night like thieves.

The unleavened dough mentioned above is an aetiological addition, explaining, retrospectively, the origin of the unleavened bread eaten in commemoration of an event that had not yet occurred, the hasty flight before the women had had time to bake their bread. Jewish custom seems to have dictated that the participants in the Passover feast not leave the house until morning (and thus they remained under the protection of the sign of the blood). In the Bible, Moses and Aaron were summoned by Pharaoh (and therefore had left the site of the feast), but in Jewish tradition, to remove this obvious problem, Pharaoh was depicted coming to Moses as a supplicant![286]

Whilst the text of *Exodus* suggests that the triumphant Hebrews extorted wealth from the Egyptians, many ancient Jewish authorities make the Egyptians voluntary contributors to their own despoilment. Josephus says "they also honored the Hebrews with gifts; some in order to get them to depart quickly, and others on account of their neighborhood, and the friendship they had with them."[287] This is an attempt to correct the unfavorable impression created by the Biblical text.

In the Quran, Pharaoh refers to the departing Hebrews contemptuously as a small troop. Surabadi would have been better advised to follow that cue instead of honoring the vast numbers attributed to the Israelites in the Bible: "And the people of Israel journeyed from Rameses[288] to Succoth, about six hundred thousand men on foot, besides women and children. A mixed multitude also went up with them, and very many cattle, both flocks and herds." (Ex. 12:37-38)[289] "The time that the people of Israel dwelt in Egypt was four hundred and thirty years. And at the end of four hundred and thirty years, on that very day, all the hosts of the Lord went out of the land of Egypt. It was a night of watching by the Lord, to bring them out of the land of Egypt; so this same night is a night of watching kept to the Lord by all

---

[286] LJ, II, 370.

[287] Josephus, Antiquities, II.14.6, p. 62.

[288] Rameses the city, identified with Tanis in the eastern Delta of the Nile. It was also known as Zoan. (ABL, p. B-7.

[289] Verse 37 giving the figure of 600,000 is a much later Priestly gloss inserted into the Yahwist text.

the people of Israel throughout their generations." (Ex. 12:40-42) The last quotation is the explanation of the origin of the Feast of the Passover.

What was the mixed multitude? Scholars have thought this to be a reference to the non-Hebrews, perhaps other Semites or even Egyptians, who accompanied the Hebrews on their flight from Egypt. This addition has a ring of authenticity to it, for it goes against the ethnocentric ideas that developed later in post-Exilic times. Whilst it probably does not, of itself, justify the interpretation Freud gave to it, that the band fleeing Egypt was actually composed of a remnant of Aton-worshippers (the monotheistic faith established by Akhenaton which had failed a century earlier), it does seem to imply that Moses' followers were not homogeneous. This did not concern the writer of this passage (J or E) as it concerned the Jews who had experienced the dispersals of the Exile. Despite all of the editing and additions that put so many injunctions towards ethnic purity in the mouth of Moses in the Pentateuch, at this time YHWH-worship was still open to all believers regardless of origin. However, its principal recruiting grounds were among the Semitic clans of southern Syria (Palestine and Jordan).

THE CENSUS: Both the Biblical figure of 600,000 men and Surabadi's more modest 300,000 are grossly overstated. The population of Egypt in Pharaonic times is not known from any census records, but in the Roman era, according to Diodorus, it was about 7,000,000.[290] (McEvedy and Jones give a more conservative figure of 4 millions for the Roman period.) During the time of Rameses II of the XIXth Dynasty, that is, the era of Moses (c. 1300 BCE), the population of Egypt is estimated by McEvedy and Jones to have been about 3,000,000. This may be too conservative, but given the state of agricultural technology, it could not have been much more by any significant factor.[291]

The Biblical figure of 600,000 men would imply a general Israelite population of 2,000,000; not counting the mixed multitude presumably not included in this figure. In other words, a majority of the inhabitants of Egypt were fleeing the country! This is already about two and one-half times the estimated population of all Palestine at the height of its prosperity under David and Solomon (c. 1000 BCE).[292] Except for

---

[290] Breasted, p. 6.

[291] McEvedy, pp. 226-277. The same authorities estimate that the population of the entire world in the time of Moses to have been no more than 50,000,000. (McEvedy, pp. 342-343.) The population figures in Surabadi and the Pentateuch are fantastically exaggerated.

[292] This comparison is based on Albright's estimate of 800,000 (Albright-Ab to Ez, p. 56). McEvedy and Jones believe that the land of Palestine had a much lower population

the credulous, the idea of such a multitude surviving for 40 weeks, much less 40 years, in the arid mountains and small oases of Sinai and northwestern Arabia is unthinkable. As we have seen, the Quran eschews such figures.

There is Biblical evidence for a more realistic appraisal of the size of the group fleeing Egypt. In the first chapter of *Exodus* (Ex. 1:15-21), as we have noted above, it is stated that there were only two midwives for the Israelites and their names are given. Just two midwives would suggest a community of several thousands, not 2,000,000.[293] It has also been suggested that the Hebrew word *eleph*, which has been translated as "thousand," in giving the above figures really means "clan," perhaps in a military sense, as the figures are always concerned with fighting men. The passage would then be rendered 600 clans, instead of 600,000 men.[294]

The first chapter of *Numbers* gives the alleged results of a census of men capable of bearing arms undertaken in the second year of the wandering. The passage is from the Priestly Document. It gives us a total of 603,550 fighting men. The usual translation of the census passages that leads to these grossly inflated figures is thus, using Benjamin as an example: "Of the people of Benjamin, their generations, by their families, by their fathers' houses, according to the number of names, from twenty years old and upward, every man able to go forth to war: the number of the tribe of Benjamin was thirty-five thousand four hundred." (Num. 1:36-37) These are the census figures by tribe:

Reuben	46,500	Ephraim	40,500
Simeon	59,300	Manasseh	32,200
Gad	45,650	Benjamin	35,400
Judah	74,600	Dan	62,700
Issachar	54,400	Asher	41,500
Zebulon	57,400	Naphtali	53,400

Of course these figures actually represent the point of view of a much later era, that of the Priestly Writer. Note that Levites, who had not yet been designated as the priestly tribe and thus exempted from military

---

of about a quarter of a million during the period of the Egyptian Empire. (McEvedy, p. 141.)

293 See Section C above.

294 BC, I, 365-367. The Arabic cognate for the Hebrew *eleph* is *alf. Ilf*, from the same root, means "friend, confidant" in Arabic, but there is no suggestion of "clan," though the root also means "assemble," "compose," and "unite."

service, are not included in the census, although the Levites are specifically mentioned as participating in bloodshed and mayhem later on in *Numbers*.

If we take the word translated as "thousand" to mean "clan" as has been suggested, the final clause would read: "the number of the tribe of Benjamin was 35 clans; 400 (men)." In support of this interpretation, it should be noted that the hundreds tend to be larger or smaller in accordance with the thousands, with the single exception of Simeon, whose large figure may be a scribal error, because the tribe of Simeon was early absorbed by the tribe of Judah. By this calculation, the total would be a more realistic 5,550 men. This would imply a total horde of some 15 to 20,000 people, much more in accord with the more recent population estimates we have already noted.[295]

It is not out of place to digress a moment about size of populations and armies in the ancient world. Our notions of these have been greatly distorted by the exaggerations of transmitters of tradition and historians. Though the Bible is rife with such exaggeration, the Greeks were no strangers to this tendency. Witness the immense figures Herodotus attributes to the Persian army invading Greece, inflated by a factor of at least ten, to several million![296] An example may be cited which is very relevant to this topic as it refers to ancient Egypt during the era we are discussing: the largest Egyptian army assembled in Pharaonic times of which we have record was that of Rameses II (the same Pharaoh whom we believe to be connected with the events of the Exodus), used in the battle of Kadesh, Syria, 1288 BCE. It had only four divisions totaling 20,000 men.[297] The Hebrew men-at-arms (not to mention the mixed multitude) would have outnumbered Rameses' grandest army 30 to 1! This historical figure is also quite different from Surabadi's 5,000,000—which would have exceeded the total population of Egypt at that time.

The *Mekilta Beshallah* also tells us of the huge forces the Egyptians had mustered against the Israelites, more than their (the Israelites') total number including women and children, that is to say an Egyptian army of more than two millions.[298] The medieval *Zohar* gives us figures even more fantastic that those of Surabadi: It was said that the Egyptians outnumbered the Israelites 300 to 1; assuming that only

---

[295] "According to scripture the Israelites were numbered at something over 2m. Ten thousand would be a better figure..." (McEvedy, p. 141.) This estimate is more conservative than our calculations based on reinterpreting the Biblical data, but probably closer to the truth.

[296] Herodotus, Bk. 7, pp. 459-461.

[297] Breasted, p. 355.

[298] LJ, III, 13.

Israel's 600,000 fighting men are to be counted, that would mean a force of some 180,000,000 Egyptian soldiers![299]

Surabadi, in this place, mentions the three-day celebration for which, according to the Bible, Moses had requested permission during his first interview with Pharaoh (Ex. 5:3). However, late Jewish tradition (the *Mekilta Beshallah*) also states that Pharaoh was under the impression the Hebrews were going away for only a three days' journey into the wilderness to offer sacrifices.[300] The Biblical text can be read to support this idea.

Surabadi continues, when the Egyptians approached the encampment of Moses, it was dark and Pharaoh decided to wait until the morning. The Israelites were very frightened. Then God sent a white cloud which descended between the two armies, so that they could not see each other.[301]

According to the Bible, the Israelites left Rameses (Tanis) and made for Succoth (Ex. 12:37), with God Personally leading them: "When Pharaoh let the people go, God did not lead them by the way of the land of the Philistines, although that was near; for God said, 'Lest the people repent when they see war, and return to Egypt.' But God led the people round by the way of the wilderness toward the Red Sea. And the people of Israel went up out of the land of Egypt equipped for battle. And Moses took the bones of Joseph with him; for Joseph had solemnly sworn the people of Israel, saying, 'God will visit you; then ye must carry my bones with you from here.' And they moved on from Succoth, and encamped at Etham, on the edge of the wilderness.

"And the Lord went before them by day in a pillar of cloud to lead them along the way, and by night in a pillar of fire to give them light, that they might travel by day and by night; the pillar of cloud by day and the pillar of fire by night did not depart from before the people." (Ex. 13:17-22) The pillar of cloud may be explained by a natural phenomenon occurring in dry, dusty lands, the whirlwind or "dust devil." Urbanites rarely see them but they are common in the Middle East, and we have seen many of them, some quite impressive, like tornadoes of dust. This explanation does not diminish the miracle; as we have said, it is often the timing—not necessarily the event itself—that is miraculous.

---

[299] The total of all the armies engaged in World War I on both sides was about 65,000,000 men; while in World War II, the figure was about 70,000,000. (World Almanac, 1968, p. 735.)

[300] LJ, III, 9.

[301] Surabadi, p. 10.

Except for the notes on the itinerary that are from the P, the passage is a conflation of the J and E accounts. The spectacle is magnificent, though perhaps primitive. YHWH, Who has come from His mountain home in Midian with Moses to bring His chosen people out of Egypt, is personally conducting the multitude out of Egypt. God's caution about leading His people along the shorter and easier shore route to Canaan is anachronistic, as the Philistines (that is, the Sea People) did not attack this corner of the Mediterranean until the 11th century BCE, two centuries after the Exodus and after the Hebrews had become established in Canaan. One wonders where a band of slaves found the all that military armament; weapons are not usually put in the hands of recalcitrant or rebellious slaves.

God then directs Moses to lead the people back to a place opposite Pi-hahiroth, between Migdol and the sea, in front of Baal-zephon, and to camp there by the sea (Ex. 14:1-2).

Thus, we see that the people, led by God, were forced marched day and night out of the cultivated regions of Egypt. It took some time (three days according to Surabadi and Jewish tradition) for the forces of Pharaoh to catch up to them. Despite the series of disasters Egypt had suffered, Pharaoh had once again changed his mind and was now in pursuit of his fleeing serfs. This is explicable only if we admit that the plagues were not as widespread and devastating as later tradition has made them out to be.

When considering these accounts we must remind ourselves, that no matter how significant they are in Jewish and later Christian and Islamic religious literature, there is no explicit reference to any of these events in contemporary Egyptian records. The only alternative to denying the historicity of these events (subject of course to the possibility that in the future some confirmation will be discovered) is to recognize that this was a local or, at most, a provincial affair involving hundreds and perhaps thousands of people rather millions. The impact of these events upon later Jewish literature is sufficient to convince us that real events lay behind these stories. However, in the Biblical narrative they have been blown out of proportion and are shrouded in the many veils of hyperbole and wishful thinking woven by later generations anxious to increase the wonder of it all.

So Pharaoh, who had previously ordered Moses to take his followers out of Egypt post haste (Ex. 13:31-32), had changed his mind: "When the king of Egypt was told that the people had fled, the mind of Pharaoh and his servants was changed toward the people, and they said, 'What is this we have done, that we have let Israel go from serving us?'"

(Ex. 14:5) Thereupon Pharaoh with 600 chariots took off in pursuit. "The Egyptians pursued them, all Pharaoh's horses and chariots and his horsemen and his army, and overtook them encamped at the sea, by Pi-hahiroth, in front of Baal-zephon." (Ex. 14:9)

As the Quran and Surabadi reflect, when the Israelites saw the Egyptian army, they were greatly frightened: "And the people of Israel cried out to the Lord; and they said to Moses, 'Is it because there are no graves in Egypt that thou hast taken us away to die in the wilderness?... For it would have been better for us to serve the Egyptians than to die in the wilderness.'" (Ex. 14:10b-11a,12b) Moses reassured the people and told them to remain calm; God would fight for them. With the two hostile camps facing each other, as in Surabadi, a cloud descended and separated the forces: "The angel of God[302] who went before the host of Israel moved and went behind them; and the pillar of cloud moved from before them and stood behind them, coming between the host of Egypt and the host of Israel. And there was the cloud and the darkness; and the night passed without one coming near the other all night." (Ex. 14:19-20) A rationalist would deem this to mean that a dense sea fog had come ashore and immobilized the camps, but in the mind of the Yahwist, it was God Himself, manifested in the cloud, Who kept the two forces apart.

CROSSING THE SEA: With morning, Surabadi tells us, Gabriel told Moses to command the people to cross the sea in safety. The people were afraid. Joshua was commanded to cross the surface of the water on a horse. When this was done, the querulous Israelites objected that Joshua had special qualities they did not have. Then Moses was commanded by Gabriel to strike the water, but whilst he was receiving the message, Aaron took the staff and struck the sea, as he wanted the honor of parting the waters. But the sea reproved him. Ashamed, Aaron returned the staff to Moses who struck the sea with it. It still did not part. Gabriel told Moses to address the sea by its proper title. Moses struck it again, calling, "Father of the Immortal, divide by God's permission." Still it would not part. Then Gabriel told him to praise the Last of the Prophets [Muhammad]. Moses uttered ten greetings of praise to him and then struck the sea, "and the sea split asunder."

Now the Israelites complained that the way was too narrow. Moses struck the sea and twelve paths appeared, one for each tribe. The people protested that they would not be able to see each other and know the fate of the other tribes. Moses (who must have possessed a truly

---

[302] Here the Elohist has an angel rather than God Himself (as in the Yahwist) intervene.

divine capacity for patience) struck the sea again and the sea formed a vast arch. Then they were afraid of the mud of the sea bottom. In response to the plea of Moses, a wind arose and dried the sea bottom. Moses struck the ground and dust arose. Only then would the people consent to pass to their salvation.[303]

This trying scene is represented by only a few verses in the Bible: "Then Moses stretched out his hand over the sea; and the Lord drove the sea back by a strong east wind all night, and made the sea dry land, and the waters were divided. And the people of Israel went into the midst of the sea on dry ground, the waters being a wall to them on their right hand and on their left." (Ex. 14:21-22)

The Psalmist describes the same scene:

> "He divided the sea and let them pass through it,
> and made the waters stand like a heap." (Ps. 78:13)

Jewish tradition also speaks of the refusal of the sea to obey Moses' command at first. In the 11th-century CE Midrash *Wa Yosha'* God orders Moses, "Take the rod that I gave unto thee, and get to the sea upon Mine errand, and speak thus: 'I am the messenger sent by the Creator of the world! Uncover thy paths, O sea, for My children, that they may go through the midst of thee on dry ground.'

"Moses spoke to the sea as God had bidden him, but it replied, I will not do according to thy words, for thou art only a man born of woman, and, besides, I am three days older than thou, O man, for I was brought forth on the third day of creation, and thou on the sixth. Moses lost no time, but carried back to God the words the sea had spoken, and the Lord said: 'Moses, what does a master to with an intractable servant?' 'He beats him with a rod,' said Moses. 'Do thus!' ordered God. 'Lift up thy rod, and stretch thine hand over the sea, and divide it.'"[304]

The earlier *Targum Yerushalmi* describes the rod: "thereupon Moses raised up his rod—the rod that had been created at the very beginning of the world, on which were graven in plain letters the great and exalted Name, the names of the ten plagues inflicted upon the Egyptians, and the twelve tribes of Jacob. This rod he lifted up, and stretched it out over the seas."[305] The involvement of Gabriel in the events of the crossing is also attested in Jewish tradition.[306]

---

[303] Surabadi, pp. 10-11.
[304] LJ, III, 18-19.
[305] LJ, III, 19.
[306] LJ, III, 20.

The refusal of the Israelites to cross the sea once it had parted for them is found in Talmudic literature. In the pre-Islamic (3rd or 4th century CE) *Fathers According to Rabbi Nathan*, there is an extensive account of this dialogue between Moses and the Israelites: "When our ancestors stood at the Red Sea, Moses said to them: 'Rise, go across!'

"'We shall not go across,' they declared, 'until tunnels are made in the sea.'

"Moses took his rod and smote the sea, and tunnels were made in it [the arches of Surabadi?]. Then Moses said to them: 'Rise, go across!'

"'We shall not go across,' they declared, 'until the sea is turned into a valley before us.'

"Moses took the rod and smote the sea, and it became a valley before them... Said Moses to them: Rise, go across!'

"'We shall not go across,' they declared, 'until it is cut asunder before us.' Moses took the rod and smote the sea, and it was cut asunder before them... Said Moses to them: 'Rise, go across!'[307]

"'We shall not go across,' they declared, 'until it is turned into clay for our benefit.' Moses took the rod and smote the sea, and it became clay... Said Moses to them: 'Rise, go across!'

(Once again, one marvels at Moses' self-control in this scene. At other times, he was not so patient.)

"'We shall not go across,' they declared, 'until it is made into a wilderness before us.' Moses took the rod and smote the sea, and it became a wilderness... Said Moses to them: 'rise, go across!'

"'We shall not go across,' they declared, 'until it is broken into many pieces before us.' Moses took the rod and smote the sea, and it turned into rocks... Said Moses to them: 'Rise, go across!'

"'We shall not go across,' they declared, 'unless it is turned into walls before us.' Moses took the rod and smote the sea, and it turned into walls Said Moses to them: 'Rise, go across!'

"'We shall not go across,' they declared, 'unless it is turned flaskshaped before us.' Moses took the rod and smote the sea, and it turned flaskshaped... As for the waters between the sundered paths, a fire came down and lapped them..."[308]

In the above, many of the elements of Surabadi's catalog of Israelite protests can be found, including the twelve paths and the final elimination of the waters separating the paths. Earlier Jewish writers such as Philo and Josephus conceived of the path between the divided

---

[307] This is the miracle of the 12 paths to which Surabadi refers. See note, ARN, p. 206.

[308] ARN, pp. 133-135. Most of our omissions are Biblical citations.

waters as a road.[309] Josephus writes: "When Moses had thus addressed himself to God, he smote the sea with his rod, which parted asunder at the stroke, and receiving those waters into itself, left the ground dry, a road and a place of flight for the Hebrews. Now when Moses saw this appearance of God, and that the sea went out of its own place and left dry land, he went first of all into it, and bid the Hebrews to follow him along that divine road, and to rejoice at the danger their enemies that followed them were in: and gave thanks to God for this so surprising a deliverance which appeared from Him."[310]

Above, we saw that Surabadi has introduced the character of Joshua into the narrative of the crossing of the sea. In the Biblical version, Joshua does not appear until the story of the battle with the Amalekites in Exodus 17. Joshua is not mentioned by name in the Quran, and there is no figure in the narrative of Moses in Egypt with whom he could be identified, just as there is not in the Bible. In *Exodus,* Aaron is also conspicuously absent from the account of the crossing of the sea.

Surabadi continues: After the Israelites had begun the crossing, the fog lifted and the Egyptians saw the Israelites in the midst of the sea. Pharaoh boasted that the waters had parted out of fear of him and started to follow. Haman reminded him that they were still the same persons who had left Pushanj,[311] and that they had not reached that degree of genuine divinity. He cautioned Pharaoh that the waters had parted because of Moses' prayer, and said: "Let us return or we shall be destroyed." Pharaoh recognized the truth of what Haman was saying and wanted to turn back, but Gabriel came to them on a mare (in heat), and the stallions of Pharaoh and Haman ran after her. Pharaoh could not get off, and he was ashamed to call for help, for could a god not control a horse? (Gabriel had previously come to Pharaoh and asked him what should be done with a servant who usurped the position of the master. Pharaoh had replied that he should be cast into the Red Sea.) [312]

On that day, Pharaoh saw his own judgment written in his own hand. The sea fell back on itself and Pharaoh and the Egyptian forces were destroyed just as the last of the Israelites reached the safety of the opposite shore. At that moment, Pharaoh wanted to recite the Declaration

309 LJ, VU, 6-7.

310 Josephus, Antiquities, II.16.3, p. 63.

311 Pūshang, to be identified with Pūshanj (in Khorasan) mentioned in Section B by Surabadi as the original home of Pharaoh and Haman.

312 Compare this with the quotation from *Wa Yosha'* cited in the text above.

of Faith[313] and be saved, but Gabriel threw a fistful of mud into his mouth, preventing him, and he was destroyed.[314]

This last is inspired by a passage found in Surah Yunus: *And We brought the Children of Israel across the sea, and Pharaoh with his hosts pursued them in rebellion and transgression, till, when the drowning overtook him, he exclaimed: 'I believe that there is no god save Him in Whom the Children of Israel believe, and I am of the believers!' What? Now? When hitherto thou hast rebelled and been of the wrongdoers? But this day We save thee in thy body that thou mayest be a portent for those after thee. Lo, most of mankind are heedless of Our portents.* (Q. 10:90-92)

In his account of the destruction of the Egyptian forces, Surabadi has reintroduced the figure of Haman. The Quran does not indicate that Haman was with Pharaoh in the final scenes. The import of the above passages seems to be that as death was coming upon Pharaoh, he repented, but it was too late. The preservation of his body would be a reference to the well-known Egyptian custom of embalming and mummifying their dead. Many Pharaonic mummies are housed in the Egyptian Museum, Cairo, including that of Rameses II. However, we must remind ourselves that historically no Egyptian monarch is known to have perished in the manner described in the Bible and the Quran. If we are concerned with historicity, we can only assume that Pharaoh in this passage describes Pharaoh's representative or governor, as discussed above.

The Bible describes the scene thus: "The Egyptians pursued, and went in after them into the midst of the sea, all Pharaoh's horse, his chariots, and his horseman. And in the morning watch, the Lord in the pillar of fire and of cloud looked down upon the host of the Egyptians, clogging their chariot wheels so that they drove heavily; and the Egyptians said, 'Let us flee from before Israel; for the Lord fights for them against the Egyptians.' (Ex. 14:23-25)

"Then the Lord said to Moses, 'Stretch out thy hand over the sea, that the water may come back upon the Egyptians, upon their chariots, and upon their horsemen.' So Moses stretched forth his hand over the sea and the sea returned to its wonted flow when the morning appeared; and the Egyptians fled into it, and the Lord routed the Egyptians in the midst of the sea. The waters returned and covered the chariots and the horsemen and all the host of Pharaoh that had followed them into the sea;

---

[313] "Declaration of Faith": Ar. *Shahādah*. "I testify that there is no god but God, (He is) One; He has no partner, and I testify that Muhammad is His servant and His Messenger."
[314] Surabadi, pp. 11-12.

not so much as one of them remained. But the people of Israel walked on dry ground through the sea, the waters being a wall to them on their right and on their left. Thus the Lord saved Israel that day from the hand of the Egyptians; and Israel saw the Egyptians dead upon the seashore." (Ex. 14:26-30)

It will be noted in the above verses from *Exodus* that there is no specific notice of Pharaoh's death, although it can be inferred—and this is the usual interpretation. However, in old sources there was a difference of opinion about his fate. According to some, he was destroyed with his forces; according to others, he survived so that he could see the power of God. The last Quranic verse quoted above (Q. 10:92) could support such an interpretation, were it not for explicit references to his drowning elsewhere.[315] In the *Pirke de Rabbi Eliezer* there is a reference to the tradition that Pharaoh repented and was saved to become the ruler of Nineveh (near Mosul in modern Iraq), where, at the behest of Jonah, he led the people in repentance for their evil behavior.[316]

A composite version of this tradition is found in the *Legends of the Jews*: "Thus all the Egyptians were drowned. Only one was spared—Pharaoh himself. When the children of Israel raised their voices to sing a song of praise to God at the shores of the Red Sea, Pharaoh heard it as he was jostled hither and thither by the billows, and he pointed his finger heavenward, and called out: 'I believe in Thee, O God! Thou art righteous, and I and my people are wicked, and I acknowledge now that there is no god in the world beside Thee.' Without a moment's delay, Gabriel descended and laid an iron chain about Pharaoh's neck, and holding him securely, he addressed him thus: 'Villain! Yesterday thou didst say, "Who is the Lord that I should hearken to His voice?" and now thou sayest, "The Lord is righteous."' With that he let him drop into the depths of the sea, and there he tortured him for fifty days, to make the power of God known to him. At the end of the time he installed him as king of the great city of Nineveh..."[317] This version would seem to owe

---

[315] For example: *(Moses) said: "In truth thou knowest that none sent down these (signs) save the Lord of the heavens and the earth as proofs, and lo, I deem thee lost, O Pharaoh." And (Pharaoh) wished to frighten them from the land, but We drowned him and those with him, all together.* (Q. 17:102-103) The destruction of "the people of Pharaoh" is referred to a number of times in the Quran, and such a term could be interpreted to exclude Pharaoh himself, but the verses just cited exclude that possibility. If we are to reconcile this judgment on Pharaoh with history, as we know it now, we must look for another explanation of the form the tradition assumed in Arabia, perhaps the use of Pharaoh as an office rather than an individual, as has been discussed above.

[316] PRE, pp. 341-343.

[317] LJ, III, 29.

something to Islamic stories, as we are sure the Muslim reader will appreciate, however none are cited by Ginsberg as direct sources.

The text of Ex. 14:21-30 is a conflation of J and P. In general, J is less supernatural than the much later P. J explicitly states that the waters were parted by an east wind: "Then Moses stretched out his hand over the sea; and the Lord drove the sea back by a strong east wind all night, and made the sea dry land, and the waters were divided." (Ex. 14:21) But P envisions walls of water standing on either side of the road made through the sea for the Israelites (Ex. 14:22, 29). Again, in the destruction of the Egyptians, J sees them mired in mud as the waters rise around them (Ex. 14:25), whereas to P, the walls of water collapsed upon the Egyptians in an overwhelming flood (Ex. 14:28). The Quranic description reflects traditions nearer to P than J in this section.

Although we can simply consider the events at the Red Sea to have been a miracle, inexplicable in terms of natural phenomena, are there possible natural explanations? Josephus reminds his readers about a similar story concerning Alexander the Great: "While, for the sake of those that accompanied Alexander, king of Macedonia, who lived, comparatively but a little while ago,[318] the Pamphylian Sea[319] returned and afforded them a passage through itself, when they had no other way to go."[320] Arrian also describes this episode: "Alexander now left Phaselis. Part of his forces he dispatched over the mountains towards Perga, along the tracks made for him by the Thracians to facilitate what was otherwise a long and difficult journey. He himself marched with his picked troops along the coast, a route that is practicable only in northerly winds—during southerlies the beach is impassable. It had been blowing hard from the south before he started; but (by the grace of God, as both he and his staff felt) the wind went round into the north and made the passage quick and easy."[321] This is very similar to the Yahwist's explanation of what happened in Egypt for Moses. Is such a natural phenomenon possible in Egypt too?

Part of the problem is geographical. The sea referred to in the Bible is popularly thought to be the Red Sea, but in these passages the Hebrew text of the Bible speaks of the Sea of Reeds, not the Red Sea. The tradition that it was the Red Sea itself arose much later. Some Biblical passages that speak of the Sea of Reeds clearly mean the Red

---

318 Josephus was writing c. 93-94 CE. Alexander the Great (356-323 BCE) lived some three and one-half centuries earlier.

319 The modern Gulf of Antalya, off southern Turkey.

320 Josephus, Antiquities, II.16.5, pp. 64-65.

321 Arrian, p. 94.

Sea, that its northeastern arm called the Gulf of Aqabah (Num. 14:25; 21:4; 1 K. 9:26) while other uses are considerably vaguer.[322] It has been noted that reeds do not grow around the Red Sea, but they do in the lagoons by the Mediterranean such as Lake Manzalah.[323]

Five place names are given in *Exodus* in the account of the flight of the Israelites from the city of Rameses (or Tanis, Ex. 13:20; 14:2,9): Succoth, Etham, Pi-hahiroth, Migdol, and Baal-zephon. All of these are from P. The Yahwist seems to imply a flight in a southerly direction in Ex. 12:37 where he says simply that Israelites went from Rameses to Succoth. Of the five place names, only Succoth seems to have been identified with reasonable certainty as Tell el-Mashkāṭah some 10 miles west of Lake Timsah.[324] Baal-zephon has been located at Tell Defneh,[325] Migdol means "tower" and may simply refer to a watchtower that the Israelites passed by. In any case, its site is still unknown as are the sites of Etham (perhaps in the Wādī Ṭumilāt) and Pi-hahiroth.[326]

If the Priestly tradition of Baal-zephon is reliable, then the crossing of the "sea" probably occurred across the southern extension of Lake Manzalah, about 6 or 9 miles northwest of modern Al-Qantarah on the Suez Canal.[327] This is the view of the editors of the *Oxford Bible Atlas*.[328] With regard to Lake Manzalah, "it is related... by an eye witness that on one occasion the waters of Lake Manzalah at the entrance to the Suez Canal were driven back by the east wind as much as seven miles."[329]

It is quite possible that some such occurrence, probably at Lake Manzalah, in which the Israelites were able to take advantage of a temporary land passage created by the unusual winds driving off the salt

---

[322] BC, I, 380.

[323] Keller, p. 126.

[324] Succoth, DB, pp. 941-942.

[325] BC, I, 381.

[326] Etham, DB, p. 270; Migdol, DB, p. 658; Pi-hahiroth, DB, p. 771.

[327] The excavation of the Suez Canal in the 19th century has, of course, considerably altered the topography and hydrology of the region.

[328] OBA, pp. 58-59.

[329] Gaster, I, p. 240. The same source also mentions similar phenomena elsewhere: "In 1485, for example, and again in 1645, a strong wind drove back the waters of the Rhone into the Lake of Geneva for a distance of about a quarter of a league [nearly a mile]. 'It looked,' says the record, 'like a wall of water'—words strikingly reminiscent of those used in the Scriptural narrative (Ex. 14:22). 'The inhabitants would go down on dry ground between the bridges and pass from one bank to the other. So too in 1738 when the Russians were fighting the Turks, they were able to enter the Crimea at the Isthmus of Perekop only because a strong wind suddenly blew upon the waters of the Putrid Sea, a the northwest corner of the Sea of Azov, causing them to recede and permit passage."

waters of the lake, lies behind the Biblical story. The cessation of those winds trapped their pursuers and their heavy chariots in the mud of the lake bottom and a returning sea. The Hebrews may also have had prior knowledge of the phenomenon, as they were resident near the lagoons of the eastern Delta. In support of this, we may mention the tradition recorded by Artapanus that Moses knew the area of the crossing well and waited to take advantage of the ebb tide.[330] If so, then this escape would nonetheless have been interpreted as an act of God, and most of us would certainly have agreed with their assessment in such a dire situation.[331]

H. IN THE WILDERNESS

...the land will surely be forbidden them for forty years that they will wander in the earth... (Q. 5:26)

With the departure of the Israelites from Egypt, the setting of the Biblical drama shifts back towards southwestern end of the Fertile Crescent and neighboring steppes and deserts, where it remains for the rest of the Old Testament's historical books.[332] As we have remarked before, the narrative portions of *Exodus* and *Numbers* are frequently in great disorder, much more so than the stories in *Genesis*. The fact that the historical narratives of these books are interrupted by longer and shorter legal and ritual codes has had the effect of masking this

---

[330] Moses, EJ, XII, 391. Prof. Hans Goedicke has proposed that the miracle of the parting of the sea and the drowning of the Egyptian army occurred nearly two centuries earlier than the generally accepted date of c. 1290 BCE. The cause, he suggests in an article in BAR, was a tidal wave generated by a catastrophic volcanic eruption of the Island of Thera in the Aegean Sea in 1477 BCE, during the reign of Pharaoh (Queen) Hatshepsut of the XVIIIth Dynasty. The wave swept across the marshes and wetlands of the northeastern Delta, destroying the Egyptians. This is not a technical impossibility, but it would have to be a very discriminating tidal wave to make a distinction between pursuers and the pursued in such circumstances. This problem was solved by the Israelites' swinging south around the marshland thereby avoiding the impact of the tidal wave. However, no such wave is reported in Egyptian annals. That aside, the date does not fit in with other evidence. Writes Charles Krahmalkov at the end of his critique of the proposal: "We may never know what really happened, but we may be sure that it did not happen on a spring day in 1477 B.C. on or near the shores of Lake Manzaleh." (Hershel Shanks, *The Exodus and the Crossing of the Red Sea, According to Hans Goedicke*, BAR, Vol. VII, No. 5, Sept/Oct 1981, pp 42-50; Charles Richard Krahmalkov, *A Critique of Professor Goedicke's Exodus Theories*, BAR, Ibid., p. 54.)

[331] One is reminded of the story of the natural, but providential, flight of sea birds hundreds of miles from the sea, which saved the Mormons in Utah in the 19th century.

[332] Being romances and fantasies, we do not count *Esther* and *Daniel*, with their exotic locations, among the historical books.

disjointedness, enabling the casual reader to miss the inconsistencies, duplications, and patching.

What we now have in the Pentateuch is a view of Moses' life assembled some eight or nine centuries after the fact, during the final post-exilic redacting processes. It is a retrospective view of Moses, designed to provide Israel with a unifying ethos to carry it through the difficulties and attacks on the concept of Israel as God's chosen people that assailed the latter-day Jews (for they had become Jews, the northern non-Judahic tribes having disappeared from history) by the immensely more powerful nations and empires they found themselves among.

Scholars face enormous difficulties when trying to reconstruct the course of events in the crucial "wandering" between and Egypt and Canaan. They have had to exercise considerable ingenuity in their efforts to establish a chronology and an itinerary that reconciles all of the contradictions and inconsistencies of the patchwork text. It is no wonder, considering the confused state of the material with which they are working, that nothing approaching unanimity of opinion about the course of events has been achieved.

We have already mentioned that it is increasingly felt that only a part of what became the later twelve tribes of Israel were actually involved in the Exodus experience, perhaps just the Josephic tribes, Manasseh and Ephraim.[333] Another reconstruction is that Moses was associated with the Judahites and Joshua with the Josephites, and that the Israelites left Egypt in at least two separate groups. The link between the Exodus and Sinai has also been questioned. There has been voluminous debate over virtually every aspect of the route from Egypt to Canaan and the exact nature of the Conquest of Canaan which followed, the very historicity of which is challenged by some authorities. It has been suggested that the forty years in the Wilderness was a period of settlement and residence, rather than aimless wandering, before a move was made towards Canaan, perhaps prompted by pressure from other tribes sharing the sparse resources of the region.

While these questions are extremely interesting—and in some respects fundamental—to the student of religious history, they are for the most part beyond the scope of this work. We shall touch upon them only as they concern the relationship between the stories in the Quran and Surabadi's Commentary on the one side and those in the Bible and other Judaeo-Christian traditional material on the other.

---

[333] Silver, p. ix.

Having described how Moses led his mixed multitude of followers across a body of water, in circumstances that might be considered miraculous, we must now look at the route to Canaan. Later editors resolved the contradictions and ambiguities by attributing the change of direction of Moses' caravan at Succoth to a stratagem to confuse the pursuing Egyptians.[334] In general, the Yahwist seems to support a view of the crossing of the sea in the region of the Bitter Lakes, whereas the later view was that Lake Manzalah had been the scene of the crossing. It should be also kept in mind that the entire region of the Sinai and Lower Syria, including Canaan, the scene of the Exodus and the wanderings, was in fact still under Egyptian control, however loosely it may have been exercised. That there is no reference to encountering Egyptian troops or even emissaries is curious, perhaps the result of editing or, more likely, Egyptian indifference to tribal affairs in the eastern steppes and deserts unless they represented a threat to the homeland. This has the effect of minimizing the historical importance of the Exodus from the Egyptian point of view.

In any event, from this point in the narrative there is even more confusion and uncertainty, leading various scholars, in their efforts to reconstruct the route of the Israelites and fit the events of the Biblical narrative into it, to propose at least three different routes (see map). The most direct route (if Canaan was really the objective) would have been what was later called the Way of the Land of the Philistines along the Mediterranean coast; but *Exodus* specifically rules that route out (Ex. 13:17). So, with what are we left?

The traditional reconstruction is the southerly one, via what is now Jabal Musa in the southern triangle of the peninsula formed by the Gulfs of Suez and Aqabah. However, this is dictated by the comparatively late location of Mount Sinai/Horeb there by 4th-century CE Christians. In addition to Jabal Musa, at least two other peaks, Jabal Katerina and Jabal Serbal, have been proposed as the Holy Mountain in that region.[335] An identification of Sinai/Horeb with Mount Seir, or even Jabal Halal, has also been proposed. This would eliminate much of the raison d'être for the southerly route.

In the proposed northern route, Moses and his followers crossed at Lake Manzalah (or perhaps Lake Sirbonis) and then followed the Brook of Egypt inland to Kadesh-barnea. Mount Sinai would be Jabal Halal.[336]

---

334 The passage mentioning this (Ex. 14:1-2) is from P.

335 OBA, pp. 58-59; Exodus, EJ, VI, 1049-1410; Exodus, DB, p. 279.

336 Exodus, EJ, VI, 1049.

The central route has at least two variations, one of which leads southward from Goshen and follows the eastern shore of the Gulf of Suez for about 20 miles before turning inland towards Kadesh. Mount Sinai could be Jabal Sinn Bishr or Jabal Ya'allaq, in this view. The second central route follows the (Muslim) Pilgrims Road from Egypt to the Hejaz after crossing the Bitter Lakes and passing the vicinity of modern Aqabah. The Holy Mountain would be in Seir, and Kadesh somewhere in Edom (Wadi Musa?).[337] The second central route would also have been the most likely for Moses to take when he fled to Midian after killing the Egyptian, and so has the added argument that he would have been familiar with it. More than one of these proposed routes may have been used by the Israelites if, as many scholars feel the present account is really a composite of the experience of at least two separate groups leaving Egypt, perhaps at different times and under different leadership.

References to these events, especially after the crossing of the sea, are scattered and episodic in the Quran. It is difficult to construct a "Quranic" history of the wandering of the Israelites because the Quran is not interested in retelling history, except insofar as it illuminates the general condition of man. Since in the Quranic view, Truth has always been available to men through either revelation or intuition, the establishment of Israel is not seen as a necessary prototype for the universal community of all human social groupings that is Islam. Rather, it was simply one more step in the process of calling mankind to self-evident truth. The Israelites are more noteworthy for their stubborn backsliding and custodial lapses whilst producing great prophets.[338]

In addition to the major historical and theological changes that occurred during the "forty years in the wilderness," there were other incidents and miracles as well, some of them alluded to in the Quran and the Quranic commentaries, such as that of Surabadi. He compares the Wilderness of Tih to a prison. The Israelites wandered there for 40 years, though it was a tract of land seven leagues in extent.[339] A horseman riding from morning to night would find himself back at his own bedroll.[340]

---

[337] Exodus, EJ, VI, 1049; OBA, pp. 58-59. (We personally are inclined to this view.)

[338] This is a theme repeated constantly by the later Israelite prophets as well, although their criticisms were grounded on the firm belief that Israel was God's Chosen People, and thereby differentiated from the rest of mankind.

[339] About 21 miles.

[340] Surabadi, pp. 56-57.

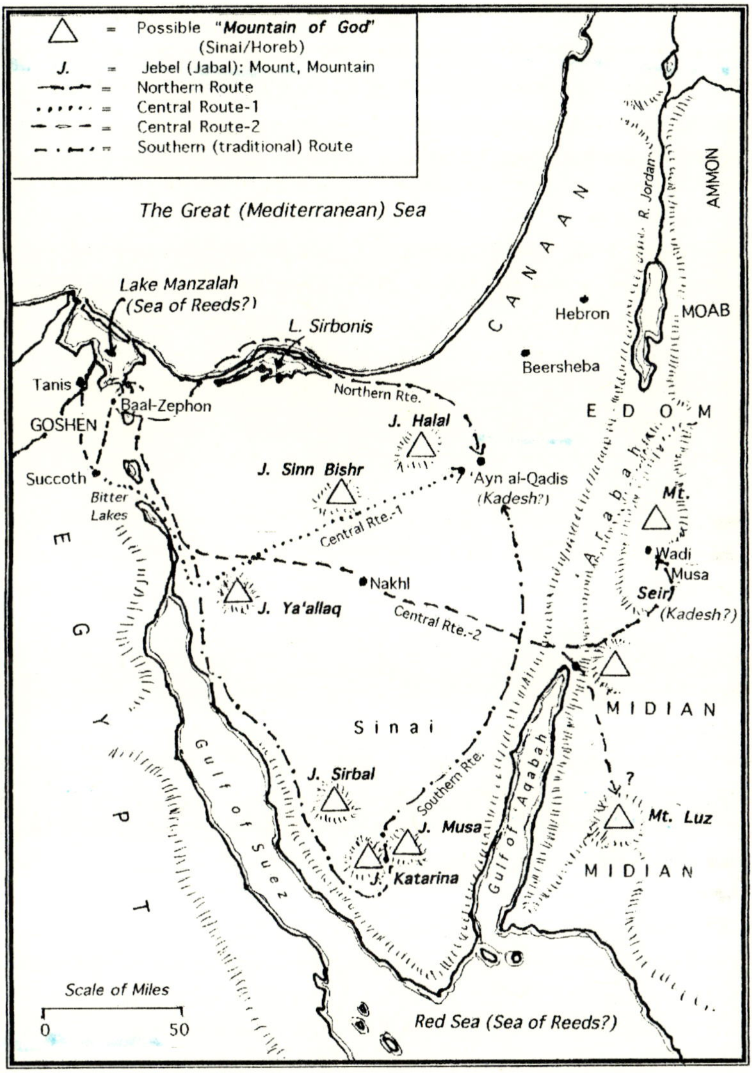

PROPOSED ROUTES OF THE EXODUS AND SITES OF THE HOLY MOUNTAIN[341]

---

341 Map based upon *Exodus*, EJ, VI, pp. 1043-1044; OBA, pp. 58-59; ABL, p. 7; National Geographic Map of Bible Lands, Dec. 1956.

The forty years of wandering is referred to in the Quran, after several verses that are doubtless related to the sending of the spies into Canaan from Kadesh, and the disheartening report that they brought about the strength of its inhabitants (Num. 13:17-14:3). This led to considerable murmuring against the leadership of Moses (perhaps referred to in Surah al-Saff, Q. 61:5[342]). As a result, according to P (the source for this), God decreed that none of those who left Egypt should live to see Canaan, and that they should remain in the wilderness forty years to implement this punishment (Num. 14:26-35).[343] As we read in the Quran: *(God) said: "For this the land will surely be forbidden them for forty years that they will wander in the earth, bewildered. So grieve not over the sinful."* (Q. 5:26)

Surabadi also writes that the people cried for sustenance and in answer to Moses' prayer, manna and quail were sent to them. They needed water and Moses struck the rock with his staff and water burst forth from it. They needed clothing and whoever was born, was born with clothing that grew with him and served at death as his shroud. When they complained of the heat, a cloud was sent to give them shade. When they complained of the darkness, a pillar of light lit the night for them.[344]

The Twelve Springs: The Quran does not mention the miraculous clothing, nor the miraculous nighttime illumination. However, the other miracles are referred to: *And We caused the white cloud to overshadow you and sent down on you the manna and quails, (saying): "Eat of the good things wherewith We have provided you—We wronged them not, but they did wrong themselves... And when Moses asked for water for his people, We said: "Smite with thy staff the rock. And there gushed out therefrom twelve springs (so that) each tribe knew their drinking-place. Eat and drink of that which God has provided, and do not act corruptly, making mischief in the earth.* (Q. 2:57, 60) The cloud mentioned in the passage need not have shaded the Israelites throughout the entire period of their wanderings, but is probably a single incident when the burning sun was blocked at a particularly critical time by a thick layer of cloud. Such things happen naturally. Again, a miracle

---

342 *And when Moses said unto his people: O my people! Why persecute ye me, when ye well know that I am God's messenger unto you? So when they went astray God sent their hearts astray. And God guideth not the evil-living folk.* (Q. 61:5)

343 Since Joshua, for example, did enter Canaan, does this mean that he did not leave Egypt with Moses? Was he born during the Wandering?

344 Surabadi, p. 57.

is often a question of timing. For the sufferer, any unexpected relief is miraculous.

Leading his thousands through a largely barren land, Moses encountered severe food and water shortages which, according to the Biblical account, were alleviated by means of divine assistance. There are several incidents of water problems. The first occurred three days after the rejoicing cause by the successful escape from Egypt: "When they came to Marah, they could not drink the water of Marah because it was bitter; therefore it was named Marah (*bitter*). And the people murmured against Moses, saying, 'What shall we drink?' And he cried to the Lord; and the Lord showed him a tree, and he threw it into the water, and the water became sweet." (Ex. 15:23-25a) Advocates of the southern route identify Marah with 'Ayn Hawarah.[345] This miracle shares none of the features mentioned in the Quran about the provision of water.

"Then they came to Elim, where there were twelve springs of water and seventy palm trees; and they encamped there by the water." (Ex. 15:27) Although in this watering there is no miracle mentioned, it does possess the twelve springs mentioned in the Quranic verse. This has caused critics to charge another instance of Quranic confusion. More will be said about this below.

The Priestly account of the manna and quails (to be discussed below) intervenes between the watering at Elim (from J) and the E version of the water from the rock, quoted here: "But the people thirsted there[346] for water, and the people murmured against Moses, and said, 'Why didst thou bring us up out of Egypt, to kill us and our children and our cattle with thirst? So Moses cried unto the Lord, 'What shall I do with this people? They are almost ready to stone me!' And the Lord said to Moses, 'Pass on before the people, taking with thee some of the elders of Israel; and take in thy hand the rod with which thou didst strike the Nile, and go. Behold, I will stand before thee there on the rock at Horeb; and thou shalt strike the rock, and water shall come out of it, that the people may drink.'" (Ex. 17:3-6)

To this a Yahwist note is appended: "and he called the name of the place Massah and Meribah,[347] because of the faultfinding of the children of Israel, and because they put thee Lord to proof by saying, 'Is the Lord among us or not?'" (Ex. 17:7) In this version, the site of the

[345] Marah, DB, p. 618.

[346] At a place called Rephidim (Ex. 17:8). This is traditionally located near Mount Sinai, but this is based upon the assumption that Sinai is the Mountain of God.

[347] Massah means "proof" and Meribah "contention."

miracle seems to be associated with Horeb, the sacred mountain. It is perhaps pertinent to ask here, are we in Seir again?

There is still another account of water from the rock, a pericope paralleling the one just quoted. In this instance, the scene is Kadesh, and the figure of Aaron is introduced. Once again, the Israelites were complaining (did they never cease?), but this time against Moses *and* Aaron (Num. 20:2). "Then Moses and Aaron went from the presence of the assembly to the door of the Tent of Meeting, and fell upon their faces. And the glory of the Lord appeared to them, and the Lord said to Moses, 'Take the rod and assemble the congregation, thou and Aaron thy brother, and tell ye the rock before their eyes to yield its water; so thou shalt bring water out of the rock for them; so thou shalt give drink to the congregation and their cattle.' And Moses took the rod from before the Lord, as he commanded him." (Num. 20:6-9)

This and the following is a conflation of J and E. Note how Aaron is introduced and then omitted, a detail obscured in the RSV translation which eschews differentiating between the 2nd-person singular "thou/thee/thy" and the 2nd-person plural "ye/you/your." In part of the passage, Aaron and Moses are on their faces before God as equals, but then the source changes, and only Moses is to take the rod, a task that Aaron often performed in Egypt. We have discussed the reasons behind these intrusions of Aaron above.

"And Moses and Aaron [together again!] gathered the assembly together before the rock, and he [Moses? Aaron?] said to them, 'Hear now, ye rebels; shall we bring forth water for you out of this rock?' And Moses lifted up his hand struck the rock with his rod twice; and water came forth abundantly, and the congregation drank, and their cattle." (Num. 20:10-11)

By this act, Moses and Aaron in some way provoked the wrath of God. Explanations by Bible commentators are admittedly educated guesses and vary considerably.[348] *Numbers* continues: "And the Lord said to Moses and Aaron, 'Because ye did not believe in me, to sanctify me in the eyes of the people of Israel, therefore ye shall not bring this assembly into the land which I have given them.'" (Num. 20:12) This appears to be an alternative explanation, albeit obscure, for the forty years of wandering in the wilderness and the reason that neither Moses nor Aaron

[348] Among those offered in the *Broadman Bible Commentary* are: Did Moses' question "shall we bring forth water for you?" imply some doubt of God's power? Was Moses' striking the rock twice instead of once a display of anger? Was God's anger at the constant complaining of the Israelites directed at Moses as their leader? The text is silent as to the specific cause. (BC, I, 136.)

ever entered the Promised Land. The passage ends with a topographical note: "These are the waters of Meribah where the people of Israel contended with the Lord, and He showed Himself holy among them." (Num. 20:13)

In *Exodus* (Ex. 17:3-7), the waters are named Massah and Meribah, and in the *Numbers* pericope (Num. 20:2-13), they are called Meribah. It should be obvious that the two passages are about the same place, and most probably the same event. They are simply another example of duplicate accounts, the like of which we have encountered before. The repetition in *Numbers* would seem to be made to account for the Wandering and for God's refusal to allow either Moses or Aaron to enter the Promise Land. The Quran refers only to one such miracle, and since it does not associate Aaron or the consequences stated in *Numbers* with it, we may say that it parallels the *Exodus* account; except for the mention of the twelve springs, which has given rise to another charge of confusion.

However, George Sale, not noted as an apologist for Islam, wrote: "Marracci thinks this circumstance [the twelve springs mentioned in the Quran] looks like a Rabbinical fiction, or else that Mohammed confounds the water of the rock at Horeb with the twelve wells at Elim [Ex. 15:27; Num. 33:9] for he says that several who have been on the spot affirm there are but three orifices whence the water issued.[349] But it is to be presumed that Mohammed had better means of information in this respect than to fall into such a mistake; for the rock stands within the borders of Arabia, and some of his countrymen must needs have seen it, if he himself did not, as it is most probable that he did. In effect, he seems to be in the right. For one who went into those parts in the end of the fifteenth century[350] tells us expressly that the water issued from twelve places of the rock. According to the number of the tribes of Israel… A late curious traveller observes that there are twenty-four holes in the stone, which may be easily counted—that is to say, twelve on the flat side, and as many on the opposite round side, every one being a foot deep and an inch wide; and he adds, that the holes on the side do not communicate with those on the other, which a less accurate spectator not perceiving (for they are placed horizontally, within two feet of the top of

---

349 Sale inserts a reference here: "Marracc. Prodr. Part IV, p.80."

350 Sale's 15th-century authority here is Breydenbach. The following "late curious traveler" was Sicard.

the rock) might conclude they pierce quite through the stone, and so reckon them to be but twelve."[351]

Jewish tradition, too, speaks of streams (in the plural) gushing from the rock that Moses struck.[352] In the old Jewish tradition of Miriam's Well, the well that accompanied the Israelites in their wanderings through the desert, there is mention of separate streams of water that went to different parts of the camp, itself arranged by tribes.[353] This traveling well is even mentioned by Paul in the New Testament: "...and (the Israelites) all drank the same supernatural drink. For they drank from the supernatural Rock which followed them, and the Rock was Christ." (1 Cor. 10:4)

Remarkably, the miracle of the water from the rock may also have a natural explanation, and has been duplicated in the same region. Major C.S. Jarvis who was the British governor of the Sinai in the 1930's actually witnessed such an occurrence: "Several men of the Sinai Camel Corps had halted in a dry wadi and were in the process of digging about in the rough sand that had accumulated at the foot of a rockface. They were trying to get at the water that was trickling slowly out of the limestone rock. The men were taking their time about it and Bash Shawish, the colored sergeant, said: 'Here, give it to me! He took the spade of one of the men and began digging furiously... One of his violent blows hit the rock by mistake. The smooth hard crust which always forms on the weathered limestone split open and fell away. The soft stone underneath was thereby exposed and out its apertures shot a powerful stream of water..."[354]

With all this evidence, we believe that the passage in the Quran reflects a strong local tradition of the caravaneers who trekked past such sites as these, which were already associated with Moses, either on the land route to Egypt across the Sinai, or the more frequented route from Makkah to Damascus. Tradition reports that the Prophet accompanied caravans to Syria. He could easily have become acquainted with the traditions of Moses and the twelve springs, as the caravan route to Syria passed close to Petra and other sites of the Wandering of the Israelites. Such stories brought back to Makkah entered the corpus of oral tradition current there at the time of the Prophet.

---

[351] Quran-Sale, pp. 9-10. Yusuf Ali also refers to this passage by Sale, and describes the rock thus: "huge mass of granite, twelve feet high and about fifty feet in circumference, where European travellers... saw abundant springs of water twelve in number." (Quran-Yusuf Ali, p. 32.)

[352] LJ, III, 312.

[353] LJ, III, 53.

[354] Quoted in Keller, p. 142.

MANNA: The providential feeding of the Israelites in the desert was considered a special sign of their favor in the eyes of God. In later times, this became an important proof supporting Israel's claim to be the "chosen people." And in Christianity, the manna given by God became a metaphor for Christ. "Jesus said to them, 'Verily, verily, I say unto you, it was not Moses who gave the bread from heaven, my Father gives you the true bread from heaven. For the bread of God is that which comes down from heaven, and gives life to the world.' They said to him, 'Lord, give us this bread always.' Jesus said to them, 'I am the bread of life; he who comes to me shall not hunger...'" (Jn. 6:32-35a)

Regardless of how the provision of manna was perceived in later times, during the wandering it became still another source of Israelite complaint and ingratitude. In *Exodus* we find the Israelites murmuring against Moses and Aaron, after just having had their thirst miraculously assuaged, because they were now hungry: "the Lord said to Moses, 'Behold I will rain bread from heaven for you; and the people shall go out and gather a day's portion every day, that I may prove them, whether they walk in My law or not.'" (Ex. 16:4) Although there was no mention of the quails in God's speech, Moses and Aaron inform the grumbling people that in the evening they will be provided with flesh to eat and on the following morning bread.

"In the evening quails came up and covered the camp; and in the morning dew lay round about the camp. And when the dew had gone up, there was on the face of the wilderness a fine, flake-like thing, fine as hoarfrost on the ground. When the people of Israel saw it, they said to one another, 'What is it?' For they did not know what it was. And Moses said to them, 'It is the bread which the Lord has given you to eat...'" (Ex. 16:13-15)

The people were enjoined to gather as much of it as they could eat but not keep any until morning, as it would spoil during the night. However, (contradicting this injunction) on the sixth day, they were to gather twice as much, and the manna was not provided on Saturday, the day of rest.[355]

"Now the house of Israel called its name manna; it was like coriander seed, white, and the taste of it was like wafers made with honey... And the people of Israel ate the manna forty years, till they came to a habitable land; they ate the manna till they came to the border of the land of Canaan..." (Ex. 16:31,35) the provision of the manna is

---

[355] This last condition is from the Priestly Document, as always concerned with ritual, in this case the sanctity of the Sabbath.

also described (in another duplication) in *Numbers*: "Now the manna was like coriander seed, and its appearance like that of bdellium. The people went about and gathered it, and ground it in mills or beat it in mortars, and boiled it in pots, and made cakes of it; and the taste of it was like the taste of cakes baked with oil. When the dew fell upon the camp in the night, the manna fell with it." (Num. 11:7-9)

There has been considerable research into the question of the nature of the manna. It may have been an edible lichen or a sweet sap exuded in early summer by the *Tamarix gallica mannifera* (the tamarisk), which grows in Sinai and elsewhere. The sap would appear during the night but melt in sunlight. Insects may have played a role in its production.[356] This identification seems quite reasonable. To the Israelites coming from Egypt who had never heard of it, its appearance would have seemed quite miraculous; however, since Moses had already traveled and lived in this region, he probably knew of its existence. It still occurs today: "In a good year the Bedouins of Sinai can today collect four pounds each in a morning, a considerable quantity, which is quite sufficient to satisfy a grown man... the Bedouins knead the globules of manna into a puree which they consume as a welcome and nourishing addition to their often monotonous diet. Manna is indeed an exportable commodity, and if carefully preserved, it forms an ideal "iron ration," since it keeps indefinitely... Tamarisks with manna still grow in Sinai and along the Wadi al Arabah right up to the Dead Sea."[357]

However the faultfinding Israelites tired of the diet of manna (the quails had only been provided once at that point) and complained wistfully: "'O that we had meat to eat! We remember the fish we ate in Egypt for nothing, the cucumbers, the melons, the leeks, the onions, the garlic; but now our strength is dried up, and there is nothing at all but this manna to look at.'" (Num. 11:4-6)[358] Once again, God sent them quails in vast numbers, and as the Israelites ate flesh again, a killing plague swept the camp, as punishment (deserved, some might say) for their constant grumbling (Num. 11:31-35).

The presence of quail in the Sinai region is also a well-attested seasonal occurrence. The quail migrate from the south during the spring, following the Red Sea, on their way to their summer grounds in Europe. They usually alight in the northern Sinai and on the Mediterranean coast

---

[356] BC, II, 115-116; Manna, DB, p. 617; Gaster, p. 242.

[357] Keller, pp. 133. 135.

[358] Cf. *And when ye said: "O Moses! We are weary of one kind of food; so call upon thy Lord for us that He bring forth for us that which the earth grows—of its herbs and its cucumbers and its corn and its lentils and its onions."* (Q. 2:61)

to rest before crossing the great expanse of the sea. Josephus also recognized the seasonal nature of the phenomenon: "Accordingly a little after came a vast number of quails, which is a bird more plentiful in the Arabian Gulf[359] than anywhere else, flying over the sea, and hovered over them, till wearied with their laborious flight, and indeed, as usual, flying very near to the earth, they fell down upon the Hebrews, who caught them and satisfied their hunger with them, and supposed that this was the method whereby God meant to supply them with food. Upon which Moses returned thanks to God for affording them His assistance so suddenly, and sooner than He had promised them."[360]

"Even today the Bedouins of this area catch the exhausted quails in spring and autumn by hand."[361] Both the quail and the manna are associated with spring, the season during which the Israelites left Egypt. However, the mention of quail seems argues a northerly route for the Israelites across Sinai, as the quail alight near the Mediterranean in large numbers, but are not common in the southern Sinai.[362]

Joshua states that after crossing the Jordan River, and entering Canaan, the Israelites camped at Gilgal a mile or two from Jericho. "And the manna ceased on the morrow, when they ate of the produce of the land; and the people of Israel had manna no more, but ate of the fruit of the land of Canaan that year." (Josh. 5:12)

Neither the Bible nor the Quran mentions the miraculous provision of clothing described by Surabadi. However, this does exist in Jewish tradition, which can be attested at least back to the time of Justin in the 2nd century CE: "During their forty years' march they had no need of change of raiment[363]. The robe of purple with which the angels clothed each one among them at their exodus from Egypt remained ever new; and as a snail's shell grow with it, so did their garments, and though they wore the same things throughout the forty years, still they were not annoyed by vermin, yes, even the corpses of this generation were spared worms."

Such durable clothing is known in other mythologies as well. For example, in the *Epic of Gilgamesh*, when the hero has reached the Spring of Youth, Utnaphistim [the Mesopotamian Noah] says: "... he shall

[359] This mention of the Arabian Gulf in reference to the Red Sea, found also in medieval Arabic literature, supports the Iranian position that the Persian Gulf should be called just that, as the Arabian Gulf already exists in the form of the Red Sea.

[360] Josephus, Antiquities, III.1.5, p. 66.

[361] Keller, p. 130.

[362] Arden, *In the Steps of Moses*, National Geographic, Vol. 140, No. 1 (Jan. 1976), p. 21.

[363] LJ, III, 237. This is a medieval version of the tale (LJ, VI, 83.).

throw off his skins and let the sea carry them away, and the beauty of his body shall be shown, the fillet on his forehead shall be renewed, and he shall be given clothes to cover his nakedness. Till he reaches his own city and his journey is accomplished, these clothes will show no sign of age, they will wear like a new garment.'"[364]

Paul also referred to the miracles of the wandering, although he gave them his own Christological interpretation: "I want you to know, brethren, that our fathers were all under the cloud, and all passed through the sea, and all were baptized into Moses in the cloud and in the sea, all ate the same supernatural food and all drank the same supernatural drink. For they drank from the supernatural Rock which followed them [the Well of Miriam], and the Rock was Christ. Nevertheless with most of them God was not pleased; for they were overthrown in the wilderness." (1 Cor. 10:1-5)

We have already quoted the verse from *Exodus* that described the Lord leading the Israelites in a pillar of cloud by day and a pillar of fire by night (Ex. 13:21-22). Even when God had taken up residence in the Tabernacle built for Him, we read: "For throughout all their journeys the cloud of the Lord was upon the tabernacle by day, and the fire was in it by night, in the sight of all the house of Israel." (Ex. 40:38)

There are numerous Jewish traditions concerning the cloud, mentioned also by the Quran, which protected them from the sun during the forty years in the wilderness. Because Abraham had bade the angels who visited him seek shade under a tree, God had spread a cloud over Israel in the wilderness.[365] In the further elaboration of this tradition, the cloud had other properties as well. It shed sunlight by day and moonlight by night, so that Israel who were surrounded by clouds, might distinguish between night and day. It also served as armor; the missiles of their enemies could not penetrate it. The cloud disappeared at the death of Aaron although it later reappeared and remained until the death of Moses when it departed forever.[366]

I. THE TABLES OF MOSES AND THE GOLDEN CALF

(Moses) threw down the tables... and broke them... (Ex. 32:19)

We read of the delivery of the tablets in Surah Al-A'raf: *And when We did deliver you from the people of Pharaoh who were afflicting*

[364] Gilgamesh, p. 112.
[365] LJ, III, 43. In the *Exodus Rabbah*.
[366] LJ, III, 49, 235.

you with dreadful torment, slaughtering your sons and sparing your women. That was a tremendous trial from your Lord. And when We did appoint for Moses thirty nights (of solitude), and added to them ten, and he completed the whole time appointed by his Lord of forty nights; and Moses said unto his brother: "Take my place among the people. Do right, and follow not the way of the corrupters. And when Moses came for Our appointed meeting and his Lord had spoken unto him, he said: "My Lord! Show (Thyself) to me that I may look upon Thee." He said: "Thou wilt not see Me, but look upon the mountain! If it stand still in its place, then thou wilt see Me."

And when his Lord revealed (His) glory to the mountain He sent it crashing down. And Moses fell down senseless. And when he woke he said: "Glory unto thee! I turn unto thee repentant, and I am the first of the believers." Said He: "O Moses! I have preferred thee above mankind by My messages and by My speaking (unto thee). So hold that which I have given thee, and be among the thankful." And We wrote for him upon the tablets [the Arabic is plural, not dual] *the lesson to be drawn from all things and the explanation of all things, then (said): "So hold it fast and command thy people: 'Take the better therein.' I shall show thee the abode of the sinful."* (Q. 7:142-145)[367]

In the Quran, this is followed by the incident of the worship of the Golden Calf by the Israelites in Moses' absence. Then: *And Moses chose of his people seventy men for Our appointed time and, when the trembling came on them, he said: "My Lord, if thou hadst willed Thou hadst destroyed them long before, and me with them. Wilt thou destroy us for that which the foolish among us did?"* (Q. 7:155) In the Biblical narrative, as we shall see, the order of events is different.

As the edition of Surabadi we are using as the basis of this study does not include the story of Moses' receiving the Law and the story of the worship of the Golden Calf by the Israelites, we use Bal'ami's version of these stories for our comparison with the Biblical version.[368] Bal'ami expands the Quranic narrative considerably, both in detail and interpretation: In the beginning an angel is introduced as the summoning agent who informs Moses that he is to go to Mount Sinai (*Ṭūr Sīnā*) and fast for thirty days so that his body will become like that of an angel; obedience will overcome his natural earthly passions.

In the Muslim commentators and historians, we see the same process of increasing the distance between God and man by means of the

---

[367] Surah Baqarah also mentions the "forty nights" Moses spent in separation from his people (Q. 2:51).

[368] Bal'ami, I, pp. 427-450.

insertion of angelic mediators that we find in the later redactions of the Bible. In this instance, the relevant Quranic text shows God communicating directly with Moses, but Bal'ami makes an angel the actual bearer of the words of God. We have already noted {in this series, in *Abraham* and *Jacob and Joseph*} several instances of this in the Bible, among them: Abraham and God before the events at Sodom; Hagar and God; Jacob's wrestling with God; God's leading the Israelites before the pursuing Egyptians. In all of these stories, the original form, as the text still betrays, was of God dealing directly with man, but later redactors, regarding this as unseemly, interposed angels acting on God's behalf. In the present example from Quran, there is no mention of an angel in the Quranic text, but Bal'ami and his fellows have thought it proper to insert one.

Bal'ami's narrative is influenced by Christian and Jewish tradition in another way. He locates the Mountain of God in Sinai. As we have seen this is a relatively late Christian tradition, though now espoused uncritically by most Jews, Christians, and Muslims. Bal'ami's reference to Moses' body becoming like an angel's may be an echo of the Priestly ending of the events concerning Moses and he giving of the Law: "When Moses came down from Mount Sinai, with two tablets of the testimony in his hand as he came down from the mountain, Moses did not know that the skin of his face shone because he had been talking with God." (Ex. 34:29) [No angel here.]

"And when Aaron and all of the people of Israel saw Moses, behold, the skin of his face shone, and they were afraid to come near him... And when Moses had finished speaking with them, he put a veil on his face; but whenever Moses went in before the Lord to speak with Him, he took the veil off, until he came out... the people of Israel saw the face of Moses, that the skin of Moses' face shone; and Moses would put the veil upon his face again, until he went in to speak with him. (Ex. 34:30,33-34a, 35)[369]

According to Bal'ami, Moses informed the Israelites that he would be absent on Mount Sinai for thirty days in order to receive the

---

[369] This rather confused and repetitious passage is quoted here partly as a good example of the awkwardness in combining divergent sources (vv. 29-33 are attributed to P, 34 and 35 to J), as well as for its content. The veil Moses used to conceal the peculiarity of his face recalls to mind Muqanna', the famous false prophet who disturbed the peace of Khorasan in the c. AH159/776CE and whose lively career fills several pages of the *History of Bukhara*. He was called Muqanna' "because he always veiled his head and face." According to the hostile historian, this was because he was so ugly, but perhaps he adopted this device as a conscious attempt to increase his remoteness, mystery, and majesty. (Bukhara, p. 90 et al.)

Law. He appointed Aaron to rule the people in his stead. The Israelites suggested to Moses that seventy righteous elders be selected to accompany him in order to be witnesses to the event. Moses agreed, but al-Samiri,[370] upon hearing this request, realized how foolish the Israelites were. [He apparently interpreted their request as an indication of doubt.] Bal'ami notes that the interval between the destruction of the Egyptians in the sea on the 10th of Muharram and the call of Moses at the beginning of Dhul-Qa'dah was eleven months.[371]

According to the Biblical text (from P), the Israelites set out from Rameses on the 15th day of the first month (Num. 33:3), and crossed the sea a few days later. The events of this section commenced on the third new moon after that (Ex. 19:1), or after an interval of about two and one-half months. Since the Hebrew calendar was (and is) lunar with the addition of an intercalary month every several years to bring it more or less in line with the solar calendar, an exact modern equivalent cannot be given; however, the Exodus began approximately in April and the Giving of the Law occurred in June. (The provision of manna and quail also supports these dates.[372])

It will be noticed that Bal'ami has already introduced the seventy elders before the worship of the golden calf. In the Quran, the seventy elders are mentioned after the golden calf, although considering the scattered nature of the allusions in the Quran, it cannot be asserted with certainty that a chronological sequence is intended. Indeed, Q. 7:154 seems to close the pericope of the Golden Calf, and Q. 7:155 with its mention of the seventy may commence a new parable. In any case, in the Bible: "the narratives attached to the delivery of the laws at Sinai are in an extraordinarily confused state,"[373] and the relevant chapters (Ex. 19,24,32,33, and 34) are a patchwork of different layers of the Yahwists, (J1 & J2) the Elohist (E), the Priestly Writer or Writers (P), with Deuteronomist (D) additions.

These are broad outlines of the Biblical narrative after this process of conflation and reaction: The Israelites agreed to accept YHWH as their God and Moses went up the Holy Mountain where he was given the Ten Commandments and the Book of the Covenant, to be

---

[370] "al-Samiri" ("the Samaritan"): more about him, his name, and his identity below.

[371] Bal'ami, I, p. 430. It would actually have been nine months, twenty days. Here Bal'ami is referring to the Pilgrimage season, which would make it a full eleven months. Such traditions would appear to be pious additions to increase the sanctity of important dates in the Islamic calendar by linking them with the ancient prophets, as we have seen Jewish tradition and exegesis link unrelated Biblical material.

[372] See previous Section.

[373] Moses, DB, p. 675.

found in *Exodus*, chapters 20-23. Sacrifices were made and the seventy elders were permitted to see God. Then Moses went up the mountain by himself and stayed for forty days and forty nights while he received the instructions concerning the establishment of the ritual of worship and the design of the sanctuary. (These instructions, Ex., chapters 25-31, are by the much later P.)

Tiring and thinking that Moses would not return, the people persuaded Aaron to make a golden calf for them to worship. When Moses returned and saw this, he was angered by the spectacle and threw down the tablets upon which God had written, breaking them. He destroyed the calf and the Levites were enlisted to slaughter the apostates. Then Moses hewed two more tablets of stone and went back up the mountain where the revelation was (obligingly) renewed by God. When Moses came down from the mountain, again after forty days and nights, he brought the tablets with him and his face shone, so that henceforth he had to veil it from the people in ordinary intercourse.

This is how the story now appears as given shape in the Bible several centuries before the Christian era. The work of separating out the original Yahwist and Elohist strands from each other and from the accretions and additions of ancient editing and revising is by no means finished in detail, and there is disagreement over the order of the text and its interpretation. However, it is useful to try to reconstruct the original Yahwist and Elohist accounts, remembering of course that these accounts themselves are composites of various traditions and do not have so simple a history as the terms *Yahwist* and *Elohist*—suggesting a single author for each—might imply.

The Yahwist's Account: According to the reconstructed Yahwist: "Then Moses told the words of the people to the Lord." (Ex. 19:9b) "And Mount Sinai was wrapped in smoke, because the Lord descended upon it in fire: and the smoke of it went up like the smoke of a kiln, and the whole mountain quaked greatly." (Ex. 19:18) "And the Lord came down upon Mount Sinai, to the top of the mountain; and the Lord called Moses to the top of the mountain, and Moses went up. And the Lord said to Moses, 'Go down and warn the people, lest they break through to the Lord to gaze and many of them perish. And also let the priests who come near to the Lord consecrate themselves lest the Lord break out upon them.'" (Ex. 19:20-22) "And the Lord said to him, 'Go down, and come up bringing Aaron with thee; but do not let the priests and the people break through to come up to the Lord, lest He break out against them.'" (Ex. 19:24) [Moses here relates what God has told him], then: "'... for on the third day the Lord will come down upon Mount Sinai in the sight of all the people. And thou shalt set bounds for the people round about, saying, "Take heed that ye do not go up into the Mountain or touch the border of it; whoever touches the mountain shall be put to death; no hand shall touch Him but he shall be stoned or shot; whether beast or man, he shall not live." When the trumpet sounds a long blast, they shall come up to the mountain." (Ex. 19:11b-13) "So Moses went down to the people and told them." (Ex. 19:25)

By noting the verse references, the reader may see how out of order the text of chapter 19 is, Dr. McNiele's reconstructed order is vv. 9-10, 18, 20-22, 11b-13, 25.[374] Verse 23 (not quoted here) is a later addition caused by the displacement of vv. 11b-13. The volcanic character of the phenomena associated with the Mountain of God is obvious and cannot be easily explained in any other away. The Mountain of God is a sacred place,[375] forbidden to ordinary people upon pain of death. Not even the priests can approach it. The Yahwist account, as preserved to us, continues:

"The Lord said to Moses, 'Cut two tables of stone... and I will write upon the tables... Be ready in the morning, and come up in the morning to Mount Sinai, and present thyself there to me on the top of the mountain. No man shall come up with thee, and let no man be seen throughout all the mountain; let no flocks or herds feed before that mountain.' So Moses cut two tables of stone... and he rose early in the morning and went up on Mount Sinai, as the Lord commanded him, and took in his hand two tables of stone. And the Lord descended in the cloud and stood with him there, and proclaimed the name of the Lord." (Ex. 34:1-5)

"And he was there with the Lord forty days and forty nights; he neither ate bread nor drank water." (Ex. 324:28a) [This is followed by a section of law from the Yahwist, incompletely preserved in Ex. 34:10-26.] Then: "And the Lord said to Moses, Write these words; in accordance with these words I have made a covenant with thee and with Israel." (Ex .34:27) "And he wrote upon the tables the words of the covenant, the ten commandments." (Ex. 34:28b)

The phrase "ten commandments," it can now be seen, does not refer to the famous ten prohibitions of Ex. 20:2-17 (which are from the Elohist history), but to the laws preserved by the Yahwist in Ex. 34:10-26. These commandments focus more on sacrifices and rituals and do not

---

[374] The reconstruction in this section is based on the analysis of Dr. A.H. McNiele in "Moses, DB, pp. 675-676.

[375] Similar to the precincts of the great mosques (*ḥarāmayn*) of Makkah and Madinah.

appear concerned with social and ethical matters. What we have quoted above is the Yahwist report of the theophany. This seems to be followed by the incident of the seventy elders referred to in Q. 7:155:

"And He said to Moses, 'Come up to the Lord, thou and Aaron, Nadab, and Abihu, and seventy of the elders of Israel, and worship afar off. Moses alone shall come near to the Lord; but the others shall not come near, and the people shall not come up with him.'" (Ex. 24:1-2) "Then Moses and Aaron, Nadab, and Abihu, and seventy of the elders of Israel went up, and they saw the God of Israel; and there was under His feet as it were a pavement of sapphire stone, like the very heaven for clearness. And He did not lay His hand on the chief men of the people of Israel; they beheld God, and ate and drank." (Ex. 24:9-11)

In addition to the anthropomorphic and primitive character of this meeting,[376] we learn that God has Feet and His guests even celebrate a meal in His presence. An indication of the age of this material is the prominence given to the two elder sons of Aaron, Nadab and Abihu. Later on, we learn that they died without issue, and the third and fourth sons, Eleazar and Ithamar became the ancestors of the Jerusalem priesthood (Num. 3:2-4). A later text would have included at least the name of Eleazar in an event of such national and religious significance.

After this, something happened to arouse the anger of God. In the present edition of *Exodus*, the worship of the golden calf is the cause, but that is from E. We do not know whether J offered this reason or some other, but it seems to have been more in the nature of a civil rebellion judging by his account of the measures taken to quell it: "And when Moses saw that the people had broken loose (for Aaron had let them break loose, to their shame among their enemies). Then Moses stood in the gate of the camp, and said, 'Who is on the Lord's side? Come to me.' And all the sons of Levi gathered themselves together to him. And he said to them, 'Thus says the Lord God of Israel, "Put every man his sword on his side, and go to and from gate to gate throughout the camp, and slay every man his brother, and every man his companion, and every man his neighbor."' And the sons of Levi did according to the word of Moses; and there fell of the people that day about three thousand men. And Moses said, 'Today ye have ordained yourselves for the service of the Lord, each one at the cost of his son and of his brother, that he may bestow a blessing upon you this day.'" (Ex. 32:25-29)

---

[376] One is reminded of Michelangelo's famous painting of God, the Creator of the Universe, in the form of a bearded man, an image itself based upon Greek and Roman depictions of their supreme god Zeus-Jupiter.

There seems to be an aetiological aspect to the above horrific account, an explanation of the status of the priestly tribe of Levites. Here they seem to have been a kind private militia for Moses.[377] The brutal slaughter of their own relatives by the Levites has been interpreted as a trial to demonstrate that their loyalty to God was stronger than human ties of kinship. The only crime of the victims, according to the version we have here, was their kinship. It is surely one of the most disturbing incidents in the entire Bible.

"The Lord said to Moses, 'Depart, go up hence, thou and the people whom thou hast brought up out of the land of Egypt, to the land of which I swore to Abraham, Isaac, and Jacob, saying, "To thy seed I will give it." And I will send an angel before thee, and I will drive out the Canaanites, the Amorites, the Hittites, the Perizzites, the Hivites, and the Jebusites. Go up to a land flowing with milk and honey; but I will not go up among thee, lest I consume thee, for thou art a stiff-necked people.' When the people heard these evil tidings, they mourned..." (Ex. 33:1-4a)

Evidence of the confused state of the text may be plainly seen in the odd reaction of the Israelites to God's promise to give them what later came to be called Palestine. The news is referred to as "evil-tidings"! Why? There does not seem to be a consensus about the answer to this question. In this passage God appears to be saying that He will remain on his mountain and not move to the land of Canaan with His people; or perhaps, that He is rejecting them as the Chosen People though He will keep His promise to give them Canaan. The preceding bloodshed does not seem to have assuaged God's anger and it persists.

The last portion of the Yahwist's account of these events deals with the sight of God which He vouchsafed Moses and His acceptance of Moses' prayer that Israel be forgiven [For which offense?]: "Moses said to the Lord, 'See, Thou sayest to me, "Bring up this people"; but Thou hast not let me know whom Thou wilt sent with me. Yet Thou hast said, "I know thee by name, and thou hast also found favor in my sight." Now therefore, I pray Thee, if I have found favor in Thy sight, show me now Thy ways, that I may know Thee and find favor in Thy sight. Consider too that this nation is Thy people.' (Ex. 33:12-13)

"And the Lord said to Moses, 'This very thing that thou hast spoken I will do; for thou hast found favor in My sight, and I know thee by name.' Moses said, 'I pray Thee, show me Thy glory,' And He said,

---

[377] Gray disagrees with the ascription of this passage to the Yahwist: "The loose connection of the passage with its context suggests that it represents an independent tradition..." Certain features make him think that it is a Northern tradition and therefore E is a more probable source. (Writing in Laymon, p. 64.)

"I will make all My goodness pass before thee, and will proclaim before thee My name "The Lord" [YHWH]; and I will be gracious to whom I will be gracious, and will show mercy on whom I will show mercy. But, 'He said, 'Thou canst not see My face; for man shall not see Me and live.' And the Lord said, 'Behold, there is a place by Me where thou shalt stand upon the rock; and while My glory passes by I will put thee in a cleft of the rock, and I will cover thee with My hand until I have passed by. Then I will take away My hand, and thou shalt see My back; but My face shall not be seen.'" (Ex. 33:17-23)

"The Lord passed before him, and proclaimed, 'The Lord, the Lord, a God merciful and gracious, slow to anger, and abounding in steadfast love and faithfulness, keeping steadfast love for thousands, forgiving iniquity and transgression and sin, but Who will by no means clear the guilty, visiting the iniquity of the fathers upon the children and the children's children, to the third and fourth generation.' And Moses made haste to bow his head toward the earth and worshipped. And he said, 'If now I have found favor in Thy sight, O Lord, let the Lord, I pray thee, go in the midst of us, although it is a stiff-necked people; and pardon our iniquity and our sin, take us for Thy inheritance.'" (Ex. 34:6-9)

"And He said, 'My presence will go with thee, and I will give thee rest.' And he said to Him, 'If Thy presence will not go with me, do not carry us from here. For how shall it be known that I have found favor in thy sight, I and Thy people? Is it not in Thy going with us, so that we are distinct, I and Thy people, from all other people that are upon the face of the earth?'" (Ex. 33:14-16)

This reconstruction of the original Yahwist account is not necessarily definitive or complete. Subsequent editing and conflation with other documents caused the loss of portions of the Yahwist's history, as for example the cause for God's anger now drawn from the Elohist. The extent of the losses and dislocations may be easily appreciated from the above version.

THE ELOHIST'S ACCOUNT: The Elohist's version is similarly disconnected, as its reconstruction shows: "And there Israel encamped before the mountain. And Moses went up to God." (Ex. 19:2b-3a) "And the Lord said to Moses, 'Lo, I am coming to thee in a thick cloud, that the people may hear when I speak to thee, and may also believe thee for ever.'" (Ex. 19:9a) "And the Lord said to Moses, 'Go to the people and consecrate them today and tomorrow, and let them wash garments, and be ready by the third day…'"(Ex. 19:10-11a)

"So Moses went down from the mountain to the people and consecrated the people; and they washed their garments. And he said to the people, 'Be ready by the third day; do not go near a woman.' On the morning of the third day there were thunders and lightnings, and a thick cloud upon the mountain, and a very loud trumpet blast, so that all the people who were in the camp trembled. Then Moses brought the people out of the camp to meet God; and they took their stand at the foot of the mountain. And as the sound of the trumpet grew louder and louder, Moses spoke, and God answered him in thunder." (Ex. 19:14-17,19) Note the resemblance of the restrictions and preparations to some of those Muslims observe for the Pilgrimage to Makkah.

"Now when all the people perceived the thunderings and the lightnings and the sound of the trumpet and the mountains smoking, the people were afraid and trembled; and they stood afar off, and said to Moses, 'Speak thou to us, and we will hear; but let not God speak to us, lest we die.' And Moses said to the people, 'Fear not; for God has come to prove you, and that the fear of Him may be before your eyes, that you may not sin.' And the people stood afar off while Moses drew near to the thick darkness where God was." (Ex: 20:18-21)

"Moses came and told the people all the words of the Lord and all the ordinances; and all the people answered with one voice, and said, 'All the words which the Lord has spoken we will do.' And Moses wrote all the words of their Lord. And he rose early in the morning, and built an altar at the foot of the mountain, and twelve pillars, according to the twelve tribes of Israel. And he sent young men of the people of Israel, who offered burnt offerings and sacrificed peace offerings of oxen to the Lord. And Moses took half of the blood and put it in basins, and half of the blood he threw against the altar. Then he took the book of the covenant, and read it in the hearing of the people; and they said, 'All that the Lord has spoken we will do, and we ill be obedient.' And Moses took the blood and threw it upon the people, and said, 'Behold the blood of the covenant which the Lord has made with you in accordance with all these words.'" (Ex. 24:3-8) This use of blood has no parallel in Muslim rituals.

Later on, we learn something more about the ritual life of the camp and the immediacy of God: "Now Moses used to take the tent and pitch it outside the camp, far from the camp; and he called it the Tent of Meeting. And every one who sought the Lord would go out to the Tent of the Meeting, which was outside the camp. Whenever Moses went out to the tent, all the people rose up, and every man stood at his tent door, and looked after Moses, until he had gone into the tent. When Moses entered the tent, the pillar of cloud would descend and stand at the door of the tent, and the Lord would speak with Moses. And when all the people saw the pillar of cloud standing at the door of the tent, all the people would rise and worship, every man at his tent door. Thus the Lord used to speak to Moses fate to face, as a man speaks to his friend. When Moses turned again into the camp, his servant Joshua the son of Nun, a young man, did not depart from the tent." (Ex. 33:7-11)

After reading these accounts, one realizes that multitudes of hundreds of thousands are simply not involved. One is left with the impression of a camp of at most a few thousand. The picture of God is more remote than that of J, and the phenomena associated with Him are atmospheric rather than geological.

The Decalogue: It is at this point that later Elohist redactor inserted the familiar Ten Commandments (as they are now called) of Northern provenance, now found in Ex. 20:1-17. These were followed by verses now found in the previous chapter: "So Moses came and called the elders of the people, and set before them all these words which the Lord commanded him. And all the people answered together and said, 'All that the Lord has spoken we will do.' And Moses reported the words of the people to the Lord." (Ex. 19:7-8)

"The Lord said to Moses, 'Come up to me on the mountain, and wait there; and I will give thee the tables of stone, with the law and the commandment, which I have written for their instruction.' So Moses rose with his servant Joshua, and Moses went up into the Mountain of God. And he said to the elders, 'Tarry here for us, until we come to you again; and, behold, Aaron and Hur are with you; whoever has a cause, let him go to them.' Then Moses went up on the mountain, and the cloud covered the mountain." (Ex. 24:12-15) "And He gave to Moses... the two tables of stone, written with the finger of God." (Ex. 31:18)

Thus begins the Elohist's account of the gift of the tables of the Law to Moses. As in Bal'ami, Moses appointed Aaron (here with Hur[378]) to act in his absence, although he does not specify how long he will be gone.

E's account then continues with the story of the Golden Calf that will be discussed below. We need only point out here that the breaking of the tables in the course of that story is a later editorial device in order to harmonize the inclusion of *two* accounts of the giving of the tables, since

[378] Hur is an attendant bearing still another probably "Egyptian name who, with Aaron, held up Moses' hands in the battle with the Amalekites so that Israel might prevail. (Hur, DB, p. 407.)

without the destruction of one set, we would have been left with two sets of tables. If we separate the two strains, we can better compare the two versions.

The Yahwist does not mention Aaron as Moses' representative, whilst E has Moses nominate him to act in his absence (as does Bal'ami). J mentions that Moses stayed forty days upon the mountain, as do the Quran and Bal'ami, but the portions of the text of E that have survived leave us only the notice that he was delayed a long time. In the J version, at one place Moses is to prepare the stones and God is to write upon them, at another God tells Moses to write the words He dictates to him upon them (Ex. 34:27). In E, they are apparently already prepared on the sacred mountain.

Both accounts associate unusual natural phenomena with the sacred mountain, and emphasize the necessity of approaching it with caution. The concept of God in both versions, though monotheistic in a general sense, is primitive and anthropomorphic, J the more so. He tells us of the seventy elders who are permitted to see God, and also of the permission granted Moses to look upon God, while in E, we see God coming to the tent of the meeting in the form of a pillar of cloud visible to all, where He converses with Moses "face to face." E mentions Joshua (destined to lead the Hebrews into Canaan), while J does not. E gives us the classical form of the Ten Commandments (the Decalogue), while those laws called the Ten Commandments by the Yahwist are largely different. Finally, the Elohist also tells of the apostasy of the Golden calf, about which the Yahwist is silent.

In the present edition of *Exodus* with its duplicate grantings of the Law to Moses in the form of stone tables, neither version associates those tables with the famous Ten Commandments![379] In their present position, the first set seems to follow the Elohist *Book of the Covenant* (Ex. 20:21-23:33), or more probably the elaborate instructions from P about the construction of the Tabernacle and the ritual of service to be

[379] The Ten Commandments are: 1. Thou shalt have no other gods before me; 2. Thou shalt not make unto thee an idol; thou shalt not bow down to them or worship them; 3. Thou shalt not take the name of the Lord thy God in vain; 4. Remember the Sabbath day, to keep it holy; 5. Honor thy father and thy mother; 6. Thou shalt not kill; 7. Thou shalt not commit adultery; 8. Thou shalt not steal; 9. Thou shalt not bear false witness against thy neighbor; 10. Thou shalt not covet the neighbor's house, thou shalt not covet thy neighbor's wife, nor his maidservant, nor his ox, nor his ass, nor any thing that is thy neighbor's. (From Ex. 20: 3-17) Of course it is not as simple as all that. The version we have given here is roughly the Judaic version. Various Christian denominations split and count them differently, though always ending up with ten. (See the chart in Robert Youngblood's article, *Counting the Ten Commandments*, BR, Vol. X, No. 6, Dec. 1994, pp. 34-35.)

established therein (Ex. 24-31:17). It is after that passage that the tablets are given to Moses (Ex. 31:18), only to be broken in the following chapter (Ex. 32:19). The second set of tables are granted after the notice of the J's commandments in Ex. 34:27-28, and they are *not* the famous ten.

The term "ten commandments" is connected to the second (J's) version in the text of *Exodus*. It is only in the Deuteronomist's preface to the older *Book of the Law* which forms the core of the present *Deuteronomy*,[380] that we find an unequivocal linking of the Decalogue to the Tables Moses received from God: "And ye came near and stood at the foot of the mountain, while the mountain burned with fire to the heart of heaven, wrapped in darkness, cloud, and gloom. Then the Lord spoke to you out of the midst of the fire; ye heard the sound of words, but saw no form; there was only a voice. And He declared to you His covenant, which he commanded you to perform, that is, the ten commandments; and he wrote them upon tables of stone: (Deut. 4:11-13) After repeating the commandments of Exodus 20 in Deut. 5:6-21 (taken from E), D continues: "These words the Lord spoke to all your assembly at the mountain out of the midst of the fire, the cloud, and the thick darkness with a loud voice; and He added no more. And He wrote them upon two tables of stone and gave them to me." (Deut. 5:22) That is what the later Israelites made of the confused accounts contained in *Exodus*.

THE SEVENTY ELDERS: Returning to the question of the difference in the order of the events of this section between the Bible and the Quran, we have seen that in the present edition of *Exodus*, the visit of the seventy elders to the mountain of God stands *before* the granting of the tables, but in the reconstruction of the Yahwist account, this episode *follows* that incident as it does in the Quran (if its position there is an indication of sequence; it may not be). In the Quran, it also follows the apostasy of Israel and the worship of the Golden Calf, but as this story is from the Elohist, its relationship to the incident of the seventy elders, if any, cannot be easily ascertained now.

The seventy elders[381] seem to have been a group whose existence can be attested before and after the affair of the theophany. Moses spoke to the elders (their number unspecified here) when he returned to Egypt

---

[380] See Introduction. {See the Foreword to this volume. In this series, see *Introduction to the Old Testament* for more information.}

[381] The seventy elders should not be confused with the seventy scholars who translated the Hebrew Bible into Greek c. 2nd century BCE (the *Septuagint*), and indicated in our text by Roman numeral LXX.

in order to secure their assent to his plan to lead the Israelites out of bondage (Ex. 3:16, 18, from J). The elders are mentioned again in connection with the instructions concerning the Passover and the last plague (Ex. 12:21, from JE). At the miracle of the turning of the bitter water to sweet on the march out of Egypt, God specifically told Moses to involve the elders (Ex. 17:5, from E). They participated in the sacrificial meal of Jethro (Ex. 18:12, from E), and may have been given judicial powers (Ex. 18:25-26, from E) upon Jethro's advice. They accepted the Covenant on behalf of the people (Ex. 19:7-8, from D).[382] In none of the foregoing is their number specified.

In the theophany, which seems to have included a ritual meal, their number is specified as seventy (Ex. 24:1-2, 9-11, from J). If this be the incident to which the Quran refers, the atmosphere is quite different. The Biblical text give us no hint of the reaction felt by the elders when they actually saw God, whilst this is the main point of the Quranic reference: the awe and fear inspired by the apperception of the presence of God. The Quranic text seems to speak of a fear of divine retribution upon the elders for some crime that Israel has committed. Since it follows the Quranic story of the Golden Calf in Q. 7, it is usually assumed that this is intention of the verses. However, this is by no means certain, as we have pointed out before, and penance had already been done for that sin. There were already plenty of causes to be found in the ample catalog of complaint and lack of faith in divine providence displayed by the Israelites on their march from Egypt to provoke the divine wrath against Israel before the incident of the Golden Calf.

The seventy elders reappear in *Numbers*, when they are again summoned by God to be consecrated to share in the responsibility of governing the Israelites (Num. 11:16-17, 24-25, from JE). This was done in the midst of grumbling by the Israelites because of the food. The miracle of the quails was repeated, but followed immediately by a retaliatory plague. Although our text of *Numbers* does not mention it, this would have been an appropriate time for the elders to disassociate themselves from the behavior of the people, as mentioned in the Quran.

Jewish tradition involves the seventy elders in the story of the Wandering further. They officiated at the sacrifice mentioned by the Elohist (see above) because the (Levite) priesthood had not yet been established.[383] They tried to prevent Moses from breaking the first set of tablets, but were unsuccessful because he was physically stronger than

---

[382]As J indicates the Yahwist, E the Elohist, JE the conflated Yahwist and Elohist sources, and P the Priestly Document, so D indicates the Deuteronomist.

[383] LJ, III, 88.

all of them put together.[384] Some traditions say that the original seventy elders were destroyed by celestial fire at Taberah (Num. 11:1-4) and had to be replaced for the consecration mentioned above (in Num. 11:16-17, 24-25).[385] The celestial fire was still another divine punishment inflicted upon the Israelites for their ingratitude.

In sum, we see there are already ample circumstances for the elders to suffer for the iniquities of the Israelites in the extant text. Others may have been omitted. The Quranic passage need not be bound to the story of the Golden Calf for want of other provocations.

ANOTHER THEOPHANY: *And when his Lord revealed (His) glory to the mountain He sent it crashing down.* (Q. 7:143) The vision of God granted to Moses in answer to his request to see Him differs in the Biblical and Islamic traditions. In the Bible, Moses is covered by the hand of God and he sees His back, for seeing His face would have caused Moses' destruction (see above). This primitive scene in which God appears to be a physical being—a much enlarged man—albeit supernatural, not unlike the pagan gods of Mesopotamia or Greece, becomes in the Quran a demonstration of the *effect* of God, that is, a demonstration of His power, the pulverization of a mountain, an act incidentally suggestive of a violent volcanic eruption—if a natural explanation be required.

In Bal'ami, this is somewhat expanded: Moses was told to look at the mountain. If the mountain could withstand the power of the immanence of God, then Moses would be able to see Him. But when the power of God was displayed, the mountain disintegrated and Moses swooned without seeing actually Him. Bal'ami adds that the mountain flew into six parts, three of which landed in Hejaz and three in Madinah.[386]

Jewish tradition records a contest among various mountains for the honor of being the site of the granting of the Torah.[387] Early sources tell us that Mount Sinai was originally part of Mount Moriah (supposed to be the present Haram and the site of the Temple of Solomon in Jerusalem), but had separated itself at the time of the sacrifice of Isaac.

---

[384] LJ, III, 129.

[385] LJ, III, 248.

[386] Is this an echo of a local Arab tradition that sacred mount, the Mountain of God, was located in Arabia, that is, Midian, or the northwestern Hejaz?

[387] LJ, III, 82-85.

In the future, it will return to its original home.[388] Another tradition asserts that God's words "break mountains into pieces."[389]

Bal'ami also tells us that when Moses was on the mountain praying, a white cloud would envelop him.[390] The seventy elders were to have been witnesses to these events, but even they could be grumblers. For after Moses recovered from his swoon at the manifestation of the power of God, and he had taken up the Tables of the Law, the cloud left him and he became visible again to the seventy. They complained (!) that they had been sent to bear witness to the speech between God and Moses, but had heard nothing. Moses asked God to let them hear Him speak, so God agreed and sent the cloud to cover all of them and spoke again with Moses so that they might hear. The seventy were so struck with terror that they died of fright. Moses prayed for them. God forgave them for their doubt, and they were revived. Then Moses picked up the Tables and descended the mountain with them.[391]

Part of this can also be traced to a Biblical source. After the Deuteronomic version of the Ten Commandments, Moses is made to say: "'And He wrote them upon two tables of stone, and gave them to me. And when ye heard the voice out of the midst of the darkness, while the mountain was burning with fire, ye came near to me, all the heads of your tribes, and your elders; and ye said, "Behold, the Lord our God has shown us His glory and greatness, and we have heard His voice out of the midst of the fire; and we have this day seen God speak with man and man still live."'" (Deut. 5:22b-24)[392]

Paralleling another episode in Bal'ami's story, the Talmudic tractate *Sanhedrin* tells us that the seventy elders died upon hearing the divine voice (in the thunder) but that the Law itself made intercession for them and they were restored to life.[393] It is interesting to note that in

---

[388] LJ, III, 84; VI, 32.

[389] LJ, II, 333; V, 425.

[390] This detail is absent from the Quranic account, but is found in the Bible: "Then Moses went upon the mountain, and the cloud covered the mountain. The glory of the Lord settled on Mount Sinai, and the cloud covered it six days; and on the seventh day He called to Moses out of the midst of the cloud. Now the appearance of the glory of the Lord was like a devouring fire on the top of the mountain in the sight of the people of Israel. And Moses entered the cloud, and went up on the mountain." (Ex. 24:15-18a, from P.) As in Bal'ami, this incident refers to the receiving of the Tables of the Law and the revelation of the Torah to Moses. Notice once again the volcanic character of the phenomena associated with the mountain. Could the fumes from the bowels of the earth have played some part in Moses' visions, as they did with the Oracle of Delphi?

[391] Bal'ami, pp. 433-435, 39-40.

[392] See also from Ex. 24:1-2, 9-11 quoted above.

[393] Cited in Tisdall, p. 114.

Bal'ami, the reason for the fear of punishment felt by the seventy is their own doubt and it is not connected with the Golden Calf. Bal'ami also cites traditions about the tables: they were made of gold and seven in number, or of ruby and emerald.

This ignores the Biblical traditions, that they were two and made of stone, but we caution the reader that the Quran always uses the *plural* (three or more) when referring to the tables, not the *dual* (two). There is a Jewish tradition that the Tables were made of sapphire,[394] but, after all, a sapphire is also a stone. There are many more Jewish traditions about these events, but they do not add much to our discussion of the relationship of the Islamic versions to those of the Bible.

THE GOLDEN CALF: We turn now to the story of the worship of the Golden Calf. The principal Biblical source for this is *Exodus*, and it is usually attributed to the Northern Elohist, There are, as we shall see, substantial differences between the E and the Quranic accounts. In its present position in the Bible, it comes between the two versions of the theophany and the promulgation of the Law. In its original context, it followed the Elohist account of the theophany, as it does in the Quran, where it follows the *single* granting of the Law to Moses. The story opens with Moses still on the mountain:

"When the people saw that Moses delayed to come down from the mountain, the people gathered themselves together to Aaron, and said to him, 'Up, make us gods, who shall go before us; and as for this Moses, the man who brought us out of Egypt, we do not know what has become of him.'" (Ex. 32:1) [This situation strongly suggests that the Israelites were accustomed to worshipping idols and had not preserved the monotheistic traditions imputed to their ancestors; in other words, they were latent idolators. Moses had come to convert them (back?) to the worship of one God, promising them freedom[395] from bondage, if they followed him. That bondage was apparently not so onerous that they did not wish to return to it in Egypt on a number of occasions before settling in Canaan.]

"And Aaron said to them, 'Take off the rings of gold which are in the ears of your wives, your sons, and your daughters, and bring them to me.'" (Ex. 32:2). "So all the people took off the rings of gold which were in their ears, and brought them to Aaron. And he received the gold at their hand, and fashioned it with a graving tool, and made a molten calf; and they said, 'These are thy gods, O Israel, who brought thee out

---

[394] LJ, III, 119; VI, 40.

[395] Or one might say: "bribing them with freedom from bondage."

of the land of Egypt!' When Aaron saw this, he built an altar before it; and Aaron made a proclamation and said, 'Tomorrow shall be a feast to the Lord.' And they rose up early on the morrow, and offered burnt offerings and brought peace offerings; and the people sat down to eat and drink, and rose up to play." (Ex. 32:3-6) Was Aaron in fact an Egyptian or a Canaanite priest? Here he does not hesitate to shrug off YHWH and lead the people in their older, idolatrous forms of worship. Not only that, the ancestor of the priesthood of YHWH actually sculpted their idol for them!

Although the story of the worship of the calf is alluded to in several places in the Quran, it is related at length in only two places. In Surah al-A'raf we read: *And the people of Moses, after (he had left them), chose a calf (made) out of their ornaments, an (empty) body which gave forth a lowing sound. Did they not see that it spoke not to them, nor did it guide them in the way?* [Creating sounds from idols and causing them to appear to speak was a well-known art in ancient Egypt. Bull worship was common in many societies of the ancient world, including Egyptian.] *They chose it and became oppressors (of themselves). And when they feared the consequences thereof and saw that they had gone astray, they said: "Unless our Lord have mercy upon us and forgive us, truly we are of the lost!"* (Q. 7:148-149)

In this place, no mention is made of al-Samiri or of Aaron. The text seems to indicate that after the calf had been made, the people realized their error, before the return of Moses in the next verse (Q. 7:150). Maulana Muhammad Ali points out that "the order here is not historical, but one connecting the repentance with the sin, mentioning the events which brought about that repentance afterwards."[396] It would be reasonable to attribute this repentance to the efforts of Aaron who, though Moses castigates him for poor stewardship of the people in his absence, is specifically exonerated of the charge of having made the idol (Q. 20:92-93), as the Biblical text would have it. Another difference here is the Quran states that the calf lowed; this detail is not mentioned in *Exodus*, but see below.

In Surah Ta Ha, the story of the Golden Calf is referred to at greater length. It is here that we find the figure of al-Samiri: Moses was away from his people, in communication with God. [This would correspond to his receiving the Tables of the Law in the Elohist history discussed above.] God informed Moses that his people had gone astray in his absence. *"What is it that has caused thee to hasten from thy people, O Moses?" He said: "They are close upon my track. I hastened unto*

---

[396] Quran-MMA, p. 349.

Thee that Thou mightest be well pleased." [If this is taken to mean that Moses has rushed ahead of the people who are following him, then it differs from the Biblical version in which the people are waiting below while Moses goes up the Holy Mountain to receive the Law. However, in Surah al-A'raf, Moses has just been described as receiving the Law. In Ta Ha too, Moses returns to his people, which would imply that they were encamped rather than in motion.] *(God) said: "Lo. We have tried the people in thine absence, and al-Samiri*[397] *has misled them."* (Q. 20:83-85)

Bal'ami substantially repeats the Quranic story, although he adds that the Israelites were worshipping by the waterside, probably because later on the ash of the Golden Calf is thrown into the water, which Bal'ami and other commentators have taken to mean the sea. Considering the disagreement over the actual site of these events, it is not clear which body of water is meant. However, most of the proposed sites for this story are situated inland at some distance from any large bodies of water such as the Red Sea, or its arms, or even the Dead Sea. More probably, a large stream or pool is meant, since the Israelites were camped by a large spring. Bal'ami also adds that God told Moses that al-Samiri had made the calf and caused it to low. Moses demurred and said that, if the calf lowed, it was by the permission of God, not the work of al-Samiri, and was therefore a test of the people. God agreed with this interpretation and said that al-Samiri had led the people in error.[398]

The parallel passage in the Bible states: "and the Lord said to Moses, 'Go down, for thy people, whom thou didst bring up out of the land of Egypt have corrupted themselves; they have turned aside quickly out of the way which I commanded them; they have made for themselves a molten calf, and have worshipped it and sacrificed to it, and said, 'These are thy gods, O Israel, who brought thee up out of the land of Egypt!'"" (Ex. 32:7-8) Note the singular here; Israel is being addressed as a unit. The tone of these verses is similar to that of the Quranic passage quoted above; however, the omission of a reference to Aaron, while not conclusive evidence that Aaron is a later addition to the text (Ex. 32:1-6, quoted above), is nonetheless striking.

In this passage, the people have made the golden calf, whilst in the former it was Aaron, another contradiction. About this, the Quran states that the instigator was al-Samiri. This assertion has two sides to it; on the one hand, it can be taken to exonerate the prophet Aaron of such a blasphemy and on the other, it names the culprit as "al-Samiri." This

---

[397] See below for the discussion of al-Samiri.

[398] Bal'ami, pp. 432-433.

would appear to represent a strong tradition about al-Samiri and the worship of the golden calf current in the Hejaz during the time of the Prophet; otherwise, there would not have been any need to introduce this figure into the text. More will be said about this below.

Bal'ami's version of these events is, as might be expected, much fuller, although in some places he differs slightly from the course of the story in the Quran. After thirty days had passed, he relates, the Israelites worriedly approached Aaron. (Thus Bal'ami seems to explain the thirty days plus ten mentioned in the Quran (Q. 7:142).) Al-Samiri seized the opportunity to say that he knew why Moses had not returned; it was because of the unclean gold and silver that the Israelites had seized as plunder from the vanquished Egyptians. He said that Moses had separated himself and the righteous elders[399] from the rest of the people so that they would not share in the imminent vengeance of God. Al-Samiri suggested that a well be dug into which the offending wealth would be buried. When Moses returned, he could decide what should be done with it. If Moses said that it was lawful, then they could dig it up again; if not, then it could be destroyed by fire.

The Israelites agreed to this proposal and Aaron had the well dug. The plunder was thrown in and the well filled up. Now al-Samiri had recognized the angel Gabriel when he had come to summon Moses to the Mountain of God, because he himself had been brought up by Gabriel. He had picked up a handful of dust from the spot where Gabriel had stood (or some say where his horse had stood) and preserved it.

When thirty days passed and Moses had not returned, al-Samiri told the people that Moses would never return until the gold and silver were burned. He told them to dig it up so that it could be destroyed by fire. Instead of destroying it, Samiri fashioned from it the calf and threw the dust which he had picked from where Gabriel had stood upon the idol, and the calf lowed. Bal'ami mentions that some add that the calf continued to low and graze like a real living animal, whilst others say that it remained metal and only lowed once. Al-Samiri told them that this was their god. Moses had gone looking for God, while he was here all the time! At al-Samiri's command, the Israelites prostrated themselves before the calf.

Aaron tried to call the people away from the idol worship to the worship of the true God, but the Israelites said that they would persist until Moses returned, and they threatened to kill Aaron if he did not

---

[399] Bal'ami seems to put the incident of the seventy elders here, perhaps under the influence of the received form of the story in the Bible where this incident precedes the revelation of the Decalogue. See above.

remain silent. They also accused Aaron of sending Moses away so that he could seize the prophethood for himself. Aaron wanted to separate himself and the 12,000 steadfast Israelites from the idol worshippers, but he was afraid that Moses, upon his return, would accuse him of dispersing his people.[400]

In the defense the Israelites made for their behavior to Moses when he returned, much of the above has Quranic support. They said: *"We broke not our appointment with thee of our own will, but we were laden with burdens of the people's ornaments, then cast them (in the fire), for thus al-Samiri proposed." Then he produced for them a calf, a mere body that gave forth a lowing sound. And they cried: "This is your god, and the god of Moses, whom he has forgotten." What? Did they not see that thing returned no speech unto them and possessed naught by which to hurt or benefit (them)? And Aaron indeed had told them before hand: "O my people! Ye are but being seduced by it, for truly your Lord is the Merciful, so follow and obey my order." They said: "We shall not cease to be its votaries until Moses returns to us."* (Q. 20:87-91)

And when Moses demanded an explanation from al-Samiri for his behavior, the latter replied: *"I perceived what they perceived not, so I seized a handful from the footsteps of the messenger, and then threw it in. Thus my self commended me.* (Q. 20:96) While the tradition repeated by Bal'ami—that the footsteps were those of Gabriel or his steed—is widely circulated, Maulana Muhammad Ali rejects it, stating instead that they were those of Moses himself. Yusuf Ali mentions both versions.[401]

Thus we see that the Quran contradicts the Biblical (Elohist) statement that Aaron was directly involved in the making of the idol; indeed, he tried to dissuade the Israelites from doing so, although he seems to have taken no action other than to warn them. Yet, in another place, there is an allusion that presupposes an intervening misunderstanding between Moses and Aaron: *And when Moses returned unto his people, angry and grieved* [because he had learned of their lapse into idolatry], *he said: "Evil is that which ye took after I had left you. Would ye hasten on the judgment of your Lord?" And he cast down the tablets, and he seized his brother* [Aaron] *by the head, dragging him toward him. (Aaron) said: "Son of my mother! Lo, the people did judge me weak and almost killed me. Oh, make not mine enemies to triumph over me and place me not among the oppressors!"* (Q. 7:150)

The literature of Jewish traditions about the golden calf is quite extensive. The Egyptian gold and silver were too highly regarded to be

---

[400] Bal'ami, pp. 430-433.

[401] Quran-MMA, p. 620; Quran-Yusuf Ali, p. 810.

considered unclean in the mainstream of Jewish tradition, as Bal'ami would have it. Even though the explicit Biblical statements about Aaron's role in the making of the calf served to constrain the apologists, nonetheless, excuses were found for Aaron's behavior—after all, he was an ancestor of the priestly caste. Indeed, several others were declared the actual fabricators of the calf. One version, based on earlier sources, is given in the *Pirke de Rabbi Eliezer*: "When Israel received the commandments they forgot their God after forty days, and they said to Aaron: The Egyptians were carrying their god, and they were singing and uttering hymns before it, and they saw it before them. Make unto us a god like the gods of the Egyptians, and let us see it before us..." [The ancient Egyptians religious processions and liturgy must have been spectacular indeed. Even today, their depictions on the walls of tombs and temples astonish the traveler who visits Egypt.]

"They betook themselves to the one who carried out the words of Moses, to Aaron his brother, and Hur, the son of his sister... But since Hur was of the tribe of Judah, and one of the magnates of the generation, he began to reprove Israel with harsh words, and the plunderers who were in Israel arose against him, and slew him.

"Aaron arose and saw that Hur, the son of his sister, was slain; and he built for them an altar... Aaron argued with himself, saying: If I say to Israel, Give ye to me gold and silver, they will bring it immediately; but behold, I will say to them, Give ye to me the earrings of your wives, and of your sons, and forthwith the matter will fail... The women heard this, but they were unwilling to give their earrings to their husbands, but they said to them: Ye desire to make a graven image and a molten image without any power in it ..." [This tradition makes Aaron's evident cooperation a stratagem to defeat their purpose.]

"The men saw that the women would not consent to give their earrings to their husbands. What did they do? Until that hour, the earrings were also in their own ears, after the fashion of the Egyptians, and after the fashion of the Arabs. They broke off their earrings which were in their ears, and they gave them to Aaron... Aaron found among the earrings one plate of gold upon which the Holy Name was written, and engraven thereon was the figure of a calf, and that plate alone did he cast into the fiery furnace... The calf came out lowing, and the Israelites saw it, and they went astray after it."

[This is a reference to Aaron's self-defense in *Exodus*: "'And I said to them, "Let any who have gold take it off"; so they gave it to me, and I threw it into the fire, and there came out this calf.'" (Ex. 32:24) as though he were surprised by it.]

"Rabbi Jehudah said: Sammael [the devil][402] entered into it, and he was lowing to mislead Israel, as it is said, 'The ox knows its owner.'"[403]

Bal'ami's tradition of the calf behaving like a living animal is also found in older Jewish tradition: "The Egyptian magicians made the calf move about as if it were alive."[404] The later Jews frequently put the blame for making the golden calf and its worship on the Egyptians who were in the "mixed multitude," although the Biblical text does not support this. The Egyptian magicians referred to are probably Jannes and Jambres. These brothers are not mentioned in the Old Testament, but in Jewish tradition, they are the sons of Balaam who took refuge in Egypt and became magicians at Pharaoh's court, and were involved in the contest with Moses. [405] They were present when Pharaoh's army was drowned in the crossing of the sea, and they made themselves wings and tried to fly away to escape.[406] However, in one version, the angel Michael caught them and dashed them against the rocks in the sea, killing them;[407] in other versions they survived this event and accompanied the Israelites out of Egypt as part of the mixed multitude, where they became the instigators of the making of the Golden Calf.[408]

Bal'ami's tradition that al-Samiri had been raised by Gabriel may be related to the Jewish tradition, mentioned in the 2nd-century CE Zadokite Fragment, that Belial (the tempting spirit) had raised Johannan (Jannes) and his brother.[409] Much has been written, by Muslim and Western scholars, about the exact significance of al-Samiri's picking up a handful of dust from the messenger's footprints and casting it into the calf. Among other things, Bal'ami's statement suggests that the calf was hollow, and al-Samiri cast something into it which made it ring, accounting for the "lowing." However, the tradition of the commentators, that al-Samiri saw the angel who had come to summon Moses and had picked up some earth from his footprints, may in some way be related to a Jewish tradition attested in the 11th-century CE *Lekah* (which does not seem to have been commented upon in this connection) that the Israelites had noticed the feet of angels were like those of calves and thus were inspired to make the image of the calf.

---

[402] See below.
[403] PRE, pp. 352-355; also LJ, III, 121-122; VI, 51.
[404] From the 6th-century CE *Song of Songs Rabbah*, quoted in LJ, VI, 52.
[405] LJ, II, 283, 287, 334.
[406] Like Daedalus and Icarus of Greek mythology.
[407] LJ, III, 28-29.
[408] LJ, III, 120.
[409] LJ, VI, 293.

In a medieval Jewish commentary, this tradition is given in a different version: The Israelites had noticed the imprints of the angels (who had come to fight the Egyptians at the Exodus) left in the sand of the shore of the sea were like those of calves; therefore they adopted the form of a calf as their idol.[410] Although these references are several centuries later than the Quran, they may represent an older tradition connected with the Quranic allusion. In the *Psalms*, a verse can be read to mean that the Golden Calf was actually alive:

"They made a calf in Horeb and worshipped a molten image.
"They exchanged the glory of God for the image of an ox that eats grass." (Ps. 106:19-20)

If the phrase "that eats grass" be taken to modify *image* rather than *ox*, it would suggest that that is what the idol did. The poet probably did not mean that; but some such interpretation could later have given rise to the tradition found in both Jewish and Islamic written and oral literature.

Other Jewish tradition names still another as the actual fabricator of the calf: Micah. Although in the Bible, he lived during the period of the Judges, after the Conquest and before the Monarchy, in the Midrashim, Micah was also alive at the time of Moses. In these traditions, Micah was the son of Delilah[411] and would have been used as building material had not Moses rescued him. (According to a Jewish tradition, Israelite children were used as building material by the Egyptians.[412]) But he was not worthy of this honor and he made idols, including the Golden Calf. Later, during the time of David and Solomon, he reformed and became a pious man; therefore, he would have lived some three hundred years.[413] He is counted among the Minor Prophets and is the reputed author of the Biblical book *Micah*. Here, however, we are concerned with Micah in his idolatrous period.

---

[410] LJ, VI, 52.

[411] The Delilah who betrayed Samson. See Part Four, I. {In this series, in *From Judges to Monarchy*.} These traditions are full of anachronisms.

[412] This gruesome accusation against the Egyptians may have been inspired by the very real infanticide that was practiced in Canaan (or transferred to them). Infant remains have been found in the foundations of structures, apparently placed there as sacrifices to the gods. As we have already noted, there is no record of ritual human sacrifice in Egypt in the historical era, although there is recent evidence that it may have occurred in the First Dynasty (c. 3000 BCE). (Galvin, pp. 106-121.)

[413] LJ, IV, 49-53.

MICAH'S GOLDEN CALF: Let us digress here and consider the story of Micah, as it is found in the Bible, for the light it will shed on the question of how the accusation of Aaron's participation in the incident of the golden calf found its way into scripture. Micah's story is told in *Judges*, chs. 17 and 18. These chapters do not seem to have been part of the original Deuteronomic recension of *Judges*, but were added somewhat later, after 731 BCE.[414] They represent traditions of the Danites, one of the twelve tribes turned, in their present form, into attacks against the supposed practices of the Danite shrine at Dan at the northern end of Palestine, near the foot of Mount Hermon, and indeed upon its right to exist. This was accomplished by giving the shrine—a potential rival to Jerusalem's Temple—a scurrilous origin. Clearly, the chapters were included by editors whose interests were identified with the primacy of the Jerusalem sanctuary. They tried to diminish its rivals, and at the same time advance the interests of the centralizing monarchical (Davidic) party, by implying that under the strong hand of a king (the story takes place during the period of the Judges, before the establishment of the monarchy) such a scandalous shrine could not have come into existence.

According to the foundation story in *Judges*, Micah was an Ephraimite (therefore a descendant of Joseph) who stole 1,100 pieces of silver from his mother. Frightened by his mother's curse, he returned the money to his mother who said: "'I consecrate the silver to the Lord from my hand for my son, to make a graven image and a molten image; now therefore, I will restore it to you.'" So his mother took 200 pieces of silver and had the images made and placed in Micah's house. Micah installed one of his sons (being a Danite, he was therefore a non-Levite) as the priest of this idol. Thus, we see in this hostile story that the idol had its origin in theft and was ministered to blasphemously by a non-priest (Jgs. 17:1-6).[415]

Then a young Levite happened to stop at the house of Micah, and Micah hired him to be priest (Jgs. 17:7-13). A little later, the Danites, who had had difficulty in claiming their original inheritance in lands inhabited by the Philistines (the region southeast of modern Jaffa), sent five scouts to find another homeland for themselves. On the way, they made the acquaintance of the young Levite priest (Jgs. 18:1-6). The scouts went on and decided to recommend the region of Laish to the Danites for their new home.[416] When the war party of 600 Danites set out

---

[414] BC, II, 451. The date has been revised.

[415] Under later Jewish law, only Levites could be priests.

[416] Laish, in northern Palestine, was renamed Dan by the Danites.

to attack Laish, they passed by way of Micah's house, and the five scouts told their brethren of the shrine and its furniture there. They decided to loot it and take the furniture to establish a new shrine at Laish after they had captured it:

"And they turned aside thither, and came to the house of the young Levite, at the home of Micah, and asked him of his welfare. Now six hundred men of the Danites, armed with their weapons of war, stood by the entrance of the gate; and five men who had gone to spy out the land went up, and entered and took the graven image, the ephod, the teraphim and the molten image, while the priest stood by the entrance of the gate with the six hundred men armed with weapons of war. And when these went into Micah's house and took the graven image, the ephod, the teraphim, and the molten image,[417] the priest said to them, 'What are ye doing?' And they said to him, 'Keep quiet, put thy hand upon thy mouth, and come with us, and be to us a father and a priest. Is it better for thee to be priest to the house of one man, or to be priest to a tribe and family in Israel?' And the priest's heart was glad; he took the ephod, and teraphim, and the graven image, and went in the midst of the people." (Jgs. 18:15-20)

When Micah saw what they had done, he pursued them, crying for the Danites to return his idols and his priest, but the Danites, who were much more powerful, threatened to kill him, so he desisted (Jgs. 18:21-26). After capturing Laish and massacring the inhabitants, the Danites renamed the place Dan and established the sanctuary. "And the Danites set up the graven image for themselves; and Jonathan the son of Gershom, son of Moses, and his sons were priests to the tribe of the Danites until the day of the captivity of the land." (Jgs. 18:30)

Now, whatever the foundation story of the shrine was, this travesty cannot have been it. "Its origin was, you could say, just about as unlawful as possible... A Jewish reader of the book would draw quite the contrary conclusion: it is a false sanctuary served by a false priest—which is exactly the impression the redactor wanted to produce by telling this story. His plea is that the first sanctuary of Dan was worthless, and was a fitting predecessor of the sanctuary into which Jeroboam I [1st king of the Northern kingdom of Israel, rgd. 931-910 BCE] brought the second golden calf."[418]

The fact that the priesthood at Dan claimed Mosaic descent (through Gershom) did not make them immune from the attacks of the Jerusalem (Aaronite-Levite) priesthood. The story itself seems to have

---

[417] See Glossary.

[418] de Vaux, II, pp. 307-308.

been inspired by the secession of the ten Northern tribes after the break up of Solomon's Empire under his incompetent son Rehoboam and Jeroboam's attempt to upgrade two sanctuaries (Dan and Bethel) within his own kingdom (Israel). As part of this effort: "So the king took counsel, and made two calves of gold. And he said to the people, 'Ye have gone up to Jerusalem long enough. Behold thy gods, O Israel, who brought you up out of the land of Egypt.'[419] And he set one in Bethel, and the other he put in Dan. And this thing became a sin, for the people went to the one at Bethel and the other one at Dan. He also made houses on high places, and appointed priests from among all the people, who were not Levites." (1 K. 12:28-31)

Now we know that the Danite priesthood claimed Mosaic origin. Does *1 Kings* then preserve a tradition that Moses himself was *not* a Levite, contradicting the statement of Ex. 2:1? Quite possibly. We have seen how Jewish tradition linked the story of Micah's idol with the incident of the Golden Calf at Horeb. Scholars have suggested that the link between the two stories is genuine, and the original inclusion of the story in *Exodus* has more than a little to do with the rivalry between Jeroboam's sanctuaries and the Jerusalem Temple establishment in the sister kingdom of Judah.

In order to understand the symbolism of these incidents, it is important to realize that both the priesthood and especially the prophets of Israel regarded the establishment of YHWH-worship in Canaan under constant threat from the earlier, but still covertly popular, local Baal-worship. Jeroboam's bulls were probably meant to be the pedestals upon which the presence of the invisible YHWH was supported, but the bulls themselves were not idols to be worshipped. This motif of a god supported by an animal is a common one in ancient Near Eastern art. Though the parallel of the worship of the sacred bull Apis in Egypt is an attractive one, neither the incident of the golden calf nor Jeroboam's bulls seem to be related to it. Rather, the symbolism is drawn from Semitic religion. The bull was the symbol of the Canaanite gods Baal and El, in their capacity as gods of fertility, as the Ras Shamra finds have shown us.

During the process of the establishment of YHWH-worship, YHWH was frequently given the attributes and titles of the gods He displaced. Equating YHWH with El, YHWH-worship probably was influenced by the bull-symbol of El. Therefore, when the Israelites

[419] This is a deliberate reference to Ex. 32:4, using the same language in order to equate Jeroboam's calves with Israel's lapse into idolatry in the Wandering. That the king would have made such a statement is almost certainly a Southern fabrication.

worshipped the golden calf, they probably thought of the calf as the symbol of El-YHWH. The incorporation of this calf as an object of worship created a strong reaction among those believers in the invisible YHWH because it compromised the purity of their concept of Him. Hence, the anger of Moses, and the shock and horror of the writer of the passage in *1 Kings* quoted above.

When Jeroboam set up the images of calves in his shrines, it is not clear whether he meant them to be thrones or symbols of YHWH.[420] However, in addition to the threat to the supremacy of the Jerusalem Temple, many saw the danger of the associations with the earlier Canaanite gods and the idolatrous practices linked to their worship that still lingered on in the land.[421]

Against this background, Jewish tradition made a bridge between the bulls of Jeroboam and the Golden Calf of the Israelites at Horeb. Even without that, the quotation from the story in *Exodus* inserted into the account of Jeroboam's making of the calves in *1 Kings* shows that such a parallel was implicit, though perhaps spurious.

Just as we have seen that scurrilous foundation story was invented by the enemies of the Danite shrine, whatever their motivation, the inclusion of Aaron in the story of the Golden Calf can probably be attributed to some similar hostility directed by the redactor towards the Aaronites. This appears to reflect the period after the exile, when the Zadokite priesthood of the Temple was trying to reestablish its primacy in Judah and engaged in a propaganda war against the local Aaronites who resisted their claims.[422] By the time the compromise had been achieved in which the Zadokites became Aaronites and the Aaronites Levites, the additions to the text of the Elohist account of the apostasy of Israel at Horeb had already acquired the sanctity of the surrounding material and later scribes did not dare to excise them.

It is also possible that Aaron's role in this story may be attributed to some other hostility directed at the Aaronites from some other phase of Israel's religious history. Our reconstruction of that history is incomplete, but the method of the *ad hominem* attack, by impugning the character of a supposed ancestor of an institution or social group, has many parallels in the Bible, such as the origin of the Danite shrine

---

[420] It may be going to far to say, with Kapelrud, that Jeroboam had identified YHWH with Baal-Hadad whose symbol was the bull. However, it would certainly have suggested such an identification (or the approval of it) to many of the more syncretizing Northerners. (Kapelrud, p. 76.)

[421] Calf, DB, p. 119; Kapelrud, pp. 37-38, 57, 76; de Vaux, II, pp. 333-335.

[422] See above in Section E.

discussed above, also the origins of the Moabites, the Hamites in *Genesis*, etc. The gratuitous nature of such vicious attacks is often self-evident. Therefore, we need feel no reservations about commending the story of Aaron's actually making the calf to the same category of maliciously inspired fabrications.[423] The rejection by the Quran of the story of Aaron's apostasy is perfectly sound in the light of the directions of modern research. More will be said about this below when we discuss the problem of the identity of al-Samiri.

As we have seen, the Jewish defense that Aaron felt threatened by the Israelites, while itself not exactly redeeming, is also reflected in Bal'ami. In the Quran, Aaron's fear is not for himself but for the division of the people: *(Moses) said (upon returning from the Mountain of God): "O Aaron! What held thee back when thou didst see them gone astray, that thou didst not follow me? Hast thou then disobeyed my order?" (Aaron) said: "O son of my mother! Clutch not my beard nor my head! I feared lest thou shouldst say: 'Thou hast caused division among the Children of Israel, and has not waited for my word.'"* (Q. 20:92-94)

This summarizes Aaron's role (in the Quranic view) in the incident: that he preached against the worship of the calf, but took no further steps, fearing the disintegration of the Israelite community. He recognized his own limitations, and knew that a greater man of action than he, that is Moses, would have to remedy the situation, so he played

---

[423] The argument often put forth supporting the authenticity of this tradition on the grounds that no one would have dared to invent such a tale about one of his ancestors can be discounted for several reasons. One is the conservative nature of the transmission of the texts. Once a story had found its way into writing, however secular, it acquired the sanctity of age and was to some extent protected by the later assertion of Mosaic authorship, whilst additions were still made both deliberately and accidentally by a copyist's incorporating notes and glosses into a text, outright suppression—an audacious move—was less frequent.

The original motivation for recording many of these stories, some of them quite damaging, was forgotten (as the difficulties faced by modern scholars trying to reconstruct these events show) and later generations were perplexed and disturbed by them, but—having retained them—were often quite ingenious in devising explanations that more or less obviated the plain unpleasantness of the pericope. Too, since authenticity of lineage and descent were more important to the post-Exilic Jews than the moral characters of their progenitors, such stories were probably not so disturbing to them as they are to the modern readers who care little for the veneration of remote ancestors but a great deal about the moral reputations of their religious teachers. In proof of this attitude, in addition to the story of Aaron's apostasy, we can cite many others: the deceitful behavior of Abraham, Isaac, and especially Jacob; Noah's drunkenness; Samson's violations of his Nazirite vows (Part Four, I), and unfavorable stories about Reuben, Levi, and Judah, David and Bathsheba, etc.

for time. He is guilty, perhaps, of timidity, but not—in the Quranic view—of the apostasy portrayed in the Bible.

Bal'ami's report of 12,000 steadfast Israelites, as well as giving support to a potential civil war among the ranks of the Israelites, seems to be an "enhanced" reference to the Levites mentioned above (Ex. 32:25-29) who massacred 3,000 of the apostates, thereby proving their own loyalty to YHWH. The connection of the passage to the worship of the Golden Calf is somewhat obscure (some scholars deny any connection), but in its present context, this blood bath was precipitated by the crisis of the Golden Calf. Jewish tradition comes down firmly in support of this view.[424] Yet, in the Bible (Ex. 32:1-8, 15-24, 35), there is no hint of popular opposition to the worship. The Quran can be read to imply that the repentance by the apostates had already begun before the return of Moses: *And when they feared the consequences thereof and saw that they had gone astray, they said: "Unless our Lord have mercy upon us and forgive us, truly we are of the lost!"* (Q. 7:149)

After being informed by God about the apostasy of his people: "...Moses turned, and went down from the mountain with the two tables of the testimony in his hands, tables that were written on both sides; on the one side and on the other side were they written. And the tables were the work of God, and the writing was the writing of God, graven upon the tables. When Joshua[425] heard the noise of the people as they shouted, he said to Moses, 'there is a noise of war in the camp.' But he said, 'It is not the sound of shouting for victory, or the sound of the cry of defeat, but the sound of singing that I hear.' And as soon as he came near the camp and saw the calf and the dancing, Moses' anger burned hot, and he threw the tables out of his hands and broke them at the foot of the mountain. And he took the calf which they had made, and burnt it with fire, and ground it to powder, and scattered it upon the water, and made the people of Israel drink it." (Ex. 32:15-20)

"And Moses said to Aaron, 'What did this people do to thee that thou hast brought a great sin upon them? And Aaron said, 'Let not the anger of my Lord burn hot; thou knowest the people, that they are set on evil. For they said to me, "Make us gods, who shall go before us; as for Moses, the man who brought us up out of the land of Egypt, we do not

---

[424] LJ, III, 94, 130, 170, 211, 404.

[425] According to the Elohist, Joshua alone had accompanied Moses up the mountain when the latter went to receive the Tables of the Law (Ex. 24:13, see above in text). This is interpreted to mean that the elders accompanied Joshua and Moses part of the way and were told to wait until the pair returned.

know what has become of him." And I said to them, "let any who have gold take it off"; so they gave it to me, and I threw it into the fire, and there came out this calf.'" (Ex. 32:21-24)

In the original version, the story was probably completed by: "And the Lord sent a plague upon the people, because they made the calf which Aaron made." (Ex. 32:35) This is plainly a syntactically awkward sentence, and it suggests the heavy-handed effort of a later redactor who added the phrase "which Aaron made" to complete his work of indicting the Aaronites. In the original version, the plague was probably the punishment, but as the chapter is now constituted, the massacre by the Levites inserted between vv. 24 and 35 appears to be the punishment of the people for their lapse into idol worship.

Paralleling this, in the Quran we read: *And when Moses returned unto his people, angry and grieved, he said: "Evil is that (course) which ye took after I had left you. Would ye hasten on the judgment of your Lord? And he cast down the tablets, and he seized his brother by the head, pulling him toward him. (Aaron) said: "Son of my mother! Lo, the people did judge me weak and almost killed me. Oh, make not mine enemies to triumph over me and place me not among the oppressors!" (Moses) said: "My Lord! Have mercy on me and on my brother; bring us into Thy mercy, Thou the Most Merciful of all who show mercy."* (Q. 7:150-151) Surah Ta Ha (Q. 20:92-94) quoted above has a slightly different exchange on the same theme. Aaron's warning to the people while Moses was away (Q. 20:90-91) has also been quoted above.

The differences between the Biblical and Quranic accounts once again are about the role of Aaron and the nature of his response to the people's demand to make the idol. In the Bible, he is the instigator, whilst in the Quran he is reproved for not taking strong enough action to stamp out the idolatry, in the other words, a lack of leadership. He is the object of Moses' wrath in both accounts.

In the Bible, Moses' simple reproof for the enormity of Aaron's own lapse into idolatry thereby encouraging that of the people seems strikingly inadequate. In one version of the punishment, 3,000 were slaughtered, and in another, the people were struck down by a plague. However, strangely, Aaron who, in the Biblical account as it stands at present, was the author of the idolatry and the manufacturer of the calf—acts which ought to have made him of all people the most culpable and subject to the righteous anger of both Moses and God—escapes scot-free after his plea not to be humiliated before the people!

What sort of justice is that? That Aaron could have directed and participated in the apostasy and afterwards not only be forgiven and unpunished for this blasphemy, but also be credited with the founding of the line of Temple priests, as related in *Exodus*, is incomprehensible. There would seem to be a grave imbalance in the scales of divine justice in this case, if we accept the veracity of the Biblical story. Fortunately, with a little understanding of the how scripture was utilized by one faction against another as a tool of propaganda during the formative period of the text (before it came to be regarded as Holy Writ), we do not have to do so.

With regard to the fate of the tables, the Quran does not support *Exodus* where it states they were broken. The words in: "and (he) broke them at the foot of the mountain" (Ex. 32:19) are probably the addition of the redactor who was conflating the J and E accounts and making their duplicated theophany two separate granting of the tables. In order to do this, the redactor was forced to dispose of one set, and he did this by having Moses not only dash the tables down on the ground, but also break them as well. The considerable blasphemy attendant upon this action—remember that it was emphasized the God himself had inscribed these tables with His Own Hand (Ex. 32:16)—did not seem to disturb the redactor.

Since, we believe, the Quran correctly speaks of only one granting of the Tables of the Law, after he had set them down in exasperation at the behavior of the people whom he was trying to enlighten, we read: *And then when the anger of Moses abated, he took up the tablets, and in their inscription there was guidance and mercy for all those who fear their Lord.* (Q. 7:154) Before the conflation of J and E, the Elohist version probably only spoke of Moses' setting down of the tables. However, later Muslim commentators, once again misled by the weight of Jewish opinion on the subject (and without the benefit of the higher criticism) also mention the breaking of the tables,[426] even though the Quran itself does not.

There are other minor differences. In the Bible, Moses grinds up the calf and throws the dust into the water and makes the Israelites drink of it. In the Quran, the fate of the calf is described thus: *(Moses said): "Now look upon thy god of which thou has remained a votary. Verily we will burn it and will scatter it dust over the sea."* (Q. 20:97) In this, the Quran has Biblical support in the words of the Deuteronomist (who also refrained from repeating that Aaron actually made and worshipped the calf): "Then I [Moses] took the sinful thing which ye had made, and burned it with fire and crushed it, grinding it very small, until it was as

---

[426] Bal'ami, p. 442.

fine as dust; and I threw the dust of it into the brook that descended out of the mountain." (Deut. 9:21)

Some commentators interpret the words in Surah Baqarah *and they drank the calf into their hearts with their unbelief* (Q. 2:93) to mean that Israelites had to drink the ashes of the calf literally, as in *Exodus*, whilst others interpret the passage metaphorically. If it is taken literally, it is not a contradiction of the speech of Moses in Surah Ta Ha (Q. 20:97) quoted above, in which he said what the intended to do with the idol. Scattering the ashes in the river does not preclude the symbolic penance by the Hebrews of drinking of the water so tainted. With regard to the punishment, Bal'ami, taking his cue form the pericope of the slaughter of the 3,000 by the Levites, relates that God would only accept the repentance on behalf of the 12,000 who had not joined in the idol worship. They were commanded to take up their swords and slaughter those who had done so. In typical medieval exaggeration, the Bible's 3,000 became the 70,000 dead in Bal'ami, of the 360,000 who, he records, had participated in the worship.[427]

Next, in Bal'ami's narrative, Moses read the Torah to the surviving Israelites. After he had finished, they commented that it would have been easier to worship the calf and be killed than to follow that which Moses had brought them.[428] This seems to parallel the reaction to the reading of the Law to the people by the 5th-century BCE prophet Ezra: "For all the people wept when they heard the words of the law... So the Levites stilled all the people saying, 'Be quiet, for this day is holy; do not be grieved.'" (Neh. 8:9, 11)

Finally, Bal'ami tells us, stronger measures had to be taken in order to coerce the reluctant Israelites to accept the provisions of the Law. The Holy Mountain was raised up over their heads and Moses threatened that if they did not accept the Torah, they would be crushed beneath it. The Israelites tried to flee, but the mountain kept pace with them. At length they accepted the Law. However, they pleaded with Moses to pray to have the Law lightened, and God responded favorably.[429]

Bal'ami's raising of the mountain over the people of Israel is based upon a literal interpretation of the Quranic text: *And We made a covenant with you and caused the Mount to tower above you...* (Q. 2:63,

---

[427] Bal'ami, pp. 446-448.

[428] Bal'ami, p. 448.

[429] Bal'ami, pp. 449-350. This reminds us of the tradition of the imposition of the numerous obligatory prayers which were reduced by God to five through the intercession of the Prophet.

93) and another text: *And when We shook the Mount above them as it were a covering, and they supposed that it was going to fall upon them...* (Q. 7:171) We have already discussed the traditions of the volcanic nature of the Mountain of God, with its towering columns of smoke, explosions of dust, fire, and rocks, etc., also echoed in the Quran. The explicit tradition is found in the Talmud and other Jewish writings: "It was not indeed quite of their own free will that Israel declared themselves ready to accept the Torah, for when the whole nation, in two divisions, men and women, approached Sinai, God lifted up this mountain and held it over the heads of the people like a basket, saying to them: 'If you accept the Torah, it is well, otherwise you will find your grave under this mountain.' They all burst into tears and poured out their hear in contrition before God, and then said: 'All that the Lord hath said, will we do, and be obedient.'"[430]

AL-SAMIRI: Before concluding this section of the story of Moses, we must return to the question of al-Samiri. We have already pointed out the dubious nature of the Biblical text which makes Aaron responsible for the actual making of the Golden Calf, and we have also discussed some of the Jewish traditions which attempted either to exonerate him by showing him coerced, or foiled in his own strategy to prevent the Israelites from relapsing into idolatry. Other individuals were accused of either stirring up the people (such as Jannes and Jambres), or actually making an idol, as did Micah.

Although some of this material may shed some light on the question of the tradition of al-Samiri, because the Bible has already accepted the guilt of Aaron, we must not expect to find much direct support for the Quranic al-Samiri in Jewish and Christian writings. We advise the reader that in the absence of external documentary evidence, much about the reference in the Quran, based upon oral tradition, remains obscure and we can only lay out what we possess, together with some speculations.

To begin, the use of the definite article tells us that al-Samiri is probably not a given personal name; it is rather in the nature of an epithet or nickname. The Arabic root *s-m-r* is associated with "spending or passing an evening," with the implication of entertainment and pleasantry. Sāmir is a general term for one enjoying himself this way and is not necessarily a proper name. For example if Ahmad is watching some entertainment, we say he is a "spectator," but that is not Ahmad's personal name; rather it is a word describing what he is doing at the

---

[430] LJ, III, 92; VI, 36.

moment. In the Quran, the word (in the accusative form) is used once with the meaning of "(someone) passing the night" (Q. 23:67). The final *i*, the *y* of relationship (*nisbah*), could mean some one associated with such an evening of entertainment. If the source of the epithet is to be found among these definitions, then we can probably pursue the question no further, for lack of relevant documentary support.

Before turning to the usual interpretation, the Samaritan, another similarity may be considered. We have seen how, according to some Jewish traditions, Satan (called Sammael or Samael in these traditions) entered the calf and caused it to low. Both the Quranic and the Jewish traditions may be oblique references to the well-known deception practiced in some ancient shrines by which an idol was made to speak by various means. One of these was the concealment of a priest either in the hollow of an idol (metal idols of any size were usually hollow because if they had been solid they would have been immovably heavy), or somewhere nearby so that the voice would seem—to a gullible public—to be proceeding from the mouth of the idol itself. That is not an aspect of the report which we wish to consider here. By a well-known linguistic rule, the frequent interchange of *l* and *r*, Samael could become Samaer. It is just possible that this tradition of Samael and the calf was known in Arabia, but with the fallen angel's name transformed from Samael to Samaer, or Samir. The Samiri would be a follower of Samir. Of course, there is no documentary evidence to support such a hypothesis, and it can only remain a possible avenue for further investigation.[431] Some have suggested that al-Samari in the Quran is actually Aaron himself, but on balance, this seems improbable.

Following the common translation of al-Samiri, the Samaritan, Western critics have made the usual charges of Quranic confusion: firstly, on the grounds that the Bible clearly states that Aaron made the calf and any other suggestion must *ipso facto* be wrong, the certainty of which we have challenged above; and secondly, on the grounds that use of the word *Samaritan* itself is anachronistic (never mind all of the Biblical anachronisms), because the Samaritans had not yet (at the time of Moses) come into existence as a people.

Who were the Samaritans? The question is better phrased: "Who *are* the Samaritans?" for a remnant the Samaritan community numbering

---

[431] Tisdall has also pointed out the possibility of a connection between Samael and the Samiri (Tisdall, p. 113), although his conclusion that Samiri is a mistake for Samael is not justified by the Arabic form of al-Samiri. It could not mean Samael himself, but rather a follower or adherent of Samael, or one who possessed his attributes, parallels of which would be on the lines of al-Mūsawī, al-ᶜĪsawī, etc.

several hundred souls still survives in central Palestine. They represent a schismatic group of YHWH-worshippers, dissenters who did not accept the primacy of the Jerusalem cult, nor many of the other principally Exilic and post-Exilic developments of official Judaism.[432]

We have noted frequently that throughout most of Israelite history a strand of rivalry and frequently hostility may be detected between the Northern tribes under the leadership of the Josephic tribes, especially Ephraim, and the Southern tribes led by Judah. To some extent, it is an accident of history that the Judahites have survived to the present day, giving their name to Judaism, whilst the Northerners, the "Samaritans," are represented only by a few hundred survivors. (It must also be remembered that the Old Testament we have today is a product of the South.) Although the threat from the Northern rivals has long since passed, during the formative period of Judaism and the scriptures, the competition between two groups of YHWH-worshippers was a very real and often acrimonious one, and the outcome by no means certain. In these circumstances, there are many direct and indirect references to this hostility, some of which we have already pointed out. The Southerners were not above using the sacred word attributed to YHWH Himself as a weapon against their Northern rivals. The picture of the North in the Bible is often a biased and negative one.[433]

Politically, this rivalry was reflected in the fact that all of YHWH-worshippers of Palestine were united only under their first three kings: Saul, David, and Solomon (although the extent of Saul's domain was not that comprehensive). After the accession of Solomon's son Rehoboam in c. 931 BCE, the North broke away and established it own line of the kings of Israel, while the South—called Judah or Judaea—continued under the Davidic line. According to *Kings*, composed in the South, every one of the 19 monarchs of the North (c. 931 to 721 BCE) was a villainous oppressor of his people and an enemy of God. In general, we are given an unfavorable view of most things Northern, religious or political, from the historical books of the Bible, all of which (not coincidentally) of are Southern redaction.

---

[432] Material from this section, including what follows, about the Samaritan comes from: Samaritans, EJ, XIV, 725-732; Gerizim, DB, p. 325; Samaria, DB, p. 879; Samaritans, DB, p. 880; Cambridge, Vol. 1, pp. 185-190.

[433] If the bitter enmity of these two tiny groups of YHWH worshippers that acknowledged kinship with each other seems a trifle ridiculous today, one may recall the bitter and bloody centuries of war and slaughter—on a much grander and sadder scale—between the world's principal adherents of the Prince of Peace, the Protestants and the Catholics, in Europe following the Protestant Reformation. I need not remind Muslim readers of the damage disputing Islamic factions have inflicted upon each other.

It was during this period of the Northern monarchy of Israel that about 880 BCE one of their kings, Omri, decided to build a new capital. "He bought the hill of Samaria from Shemer for two talents of silver; and he fortified the hill, and called the name of the city which he built, Samaria, after the name of Shemer, the owner of the hill." (1 K. 16:24) From the name of this city, the central hill country of Palestine, primarily inhabited by the Josephic tribes of Ephraim and Manasseh, came to be called Samaria. This was the name applied to the region in Roman times, with Galilee to the north and Judaea to the south.

In 721 BCE, after a three-year siege, Samaria fell to the Assyrians and the kingdom of Israel became a province of their empire. The inhabitants, according to the Southern record, were transported to other parts of the Assyrian Empire, and were replaced by non-Israelite colonizers, who corrupted the purity of YHWH-worship in the North (2 K. 17:32-41). For centuries, this passage condemning the Samaritans on the grounds of impure race (mixed origins!) and impure religious practices has been the starting point for assessments of these schismatics. However, the passage is almost certainly post-Exilic[434] and is another salvo in the long war of propaganda between the North and the South that resumed with the Return of the Southerners and the rebuilding of the Temple in Jerusalem, after Judah had suffered the same fate as Israel at the hands of the Babylonians in 586 BCE. There is no *a priori* reason to believe that the Samaritans were any more ethnically mixed than the Judahites, and their still-surviving religion is uncompromisingly monotheistic, contradicting the accusations found in *2 Kings*.[435]

As has been remarked above, the claims of the Jerusalem cult gradually evolved from primacy to exclusivity. Jerusalem was the latest of the YHWH-shrines to be established (by David after 1000 BCE), but in the period before and during the United Monarchy of David and Solomon a number of YHWH-sanctuaries had already been established much earlier: Dan, Shechem, Bethel, Shiloh, Hebron, Beersheba, etc.

---

[434] BC, III, 269-271.

[435] Sargon of Assyria, in his own records of the event, claims to have transported 27,290 Israelites into captivity. (Albright-Ab to Ez, p. 73.) This does not support the Bible's assertion than the entire population of the ten tribes of Northern Israel was carried off. The population of Israel must have been considerably more than 27 thousand, probably closer to 200,000. Sargon may simply have carried of the people of the city of Samaria and its environs, and the Biblical statement is simply another slanderous attack on the Northerners, making them the descendants of non-Israelites. Though there was considerable depopulation, doubtless many if not most of the villages where the bulk of the people lived were relatively untouched. After all, cultivators are economically profitable and it would not have served Assyria to lose the potential revenue.

The Jerusalem, sanctuary, though the youngest, enjoyed royal patronage and the considerable prestige of possessing important national relics such as the Ark of the Covenant and the Tables of the Law given to Moses. From its beginnings, therefore, Jerusalem enjoyed certain advantages none of the others could claim, but as long as the sanctity of the older shrines was recognized, regardless of political conditions, there was a feeling of community among YHWH worshippers, both Northern and Southern.

The collapse of the Northern kingdom in 721 BCE changed matters. Simultaneously in the Southern kingdom, the exclusivist claims of the Jerusalem shrine gained royal support, especially under Hezekiah (716-687 BCE) and later Josiah (640-609 BCE). Judah was now the sole political representative of the YHWH cult, and steps were taken to suppress rival sanctuaries throughout the land and to completely centralize the sacrificial and ritual aspects of YHWH-worship at Jerusalem. Whenever circumstances permitted, the Judahites extended this policy of suppression of rival shrines to the lands of the former kingdom of Israel, that is, Samaria.[436]

With the destruction of Jerusalem and the Temple by the Babylonians in 586 BCE, the situation was reversed. Sanctuaries at Shechem and other places flourished freely while the Jerusalem Temple lay in ruins, its leadership and its priesthood carried off in captivity (the Exile) to Babylonia. Despite the impression created in the Bible, the depopulation of Judah by the Babylonians—Judah was after all half the size of its former rival, the kingdom of Israel—was much more sweeping than that of Israel by the Assyrians a century and a half earlier.

When the Persian king Cyrus, history's first world emperor, generously permitted the exiles to return and rebuild the Temple at Jerusalem, the priesthood was determined to reassert its exclusivity and primacy in all Palestine—North and South—with the renewal of its interpretation of the YHWH cult. This resulted in a series of political and priestly squabbles that eventually led to a rejection of the legitimacy of the priesthoods of the (primarily) Northern sanctuaries by the Southerner Ezra in the middle of the 5th century BCE. Schism between the two rival cults was inevitable, just as the division of Solomon's kingdom had become inevitable through Rehoboam's mismanagement nearly five centuries earlier. (This rivalry goes back even further, to the ancient competition between the southern Judahic and northern Josephic tribes for domination in Canaan.)

---

[436] As under Josiah. (See 2 K. 23:15, 19; 23 Ch. 34:6.7.)

For their part, the Northerners rejected the claims of the Jerusalem cult and completely focused their attention upon the ancient sanctuary at Shechem and the sacred mountain of Gerizim. Henceforth, it became their religious center, as it has remained to the present day for the Samaritans, the descendants of those Northerners of ancient times. That the claims of the Samaritans had considerable validity is shown by the degree of the hostility directed at them by the (Southern) Jews. The Samaritans rejected all scripture save the Torah (the Pentateuch). Their own version has numerous minor and major readings that differ from the received Massoretic text of the Old Testament that was finally established c.700 CE[437] (a date *later* than the establishment of the received text of the Quran).

The Samaritans' claim that Gerizim (in the heart of Ephraim, the dominant Josephic tribe) was the mountain of the Lord, rather than the upstart Mount Moriah at Jerusalem, seems also to be well-grounded in the present text of the Old Testament despite several alterations and the probable deliberate suppression of the role of Shechem. The great national covenant after the Conquest is set at Shechem (Josh. 24:1-28). Joseph was buried there, and the shrine has Jacobite associations. When Solomon's kingdom split up under his son, "Rehoboam went to Shechem, for all Israel had come to Shechem to make him king."[438] (1 K. 12:1) Shechem was also the first capital of Israel (1 K. 12:25). More importantly, the Samaritan Pentateuch makes Mount Gerizim the scene of the sacrifice by Abraham.

The Samaritans built a temple on Mount Gerizim that was destroyed by the (Southern) Maccabean John Hyrcanus in 126 BCE. Nonetheless, the Samaritans survived and towards the end of the 2nd century CE, some 300,000 were living in their central Palestinian homeland.[439] During the Christian and Islamic periods, their numbers gradually dwindled to the remnant remaining today.

Mainstream Jews regarded them as a pariah people. Their origins, their customs, and religious practices were cruelly misrepresented. However, Ackroyd writes: "There is nothing to suggest that they were involved in alien religious practices or belief as some of the stories about them state. Such stories are part of a propagandist

---

[437] Text of the Old Testament, DB, p. 972. {See summary in the Foreword. For more, in this series, see *Introduction to the Old Testament.*}

[438] His purpose was to prevent his rival Jeroboam, who was away in Egypt, from establishing a secessionist Northern kingdom of Israel. Rehoboam failed in this and Jeroboam became the first king of Israel.

[439] Samaritans, EJ, XIV, 731.

tradition in some Jewish circles... All this suggests the possibility that the Samaritan community was in origin a conservative protest against Jerusalem practice."[440]

More than a hint of this animosity between the Jews and the Samaritans during New Testament times can be gained from the encounter between the Jew Jesus and the Samaritan woman at the well: "There came a woman of Samaria to draw water. Jesus said to her, 'Give me drink.' For his disciples had gone away into the city to buy food. The Samaritan woman said to him, 'How is it that thou, a Jew, askest a drink of me, a woman of Samaria?' For Jews have no dealings with Samaritans...'" (Jn. 4:7-9)

This relationship between the Jews and the Samaritans has led Golziher and others to interpret the statement of Moses in the Quran to al-Samiri: *"Then go! And lo, in this it is easy for thee to say: Touch me not! And lo, there is for thee an appointment thou canst not break..."* (Q. 20:97) as a reference to the pariah status of the Samaritans (and hence as further proof of the anachronism involved in the figure of Quranic al-Samari).[441] This is an attractive and facile view, however, a little consideration will show that there are problems in our accepting it. Schismatics, even with the heritage of enmity that the Samaritans and the Jews felt for each other, do not go around warning their opponents to avoid pollution (literally or figuratively) by crying out "Touch me not!" The story of Jesus and the woman at the well, quoted above, shows that though the Jews regarded the Samaritans as ritually impure, as were *all* non-Jews (Romans, Greeks, Egyptians, etc.), the feeling was not so strongly reciprocated by the Samaritans, at least this woman expressed no concern about becoming ritually impure through contact with a Jew.

There is, however, a class of people who from ancient times until comparatively recently were obliged by law and custom to warn people of their approach and who were isolated from society: lepers. It would seem that al-Samiri's punishment in this life was leprosy. There are numerous traditions of leprosy associated with Moses. When Miriam, his sister, criticized him, she was afflicted with leprosy that was only cured through her brother's prayer (Num. 12). The white hand of Moses and his shining face both have leprous connotations (see above). Others connected with the story of Moses who were supposed to have been afflicted with leprosy at one time or another include Aaron, Bithiah, the Egyptians at the time of the birth of Moses, Job, Pharaoh, *and* Samael.[442]

---

[440] Ackroyd, p. 170.
[441] Samiri, SEI, 501-502.
[442] LJ, VII, 283.

Jewish tradition also makes Moses capable of inflicting leprosy (on the Egyptians)[443] as well as knowing how to cure it.[444] While this explanation helps us to understand the possible implication of the Quranic verse in question, it does not advance our enquiry into the identity of al-Samiri in any particular direction, save perhaps that of Samael. However, in Jewish tradition, his leprosy will occur at the last judgment,[445] so perhaps too much should not be made of that aspect of the connection in this life, although a different tradition about him may have been circulating in the Hejaz.

Returning to the meaning of "Samiri," the evidence of the Samaritan community in this regard is important. The Samaritans called themselves *Shamerim*, meaning "keepers or observers" (of the truth). They do not derive their name from the city or country of Samaria which they call *Shomron*, and its people *Shomronim*. This name is, according to the passage from *2 Kings* cited above, derived from the former owner of the site of the city, one Shemer, whose name, from the same root as *shamer*, is taken to mean "guardian."[446] (The Hebrew root *sh-m-r* is the cognate of the Arabic root *s-m-r*.)

The Samaritan priesthood claimed descent from Phinehas, the son of Eleazar, the son of Aaron, and the line survived until the 17th century CE.[447] Phinehas bears an Egyptian name and became high priest after Eleazar.[448] *Chronicles* preserves a tradition associating Phinehas with Korah: "And Phinehas the son of Eleazar was the ruler over them [the Korahites] in time past; the Lord was with him." (1 Ch .9:20) Both Eleazar and Phinehas were buried at Gibeah, in the hill country of (Josephic) Ephraim, that was later called Samaria (Josh. 24:33).[449] Neither Eleazar not Phinehas figured in any rebellious activity against

---

443 LJ, II, 354.

444 LJ, III, 260.

445 LJ, V, 101.

446 Samaritans, EJ, XIV, 728.

447 Samaritans, EJ, XIV, 727.

448 Phinehas, DB, 768. Yusuf Ali also speculates that "Samiri" could be of Egyptian derivation, from *shemer* meaning "stranger, foreigner." (Quran-Yusuf Ali, p. 807, Note 2605.) As a given name used by Israelites, it appears in both *Kings* and *Chronicles*, though no one of that name is associated in the Bible with the events of the Exodus or the Wandering. Perhaps he was an Egyptian in the "mixed multitude."

449 Gibeah was actually in the territory of the other Rachel tribe (Joseph was also Jacob's son by Rachel) Benjamin. This tradition may reflect a time before the Benjaminites had become established there. In the Biblical text cited (Josh. 24:33), it is specifically said that Gibeah was "in the hill country of Ephraim." It is thought that the Benjaminites, a small tribe, were late in seizing the territory in Canaan allotted to them, as has been discussed in the text above.

Moses in the Pentateuch; indeed, the oldest sources, the Yahwist and the Elohist, hardly mention them.

There is an old Jewish tradition of an abortive attempt by the Ephraimites to leave Egypt under the leadership of one Ganon or, as he was also called, Jair. The leader is depicted as a false prophet, and the expedition ended in disaster.[450] However, if he is to be identified with Jair, there is nothing else unfavorable about him. Aaron had two other sons, Nadab and Abihu, both of whom were reported accompanying Moses to the top of Mount Sinai (Ex. 24:1) and being made priests (Ex. 28:1). However, they were guilty of making a sacrifice with "unholy fire" "and fire came forth from the presence of the Lord and devoured them, and they died before the Lord." (Lev. 10:2) They are not mentioned in the story of the Golden Calf and one can only speculate about whether one of their names was originally in place of that of Aaron, or the term "son of Aaron" for "Aaron." In any case, such speculation does not explain the use of the Quranic term al-Samiri.

Trying to solve the problem by resorting to the North-South controversy is difficult. If, as is supposed, the Mosaic tradition really originated with the South, Moses was certainly honored in the North. Indeed, the only priestly line claiming Mosaic descent was to be found there (at Dan). As an aspect of the Levite/Aaronite competition, the Levites rallied to Moses after the incident of the Golden Calf, whilst on the other hand, the Levite Korah opposed him—although the Korahites may originally have been (despised) Edomites and not Levites (or even Hebrews) at all![451]

If we are to regard *al-Samiri* as a reference to someone in the Northern tradition of YHWH-worship, as opposed to the Southern tradition represented by Moses, not enough seems to be found in the Biblical data to help us make a positive identification. The weight of the role of the Aaron, however spurious, has obscured any other traditions of leadership in the affair of the Golden Calf. That the term Samiri, if it is to be equated with either *shamerim*, the keepers, or *shomronim*, the Samaritans, is an anachronism in this situation is not a serious obstacle. A representative of the Northern tradition that became the *shamerim* would be meant.[452] This is supported by the evidence of the persistence of calf worship in the North (Jeroboam's calves) and some leader of the

---

[450] LJ, III, 899; VI, 2,3.

[451] Korahites, DB, p. 560.

[452] We commonly speak of Judaism as including the periods of David and Solomon, or even Abraham, when the history of the term properly begins with the Exile. A person of English descent in the United States considers himself an American, not an Englishman.

(Northern) Josephic tribes whose name has been lost to us may have led the opposition to Moses and proposed the construction of the idol along familiar Egyptian lines. The story would then reflect the tensions between the Judahic and Josephic tribes before they settled in Palestine. The Samiri's seizure of the dust could be interpreted to mean that he was imitating the acts of Moses and had set himself up as a rival leader. Moses rallied his Levites and crushed the rebellion. In later times for other reasons, the name of the leader was replaced by that of Aaron.

On the other hand, equating al-Samiri with the Samaritans or the Samarians may be a false lead. Perhaps we should look to the meaning of the word. Perhaps al-Samiri was in some way connected with keeping the watch (mixing the Hebrew and Arabic meanings of the word); or it was connected with an earlier corruption of one of the names of the Hebrew Satan, Samael. From this distance, we can only offer these lines of investigation. However, it is necessary to remark again, the use of the term "al-Samiri" in this Quranic text is very firm and unhesitating, reflecting a well-known tradition among its auditors. The accusation made by Westerners that it is an echo of Jewish hostility towards the Samaritans learned by Muhammad is obviated by the fact that the term never occurs in the Quran in any context other than the story of the Golden Calf, and there are no important Jewish traditions associating that story with the later Samaritans. (The bulls installed by Jeroboam belong to a time before the term Samaritan had come into use.) However, in the 8th century BCE, Hosea wrote:

> "The inhabitants of Samaria tremble
> for the calf of Bethaven. [Bethel?]
> Its people shall mourn for it,
> and its idolatrous priests shall wail over it,
> over its glory which has departed from it.
> Yea, the thing itself shall be carried to Assyria,
> as a tribute to the great king.
> Ephraim shall be put to shame,
> and Israel shall be ashamed of his idol."
> (Hos. 10:5-6)

Nonetheless, in later times there does not seem to have been any stress on the association of the Samaritans with the worship of the golden calves, because the schism occurred long after the disappearance of those idols and they do not figure prominently in the polemics the two rivals directed against each other.

For the present, the story of al-Samiri, like those of Hud, Shu'ayb, and others whose names would have recalled a network of associations familiar to the first audience of the Quran but now lost, is unfinished. It remains clothed in ambiguity because in varying degrees the context of the oral tradition has vanished, pending any new discoveries. So, who was al-Samiri? Samael? We do not yet have a definitive answer. We do not, or no longer, know. We have no reason to doubt that, based upon other parts of our examination of the stories, the people of the Prophet knew. *And God knows best.*

J. KORAH

"I don't want the treasure of Qarun!" (Persian song)

Now Korah was of the people of Moses, but he oppressed them; and We gave him so much treasure that his keys[453] *thereof would truly have been a burden for a number of strong men. When his own people said unto him: "Exult not! God loves not the exultant. Rather seek the abode of the Hereafter in that which God has given thee and neglect not thy portion of the world, and be thou kind even as God has been kind to them and seek not corruption; lo, God loves not the corrupters." He said: "I have been given it only on account of a knowledge which I possess."*

Did he not know that God had destroyed generations of men before him, mightier than he in strength and more numerous? And the guilty are not to be questioned about their sins! Then he went forth before his people in his finery. Those who desired the present life said, "Would that we had what Korah has been given! Truly he is a man of great fortune!"

So We caused the earth to swallow him and his dwelling. Then he had no host to help him, save God, nor was he of those who can save themselves. And in the morning those who had longed to be in his place

---

[453] *keys*: some translate the Arabic word here, *mafātīḥ*, as "hoards." The Arabic word is a plural of either *maftaḥ* or *miftāḥ*, the former meaning "hoard," "stores"; the latter meaning "key." As the great number of keys for Korah's treasure is referred to in older Jewish writings, it is the preferred reading here. The attached possessive pronoun is masculine singular and cannot refer to "treasure" (*kunūz*), which is a broken plural and grammatically feminine. Consequently it refers to Korah, and is translated "his." In the Islamic world Korah is known as *Qārūn*. We feel that the exaggeration here is deliberate, emphasizing the parabolic nature of the passage, an illustration of the proverb from *Proverbs*: of "pride goeth before destruction, and an haughty spirit before a fall." (Prbs. 41:18)

were saying: "Ah! God spreads out and narrows His provision for whom He will of His servants. If God had not been gracious to us, He would have caused us to be swallowed up (too). Ah! The unbelievers never prosper!" (Q. 28:76-82)

This is the principal Quranic text of the parable of Korah. He is mentioned in two other places (Q. 29:39; 40:24), with Pharaoh and Haman, as an opponent of Moses. In the Quran, his story is a cautionary tale of the futile arrogance of wealth and the delusions of temporal power.

Once again, the later Muslim commentators have laden the Quranic story with more details and incidents, some of them quite out of harmony with the moral of the pericope. In Surabadi's expansion, Korah was very wealthy, and—it is said—the treasurer of Pharaoh. His wealth was derived from Pharaoh's treasury. When he saw all the honor the Israelites were giving Moses, he became jealous. He approached Moses and asked him what was left for him (Korah), as Moses had been given the honor of prophethood, and Aaron chieftainship. Moses replied that the giving belonged to God. Korah was displeased and became a hypocrite.[454] Moses told him to bring him his staff. Korah brought the staffs of 360 Israelite nobles, and they were placed in Moses' leather tent. The next day the staffs of Moses and Aaron were found to have grown and sprouted branches. Korah accused Moses of sorcery, and Moses, angered, prayed that the earth would swallow Korah up.[455]

This seems to make Korah's destruction the result of a fit of pique by Moses. The incident of the staffs was doubtless ultimately dependent upon the tradition of the staffs found in Num. 17:1-11, wherein a similar contest is described with twelve staffs, one for each tribe, with Aaron's staff representing the tribe of Levi. It is meant as the assertion of the rights of the priestly tribe of Levi represented by Aaron. "The Lord said to Moses, 'Speak to the people of Israel, and get from them rods, one for each fathers' house… twelve rods. Write each man's name upon his rod, and write Aaron's name upon the rod of Levi. Then thou shalt deposit them in the tent of the meeting before the testimony, where I meet with you. And the rod of the man whom I choose shall sprout…'" (Num. 17:1-5)

This was done. As in Surabadi: "and on the morrow Moses went into the tent of the testimony; and behold, the rod of Aaron for the house of Levi had sprouted and put forth buds, and produced blossoms, and it

---

[454] The use of the word "hypocrite" by the Surabadi is a strong condemnation, because of its association with the opponents of the Prophet during his mission.

[455] Surabadi, pp. 306-307.

bore ripe almonds..." (Num. 17:8) This device has been used in other places by both Muslim[456] and Jewish commentators. In the Bible, this test immediately follows the account of the destruction of Korah and his party, so Surabadi's use of the incident is not out of place.

In the description Surabadi gives us of Korah's wealth, he says that Korah's treasure was 400,000 dirhams, carried by 40 men whom he kept with him always. When Moses came down from the Holy Mountain and found them worshipping the Golden Calf, he threw down the tables (of the Law) and broke them. Then God commanded him to fashion two tablets of gold to replace them.[457] Moses asked where he could get so much gold. Then Gabriel taught him about three plants which, when mixed with iron, copper, and tin, would turn those metals into gold.

Moses then fashioned the tablets and separately disclosed the secret of one plant each to Korah, Aaron, and to Miriam, who was married to Korah. Aaron gave his secret to Korah, and Korah got Miriam's so that he (now possessing the knowledge of all three plants) could then make as much gold as he wished. While Moses went without food for three days, Korah paraded about in worldly splendor. It is also said that there was never such rejoicing as at the birth of Korah because of his great fortune, and never such sorrow as at the birth of Jesus.[458]

Josephus also speaks of Korah's great wealth and his envy of Moses: "Korah, a Hebrew of principal account, both by his family and his wealth, one that was also able to speak well, and one that could easily persuade the people by his speeches, saw that Moses was in an exceeding great dignity, and was uneasy at it, and envied him on that account, (he was of the same tribe with Moses, and of kin to him,) and was particularly grieved, because he thought he better deserved that honorable post on account of his great riches, and not inferior to him in birth."[459]

In Talmudic tradition, Korah's wealth was given the following origin: "(Korah) had been the treasurer of Pharaoh [as in Surabadi], and possessed treasures so vast that he employed three hundred white mules to carry the keys of his treasures... when Joseph, during the lean years,

---

456 See Joseph, Part Two, VI.B. {In this series, in *Jacob and Joseph.*}

457 This contradicts the Quranic silence on the breaking of the tables of the law by Moses, but it entered the commentaries anyway; perhaps it was too good a story to pass over. The conflated nature of the accounts in the Pentateuch was of course unknown when Surabadi was writing. In this instance, two separate, somewhat different, versions of the same story found their way into *Exodus*, creating the erroneous impression that there were two deliveries of the tables of the law to Moses.

458 Surabadi, pp. 308-309.

459 Josephus, Antiquities, IV.2.2, p. 85.

through the sale of grain amassed great treasures, he erected three great buildings, one hundred cubits wide, one hundred cubits long, and one hundred cubits high, filled them with money and delivered them to Pharaoh, being too honest to leave even five silver shekels of this money to his children. Korah discovered one of these three treasuries."[460] Korah was the richest man who ever lived.[461]

The discovery of Joseph's treasure is the usual explanation given as the origin of Korah's immense wealth in Jewish tradition, and alchemy does not seem to be connected with it, as Surabadi would have it, but then Surabadi lived in a world preoccupied with the transformation of base metals to gold. If they had been successful, it would paradoxically have immediately made gold almost worthless. There is also mention of Miriam's husband in the Bible. In Jewish tradition, he was not Korah. She is sometimes said to have been the wife of Caleb of the tribe of Judah, or the clan of Kenizzites, thought to have been absorbed by Judah.[462]

The Quran uses the story of Korah, in its popular form well known to the Prophet and his contemporaries, as a parable on the folly of the arrogance of wealth and man's reliance upon the material. Its lesson is eternal, and we should avoid taking the story too literally. The Biblical purpose of the story was quite different, and is connected with the rather unedifying struggles between the Levites and Aaronites for supremacy in the Israelite priesthood, as is so much else in the extant Biblical version of the story of Moses.

Scholarly analysis of Num. 16 has identified two separate stories of rebellion in three different strata.[463] The oldest, from the JE conflated history, deals with the rebellion of Dathan and Abiram of the tribe of Reuben against the civil authority of Moses.[464] Impatient with the delay in reaching the land of milk and honey promised to them, they rebelled against Moses. Angered, Moses isolated them from the rest of Israel and prayed that they be swallowed up by the earth: "And as he finished speaking all these words, the ground under them split asunder; and the earth opened its mouth and swallowed them up..." (Num. 16:31-32a) "So they and all that belonged to them went down alive into Sheol; and the earth closed over them, and they perished from the midst of the

---

[460] LJ, III, 286.
[461] LJ, IV, 393.
[462] LJ, II, 253. In this view, Miriam and Caleb were counted among the ancestors of the house of David.
[463] Korah, DB, p. 560.
[464] It is to be found fragmented into Num. 16:1b-2a, 12-15, 25-26, 27b-32a, 33-34.

assembly. And all Israel that were round about them fled at their cry; for they said, 'Lest the earth swallow us up!'" (Num. 16:33-34) Thus, in the original version, Dathan and Abiram, and their families, were punished by being swallowed up for their rebellion against Moses' authority.

The story of Korah in this chapter is in two strata, both from the Priestly tradition.[465] In the first version, when the story probably stood independently, Korah and 250 leaders of the people contested the priestly authority of the Levites. They agreed to a trial by censers. Each man of the 250 plus Aaron and Moses appeared at the tent of the meeting with incense in his censer. "And the Lord said to Moses and Aaron, 'Separate yourselves from among this congregation, that I may consume them in a moment.' …And the fire came forth form the Lord, and consumed the two hundred and fifty men offering the incense.'" (Num. 16:20-21,35) In a sequel to this, a plague struck the people killing 14,700 (Num. 16:49). The superiority of the Aaronites was further demonstrated in the story of the rods (correctly introduced into the narrative of Korah by Surabadi, but in the wrong place) in which Aaron's rod sprouted branches (Num. 17).

Thus, the original version reflects a challenge to the special status of the Levites as the only priests acceptable to YHWH. In that version, Korah was destroyed by fire at the tent of meeting. The next step was the conflation of these two accounts of rebellion into one by another redactor of the Priestly school. In the process, he made certain additions.[466] In the resulting account, Korah became a co-conspirator with Dathan and Abiram at the head of 250 Levites against the religious monopoly of the Aaronites; or perhaps it was an intercollegiate struggle between the Zadokites and the Korahites who, despite this story of their progenitor, were in the Temple service in later times. In this edited version, Korah shared the fate of Dathan and Abiram and was swallowed up by the earth, while the 250 rebel Levites were consumed by fire. Num. 16 is an interesting example of the process that shaped the present text of the Bible. Although the Bible mentions the men and goods that belonged to Korah (Num. 16:32b), there is no emphasis upon his wealth. That was a later development of Jewish tradition. In this conflated form, it entered Arab oral tradition and supplied a parable for the Quran.

Surabadi mentions another incident leading up to the destruction of Korah. Prompted by his envy of Moses, Korah bribed a woman to stand up in the assembly and accuse Moses of having had carnal intercourse with her. But when she attended the assembly, she regretted

---

[465] It is to be found in Num. 16:1a, 2b-7a, 18-24, 27a, 32a, 35, 41-50, and ch. 17.
[466] Num. 16:7-11, 16-17, 36-40.

this arrangement, and instead of accusing Moses, she related Korah's proposal to the congregation. Moses complained to God that he could not tolerate this. God granted him power over the earth. Moses went to Korah, who had surrounded himself with all of his servants and dependents, and ordered the earth to swallow them up. When Korah had sunk to his head, Aaron rushed up and tried to save him as he was a relative, but Moses threatened him as well. Aaron turned aside, and Korah disappeared under the earth.[467]

This pericope seems to be in some way connected with the story of the sedition of Miriam and Aaron against a marriage of Moses: "Miriam and Aaron spoke against Moses because of the Cushite woman whom he had married, for he had married a Cushite woman..." (Num. 12:1) Why this act aroused such anger—other than that Cush was an African and we may presume that the woman was black or dark—we do not know. The punishment meted out to Miriam (she became leprous) seems unduly harsh if this was all there was to the story. (As usual Aaron escaped without any punishment.) As a result of Moses' prayer, she was cured after seven days (Num. 12:13-15).

Who was the Cushite woman? Some have proposed that she is the same as Zipporah, a Midianite. However, this identification meets this criticism: Why had not Miriam and Aaron objected to her earlier? There is a possibility that the Cushite is an error for Cushanite because Cushan (not Cush) was a tribe in Midian, but the obvious meaning that would have first occurred to the reader was that she was a woman of Cush; that is, Ethiopia.[468] More will be said about this in the Section L below.

Many of the developments in the story of Korah appear to be Islamic additions, as the story caught the imagination of the Muslim public from early times and his wealth became proverbial, as has the wealth of Croesus in the West. The differences between the Talmudic and Islamic traditions suggest that this embellishment took place without a great deal of dependence upon the form the Jewish traditions took, as the stories borrowed from or suggested by other Biblical passages indicate. The exaggerations of medieval Muslim exegetes have to some extent obscured the point of the Quranic parable.

---

[467] Surabadi, pp. 307-308.
[468] BC, II, 1180119; Cush, Cushan, Cushite, DB, pp. 194-195.

K. THE ISRAELITES AND THE COW

God commands you that ye sacrifice a cow. (Q. 2:67)

In this section, Surabadi relates at some length the story of an unsolved murder. During the time of Moses there was a rich Israelite named 'Amil (ᶜĀmīl) who had a daughter whom his nephew desired to marry. 'Amil would not agree to the match, as the lad was poor. The nephew developed a hatred for his uncle and plotted to kill him, seize his wealth, and then marry his daughter. By means of a ruse, telling his uncle that there was a merchant in a neighboring town who had received a large quantity of goods for sale, the nephew enticed 'Amil out of his own town where he killed him on the road. He then returned to town displaying the signs of mourning. No one was able to discover the killer. The people swore to accept blood money[469] and the people of both towns quarreled over the matter. Finally, they approached Moses and asked that he intercede with God so that He might reveal the culprit. In reply God said that they must find a cow which fitted a certain description, slaughter it, and strike the meat on the corpse of 'Amil, who would revive and reveal the identity of his murderer.[470]

Surabadi offers several versions of the purchase of the cow. In one, the only animal fitting the description belonged to a jewel merchant. The merchant was asleep and his son refused to awaken him. Finally, the Israelites were forced to agree to pay for the cow by filling its hide with gold. In another version, the same price had to be paid to a woman who had lost all of her herds to an epidemic, except one, which fitted the divine description. In still another version, the cow was the last remaining property of a widow with one pious son. She told him one day to go and bring the cow in, telling him that no one was to sit upon it. The boy found the cow and the animal invited him to ride her, but he remembered his mother's injunction and refused. Then Iblis came along feigning illness and asked to ride the cow, but once again, the boy refused. An angel came and tested him by trying to get him to sell the cow without his mother's consent. Again, he refused. Then the angel told

[469] That is, they agreed that they would not demand that the murderer be executed and would accept the blood money, or indemnity, for the crime. This was done in the hope that the murderer, fearing retribution, would confess and indemnify the victim's family.
[470] Surabadi, pp. 12-13.

him the Israelites would come and offer its hide filled with gold. And so it happened the next day.[471]

After securing the cow, they slaughtered it and struck the corpse of 'Amil with its flesh. He revived, as did the cow, and named his murderer. The cow confirmed his statement, and they both expired again.[472]

This story is offered by the Muslim commentators in explanation of the passage in Surah Baqarah[473] that gives the surah its name. It has two parts. This is the first part:

And when Moses said unto his people: "Lo, God commands you that ye sacrifice a cow." They said: "Dost thou make game of us?" He answered: "God forbid that I should be among the foolish!" they said: "Pray for us unto thy Lord that He make clear to us what (cow) she is." (Moses) said: "Lo, He says that she is a cow neither with calf nor immature; between the two conditions. So do that which ye are commanded." They said: "Pray ye for us unto thy Lord that He make clear to us of what color she is." (Moses) said: "Lo, He says that she is a yellow cow. Bright is her color, gladdening beholders." They said: "Pray for us unto thy Lord that He make clear what (cow) she is. Lo, cows are much alike to us; and lo, if God wills, we may be led aright." (Moses) said: "Lo, He says that she is a cow unyoked; she ploughs not the soil nor waters the tilth. Whole and without any mark." They said: "Now thou bringest the truth." So they sacrificed her, though they almost did not. (Q. 2:67-91)

Taken by itself, the passage is so similar to the sacrifice of the red heifer in *Numbers* that it is most likely connected with it. In that passage (from P), God told Moses and Aaron: "'This is the statute of the law which the Lord has commanded: Tell the people of Israel to bring thee a red heifer without defect, in which there is no blemish, and upon which a yoke has never come. And ye shall give her to Eleazar the priest, and she shall be taken outside the camp and slaughtered before him; and Eleazar the priest shall take some of her blood with his finger, and sprinkle some of her blood toward the front of the tent of meeting seven times. And the heifer shall be burned in his sight; her skin, her flesh, and her blood, with her dung, shall be burned; and the priest shall take cedarwood and hyssop and scarlet stuff, and cast them into the midst of the burning of the heifer.'" (Num. 19:2-6)

---

[471] Surabadi, pp. 13-15.

[472] Surabadi, pp. 15-16.

[473] *Baqarah* means *cow*.

There follow some instructions about the ritual purification of those involved in the slaughter of the heifer, then: "'And a man who is clean shall gather up the ashes of the heifer, and deposit them outside the camp in a clean place; and they shall be kept for the congregation of the people of Israel for the water of impurity, for the removal of sin.'" (Num. 19:9)

The remainder of the chapter explains the use of this "water of impurity" (it is to be prepared by mixing the ashes of the heifer with running water). Its purpose is to remove the ritual uncleanness caused by contact with the dead. "But the man who is unclean and does not cleanse himself, that person shall be cut off from the midst of the assembly, since he has defiled the sanctuary of the Lord; because the water of impurity has not been thrown upon him, he is unclean." (Num. 19:20)[474]

As they stand in the Quranic text, the verses quoted above (Q. 2:67-71) form a complete unit. The purpose of the text, considered as a self-contained unit, would then become a perhaps wry criticism of the excessive nit-picking of rabbinical writings, of which the red heifer is cited as an example. A tractate of the Talmud (*Parah* of the *Order Tohorot*) is devoted to the Red Heifer, and its qualifications were so elaborated by the rabbis that, according to Rabbi Nisin, no one had been able to find such a cow since the days of Moses.[475] In the pestering questions of the Israelites in their dialogue with Moses, there is more than a hint of satire, as the Israelites keep trying to find an excuse for not making the sacrifice.

In order to tie the above into Surabadi's story of murder, one most read the following two verses with them: *And (remember) when ye slew a man and disagreed concerning it and God brought forth that which ye were hiding. And We said: "Smite him with some of it. Thus God brings the dead to life and shows you His portents so that ye may understand.* (Q. 2:72-73)

These verses are extraordinarily difficult. How the story of 'Amil developed from them is easy to see. Nevertheless, the verses do not necessarily support the interpretation of the commentators. The order of

---

[474] Jewish tradition gives further details about the use of the red heifer's ashes and the practice was continued throughout the ages: "Although, beside this one, a number of other red heifers were provided in future generations, this one was distinguished by having its ashes kept forever, which, mingled with the ashes of other red heifers, were always used for the purification of Israel." *Mishna Parah* also states that from the time of Moses until the Second Temple nine such heifers were furnished. The tenth will be supplied by the Messiah. (LJ, III, 216; VI, 79.)

[475] Cited by MMA, Quran-MMA, and p. 33.

events is: 1, a murder committed by three or more persons[476]; 2, a dispute concerning the crime, not necessarily over the identity of the murderer; 3, a parenthetical expression stating that God is the revealer of what they had concealed; 4, the divine order to strike something (the corpse?) with something (a part of the cow?); 5, a general statement that may be allegorical that God resurrects the dead (plural).

A passage in the Bible cited in connection with these two verses is found in *Deuteronomy*. It describes the rites of absolution in the case of finding a person whose slayer is unknown. "'If in the land which Lord God gives thee to possess, any one is found slain, lying in the open country, and it is not known who killed him, then thy elders and thy judges shall come forth, and they shall measure the distance to the cities which are around him that is slain; and the elders of the city which is nearest to the slain man shall take a heifer which has never worked and which has not pulled the yoke. And the elders of that city shall bring the heifer down to a valley with running water, which is neither ploughed nor sown, and shall break the heifer's neck there in the valley." (Deut. 21:1-4)

"And the priests of the sons of Levi shall come forward, for the Lord thy God has chosen them to minister to Him and to bless in the name of the Lord, and by their word every dispute and every assault shall be settled. And all the elders of that city nearest to the slain man shall wash their hands over the heifer whose neck was broken in the valley; and they shall testify, 'Our hands did not shed this blood, neither did our eyes see it shed. Forgive, O lord, Thy people Israel, whom Thou hast redeemed, and set not the guilt of innocent blood in the midst of Thy people Israel; but let the guilt of blood be forgiven them.' So thou shall purge the guilt of innocent blood from your midst, when thou shalt do what is right in the sight of the Lord." (Deut. 21:5-9)

Q. 2:72-73 seems to refer to a story well known among the Hejazi Arabs. Is it the story that Surabadi has given us, linking both passages of the Quran? If it is unconnected with the preceding verses, it is not even certain that the addressees are Israelites. Maulana Muhammad Ali denies any connection between the two parts, but Surabadi and other commentators plainly thought there was such a link, as the story of 'Amil shows. Indeed, if one interprets the verses about the killing to mean an unsolved crime, then the dependence is certain. The Quran in the first part makes no reference to the rites of burning the heifer and mixing the ashes with water to make the "water of impurity," as in *Numbers*.

---

[476] The Quran uses the plural "ye slew."

On the other hand, no color is specified in the case of the unsolved murder, whilst it is in the case of the heifer whose ashes are to be used to remove ritual uncleanness. In this respect, the passage is closer to *Deuteronomy* than *Numbers*. Maulana Muhammad Ali denies a connection and suggests that Q. 2:72-73 is a reference to the attempted crucifixion of Jesus.[477] He makes the feminine pronoun *hā* translated here as "it" in the phrase "some of it" a reference to the act of killing rather than the cow. Not very many have followed him in this explanation. He also denies any relationship between these passages and the Biblical passage in *Numbers* above and that in *Deuteronomy* below.

It is conceivable that the two Quranic verses refer to this aspect of the sacrifice, that is, as a dispute over the purification procedure after a killing and the resultant uncleanness therewith created. *Thus God brings the dead to life* would therefore be a metaphor for the removal of the uncleanness and rejoining the community. Against this interpretation is the fact that the object of "smite" appears to be the corpse, not the perpetrators of the crime. (*Jalalayn* says that it was struck with the tongue or tail of a cow, bringing the corpse to life to identify his assassins.[478]) The passage seems to be a reference to some well-known circumstance, now lost. Again, it may be completely independent of the preceding parable of the heifer and simply deriding extremes of scrupulousness. Whatever the basis of the second part, its point seems to be a parable of resurrection and the omniscience of God, not just the disclosure of a murderer.

It must also be noted that neither Biblical passage is concerned with the solution of an unsolved murder. *Numbers* is only concerned with the removal of ritual impurity caused by contact with the dead, while *Deuteronomy* is concerned with the removal of bloodguilt from a community created by an unknown killer. In the Quran, the same people who were responsible for the death are told to perform the action of striking the corpse (?) with something, and the whole is seen as a proof of God's ability to resurrect the dead, perhaps in this case for the slain man to name his killers, as Surabadi would have it. In the Quran, they are known to God, but not to man. Indeed, the circumstances may not be homicide, but an accidental death and some expiatory ritual connected with it. The problem remains unresolved. *And God knows best.*

---

[477] Quran-MMA, pp. 33-35.
[478] Jalalayn, p. 11.

L. THE JOURNEY OF MOSES

"I will not give up until I reach the point where the two seas meet..." (Q. 18:60)

Our edition of the Quranic Stories from the Commentary of Surabadi does not include an account of Moses' journey to the "meeting of the two seas." In view of its importance in the story of Moses and the considerable controversy that surrounds it, we feel obliged to examine it, however briefly. Although it probably relates to his youth in Egypt, before the flight to Midian, we place it here as a kind of appendix, so as not to interrupt the traditional, Biblical sequence of events. We shall begin with Quranic version. This is found in Surah al-Kahf and belongs to the Makkan period. Other details for the amplified Islamic version will be drawn from Bal'ami's account.[479] Some commentators, as Bal'ami notes, have suggested that this story is not about the Moses of the Exodus, but another, one Moses the son of Manasseh the son of Joseph, but this is not the prevailing view.[480] In his history, Bal'ami places this story after the destruction of the Egyptians in the Red Sea and before the rebellion of Korah.

The story in the Quran begins thus: *And when Moses said unto his servant: "I will not give up until I reach the point where the two seas meet, though I march on for ages."* (Q. 18:60)[481] Bal'ami explains that his companion was Joshua the son of Nun and the place of the meeting of the two seas was three days journey from Egypt. The geographical directions he gives seem to point to some place in the Gulf of Oman or the Arabian Sea.[482]

And when they reached the point where the two met, they forgot their fish, and it took its way into the waters, being free. And when they had gone further, he said to the servant: "Bring us our breakfast. We

---

[479] Bal'ami, I, pp. 461-477. Because of the extensive elaboration of this story in Islamic tradition, which would entail a separate volume in itself to do the material justice, we shall generally confine ourselves to the parallels and sources of the Quranic version, supplementing it only with details from Bal'ami that are closely related to the original Quranic text.

[480] Bal'ami, I, p. 462. There is no Moses among the sons of Manasseh listed in the Bible. The closest to "Moses" in form, and not very close at that, would be Machir, who settled east of the Jordan.

[481] This verse always reminds us of Alfred Lord Tennyson's *Ulysses*: "I cannot rest from travel; I will drink life to the lees...To sail beyond the sunset... To strive, to seek, to find, and not to yield."

[482] Bal'ami, I, pp. 467-468.

have truly found fatigue in this our journey." (Q. 18:61-62) In Bal'ami, the fish had swum away and the waters parted, leaving land in the middle upon which the fish sat.[483] The sudden introduction of the fish (see below) in this passage, without preamble, is proof that the story that forms the basis of the parable was already well known to its early 7th-century CE Arab audience.

He said: "Didst thou see, when we took refuge on the rock, and I forgot the fish—none but Satan caused me to forget to mention it—it took its way into the waters by a marvel." He said: "This is that which we have been seeking." So they retraced their steps again. (Q. 18:63-64) Bal'ami says that Moses and Joshua followed the fish back to the rock.[484]

They found one of Our servants, unto whom We had given mercy from Us, and had taught him knowledge from Our presence. (Q. 18:65) Bal'ami identifies this servant as Khidr.[485]

Moses said unto him: "May I follow thee, to the end that thou mayest teach me right conduct of that which thou hast been taught?" Said he: "Lo, thou canst not bear with me patiently. How canst thou bear with that whereof thou hast never encompassed in thy knowledge?" (Moses) said: "Thou shalt find me, God willing, patient and I shall not rebel against thee in anything." Said he: "Well, if thou go with me, ask me not concerning anything till I myself mention it unto thee." (Q. 18:66-70)

From this point on Moses and the "servant of God" seem to be by themselves; no further mention is made of Moses' traveling companion, and the verbs in the Quranic text are dual.[486] We are left to speculate as to whether he was with them or not. The nature of the following events and the absence of any response or comment by the former companion suggest that he was not a participant in them. The first of the mysterious incidents to follow the servant of God's agreement to let Moses accompany him was his holing of the boat in which they had set out (Q. 18:71-73). Moses was astonished. Forgetting his promise not to question anything the servant of God did, he asked about it. *(The servant of God) said: "Did I not say unto thee that thou couldst never bear with me?"* (Q. 18:72)

---

[483] Bal'ami, I, p. 468.

[484] Bal'ami, I, p. 470.

[485] Bal'ami, I, p. 470.

[486] We remind the reader that classical Arabic has three "numbers": singular, dual, and plural (three or more). This is reflected in the conjugations of verbs and the declensions of nouns and adjectives.

They went on and met a boy whom the servant of God slew (Q. 74-76). Once again, Moses forgot his promise and asked, using words of condemnation, the meaning of the act. *He said: "Did I not say unto thee that thou couldst never bear with me?"*

Nevertheless, he accepted Moses' renewed promise that he would not repeat his behavior. They went on until they reached a town that refused them hospitality. Nonetheless, the servant of God stopped to repair a wall that was on the point of collapsing. Once again, Moses forgot his promise and commented upon the servant of God's action (Q. 18:77). *Said (the servant of God): This is the parting between me and thee! Now I shall tell thee the interpretation of that thou couldst not bear with patience. As for the ship, it belonged to poor people working on the sea, and I wished to mar it, for there was a king behind them who was taking every ship by force."* (Q. 18:78-79) Bal'ami relates that the king was Mandal bin Khaland al-Azdi of Antioch in Syria.[487]

"As for the lad, his parents were believers and we feared lest he should oppress them by rebellion and disbelief. And we intended that their Lord should change him for them for one better in purity and nearer to mercy." (Q. 18:80) Bal'ami observes that the boy was a secret idolator.[488]

"As for the wall, it belonged to two orphan boys in the city, and there was beneath it a treasure belonging to them, and their father had been righteous, and thy Lord intended that they should come to their full strength and should bring forth their treasure as a mercy from their Lord. I did it not at my (own) bidding. Such is the interpretation of that wherewith thou couldst not bear." (Q. 18:81-82)

Bal'ami adds that the treasure was a golden tablet upon which were written five lines in the manner of Wisdom: "I wonder at him who is certain to die and rejoices. I wonder at him who is certain of merit and is lazy. I wonder at him who is certain of retribution yet disobeys. I wonder at him who is certain of sustenance yet seeks it. I wonder at him who is certain of the world and its perishing, yet relies upon it." After Khidr [for Bal'ami identifies him as Khidr, see below] had finished speaking, he vanished and Moses and Joshua (who has rejoined Moses) returned to the Israelites.[489]

This is the Quranic version of this story with the comparatively restrained additions of a reputable commentator. The elaborations seem

---

487 Bal'ami, I, pp. 474-475. The word translated as "sea" (*baḥr*) could also mean "large river."

488 Bal'ami, I, p. 475.

489 Bal'ami, I, pp. 476-477.

to be in the direction of treating the parables as history rather than as moral lessons that emphasize the necessity of trusting in the plan of God in preference to our own shortsightedness. "The Lord moves in mysterious ways his purposes to accomplish" is the spirit of this passage. No personal names are used except that of Moses, and that but twice. Treating it as literal history, explaining everything, giving the characters names, and introducing extraneous figures and events, as the commentators were wont to do, detracts from the deceptive simplicity and directness which harbor many layers of lessons for believers.

However, there is nothing in the Biblical story of Moses that even closely resembles this. It has a visionary quality, but it does not seem to be related to any of the several accounts of ascensions by Moses to heaven or the revelations of the workings of the universe in the apocalyptic spectacles to be found in later Judaeo-Christian religious writings. But, as we shall see, some of the material for the framework of the story in this episode has an ancestry that once again takes us back to ancient Babylonia. How that became part of the oral tradition of the Hejazi Arabs in the 6th and 7th centuries CE is uncertain; possibly it coalesced earlier with another tradition about the expedition of Moses to Ethiopia not found in the Bible, but attested in Hellenistic literature as early as Artapanus, writing in the 1st century BCE. This story seems to have been an alternative explanation of the cause of Moses' flight to Midian; at least it precedes it in those versions.

Artapanus, tells us: "Chenephres,[490] the husband of Moses' foster-mother, became envious of Moses, and sought to slay him on some plausible pretext. And so when the Ethiopians invaded Egypt, Chenephres sent Moses in command of a force against them, and enrolled a body of husbandmen for him, hoping that through the weakness of his troops, Moses would be easily destroyed by the enemy. Moses, however, was victorious in his campaign that lasted ten years, and on account of his excellence even the Ethiopians became so fond of him that they learned from him the custom of circumcision. Moses built a city as quarters for his vast army, and therein he consecrated the ibis, because this bird destroys the animals that are noxious to man. When Moses returned to Egypt, he was welcomed by Chenephres, who in reality continued to plot against him."

This narrative is followed by the circumstances leading to Moses' seeking refuge in Midian.[491] So, here we have the tradition of

---

[490] Chenephres is called the king of Memphis (LJ, V, 398), a longtime capital of Egypt, situated about fifteen miles south of Cairo, on the left bank of the Nile.
[491] Quoted in LJ, V, 407.

Moses' making an expedition, the frame of the Quranic story, already well established.

In Josephus, too, Moses' expedition to Ethiopia takes place in his youth, before his flight to Midian. The circumstances leading up to the participation of Moses in the expedition are somewhat different. In Josephus' account, the Ethiopians had invaded Egypt from the south and proceeded as far north as Memphis and in places had even reached the (Mediterranean) sea. The Egyptian forces were crushed and the priests consulted their oracles for divine advice. The oracles, directed by God, answered that the Egyptians were to put Moses in command of the army. Moses had been protected from his enemies at the court of Pharaoh by his foster-mother, the princess Thermuthis. When approached by the leaders of Egypt to let them have Moses, she refused to release him until they swore to do him no harm.

"So Moses, at the persuasion both of Thermuthis and the King himself, cheerfully undertook the business: and the sacred scribes of both nations were glad: those of the Egyptians, that they should at once overcome their enemies by his valour, and that by the same piece of management Moses would be slain; but those of the Hebrews, that they should escape from the Egyptians, because Moses was to be their general; but Moses prevented the enemies, and took and led his army before those enemies were apprised of his attacking them, for he did not march by the river, but by land...

"When he had therefore proceeded thus on his journey, he came upon the Ethiopians before they expected him; and, joining battle with them, he beat them and deprived them of the hopes they had of success against the Egyptians, and went on in overthrowing their cities, and indeed made a great slaughter of the Ethiopians."

Victory heartened the Egyptians and Josephus describes further success under Moses' generalship: "Now when the Egyptian army had once tasted of this prosperous success, by the means of Moses, they did not slacken their diligence, insomuch that the Ethiopians were in danger of being reduced to slavery, and all sorts of destruction; and at length they retired to Saba, which was the royal city of Ethiopia, which Cambyses[492] afterwards named Meroe,[493] after the name of his own sister.

"The place was to be besieged with very great difficulty, since it was both encompassed by the Nile quite round, and the other rivers, Astapus and Astaboras, made it a very difficult thing for such as

---

492 Cambyses, the Persian king who conquered Egypt c. 525 BCE.

493 Meroe was the Nubian capital located on the Nile between the 5th and 6th cataracts, some 40 miles south of Atbara in Sudan.

attempted to pass over them: for the city was situate in a retired place, and was inhabited after the manner of an island, being encompassed with a strong wall, and having the rivers to guard them from their enemies, and having great ramparts between the wall and the rivers, insomuch, that when the waters come with the greatest violence it can never be drowned; which ramparts make it next to impossible for even such as are gotten over the rivers to take the city."[494]

Where arms will not succeed, passion often does, as Josephus continues the story: "However, while Moses was uneasy at the army's lying idle, (for the enemies durst not come to battle,) this accident happened:—Tharbis was the daughter of the king of the Ethiopians: she happened to see Moses as he led the army near the walls, and fought with great courage; and admiring the subtlety of his undertakings, and believing him to be the author of the Egyptians' success, when they had before despaired of recovering their liberty, and to be the occasion of the great danger the Ethiopians were in, when they had before boasted of their great achievements, she fell deeply in love with him; and upon the prevalency of that passion, sent to him the most faithful of all her servants to discourse with him about marriage. He thereupon accepted the offer, on condition she would procure the delivering up of the city, and gave her the assurance of an oath to taker her to his wife; and that when he had once taken possession of the city, he would not break his oath to her. No sooner was the agreement made, but it took effect immediately; and when Moses had cut off the Ethiopians, he gave thanks to god, and consummated his marriage, and led the Egyptians back to their own land."[495]

This is all that Josephus tells us about the matter, but in it he adds to Artapanus' notice about Moses' leading an expedition up the Nile into Cush/Ethiopia, and he puts Moses in the vicinity of the confluence of two great rivers. Josephus' geographical details seem to be based upon Diodorus, who also describes Meroe as an island and attributes its founding to Cambyses. The legend of the Island of Meroe seems to be derived from the fact that the region of Nubia, of which Meroe is the center, is bounded by southwest by the Blue Nile, on the northwest by the Nile and on the northeast by the Atbara, the Astaboras of Josephus.[496]

---

[494] The rivers mentioned flow from Ethiopia, the Astapus into the Astaboras (the modern Atbara) and then into the Nile 40 miles above Meroe. No perennial rivers flow into the Nile after the Atbara. See text below.

[495] Josephus, Antiquities, II.10.2, p. 58.

[496] Shinnie, p. 16.

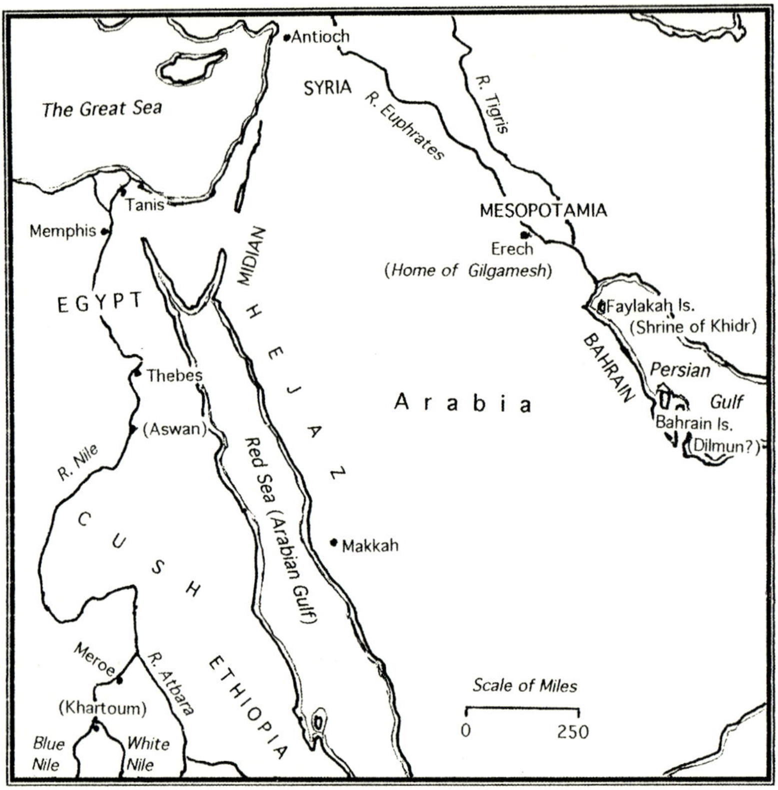

PLACES MENTIONED IN THE *JOURNEY OF MOSES*

There are two major junctions of rivers in the Sudan, that of the Blue and White Niles at modern Khartoum, the other being the meeting of the Nile and the Atbara at Atbara. One of these may lie behind the tradition of Moses and the meeting of the seas (large rivers). If, indeed, Josephus' story be related to it at all, it would be no great stretch to suppose that Moses traversed the entire country, as far as these confluences, of which the locals would surely have informed him.

These characteristics of the story can also be found in the Quranic pericope: the idea of the journey itself, the meeting of the two waters, and the youth of Moses. The Quranic story is redolent of youth, of the incipient prophet being taught the ways of God. The expedition of Moses to Ethiopia in Artapanus and Josephus is the first major incident of his adult life, although not mentioned in the Bible. Furthermore, Josephus' more detailed version, though later than Artapanus', presupposes a much longer history of transmission, as he did not invent stories for his *Antiquities*, but preserved many extra-Biblical traditions that would other wise have been lost, much as the Quran preserves and refers to otherwise lost Arab lore.

The Talmud ignores Moses' journey, and the earliest notice in rabbinic literature is in the *Targum Yerushalmi* of the 7th and 8th centuries CE. Because of its conflict with the text of the Pentateuch, it does not seem to have received much attention until medieval times, when it attracted considerable elaboration (perhaps prompted by Muslim interest in the Quranic story): After the death of the king of Ethiopia Quqanos, Moses was crowned king and married the widow of the former king, Adoniah. (Artapanus made no mention of a wife, though Josephus did.) But because it was not seemly for a Jew to cohabit with a non-Jewish woman, he refrained from having sexual relations with her (contradicting Josephus who explicitly says that Moses consummated the marriage). Eventually, after forty years, she complained of this, and the Ethiopians selected another king in his place and sent him away with presents.[497]

As have already noted, the Bible knows nothing of this episode in the life of Moses, but then it is silent about Moses' "lost years" as an Egyptian princeling until he killed the Egyptian, an act which precipitated his flight to Midian. However, the complaint of Aaron and Miriam about the Cushite woman whom Moses had married may have a connection with this story: "Miriam and Aaron spoke against Moses because of the Cushite woman whom he had married, for he had married a Cushite woman." (Num. 12:1) This sedition resulted in Miriam's leprosy, as we have noted above.[498] The presence of this Cushite woman that excited this protest is one of the mysteries of the Bible. This tradition may be its solution.

To the ancient Egyptians, Cush meant the territory south of the first cataract of the Nile, near the modern Aswan, and though the name is usually translated as Ethiopia, Nubia (the modern northern Sudan), with a general extension to the Horn of Africa, would be a better equivalent. This is the usual meaning of the name in the Bible, but the Table of Nations appears to locate the descendants of Cush in southern and central Arabia, a possible confusion with the Kassites or Cossaeans. In one place, a tribe called Cushan is associated with Midian (Hab. 3:7). It is also known that there were Cushite slaves in both Egypt and Palestine.[499]

---

[497] LJ, II, 286-289.

[498] See Section J above.

[499] Cush, DB, pp. 194-195; Cushite, DB, p. 195.

Jewish tradition frequently identifies this Cushite woman with Zipporah, the daughter of Jethro whom Moses married during his first stay in Midian, but modern scholars favor the view that they were not identical, and that the Cushite was probably of Nubian/Sudanese origin.[500] We do not know whether the story of Moses' journey was suggested by the verse in *Numbers*, or whether both are related to some tradition of Moses' participation in an Egyptian military expedition to the south. Such expeditions were not uncommon during the period of the Egyptian New Empire, although the Ethiopians did not invade Egypt successfully until the middle of the 8th century BCE when they founded the XXVth Dynasty. The Cushite woman may have been married by Moses in some other circumstance.

Could Moses have made such a journey? Certainly. Such travel was possible in his era. Is there evidence that he did? Just the Arab tradition remembered in the Quran, and the tantalizing paragraphs of Artapanus and Josephus. As it was feasible and could have occurred whilst he was in Midian, we may choose to believe that he did—or we may read the story as a parable. There is no evidence, other than the Bible, that Abraham lived and journeyed from Ur to Canaan, but most of us accept his reality. For our purposes, the historicity of Moses' expedition is perhaps not so important as is the question: How did these traditions travel to Arabia? In the centuries between Josephus' evidence and that of the Quran, there was ample opportunity for the creative aspect of oral transmission to do its work and for other traditions to coalesce about a basic tradition of Moses' journey to a distant and somewhat mysterious land, where the two seas met.

In Arabia at least, more traditions, this time from Mesopotamia and the Persian Gulf also collected about Moses in pre-Islamic times, as the nature of the necklace of parables in the Quran demonstrates. The text of the Bible itself proves that traditions of great antiquity have survived in oral transmission. Generally, there is a subtle process of editing; oral tradition is a growing organism until petrified by writing.

Something of this sort may have occurred in Arabia with the reputation of Moses. The Hejazi Jews had probably heard of the journey of Moses, though in the absence of strong confirmation this can only be a guess. Moses himself was not unknown in the Arabian Peninsula, and none of the varied ingredients in the story of Moses' journey appear to have been startling or new, though of course as with any old story, some may have been hearing if for the first time in its Quranic version. The

[500] Ethiopian Woman, DB, p. 273.

journey itself does not seem to have been unfamiliar. There was already a tradition in circulation linking Moses with the meeting of the seas.

But in Arabian version, perhaps the tradition of another powerful figure from past became mingled with that of Moses. This conflated version may have become the basis for the parables in the Quran. The tradition was of the young Moses on his way to becoming a prophet, the journey a mystical excursion with its lessons about the obscure manner in which divine providence fulfills its aims. It fitted into the period when Moses was in Egypt, before the Exodus and his taking up the burden of leading the fractious and often unwilling Israelites out of captivity and delivering the Law that turned them into the people of YHWH. In the Quran, too, in this story, Moses seems to be a young man; he has the impatient curiosity of youth. There are the three elements in common between the Quranic story and that of Josephus: the journey itself, the confluence of the waters, and youth.

Where do the other elements come from? The reader may recall references to and excerpts from the ancient *Epic of Gilgamesh* in the story of the Creation and that of Noah and the Flood. {In this series, discussed in *From the Creation to the Flood.*} This epic assumed literary shape in Sumerian times and, in its (Semitic) Akkadian recensions, achieved wide circulation in the ancient Near East, contributing directly and indirectly to what later became the Yahwist and Priestly histories of the world before Moses, as found in the *Genesis.*

Much of the *Epic of Gilgamesh* has to do with search and wandering. Gilgamesh and his companion Enki traveled westward in search of adventure. When they returned to Erech,[501] the goddess Ishtar attempted unsuccessfully to seduce the hero Gilgamesh. Furious, she persuaded another god to create the Bull of Heaven, which was supposed to wreak havoc upon Gilgamesh's people. Instead, Gilgamesh killed it, and the gods decided that for this act Enki [not Gilgamesh!] must die. Struck by the reality of death for the first time, Gilgamesh set out alone to find his ancestor Utnapishtim [the Mesopotamian Noah], the only mortal who had been granted immortality. After many more adventures, Gilgamesh found him in a place called Dilmun [Eden?]. Utnapishtim taught him how to find the plant at the bottom of the sea that bestowed immortality.[502]

---

[501] Erech, or Uruk (the modern Warka), lies about 150 miles NW of Basrah (Iraq) near the Euphrates River. Once the largest city in Mesopotamia (and probably the entire world), it was founded in the 5th millennium BCE. (Erech, CE, p. 666; et al.)
[502] Hooke, pp. 36, 37, 49-55.

Although there are other epics involving travel and wandering in ancient literature, the *Odyssey* perhaps the most famous, this one seems to stand in some sort of a relationship to the story of Moses in the Quran and the "immortal" man. In addition to the theme of the journey, we also have a traveling companion (Enki = Joshua in Bal'ami?) for part of the story, though missing in much of it.[503] There is also the figure of wise man. In the Quran, he and Moses travel together for a while (during the three "lessons"), whilst in the *Epic of Gilgamesh* he is the goal of Gilgamesh's journey. There is an atmosphere of the marvelous in both stories, and the goal of the journey is knowledge, but in the Quran, it is the knowledge of the workings of God, whilst for Gilgamesh it is the secret of eternal life to be found in Dilmun.

And Dilmun is believed to be Bahrain.[504] The Arabic name, *Baḥrayn*, meaning "two seas," has always been a bit of a mystery.

The ancient Mesopotamians believed that there were two seas: one sweet, the other salt, and the sweet water underlay the salt water. Their separation was the first step in creation, which the Babylonians conceived to have been the replacement of chaos by order.[505] We have also seen how the Babylonian paradise at first possessed everything except sweet water, which the sun god Utu provided by causing it to well up from under the earth.[506] This still occurs in a startling fashion around Bahrain. The undersea freshwater springs were for centuries the principle source of drinking water for the island.

Bahrain—the name originally applied to the adjacent coastal region of modern Saudi Arabia as well, as its waters shared the same characteristics—does not stand at the junction of any geographical bodies of water as a glance at a map of the Persian Gulf will show. Yet, Bahrain, according to a belief of the greatest antiquity, was located at the junction of two seas: the salt sea on the surface and the sweet sea that lay beneath earth. The sweet sea came to the surface around that fortunate island, and mingled, or "met": the "meeting of the two seas." There is probably no need to look further for the source of the Quranic phrase.[507]

---

[503] Wensinck, writing in SEI, has apparently forgotten about Enki when he states: "The figure of the travelling companion is not connected with the Gilgamesh Epic." (Khadir, SEI, p. 232.) It is true that Gilgamesh was not along in this part of the epic, but he was very much present in the Sumerian hero's earlier adventures, and it was his death that prompted Gilgamesh to go upon his quest.

[504] See Part One, II, C. {In this series, in *From the Creation to the Flood.*}

[505] See Part One, I. {In this series, in *From the Creation to the Flood.*}

[506] See Part One, II, C. {In this series, in *From the Creation to the Flood.*}

[507] Bibby-Dilmun, p. 236-238.

Whether this meeting of the branches of the Nile in the story of Moses and the meeting of the two "seas" at Dilmun/Bahrain in the *Epic of Gilgamesh* are related is not easy to say. Probably, the Arabic Bahrain is the latest translation of a name meaning "two seas" that has been applied to the area from ancient times. Geoffrey Bibby even speculates that the word Dilmun itself may have originally meant "two seas."[508]

The distance from Lower Egypt (if that is taken as the starting point for Moses' journey) to the region of Bahrain is shorter than the distance up the Nile to the confluence of the Atbara and the Nile. If the journey is associated with his religious conversion in Midian and began there, it would be even shorter. Such journeys were not unusual and the Midians were experienced traders, traveling throughout the region. If such a trip lies behind the tradition of the journey, then it would be another point of contact between Moses and the Prophet who is reported have accompanied caravans to Syria in his youth, broadening his own experience thereby.

All of this is striking enough, but there is another point of contact: the Quranic figure of the "servant of God" with whom Moses traveled in search of knowledge. This servant is identified with the mysterious figure of Khidr by the strongest Muslim tradition. Khidr is not mentioned in the Quran by name; this may indicate that he was not meant to be an historical figure per se. In any case, in popular tradition, Khidr is immortal[509]; in the *Epic of Gilgamesh*, Utnapishtim is immortal. Utnapishtim is associated with Dilmun-Bahrain and the saint Khidr has a shrine of unknown age (though presumably Islamic in its present form) on the small island of Faylakah off the coast of Kuwait, at the northern end of the classical Bahrain.[510] According to local traditions, Khidr was the companion of Moses. He normally resides at Karbala,[511] but on Tuesdays he flies to the Island of Faylakah where he spends the night. Petitioners often spend that night at the shrine.[512] In the *Epic of Gilgamesh*, Utnapishtim is called "Exceeding Wise."[513] Is this not reminiscent of the Quranic description (Q. 18:65) of the servant as one to whom "God had taught knowledge"?

---

[508] Bibby-Dilmun, p. 238.

[509] Khidr, or perhaps more properly *Khaḍir*, means "green," the color signifying eternal life.

[510] Bibby-Dilmun, p. 238.

[511] Karbala is located by the Euphrates River, about 120 miles NW of the site of Gilgamesh's home city of Erech.

[512] Bibby-Dilmun, p. 195.

[513] ANE, I, p. 71.

The incident of fish is a still bit of a puzzlement; besides Bal'ami's story, some commentators have also allegorized it. There is the suggestion that it may be traced to the *Alexander Romance*, which is itself indebted to the *Epic of Gilgamesh*, substituting Alexander for Gilgamesh, and considerably elaborating the story of Alexander's quest for the spring of eternal life, but the connection with the Quranic fish is tenuous.[514]

That the quest for eternal life, the theme of the latter part of the *Epic of Gilgamesh* as well as the *Alexander Romance*, is not hinted at in the Quranic version is further evidence of a selective union of the features of one story or another in the fashioning of the extended parable. One may adduce a story circulating before the time of the Prophet with the features of the pericope in the Quran, but probably without the three tests. Clearly, at some point in pre-Islamic times, the traditions drawn from those that went into the Gilgamesh and Alexander stories became conflated with the tradition of the journey of Moses. However, if the story as it was known in the Hejaz had simply contained these elements, it would not have earned notice in the Quran. They are interesting, but their entertainment value far exceeds their moral value.

The reason for the story's inclusion in the Quran is the unique twist given to it as a parable in patience and trust in the wisdom of God; that is, the episode of the three tests. We now return to Jewish literature. There is a fable about one Joshua ben Levi who accompanied the prophet Elijah on a trip in which there were incidents similar to these in the Quran. There are four tests instead of the three in the Quran. It is worthwhile to quote the story in full:

"Among the many and various teachings dispensed by Elijah to his friends, there are none so important as his theodicy, the teachings vindicating God's justice in the administration of earthly affairs. He used many an opportunity to demonstrate it by precept and example. Once he granted his friend Rabbi Joshua ben Levi the fulfillment of any wish he might express, and all the Rabbi asked for was, that he might be permitted to accompany Elijah on his wanderings through the world. Elijah was prepared to gratify this wish. He only imposed the condition, that, however odd the Rabbi might think Elijah's actions, he was not to

---

[514] Khadir, SEI, p. 232. On the fantastic journey Alexander came upon a river: "And there were... many kinds of fish which were cooked not by fire but rather by cold spring water. For one of the soldiers washed one in cold water, put it in a pan and left it, and then he found the fish cooked in the pan. And an hour after he had tried this, he showed it to the others." (PseudoCal, p. 114.)

ask any explanation of them. If ever he demanded why, they would have to part company."

As in the Quran, in this story we find the condition of trust imposed upon the accompanier.

"So Elijah and the Rabbi fared forth together, and they journeyed on until the reached the house of a poor man, whose only earthly possession was a cow. The man and his wife were thorough good-hearted people, and the received the two wanderers with a cordial welcome. They invited the strangers into their house, set before them food and drink of the best they had, and made up a comfortable couch for them for the night."

"When Elijah and the Rabbi were ready to continue their journey on the following day, Elijah prayed that the cow belonging to his host might die. Before they left the house, the animal had expired. Rabbi Joshua was so shocked by the misfortune that had befallen the good people, he almost lost consciousness. He thought: 'Is that to be the poor man's reward for all his kind services to us?'

"And he could not refrain from putting the question to Elijah. But Elijah reminded him of the condition imposed and accepted at the beginning of their journey, and they travelled on, the Rabbi's curiosity unappeased." This test is not found in the Quranic story.

"That night they reached the house of a wealthy man, who did not pay his guests the courtesy of looking them in the face. Though they passed the night under his roof, he did not offer them food or drink. This rich man was desirous of having a wall repaired that had tumbled down. There was no need for him to take any steps to have it rebuilt, for, when Elijah left the house, he prayed that the wall might erect itself, and lo! it stood upright. Rabbi Joshua was greatly amazed, but true to his promise he suppressed the question that rose to his lips." This of course resembles one of the tests in the Quranic pericope.

"So the two travelled on again, until they reached an ornate synagogue, the seats in which were made of silver and gold. But the worshippers did not correspond in character to the magnificence of the building, for when it came to the point of satisfying the needs of the way-worn pilgrims, one of those present said: 'There is no dearth of water and bread, and the strange travellers can stay in the synagogue, whither these refreshments can be brought to them.'

"Early the next morning, when they were departing, Elijah wished those present in the synagogue in which they had lodged, that God might raise them all to 'heads.' Rabbi Joshua again had to exercise great self-restraint, and not put into the words the question that troubled him profoundly." This has no equivalent in the Quranic story.

"In the next town, they were received with great affability, and served abundantly with all their tired bodies craved. On these kind hosts Elijah, on leaving, bestowed the wish that God might give them but a single head. Now the Rabbi could not hold himself in check any longer, and he demanded an explanation of Elijah's freakish actions. Elijah consented to clear up his conduct for Joshua before they separated from each other. He spoke as follows:

"'The poor man's cow was killed, because I knew that on the same day the death of his wife had been ordained in heaven, and I prayed to god to accept the loss of the poor man's property as a substitute for the poor man's wife.

"'As for the rich man, there was a treasure hidden under the dilapidated wall, and, if he had rebuilt it, he would have found the gold; hence I set up the wall miraculously in order to deprive the curmudgeon of the valuable find.

"'I wished that the inhospitable people assembled in the synagogue might have many heads, for a place of numerous leaders is bound to be ruined by reason of the multiplicity of counsel and disputes.

"'To the inhabitants of our last sojourning place, on the other hand, I wished a "single head," for with one to guide a town, success will attend all its undertakings.

"'Know, then, that if thou seest an evil-doer prosper, it is not always unto his advantage, and if a righteous man suffers need and distress, think not God is unjust.' After there words Elijah and Rabbi Joshua separated from each other, and each went his own way."[515]

The resemblance of this story to that of Moses the servant of God in the Quran is readily apparent. Elijah plays the same roles as the "servant of God" (Khidr?),[516] and Rabbi Joshua ben Levi that of Moses. Wensinck, in the SEI, and Ginzberg, in the *Legends of the Jews*, assert the dependence of the Quranic pericope account upon this story.[517] There is clearly some sort of dependency, but it is not immediately clear which is dependent upon which; for, as far as written evidence goes—according to Ginzberg, the Quranic story's appearance is earlier by several centuries than its appearance in Jewish literature. The text we have just

---

[515] LJ, IV, 223-226.

[516] Surabadi identifies or links Elijah with the Khidr, by which link Elijah is also thought to be immortal. (See Elijah in Part Six below, I.) {In this series, in *From Monarchy to Hellenism*.}

[517] Khadir, SEI, p. 232; LJ, VI, 334.

quote is from the medieval *Hibbur Yafeh*; it also appears in the *Ma'asiyot*.[518] If this be taken as an Islamic borrowing from the Joshua ben Levi cycle, it would be the only one in Islamic tradition.[519]

Only one of the acts of Elijah has a parallel in the Quranic story; that of the collapsing wall. If there were a close connection, surely one of the others would also have been echoed in the Quran. But that is not the case. Perhaps both the Jewish and the Quranic stories were influenced by older oral traditions of which the written evidence—if such ever existed—has been lost. Such traditions may have been associated with some one else. They bear the stamp of folk wisdom. Ginzberg's argument that the story is of Jewish origin because Elijah appears in pre-Islamic Haggadah as the vindicator of God's justice is hardly conclusive. Such a theme can scarcely be said to have been a monopoly of Elijah in ancient literature. And the fact of the greater antiquity of the Quranic text remains. There is certainly a relationship, but it may be one of a common source from which both the Jewish and Arabian versions took form in pre-Islamic times, one associated with Elijah and the other with the Moses, who was better known among the Arabs.

It is reasonably clear that the Quranic story represents a cluster of traditions that must have developed over a considerable time. We have identified here at least three strands woven together in its development: the journey of Gilgamesh in search of the secret of eternal life, the expedition of Moses to the regions of Cush/Ethiopia cited in Artapanus and Josephus, and the tradition of the tests of patience by a mysterious figure endowed with supernatural prescience (Utnapishtim/servant of God-Khidr/Elijah) represented in Sumerian, Islamic, and Jewish versions, probably from an earlier source. The principal elements of the story were apparently well known among the Arabs (the journey, the fish, the two seas); the tests, perhaps less so.

The result in the Quran is a quest for knowledge that may be understood by all of us, who are on our own journeys, at many levels of spirituality. We are taught patience and to look beyond the obvious. We are taught that things are not always as they seem. We must trust in the providence of God with its corollary of hope, and we must persevere in adversity.

The secret of everlasting life that Gilgamesh sought is found here in trust in the wisdom of God. The search for everlasting life is not a wrong one. Gilgamesh was simply looking in the wrong place. It is a

---

[518] LJ, VI, 334. The composition of the *Ma'asiyot* last from the 7th to 11 centuries CE and cannot be necessarily free of Islamic influence.
[519] Khadir, SEI, p. 232.

long quest, but success does not lie on a mountaintop or beneath the sea. In fact, the secret of immortality is found in each one of us, in the soul and in the heart. And perhaps the final lesson to be derived from these few verses describing the journey of Moses is one of humility: even a prophet and lawgiver as great as Moses had to learn before he could teach.[520]

M. BALAAM

"What have I done unto thee, that thou hast smitten me three times?"
(Num. 22: 28)

Several verses in Surah Al-A'raf are taken by many commentators, among them Surabadi, to refer to Balaam, a seer mentioned in the Bible: *And recite unto them the tale of him to whom We gave Our revelations, but he sloughed them off, so Satan overtook him and he became of those who lead astray. And had We willed, We could have raised him by their means, but he clung to the earth and followed his own lust. Therefore his likeness is as the likeness of a dog; if thou attackest him, he panteth with his tongue out, and if thou leavest him, he panteth with his tongue out...* (Q. 7:175-176)

This identification with the Biblical Balaam of *Numbers* is by no means certain, but once again the Quran seems to be alluding to a story familiar to its initial audience. Whoever the person may be, in the Quran his story has become a parable condemning those who would cling to the world rather than climb the precipitous heights of spirituality.

According to Surabadi, the protagonist of the Quranic verses is Balaam the son of Beor, the religious leader of Jericho. He lived during the time of Moses. When Moses made to attack Jericho,[521] he was opposed by Og the son of Anak.[522] Og was so huge that he could pluck a fish from the bottom of the sea and fry it on the sun. During the Flood, when all the mountains were covered by at least forty cubits (c. 60 ft.) of water, the waters only reached his knees. When he went to a city the people had to prepare an immense amount of food for him, or he would destroy them.

---

[520] In the Quran, this story is followed immediately by the story of Dhul-Qarnayn with which it shares many features, including possible associations with Alexander. See *Miscellaneous Stories* in Vol. 2, IV. {In this series, in *From Monarchy to Hellenism.*}

[521] According to the Bible, Moses never crossed the Jordan into Palestine, therefore he never attacked Jericho. Joshua was responsible for that (Josh. 6).

[522] The Arabic form of these names: Beor, *Bā^{c}ūrā*; Og, *^{c}Awj*; and Anak, *^{c}Unuq*.

During the fight between Og and Moses, Og tore up a mountain of granite one parasang square[523] and carried it up to drop on the camp of Moses. God ordered a hoopoe with a diamond beak to chip away at the rock. Gabriel came to Moses and told him to fight Og, whom he would defeat with one blow. When Moses went out to fight him, the hoopoe had carved a hole in the mountain Og was carrying, and it slipped down upon his neck. Moses, who was twelve cubits (c. 18 ft.) tall and his staff the same, leaped the same distance and struck Og's ankle with the head of his staff and killed him. Thus Surabadi.[524]

The Biblical Og was the king of Bashan, and his defeat by the Israelites under Moses seems to have made a particularly deep impression upon them. There are scattered references to Og and his defeat in the books of *Numbers*, *Joshua*, and *Psalms* (135 and 136), which add little information to the principal narrative found in *Deuteronomy* (Deut. 3:1-13).[525]

The Israelites, having defeated the Amorite king Sihon, turned north and defeated Og, king of Bashan, at the battle of Edrei (modern Der'a in Syria). Before the battle, the Israelites were afraid of the strength of Og, but God promised them victory. "So the Lord our God gave into our hand Og also, the king of Bashan, and all his people; and we smote him until no survivor was left to him. And we took all his cities at that time—there was not a city which we did not take from them—sixty cities, the whole region of Argob, the kingdom of Og of Bashan. All these were cities fortified with high walls, gates, and bars, besides very many unwalled villages. And we utterly destroyed them, as we did to Sihon the king of Heshbon, destroying every city, men women, and children. But all the cattle and the spoil of the cities we took as our booty." In this manner, Moses is said to have described the defeat of Og (Deut. 3:3-7). The genocidal massacre of the defeated was in accordance with the divine commandment about dealing with the vanquished peoples whose lands the Israelites were seizing: "And when the Lord thy God gives them over to thee, and thou defeatest them; then thou must utterly destroy them and show no mercy." (Deut. 7:2)[526] No comment is

---

[523] "a parasang square": about 3 miles square, or 9 square miles.

[524] Surabadi, pp. 88-89. This resembles the story of Achilles, the Greek hero. See below.

[525] In a reversal of the usual pattern, the passage in *Numbers* is thought to have been borrowed from *Deuteronomy*, not the reverse. (BC, II, 141.)

[526] For the Mosaic Law about holy war we may quote from the 20th chapter of *Deuteronomy*: "When thou drawest near to a city to fight against it, offer terms of peace to it. And if its answer to thee is peace and it opens to thee, then all the people who are found in it shall do forced labor for thee and shall serve thee. But if it makes no peace with thee, but makes war against thee, then thou shalt besiege it; and when the Lord thy

needed about the barbarity of these scenes, and the knavery of ascribing them to God in a war of conquest.

Og's kingdom, Bashan, was located east of the Sea of Galilee and the Jordan valley, in the southwestern portion of modern Syria, extending as far as modern Salkhad (Biblical Salecah) in the east and almost reaching Damascus in the north. The capital was probably Ashtaroth. Bashan became the inheritance of the eastern half of the tribe of Manasseh. Its cattle were famous for their quality in Biblical times. Quite possibly, it was one of the last remaining Hyksos principalities in the region of Canaan.[527]

Deuteronomy also notes Og's gigantic stature, or at least the size of his tomb: "For only Og the king of Bashan was left of the remnant of the Rephaim; behold, his bedstead of iron[528]; is it not in Rabbah of the Ammonites? Nine cubits was its length, and four cubits its breadth, according to the common cubit." (Deut. 3:11) This verse seems to imply that something called Og's bedstead could still be seen in the day of the

---

God gives it into thy hand thou shalt put all its males to the sword, but the women and the little ones, the cattle, and everything else in the city, all its spoil, thou shalt take as booty for thyself; and thou shalt enjoy the soil of thy enemies, which the Lord has given thee. Thus thou shalt do to all the cities which are very far from thee, which are not cities of the nations here.

"But in the cities of these people that the Lord thy God gives thee for an inheritance, thou shalt save alive nothing that breathes, but thou shalt utterly destroy them, the Hittites and the Amorites, the Canaanites and the Perizzites, the Hivites and Jebusites, as the Lord thy God has commanded; that they may not teach thee to do according to all their abominable practices which they have done in the service of their gods, and so to sin against the Lord thy God." (Deut. 20:10-18)

When discussing the treatment of the Jewish Qurayzah after they had acted treacherously to the Muslims of Madinah at the time of war, Phipps argues that according to the Mosaic Law those who surrendered should not have been executed, just enslaved, and that therefore Muslim apologists are ignoring that provision of the (Mosaic) Law. But he ignores the two-tier approach of the Mosaic Law, or rather twists it on its head: clemency in surrender for those outside of 'inheritance of Israel,' but annihilation for those within the 'inheritance.' (Phipps, p. 89.) By that criterion, Madinah lay within the Islamic 'inheritance,' and the annihilation of the Jews without any provocation or cause would have been justified, whether they had acted treacherously or not. According to this interpretation of the Mosaic dictum, they should simply have been slaughtered in any case. In wartime Madinah, however, it was their own treason that brought this fate upon themselves; moreover, the arbiter of their fate was not a Muslim, but one of their own Jewish chiefs, Sa'd bin Mu'adh.

527 Bashan, DB, p. 91; Og, EJ, XII, 1341; ABL, p. 6.

528 At that time, before the development of high-temperature smelting techniques, iron was a precious metal and used decoratively as gold, silver, and ivory were. The bed was probably decorated with iron, not made of solid iron. (See Alan R. Millard's article, *King Og's Bed—Fact or Fancy?* BR, Vol. VI, No. 3, April 1990, pp. 16-21, especially p. 20.) The Biblical measurements would indicate a bed 14.5 ft. in length, and 6 ft. wide.

writer. The Rephaim were a pre-Israelite people living east of the Jordan: "The Emim formerly lived there, a people great and many, and tall as the Anakim; like the Anakim they are also known as Rephaim, but the Moabites call them Emim." (Deut. 2:10-11) The Rephaim appear, from this passage, to be inclusive of the Anakim and Emim.

Not a great deal is known about these peoples who appear in the Bible as opponents of the occupation of their lands by the incoming Israelites. They were all defeated, and the scope of these victories was magnified by making them of gigantic stature, somewhat as a precursor to the David vs. Goliath tradition. This interchangeability of tribal names also includes the Nephilim.[529] In Num. 13, spies sent out to survey Canaan before the Conquest reported: "the land... is a land that devours its inhabitants; and all the people that we saw in it are men of great stature. And there we saw the Nephilim (the sons of Anak, who come from the Nephilim); and we seemed to ourselves like grasshoppers, and so we seemed to them." (Num. 13:32-33) Thus, the demigod Nephilim of *Genesis* (Gen. 6:4) are related to the Anakim who are, in turn, related to the Rephaim and Og.

Since Surabadi uses the phrase "'Awj (Og) son of 'Unuq," let us consider the word *'Unuq* for a moment. The father (or ancestor) of Og would appear to be one 'Unuq, the Anak of *Joshua*: "According to the commandment of the Lord to Joshua, he gave Caleb the son of Jephunneh a portion among the people of Judah, Kiriath-arba, that is Hebron (Arba was the father of Anak), and Caleb drove out from there the three sons of Anak, Sheshai and Ahiman and Talmai, the descendants of Anak." (Josh. 15:13-14) Thus Anak was associated with Hebron. His father Arba was said to be the founder of Hebron, whilst Anak was the father of the three clans of Anakim. However, this genealogy is not given much credence by scholars.[530]

In the Biblical context, these traditions are connected with southern Palestine (Judah) and not with Bashan, some 120 miles to the northeast. However, another passage in *Joshua* (Josh. 11:21-22)[531] suggests that the Anakim were far more widespread than Josh. 15:13-14 indicates. The name itself (Ar. *'unuq*, a cognate of Hebrew *'anāq*, both

---

[529] See Part One, IV, "Harut and Marut." {In this series, in *From the Creation to the Flood.*}

[530] Kiriath-arba means "village of Arba." (Anak, DB, p. 30; Arba, DB, p. 49.)

[531] "And Joshua came at that time and wiped out the Anakim from the hill country, from Hebron, from Debir, from Anab, and from all the hill country of Judah, and from all the hill country of Israel; Joshua utterly destroyed them with their cities. There was none of the Anakim left in the land of the people of Israel; only in Gaza, in Gath, and in Ashdod, did some remain." (Jgs. 11:21-22)

associated with the neck) would imply that there was something significant about the necks of these people. They may have been "long-necked" or tattooed on their necks, or perhaps they wore conspicuous necklaces. The passages cited above indicate a relationship between the Anakim of the Hebron region and Og of Bashan, but it is probably one of kinship rather than direct descent, as Surabadi asserts.

The most noteworthy feature of these peoples: the Nephilim, the Anakim, and the Rephaim—according to their Israelite enemies who perhaps interested in magnifying their victories over them and the glory of their extermination—was their gigantic size and strength. The dimensions of Og's bed make it about five yards long. Commentators have suggested that this was in reality a reference of a prehistoric dolmen in the neighborhood of Rabbah, the modern Amman, capital of Jordan. This would seem to be based upon the idea that the writer, who was referring to a well-known relic, did not know the difference between iron and stone. In any event, the text makes about 14 ft. the upward limit of Og's height.

Jewish tradition joins in the exaggeration of Og's stature. In the Talmud, it is said that his thighbone was three leagues long (nine miles!).[532] He was born either before the Flood or before Abraham and lived either 800 or 500 years until killed by Moses.[533] He consumed one thousand oxen a day or an equal quantity of other animals,[534] and his death is described in the Talmud in the following fashion: "When he discovered that Israel's camp was three parasangs [9 miles] in circumference, he said: 'I shall now tear off a mountain of three parasangs, and cast it upon Israel's camp, and crush them.' He did as he had planned, pulled up a mountain of three parasangs, laid it upon his head, and came marching in the direction of the Israelite camp, to hurl it upon them. But what did God do? He caused ants to perforate the mountain, so that it slipped from Og's head down upon his neck, and when he attempted to shake it off, his teeth pushed out and extended to left and right, and did not let the mountain pass, so that he now stood there with the mountain, unable to throw it from him. When Moses saw this, he took an axe twelve cubits [18 ft.] long, leaped ten cubits [15 ft.] into the air, and dealt a blow to Og's ankle, which caused the giant's death."[535]

---

[532] LJ, III, 344; VI, 119.
[533] LJ, III, 343; VU, 120.
[534] LJ, III, 344.
[535] LJ, III, 245-246; VI, 120.

The dependence of Surabadi's story upon this legend is obvious. Later Jewish Midrashim have a version in which birds, the hoopoe (as in Surabadi) or the raven, are substituted for the ants, perhaps under Islamic influence.[536] Og's manner of death, killed by a wound in the ankle, is reminiscent of the death of Achilles in Greek legend—quite possibly the inspiration of both the Jewish and Islamic versions—who was killed by an arrow shot into his heel, the only vulnerable part of his body.[537] In one Jewish tradition Og (and his brother Sihon) are represented as being so tall that the Flood did not reach to their ankles, as in Surabadi.[538] However, in another place, Og saved himself by riding on the Ark.[539]

Now Balaam makes his appearance. According to Surabadi, after the people of Jericho learned of the death of Og, they were frightened and they approached Balaam who was a learned man and whose prayers were answered. They asked him to pray to Moses. Balaam replied that Moses was a prophet and that they should submit themselves to him. The Jerichoans, knowing that the greatest man can be deceived by a woman, decided to offer a treasure to Balaam's wife to persuade her husband to pray against Moses. She agreed and approached her husband. At first Balaam would not agree to do so, but finally he did. He left for his retreat outside the city. On the road, he came to a sea that had never been there before. Taking it as a sign, he returned home, but his wife sent him out again. The second time the road was blocked by a high wall. Again he returned home and again his wife persuaded him to start out again. The third time, a lion blocked his way. In this fashion, he was obstructed seventy times, until at least he reached the retreat and was able to pray against Moses.[540]

When Moses found himself and his people lost in the wilderness, he asked who had caused it. The answer came that Balaam had done this. Moses prayed that the best thing Balaam had been given be taken away from him. So, when Balaam was praying to the Muslim qiblah with his wife behind him, he stood up and became an infidel, something that he

---

[536] LJ, VI, 120.

[537] Graves, Vol. 2, p. 316. According to the myth, his mother Thetis dipped the infant Achilles into the River Styx in order to make him invulnerable. But the waters did not touch the heel by which she was holding him, and that was his only vulnerable spot.

[538] LJ, III, 469.

[539] LJ, I, 160.

[540] Surabadi notes that some say Balaam was to pray against Joshua rather than Moses. This perhaps is an indication of some confusion about the identity of the prophet involved in this story. Moses is not recorded as having proceeded north into the Bashan, so presumably Joshua was the commander in that war, or more probably it was fought independently by the Israelite tribes trying to wrest the land from its occupants.

should have done seventy years earlier. It is said that a white bird flew out of his throat, and that that was his "light of spiritual knowledge"[541]; and a black bird flew in to replace it. It is also said that God took away from him His Greatest Name (or the Torah, or the Books of the Prophets, or His miraculous power (*karāmat*). He was likened to a dog whose tongue is extended in love of the world unnecessarily (compare Q. 7:176 quoted above).

When they saw that a man such as Balaam, who had been so near to God, had fallen into error, 70,000 Jewish scholars gathered to discuss the matter. They decided that the loss of divine knowledge came from four things: irresolution, dishonor, boldness, and neglect. If Balaam had prayed: *Our Lord, make not our hearts to swerve after Thou hast guided us,* (Q. 3.8) he would have avoided ruin.[542]

In the Bible, the story of Balaam has nothing to do with the fall of Jericho; that story is associated with Joshua (Josh. 6). Nor is Balaam associated with Jericho itself, although the main source for his story, (Num. 22-24), begins with a statement that Israel was encamped in the plains of Moab beyond the Jordan at Jericho. This verse (Num. 22:1) is from P and is designed to tie the next three chapters about Balaam and his oracles to the events of the Conquest. Moses is not mentioned once during the three chapters, nor is his lieutenant Joshua. A redactor has simply inserted in this place the independent tradition of Balak and Balaam, as it is sometimes called. It is a conflation of accounts from the J and E, in which are embedded several oracles in poetic form from another source, probably of greater antiquity.[543] It is only in the Priestly material of Num. 31 that a link between Moses and Balaam is provided.[544]

There is little in the Balak-Balaam chapters to justify the abhorrence in which Balaam was held by later writers such as John in the New Testament *Revelation*. In that book, the last in the Christian Biblical canon, we read (Jesus is the putative speaker): "'But I have a few things against thee: thou hast some there who hold to the teaching of Balaam, who taught Balak to put a stumbling block before the sons of Israel, that they might eat food sacrificed to idols and practice immorality.'" (Rev. 2:14) And in *Jude*: "Woe to them! For they walk in the way of Cain, and

[541] "light of spiritual knowledge": Per. *nūr-i maᶜrifat*.

[542] Surabadi, pp. 89-92.

[543] Albright suggests that the oracles date from the 13th or 12th centuries BCE in an oral form. (Balaam, DB, p. 85.)

[544] However, see the description of Balaam's death below.

abandon themselves for the sake of gain to Balaam's error, and perish in Korah's rebellion." (Jude 11)

In the Priestly tradition of Num. 19, it was the counsel of Balaam that was responsible for leading the Israelite men into a disaster which cost them 24,000 lives. Although the principal narrative is concerned with Moab (east of the southern half of the Dead Sea), in this chapter the scene is the aftermath of a battle with Midian farther to the south in which the Israelites were victorious: "They slew the kings of Midian... and they also slew Balaam the son of Beor with the sword." (Num. 31:8) The reason is made clear a little further on: "Moses said to them, 'Have ye saved all the women alive? Behold, these caused the people of Israel, by the counsel of Balaam, to act treacherously against the Lord in the matter of Peor, and so the plague came among the congregation of the Lord. Now therefore, kill every male among the little ones, and kill every woman who has known man by lying with him. But all the young girls who have not known man by lying with him, keep alive for yourselves.'" (Num. 31:15-18) This brutal, sanguinary reprisal wreaked by the Biblical Moses, extending even to male children, was in response to the defeated people's having followed the counsel of Balaam "in the matter of Peor."

But what was Peor? Peor should not be confused with Beor, Balaam's father. Peor was a mountain in the neighborhood of Mount Nebo east of the Jordan, where Baal-worship was long established.[545] So, what was the affair of Peor? "While Israel dwelt in Shittim the people began to play the harlot with the daughters of Moab. These invited the people to the sacrifices of their gods, and the people ate, and bowed down to their gods. So Israel yoked himself to Baal of Peor." (Num. 25:1-3) In Jewish tradition, the explanation given is that this was a deliberate seduction by the Moabite women upon the advice of Balaam. However, in this passage Balaam is not mentioned at all, and the women are Moabites, not Midianites as in Num. 31, where Balaam is mentioned. Though neighbors, the Moabites and Midianites were distinct peoples. Why was Moses wreaking vengeance upon the Midianites for the alleged crime of the Moabites? In any case, the result was that the Lord, angered by still another example of Israel's easy apostasy, sent a plague that took 24,000 lives.

Following these Biblical hints, many unfavorable notices about Balaam are to be found in Jewish tradition, associating him with the

---

[545] See also the Story of Job, Part Three, II, which follows the Story of Moses. {In this series, in *From Judges to Monarchy.*}

hated Pharaoh and the oppression of the Hebrews in Egypt.[546] He incited nations against Israel,[547] and counseled the Israelites to immorality.[548]

In the Bible, as in Surabadi, a victory precedes the appeal to Balaam. The role played by the people of Jericho in Surabadi is instead assigned to the Moabites and their king Balak. The Israelites had just defeated the Ammonites under Sihon and the Bashanites under Og. The Moabites were terrified and their king, Balak, son of Zippor, sent messengers to bring Balaam, son of Beor, from his home at Pethor[549] to come and curse the Israelites. It was believed that such a curse would aid in the defense of Moab. "God said to Balaam, 'Thou shalt not go with them; thou shalt not curse the people, for they are blessed.'" (Num. 22:12) The messengers returned to Moab without Balaam.

Balak sent another embassy, this time consisting of more important personages, and with offers of greater rewards. Balaam replied to their entreaties: "'Though Balak were to give me his house full of silver and gold, I could not go beyond the command of the Lord my God, to do less or more.'" (Num. 22:18) Balaam entertained the emissaries for the night and during the night God told Balaam to go with them, but to do only what He instructed him to do. "So Balaam rose in the morning, and saddled his ass, and went with the princes of Moab." (Num. 22:21)

In another of those improbable contradictions that are a commonplace in portions of the Bible, after just having been commanded by God to go with the Moabites, we read: "but God's anger was kindled because he went; and the angel of the Lord took his stand in the way as his adversary. Now he was riding on the ass, and his two servants were with him." (Num. 22:22) The princes of Moab have vanished from the narrative and have been replaced by two servants! This is caused by the awkward (and careless) joining of the Elohist source to Yahwist source in v. 22.

Visible only to the ass, the angel stood with a drawn sword at three points on the road. Not knowing the cause for the animal's stopping, on each occasion Balaam abused the beast until on the third halt it was given the power of speech. The ass reproached him, saying: "'What have I done to thee, that thou hast struck me these three times?'" (Num. 22:28) Showing no amazement at the prodigy of a talking ass,

---

546 LJ, II, 255-256.
547 LJ, III, 354, 411.
548 LJ, III, 355, 362, 410, 411, etc.
549 Pethor: probably a town on the upper Euphrates south of Carchemish (Pethor, DB, p. 759). That would make Balaam a man of the same region, Harran, from which Abraham and his clan had set out for Canaan several centuries earlier.

Balaam threatened to kill the animal in the short dialogue which ensued. "Then the Lord opened the eyes of Balaam, and he saw the angel of the Lord standing in the way, with his drawn sword in his hand; and he bowed his head, and fell on his face." (Num. 22:31)

Excusing himself for not understanding the behavior of the ass as a sign, Balaam offered to turn back. "And the angel of the Lord said to Balaam, 'Go with the men; but only the word which I bid thee, that shalt thou speak.' So Balaam went on with the princes of Balak." (Num. 22:35)

Thanks to a quick change from J to E, the princes have reappeared! The point of including this episode would appear to be to emphasize that the oracles and prophecies that Balaam will soon be called upon to utter in the text have come from God, and perhaps secondarily to justify his death because of the unsanctioned advice he is reported to have given the Midianites (not the Moabites) in chapter 31, although that episode belongs to a redaction several centuries later than the chapters we are now considering.

Balak honored Balaam by greeting him on the boundary of his territories. After making animal sacrifices and building altars, Balak asked Balaam to pronounce the curses. But instead of a curse, God made Balaam pronounce a blessing upon Israel. Balak and Balaam tried three different places, but in each, the result was the same. [In other words Balaam had actually come to curse Israel as in the original story, despite the divine instructions received in the incident of the balky ass. Could Balaam have forgotten his promise to God so quickly?]

Exasperated, Balak "struck his hands together; and... said to Balaam, 'I called thee to curse mine enemies, and behold, thou hast blessed them these three times. Therefore now flee to thy place; I said, "I will certainly honor thee," but the Lord has held thee back from honor.' And Balaam said to Balak, 'Did I not tell thy messengers whom thou didst sent to me, "If Balak should give me his house full of silver and gold, I would not be able to go beyond the word of the Lord, to do either good or bad of my own will; what the Lord speaks, that will I speak"?'" (Num. 24:10-13)

With several more dire predictions by Balaam concerning the fate of Israel's enemies, the Balak-Balaam chapters end somewhat ambiguously. The reader is left with the impression that Balaam is not firmly on the side of the Lord. If the Quranic verses cited at the beginning of this section do indeed refer to Balaam, then they are based upon the edition of the story in which Balaam later acts against Israel and Moses. As we have seen in the above, these chapters are associated neither with Moses nor Joshua; it is only in the late account of Balaam's death (by P, quoted above) that a connection is made.

Albright suggests that though the Priestly context of the defection and slaying of Balaam is late, it represents an oral tradition going back to the same period as that of the material in Num. 22-24. This is not unreasonable and would account for the strength the Jewish tradition that, though he was originally favored by God with prophetic powers, he later apostatized.[550]

The Balaam stories quite probably are related to a real historical personality. The name Balaam is Northwest-Semitic, and was originally *Yabil-'ammu*, probably meaning, "May the clan lead." Similarly, the name of his father Beor is probably a shortened form of a name such as *Ba'al-ram*, "Baal is exalted."[551] His country, Pethor in the land of the 'Amau, is also attested in 15th century BCE Egyptian inscriptions.[552]

Many of the elements of Surabadi's story are obviously Islamic, such as the mention of Balaam's praying in the direction of the Muslim direction of prayer (*qiblah*). Indeed, there is considerable evidence that Surabadi's story of Balaam is only inspired in a vague way by the Biblical and later Jewish versions. Because the story is given in considerable (albeit confused) detail in *Numbers*, later Jews could not stray too far from the general outline. Perhaps the most conspicuous feature of the Biblical story and the later developments of it in Jewish traditions is the talking ass, but that is not even mentioned by Surabadi. The angel blocking Balaam's way is also absent from Surabadi. On the other hand, neither the Bible nor Jewish tradition assigns a role to Balaam's wife.

In Jewish tradition it is Balaam's own avarice which leads him on.[553] There is no mention of a sea or a lion as obstacles; however, there is a point of similarity in the matter of the wall. The Bible relates: "Then the angel of the Lord stood in a narrow path between the vineyards, with a wall on either side. And when the ass saw the angel of the Lord, she pushed against the wall, and pressed Balaam's foot against the wall; so he struck her again." (Num. 22:24-25) This similarity may be an accident rather than dependence, in view of the wide range of differences throughout the rest of the narrative. Jewish tradition also lists three faults of Balaam's character that led to his downfall: a jealous eye, a haughty

---

[550] Balaam, EJ, IV, 121.
[551] Balaam, EJ, IV, 122.
[552] Balaam, EJ, IV, 122.
[553] LJ, III, 361.

spirit, and a greedy soul. This may be compared with the list of four causes attributed to the 70,000 Jewish scholars in Surabadi.

The Islamic tradition of Balaam, as found in Surabadi, seems to be dependent upon the Biblical and rabbinic accounts in only its broadest outlines. The reader may not be satisfied that the Quranic passage refers to Balaam at all, but perhaps to someone else. Most of the detail does not seem to owe much to the material in available sources. This contrasts with other stories also suggested by brief Quranic references that correspond much more closely to their Biblical or later counterparts, as the following section will demonstrate. *And God knows best.*

N. THE DEATH OF AARON

And Aaron died there on top of the mountain. (Num. 20:28)

The Quran does not comment upon the death of Aaron, but Surabadi in his Commentary describes it: When the time for his death had come, instead of his going to Moses as he was wont to do each morning, "Moses, peace be upon him, came to him and took his hand and said: 'Come, let us enter this mountain and admire the wonders of the handiwork of God Most High.' They went in, taking Eleazar[554] the son of Aaron with them. Upon entering the mountain, a luxuriant garden appeared in the midst of which was a mansion. Atop the mansion was a copula, and upon it there was an adorned couch. Aaron said: 'Behold, what a pleasant place to sleep!' Moses, peace be upon him, said: 'If thou dost wish it, sleep on that couch.' Aaron removed his clothing and lay upon the couch. God Most High took his soul. Moses and Eleazar returned."[555]

The Israelites preferred Aaron to Moses and they accused Moses of killing him out of jealousy because of Aaron's popularity and eloquence. Moses denied that he could slay his own brother. When the Israelites threatened to kill Moses, "God Most High commanded the angels to take Aaron's couch and bring it to the Children of Israel. It is said that God revived Aaron. Until the return of Moses [who had gone off to pray to God for His aid in this difficulty] Aaron chastised the Children of Israel, saying: 'Why do ye accuse Moses, the Word of God, of killing me? Nay, rather I died as was my destiny.' Having spoken thus

---

[554] Surabadi calls him *ᶜĀzar*.

[555] Surabadi, p. 57.

Aaron died again and was returned to his place. Then the Children of Israel believed Moses and they mourned Aaron for many years."[556]

The Biblical narrative of the death of Aaron makes no such accusation against Moses: "And they journeyed from Kadesh, and the people of Israel, the whole congregation, came to Mount Hor. And the Lord said to Moses and Aaron at Mount Hor, on the border of the land of Edom, 'Aaron shall be gathered to his people; for he shall not enter the land which I have given unto the people of Israel, because ye rebelled against My command at the waters of Meribah [see following section]. Take Aaron and Eleazar his son, and bring them up to Mount Hor; and strip Aaron of his garments and put them on Eleazar his son; and Aaron shall be gathered to his people and shall die there.'

"Moses did as the Lord commanded and they went up Mount Hor in the sight of all the congregation. And Moses stripped Aaron of his garments, and put them upon Eleazar his son; and Aaron died there on the top of the mountain. Then Moses and Eleazar came down from the mountain. And when all the congregation saw that Aaron was dead, all the house of Israel wept for Aaron for thirty days." (Num. 20:22-29)

The transfer of the garments symbolized, of course, the transfer of the office of the high priest of Israel from Aaron to his son Eleazar, thereby strengthening the claims of that branch of the Temple priesthood centuries later. (Not surprisingly, this passage—of doubtful historicity—is from the hand of the Priestly Writer.) Surabadi's account mentions the same three at the final scene: Moses, Aaron himself, and his son, but does not appear to know the reason for Eleazar's presence.[557]

The scene of Aaron's death in the Bible is Mount Hor. Since the time of Josephus at least, Mount Hor has been identified with Jabal Harun, a peak in Mount Seir, above the fabled ruins of Petra in western Jordan. A tomb there is still pointed out to the traveler as that of Aaron.[558] Josephus writes: "And when he came to a place which the Arabians esteem as their metropolis, which was formerly called Arce, but has now the [Greek] name of Petra, at this place, which was encompassed with high mountains, Aaron went up one of them in the sight of the whole army, Moses having before told him that he was to die, for this place was over against them. He put off his pontifical

---

[556] Surabadi, pp. 57-58. The reader may be reminded of the murder of 'Amil in Section K above where 'Amil was also revived, albeit not to exonerate, but rather to accuse.

[557] Aaron had four sons: Nadab, Abihu, Eleazar, and Ithamar. The first two died without issue after being struck down for some ritual offense against YHWH (Lev. 10:1-2; Num. 3:2-4). Therefore Eleazar, now the eldest, was Aaron's successor. See Section I above.

[558] Hor, DB, p. 396. We have also seen the peak where Aaron reputedly rests.

garments, and delivered them to Eleazar his son, to whom the high priesthood belonged because he was the elder brother; and died while the multitude looked upon him."[559]

In the Biblical account, Aaron's death is announced to Moses and Aaron together, but in Josephus, Moses knows of it before Aaron. This also seems to be also the assumption of Surabadi. A version of Aaron's death found in the 8th-century CE Midrash *Petirat Aharon* seems to stand behind Surabadi's story. In the *Petirat Aharon*, God asks Moses to prepare Aaron for death. "Ascend thou also with them, and there speak with thy brother, sweet and gentle words, the burden of which will, however, prepare him for what awaits him...[560]

"Now it had been customary during the forty years' march through the desert for the people daily to gather, first before the seventy elders, then under their guidance before the princes of the tribes, then for all of them to appear before Eleazar and Aaron, and with these to go to Moses to present him their morning greeting. On this day, however, Moses made a change in this custom, and after having wept through the night, at the cock's crow summoned Eleazar before him and said to him: 'Go and call to me the elders and the princes, for I have to convey to them a commission from the Lord.' Accompanied by these men, Moses now betook himself to Aaron who, seeing Moses when he arose, asked: 'Why hast thou made a change in the usual custom?'"[561]

Moses persuaded Aaron to go up the mountain with him in his priestly robes. On the mountain a cave opened up and they both entered it. Aaron divested himself of his clothes, though he still did not know that death awaited him, and Eleazar put them on. Gradually Aaron came to understand that his end was near. He lay down upon the "adorned couch in the cave and God received his soul." Then Moses left the cave, and it immediately disappeared.

"When the people saw Moses and Eleazar return without Aaron, they were not at all in the mood to lend faith to the communication of Aaron's death... Some declared that Moses had killed Aaron because he was jealous of his popularity; some thought Eleazar had killed his father to become his successor as high priest; and there were also some who declared that he had been removed from the earth to be translated to heaven. Satan had so incited the people against Moses and Eleazar that they wanted to stone them.

---

[559] Josephus, Antiquities, IV.4.7, p. 89.
[560] LJ, III, 321.
[561] LJ, III, 322.

"Moses hereupon prayed to God, saying: 'Deliver me and Eleazar from this unmerited suspicion, and also show to the people Aaron's bier, that they may not believe him to be still alive, for in their boundless admiration of him they may even make a God of him.' [This is an oblique criticism of the Christian deification of Jesus.]

"God then said to the angels: 'Lift up on high the bier upon which lies My friend Aaron, so that Israel may know he is dead and may not lay hands upon Moses and Eleazar.' The angels did as they were bidden, and Israel then saw Aaron's bier floating in the air, while God before it and the angels behind intoned a funeral song for Aaron."[562]

Jewish tradition describes the mourning for Aaron as even greater than that for Moses. In the *Fathers According to Rabbi Nathan* we read: "Why did all Israel weep for Aaron thirty days while for Moses only the men wept? Because Moses rendered judgment strictly according to the truth; but Aaron never said to a man, 'Thou hast acted offensively,' or to a woman, 'Thou hast acted offensively.' That is why it is said, 'And all the house of Israel wept for him.' But of Moses, who reproved them with strong words, it is said, 'And the men of Israel wept for Moses.' (Deut. 34:8) Moreover how many thousands there were in Israel named Aaron! For had it not been for Aaron these children would not have come into the world."[563]

The same source shows Moses overwhelmed by the splendor of Aaron's death: "At that time Moses begged for a death like Aaron's death; for he saw Aaron's bier laid out with great honor, and bands and bands of ministering angels mourning him."[564]

This exaltation of Aaron, even over Moses, must strike the reader as curious. Had Aaron not been accused in the Bible of abetting apostasy and rebellion against the pure worship of YHWH? Clearly, there is a contradiction here which probably originates in a much more benign popular view of Aaron, possibly encouraged by the Aaronite priesthood, in contrast to the negative traditions hostile to him preserved in *Exodus* and *Numbers*.

The correspondence between these traditions and the story of Surabadi is quite close, contrasting strongly with his story of Balaam in the previous section that is a much freer in its adaptation.

---

[562] LJ, III, 324-327.
[563] ARN, p. 64.
[564] ARN, p. 65.

O. THE DEATH OF MOSES

And there hath not arisen a prophet since in Israel like Moses... (Deut. 34:10)

As in the case of Aaron, the Quran gives no special notice of the death of Moses, but Surabadi gives us an elaborate account of the at event: When Moses' time had come, the Angel of Death accosted him on the road. Moses protested that he had requested that he be given a warning of his death. The angel replied that each grey hair and the weakening of his body were warnings. Moses asked permission to bless his family; his request was granted. He returned home and knocked on his door. When the people in the house asked who it was, Moses replied that it was he. They said it could not be Moses, because he had gone for three days of meditation and was not yet due back. Moses replied that he had returned with the Angel of Death. The inhabitants began to weep and mourn.

Moses asked Gabriel what would be the fate of his three children after his death.[565] Gabriel told him to go to the seashore and strike the sea with his staff. He did and saw a stone at the bottom of the sea. He was told to strike the stone; when he did, it split apart revealing a red worm with a green leaf in its mouth. Gabriel said that if God had provided for this worm, how would He not provide for the children of His friends?

Moses returned and appointed Joshua son of Nun as his successor. Then he went with the Angel of Death to the place appointed for his death. Moses asked from what part of the body his life would be taken, that which had spoken with God, or the eyes which had beheld Him, or the hand which had grasped the Tables of the Law, or the feet which had gone to the Place of Prayer? The angel remarked that Moses did not want to die and commanded him to sigh. When he did so, the angel seized his soul.

In another version, Surabadi relates that when the Angel of Death came to Moses, the angel said that it was not proper that he take Moses' life without his agreement, and (the angel) retired to await that. Then Moses passed four angels in human form digging a grave. He learned it was for a friend of God, and the scent of Paradise rose out of it.

---

[565] The Bible mentions only two of his children, his sons Gershom and Eliezer. (Ex. 18:3-4.)

Moses entered the grave and lay down, saying that he wished it were his own grave. He sought death and he died.[566]

These stories have little in common with the Biblical version of Moses' death, although both share an atmosphere of the miraculous. In the Biblical account, Moses, when his time came, went willingly to the place appointed for his death. Like the rest of his generation, he was prohibited from entering the Promised Land. *Deuteronomy*, which is our source for the last days of Moses, gives the reason for this prohibition: God told Moses: "'Ascend this mountain of Abarim, Mount Nebo, which is in the land of Moab, opposite Jericho; and view the land of Canaan, which I give to the people of Israel for a possession; and die on the mountain which thou ascendest, and be gathered to thy people, as Aaron thy brother died in Mount Hor and was gathered to his people; because thou didst break faith with Me in the midst of the People of Israel at the waters of Meribah-kadesh, in the wilderness of Zin; because thou didst not revere Me as holy in the midst of the people of Israel. For thou shalt see the land before thee; but thou shalt not go there, into the land which I give unto the people of Israel.'" (Deut. 32:49-52)

It is presumed that this offense was the striking of the rock and producing water without first securing God's permission for the performance of this miracle. The punishment, considering some of the barbarous activities attributed to Moses in the Bible, seems rather disproportionate, and suggests that it is an interpretation of these events invented in a later time to explain how it was that a prophet and leader as favored by God as Moses had never set foot in Canaan.

JOSHUA: As Surabadi reports, in the Bible Joshua was appointed Moses' successor. The book immediately following the Pentateuch is called by his name, and belongs to the same literary tradition as the five preceding books. Hence, the six books taken together are often spoken of as the Hexateuch.[567] They relate the history of Israel from the beginning of the world to the Conquest of Canaan under Joshua.

Joshua is first mentioned at the battle with the Amalekites (Ex. 17:8-14). His name, according to the Priestly tradition to be found in *Numbers*, was originally Hoshea, and under that name he was one of the spies sent out to Canaan to survey the strength of its defenses: "from the tribe of Ephraim, Hoshea the son of Nun." (Num. 13:7) Later on Moses changed his name to Joshua: "And Moses called Hosea the son of Nun

---

[566] Surabadi, pp. 58-59.

[567] As Pentateuch is from the Greek and means "Five Books," so Hexateuch means "Six Books."

Joshua" (Num. 13:16), still another Biblical name change. The mention of Ephraim shows that Joshua was of the Josephic tribes, and the tradition is probably a Northern one. Joshua was also expressly exempted by God (as was Caleb of Judah) from the punishing prohibition against the entrance into Canaan of all Israelites over twenty that had prevented Moses and Aaron from doing so (Num. 14:28-20).

Joshua is not mentioned by name in the Quran, but he is probably one of the two men referred to in Surah al-Ma'idah: *Then two of the men who feared (God) unto whom God had been gracious spoke out: "Enter in upon them by the gate, for if ye enter by it, lo, ye will be victorious. So put your trust (in God) if ye are indeed believers.* (Q. 5:23) The other man, if this identification be correct, would be Caleb, and the incident would be their attempt to give heart to the Israelites who had been disheartened by the reports of the strength of the inhabitants of Canaan: "And Joshua the son of Nun and Caleb the son of Jephunneh, who were among those who had spied out the land, rent their clothes, and said to all the congregation of the people of Israel, 'The land, which we passed through to spy it out, is an exceedingly good land. If the Lord delights in us, He will bring us into this land and give it to us, a land which flows with milk and honey. Only do not rebel against the Lord; and do not fear the people of the land, for they are bread for us; their protection is removed from them, and the Lord is with us; do not fear them.' But all the congregation said to stone them with stones." (Num. 14:6-10)

But Joshua and Caleb were not stoned, and later, at the command of God, Moses appointed Joshua his successor: "And the Lord said to Moses, 'Take Joshua the son of Nun, a man in whom is the spirit, and lay thy hand upon him; cause him to stand before Eleazar the priest and all the congregation, and thou shalt commission him in their sight. Thou shalt invest him with some of thy authority, that all the congregation of the people of Israel may obey…' And Moses did as the Lord commanded him; he took Joshua and caused him to stand before Eleazar the priest and the whole congregation, and he laid his hands upon him, commissioned him as the Lord directed through Moses." (Num. 27:18-20, 22-23) A charismatic leader, Joshua went on to lead the Israelites into Canaan. Although the military prowess attributed to him in the Bible may be exaggerated, there is little doubt that he was a real person. He was buried in the territory of the Ephraimites. As he does not figure prominently in Islamic tradition, we shall content ourselves with this much about him.

In the final scenes of his life, after blessing the tribes of Israel in fulfillment of the command cited earlier: "...Moses went up from the plains of Moab to Mount Nebo, to the top of Pisgah, which is opposite Jericho. And the Lord showed him all the land, Gilead as far as Dan, all Naphtali, the land of Ephraim and Manasseh, all the land of Judah as far as the Western Sea [the Mediterranean], the Negeb, and the Plain, that is the valley of Jericho the city of palm trees, as far as Zoar. And the Lord said to him, 'This is the land of which I swore to Abraham, to Isaac, and to Jacob, "I will give it unto thy seed." I have let thee see it with thy eyes, but thou shalt not go over there.'

"So Moses the servant of the Lord died there in the land of Moab, according to the word of the Lord, and He buried him in the valley in the land of Moab opposite Beth-peor; but no man knows the place of his burial to this day. Moses was a hundred and twenty years old when he died; his eye was not dim, nor his natural force abated. And the people of Israel wept for Moses thirty days; then the days of weeping and mourning for Moses were ended... And there has not arisen a prophet since in Israel like Moses, whom the Lord knew face to face, none like him for all the signs and the wonders which the Lord sent him to do in the land of Egypt, to Pharaoh and to all his servants and to all his land, and all the mighty power and all the great and terrible deeds which Moses wrought in the sight of all Israel." (Deut: 34:1-8, 10-12)

This is the Biblical account of the death of Moses and its summary of his accomplishments; his epitaph by the Elohist. He was buried by God Himself in an unknown place in Moab, in what later became the territory of the tribe of Reuben. Mount Nebo is traditionally identified with Jabal al-Naba, about fifteen miles southwest of Amman, the capital of Jordan.[568] It rises 3907 ft. above the surface of the Dead Sea, the northern end of which lies less than ten miles due west of its peak. On a clear day, the view can be as described in the passage above from the northern end of Palestine to the Negeb, although the Mediterranean Sea is not visible from any point in the region.

Beth-peor has been identified with Baal-peor, the modern Khirbat al-Shaykh Jāyil, about 3 miles northwest of Mount Nebo.[569] If the Deuteronomic tradition be correct, the grave of Moses would have been located in the valley that lies to the north of Mount Nebo. (The Talmud says that Moses' grave can never be discovered, because from the top of the mountain it looks as though it were in the valley, but from

---

[568] Nebo, DB, p. 693.
[569] OBA, pp. 63, 69; Beth-peor, DB, p. 101.

the valley it looks as though it were on the top of the mountain.[570]) No Muslim shrine in the area seems to be associated with Moses, although there is one called Nabī Mūsā in a valley east of the Jordan, visible from the road between Jericho and Jerusalem.

The traditions in Surabadi about the death of Moses show greater independence of the Bible and Jewish literature than do those of Aaron cited in the previous section, although Surabadi's anecdotes about Moses' evasiveness when his hour had come are confirmed by Jewish tradition, much of it stemming upon Moses' great desire to live a few more years and enter the Promised Land. When Moses prayed for this, God told the angel Akrazaiel to lock all the gates of heaven so that Moses' prayer could not ascend into it.[571] God tried to comfort Moses concerning his death,[572] but he would not be comforted and he pleaded with the Earth, the Heavens, the Sun and the Moon, the Stars and the Planets, the Hills and the Mountains, Mount Sinai, the Rivers, the Deserts and all the Elements of Nature, and even the Great Sea to intercede with God on his behalf, but they all refused.[573] He then approached Joshua, Eleazar, and Caleb, but also in vain,[574] and ultimately the Angel of the Face, who told him: "'Why, Moses dost thou exert thyself in vain? Standing behind the curtain that is drawn before the Lord, I heard that thy prayer in this instance is not to be answered.' Moses now laid his hand upon his head and wept bitterly, saying, 'To whom shall I not go, that he might implore God's mercy for me?'"[575]

All of this is rather undignified and inconsistent with Moses' role as the founder of a nation and a religion. Of course, it is partly to be explained by a desire to show Moses' concern for his people who settled in the Promised Land after his death, and his burial outside of it seemed to orphan them.

Another view is reflected in *Deuteronomy Rabbah*. In this passage, Moses actually seems to fear death at the hands of the Angel of Death: "A voice from heaven resounded, saying, 'Why, Moses, dost thou strive in vain? Thy last second is at hand.' Moses instantly stood up for prayer, and said. 'Lord of the world! Be mindful of the day on which Thou didst reveal Thyself to me in the bush of thorns, and be mindful also of the day which I ascended into heaven and during forty days

---

[570] Moses, EJ, XII, 398.
[571] LJ, III, 418-419.
[572] LJ, III, 428-431.
[573] LJ, III, 431-433.
[574] LJ, III, 433-435.
[575] LJ, III, 435.

partook of neither food nor drink. Thou, Gracious and Merciful, deliver me not into the hand of Samael." God replied, 'I have heard thy prayer. I Myself shall attend to thee and bury thee.'

"Moses now sanctified himself as do the Seraphim that surround the Divine Majesty, whereupon God from the highest heavens revealed Himself to receive Moses' soul. When Moses beheld the Holy One, blessed be His Name, he fell upon his face and said, 'Lord of the world! In love didst Thou create the world, and in love Thou guidest it. Treat me also with love, and deliver me not into the hands of the Angel of Death." A heavenly voice sounded and said, 'Moses, be not afraid. "Thy righteousness shall go before thee; the glory of the Lord shall be thy reward."'

"With God descended from heaven three angels, Michael, Gabriel, and Zagzagel. Gabriel arranged Moses' couch, Michael spread upon it a purple garment, and Zagzagel laid down a woolen pillow. God stationed Himself over Moses' head, Michael to his right, Gabriel to his left, and Zagzagel at his feet, whereupon God addressed Moses, 'Cross thy feet,' and Moses did so. He then said, 'Fold thy hands and lay them upon thy breast,' and Moses did so. Then God said, 'Close thine eyes,' and Moses did so. Then God spoke to Moses' soul, 'My daughter, one hundred and twenty years had I decreed that thou shouldst dwell in this righteous man's body, but hesitate not now to leave it, for thy time is run.'"[576] (The soul is addressed as "daughter" because the word is feminine.)

The soul pleaded to remain in Moses, but "when Moses saw that his soul refused to heave him, he said to her, 'Is this because the Angel of Death wishes to show his power over thee?' the soul replied, 'Nay, God doth not wish to deliver me into the hands of death.' Moses: 'Wilt thou, perchance, weep when the others will weep at my departure?' The soul: 'The Lord "hath delivered mine eyes from tears."'; Moses: 'Wilt thou, perchance, go into Hell when I am dead?' The soul: 'I will walk before the Lord in the land of the living.' When Moses heard these words, he permitted his soul to leave him, saying to her, 'Return unto thy rest, O my soul; for the Lord had dealt bountifully with thee.'"[577] Another source, the Talmudic tractate *Baba Batra*, adds that God took Moses' soul by kissing him on the mouth.[578]

As may be seen, Surabadi's traditions have little in common in detail with these Jewish traditions. Ginzberg records a version from the

---

[576] LJ, III, 471-472.
[577] LJ, III, 472-473.
[578] LJ, III, 473.

Falashas (of Ethiopia) very similar to Surabadi's account, but can find no pre-Islamic source for it.[579] In the Talmud, the Angel of Death also has to resort to trickery in order to claim the soul of David,[580] but the parallel ends there.

Whilst the Bible makes Moses' death a solitary affair, away from the eyes of men, Josephus gives us a different version in which the people, who knew that Moses was going to die as he had told them so, were weeping and lamenting. Then with the elders, Eleazar and Joshua, Moses ascended the mountain. "He dismissed the senate [the elders]; and as he was going to embrace Eleazar and Joshua, and was still discoursing with them. A cloud stood over him on the sudden, and he disappeared in a certain valley, although he wrote in the holy books that he died, which was done out of fear, lest they should venture to say that, because of his extraordinary virtue, he went to God."[581] That is how Moses came to be credited with writing the passage in *Deuteronomy* describing his own death and the subsequent mourning—although modern scholars consider the last chapter to be a pastiche with verses from all three of the principal sources of the Pentateuch: J, E, and P.

Thus died one of the most influential men who ever lived. His life, acts, and teachings have affected half of modern mankind: the Jews, the Christians, and the Muslims. Though some critics have doubted the reality of his existence because of the legendary nature of much of the material about him in the Bible, it would be as easy to doubt the historicity of Alexander simply because of the development of the Alexander romances of a later era. No, Moses was a real man, physically strong and impressive, yet meek (Num. 12:3); a leader who could rise to tremendous anger and passion when he saw his people violating their covenant with God.

We have already quoted the Deuteronomist's judgment that "there has not arisen a prophet since in Israel like Moses." Josephus also commented upon his life: "He was one that exceeded all men that ever were in understanding, and made the best use of what that understanding suggested to him. He had a very graceful way of speaking and addressing himself to the multitude: and as to his other qualifications, he had such a full command of his passions, as if he had hardly any such in his soul, and only knew them by their names, as rather perceiving them in other men than in himself. He was also such a general of an army as is seldom

---

[579] LJ, VI, 162-163.
[580] LJ, IV, 113-114.
[581] Josephus, Antiquities, IV.8.48, p. 103.

seen, as well as such a prophet as was never known, and this to such a degree, that whatsoever he pronounced, you would think you heard the voice of God himself."[582]

Is it any wonder then that Muslims, when reflecting upon the life of the Prophet Muhammad, have so often seen in Moses his prefigurement?

---

[582] Josephus, Antiquities, IV.8.49, p. 103.

GLOSSARY

Aetiology: adj. *aetiological*: the study of causes. Also, *etiology*, *etiological.*

Apocrypha: non-canonical religious writings.

Apology: in literary language it signifies a defence, rather than an admission of regret for an error as it is more frequently used in modern speech.

Aramaic: the Semitic language spoken by the people of the New Testament Near East. It replaced several other Semitic languages, including Hebrew among the Jews.

Assyria: a Semitic empire based in northern Iraq. In its imperial phase (883-626 BCE) it was a world power.

Babylon: the chief city of Semitic peoples of southern Iraq in ancient times. Its ruins lie some 70 miles south of Baghdad.

Babylonian Captivity (*Exile*): the period that the Jews of Jerusalem spent in Babylon after being carried off by Nebuchadnezzar in 586 BCE. The Edict of Cyrus (538 BCE) permitted the Jews tot return and officially ended the "Captivity" or "Exile."

Canon: the list of books officially accepted for inclusion in the Bible. It varies according to the faith. The Jews, for example, only recognize the books of the Old Testament as canonical.

Daniel: an Old Testament prophet; the Biblical book (Dan.) bearing his name.

Elohist: also designated E; the second earliest strand in the Pentateuch representing Northern traditions, and its writer.

Ephod: priestly vestment, often adorned with precious stones.

Ezekiel: an Old Testament prophet; the Biblical book (Ezek.) bearing his name.

Fertile Crescent: a term applied to the agricultural lands than arch around the northern deserts of Arabia; modern Palestine, Syria, and Iraq.

Gentile: non-Jewish persons or practices.

Graven image: an idol carved of wood or stone.

Haggada(h): that part of the Talmud containing the stories, legends, parables, and tales that illustrate the Halakah (the legal part of the Talmud).

Hellenization: an ancient parallel to modern Westernization or Europeanization; the adoption of Greek modes of thought, customs, dress, culture, and worldview—sometimes by force and sometimes voluntarily.

Hexateuch: the Pentateuch plus *Joshua*; the first six books of the Jewish Bible and the Christian Old Testament.

Higher Criticism: in Biblical studies, the discipline that examines the text produced by the lower criticism in order to answer questions of authorship, date, the circumstances of composition, historicity, literary sources, relationships to other writings, theological development, the influence of other factors, types, forms, etc.

Isaiah: an Old Testament prophet and the Biblical book (Is.) bearing his name.

Israelite: adj., related to the descendants of Abraham through Jacob in Canaan (Palestine); also applied particularly to the people of the Northern Kingdom of Israel (the ten northern tribes).

Jeremiah: an Old Testament prophet active from c. 627 to some time after 586 BCE, and the Biblical book (Jer.) bearing his name.

Judah (*Judaea*): the southern part of Palestine, usually not including the Negev desert to the south. Jerusalem is its chief city.

Lacuna, pl., lacunae: a gap or missing part, often of a manuscript or chain of transmission.

Lower Criticism: in Biblical studies, the discipline that strives to achieve the best possible text in the original languages of composition.

LXX: an abbreviation for the Greek Bible, the *Septuagint.*

Mesopotamia: the Land Between the Rivers, the name given by the Greeks to the plains of the eastern end of the *Fertile Crescent* (q.v.) between the Tigris and Euphrates Rivers, roughly coterminous with modern Iraq.

Micah: an 8th-century BCE Old Testament prophet and the Biblical book (Mic.) bearing his name.

Mishnah: that part of the Talmud containing the Oral Law, secondary in importance only to the Mosaic Torah. Sometimes written *Mishna.*

Molten image: an idol cast of bronze or some other metal.

Mount of Olives: the mountain to the east of ancient of Jerusalem.

Nazirite: one who had separated himself by a special vow to Yahweh (God). This could be lifelong or for a limited period.

Nebuchadnezzar: 6th century BCE Babylonian king who carried off the Jews from Jerusalem and Judaea to Babylon. Sometimes written *Nebuchadrezzar*, (See *Babylonian Captivity* above.)

Non-canonical: writings (religious in this context) not included in the canon and not regarded as authoritative.

Oracle: a divinely inspired utterance, usually of a prophetic nature.

Oral Law: the traditional legal teachings now found in that part of the Talmud called the Mishna(h).

Pauline: pertaining to Paul and his doctrines.

Pentateuch: the first five books of the Jewish Bible and the Christian Old Testament: *Genesis*, *Exodus*, *Leviticus*, *Numbers*, *and Deuteronomy*. They are traditionally ascribed to Moses.

Pericope: a selection from a longer text, often a brief narrative or incident.

Provenance: origin, source; pedigree.

Psalms: (Ps.) the "hymnal" of the Old Testament, perhaps containing the Quranic *Zabūr*.

Pseudepigrapha: writings falsely or spuriously attributed to personages significant in religious history, especially Biblical characters.

Seraphim (sing. *seraph*): 6-winged angels standing in the presence of God.

Shahādah: the Muslim Testimony of Faith.

Sumeria: the seat of the world's oldest civilization; roughly, the Tigris-Euphrates plain below Baghdad in modern Iraq. The ethnic and linguistic affinities of the Sumerians are still unknown.

Surah: Ar., a chapter of the Quran. The Quran contains 114 chapters, or *surahs*.

Talmud: "The principal literary production of post-Biblical Judaism," divided into two parts: the *Mishnah* ("second law") and the *Gemara* ("completion). (DB, p. 954)

Targum: an Aramaic paraphrase of the Jewish Bible (the Old Testament), made necessary by the change of the Jewish vernacular from Hebrew to Aramaic in the centuries before the beginning of the Common Era.

The Temple: the Temple of Jerusalem, reconstructed by Herod the Great in the 1st century BCE and destroyed by the Romans in 70 CE after a Jewish insurrection.

Teraphim (sing. *teraph*): household gods, often associated with fertility.

Theodicy: the defense of God's goodness and omnipotence in view of the existence of evil. (Webster)

Theophany: the visible manifestation of a deity to a human being.

Theophorous, *theophoric*: adj., describing a name compounded with the name of God or a god.

Traditionist: (*muḥaddith*), capitalized to distinguish it from "traditionist" or "traditionalist" used in the general sense of a supporter of tradition and custom; a student or narrator of religious traditions and stories, especially the Traditions of the Prophet.

Umayyad: pertaining to the Umayyad dynasty based at Damascus in Syria, rgd. AH 41-132/661-750 CE. Overthrown by the Abbasid revolution.

Yahwist: also designated J; the writer of the earliest of the component documents of the historical books of the Bible. Scholars believe the J document is a combination of and earlier J (J1) and another of the same tradition about a century later (J2).

YHWH: the Tetragrammaton; the four consonants of the unutterable name of God in the Old Testament. Now vowelized as *Yahweh*, usually translated as "the Lord." It may mean, "I am Who I am," or "O He!"(God, DB, pp. 334-335.)

Ziggurat: a Mesopotamian pyramidal temple, usually constructed in steps or platforms.

Zoomorphic: concerning a deity conceived of as an animal.

BIBLIOGRAPHY (CODED)

(AAWH) Kinder, Herman & Hilgeman, Werner. *The Anchor Atlas of World History*. 2 vols. Mew York: Bantam, Doubleday, Dell Publishing Group, 1974.

(ABD) Freedman, David Noel, ed. *The Anchor Bible Dictionary*, 5 vols. New York: Doubleday, 1992-.

(ABL) *Atlas of the Bible Lands*. Maplewood: Hammond, 1959.

(Ackroyd) Ackroyd, Peter R. *Israel under Babylon and Persia*. New Clarendon Bible, Old Testament, Vol. 4. London: Oxford Univ. Press, 1970.

(Albright-Ab to Ez) Albright, William F. *The Biblical Period From Abraham to Ezra*. New York: Harper Torchbooks, Harper & Row, 1963.

(Albright-Arch) Albright, William F. *Archaeology, Historical*

(Albright-Stone Age) Albright, William F. *From Stone Age to Christianity*. Second edition. Garden City: Doubleday Anchor Books, 1957.

(Anderson) Anderson, G.W. *The History and Religion of Israel*. New Clarendon Bible, Vol. I. London: Oxford Univ. Press, 1966.

(ANE) Pritchard, James B., ed. *The Ancient Near East*. 2 vols. Princeton: Princeton Univ. Press, 1958, 1975.

(Arberry) Arberry, Arthur J. *The Koran Interpreted*. London: Oxford Univ. Press, 1964.

(Arden) Arden, Harvey. "In the Steps of Moses." *National Geographic Magazine*. Vol. 149, No. 1, Jan. 1976, pp. 21.

(Arrian) Arrian: *the Campaigns of Alexander*. Revised edition. Trans. Aubrey de Selincourt. Harmondsworth: Penguin Books, 1971.

(Asimov-OT) Asimov, Isaac. *Asimov's Guide to the Bible: The Old Testament*. New York: Avon Books, 1971.

(BA) *Biblical Archeologist*. Magazine.

(Bal'ami) Bal'ami, Abu 'Ali Muhammad bin Muhammad bin. *Tarikh-i Bal'ami*. 2 vols. Dr. Muhammad Taqi Bahar, ed. (Persian) Tehran: Kitabfurushi-yi Zawwar, AHS 1353.

(BAR) *Biblical Archaeology Review* (periodical)

(BC) Allen, Clifton J., gen. ed. *Broadman Bible Commentary, The*.12 vols. London: Marshall, Morgan & Scott, 1970-72.

(Bibby-Dilmun) Bibby, Geoffrey. *Looking for Dilmun*. New York: New American Library, 1974

(BR) *Bible Review* (periodical)

(Breasted) Breasted, James Henry. *A History of Egypt*. New York: Bantam Books, 1964; reprint of revised edition of 1909.

(Breasted-Religion) Breasted, J.H. *Development of Religion and Thought in Ancient Egypt*. New York: Harper & Row, 1959. Orig. Edition Scribner's, 1912.

(Buber) Buber, Martin. *Moses*. New York: Harper & Row, 1958.

(Budge-Gods) Budge, E.A. Wallis. *The Gods of the Egyptians*. 2 vols. New York: Dover Publications, 1969. Reprint of 1904 edition.

(Bukhara) Al-Narshakhī, Abū Bakr Muḥammad. *Tārīkh-i Bukhārā* (History of Bukhara). Abū Naṣr Aḥmad bin Muḥammad al-Qibāwī, trans. from Arabic into Persian. Ed. & notes by Mudarris Ridawi. (Persian) Tehran: Bunyad-i Farhang-i Iran, AHS1351/1972 CE.

(Bukhari) Bukhari, Imam. *Sahih al-Bukhari.* Dr. Muhammad Muhsin Khan, translator. Nine volumes. Lahore: Kazi Publications, 1979.

(Burhan) Bidokht, Nahid, *Burhan-i Qati',* Muhammad Husayn ibn Khalaf Tabrizi 'Burhan,' dtd AH 1062, ed. Dr. Muhammad Mu'in Tehran: Ibn Sina, 2nd printing, AHS 1342.

(Campbell) Campbell, Joseph: *The Masks of God.* 4 vols. New York: Viking Press, 1970.

(CE) *Columbia Encyclopedia, The.* Wm. Brigwater and Seymour Kurtz, eds. New York: Columbia Univ. Press, 1968.

(DB) Hastings, James, ed. *Dictionary of the Bible*, rev. Ed. Frederick C. Grant & H.H. Rowley. New York: Charles Scribner's Sons, 1963.

(de Vaux) de Vaux, Roland. *Ancient Israel*, 2 vols. New York: McGraw-Hill, 1965.

(Doughty) Doughty, Charles M. Passages from *Arabia Deserta*, selected by Edward Garnett. Harmondsworth: Penguin Bks, 1956 (1931).

(EB) *Encyclopædia Britannica.* Chicago: Encyclopædia Britannica, 1960 ed.

(EB, EB-Mac, EB Mic) *New Encyclopædia Britannica.* Univ. of Chicago. 15th edition. Chicago: Enc. Britannica, 1967. Micropædia and Macropædia.

(EI) *Encyclopædia of Islam, The.* 11 vols. + indices. Leiden: E.J. Brill, 1960-2002.

(EJ) *Encyclopædia Judaica.* 16 vols. New York: Macmillan & Co, 1971.

(ERE) Hastings, James, ed. *The Encyclopædia of Religion and Ethics.* 12 vols. + Index. New York: Scribner's, 1961.

(Fairservis) Fairservis, Walter A., Jr. *The Ancient Kingdoms of the Nile.* New York: Mentor Books, 1962.

(Freud) Freud, Sigmund. *Moses and Monotheism.* Trans. Katherine Jones. New York: Vintage Books, 1939.

(Gager) Gager, John G. *Moses in Greco-Roman Paganism.* Society of Biblical Literature Monograph Series, Vol. 16, Robt. A. Kraft, ed. Nashville, Abdingdon Press, 1972.

(Galvin) Galvin, John. "Egypt's First Pharaohs." *National Geographic Magazine.* Vol. 207, No. 4, Apr. 2005, pp. 106-121.

(Gaster) Gaster, Theodor H. *Myth, Legend, and Custom in the Old Testament.* 2 vols. New York: Harper & Row, 1975.

(Gilgamesh) Sandars, N.K., trans. *The Epic of Gilgamesh.* Harmondsworth: Penguin Books, 1964, revised ed.

(Graves) Graves, Robert. *The Greek Myths.* Two volumes. Harmondsworth: Penguin Books, revised edition, 1960.

(Halley) Halley, Henry H. *Bible Handbook.* 24th edition. Grand Rapids: Zondervan Publishing House, 1965.

(Herodotus) Herodotus. *The Histories.* Trans. Aubrey de Selincourt. Harmondsworth: Penguin Books, 1972.

(Hooke) Hooke, S.H. *Middle Eastern Mythology.* Harmondsworth: Penguin Books, 1963.

(Hughes) Hughes, Thomas Patrick. *A Dictionary of Islam.* Chicago: Kazi Publications, 1994 reprint of 1886 edition.

(IB) *Bible, The Interpreter's.* 12 volumes. Nashville: Abington Press, 1951-57.

(IDB) Buttrick, George Arthur, ed. *The Interpreter's Dictionary of the Bible*, 4 vols. plus Supplementary volume. Nashville: Abdingdon Press, 1962, 1976.

(Jalalayn) *Tafsir al-Jalalayn.* (The Commentary by the Two Jalals: Jalal al-Din al-Mahalli and Jalal al-Din al-Suyuti). Eighth edition (Arabic). Beirut: Dar al-Jil, AH1415/1995 CE.

(James) James, Montague Rhodes. *The Apocryphal New Testament.* London: Oxford Univ. Press, 1953.

(JB) *Bible, The Jerusalem.* Jones, Alexander, gen. ed. Standard edition. London: Barton, Longman & Todd, 1966.

(Josephus) Josephus. *Complete Works.* Trans. William Whiston. Grand Rapids: Kregel Publications, 1967; orig. Published in Edinburgh, 1867.

(Kapelrud) Kapelrud, A.S. *The Ras Shamra Discoveries and the Old Testament.* Oxford: Blackwell, 1965.

(Keller) Keller, Werner. *The Bible as History.* Trans. William Neil. New York: Bantam Books, 1974.

(Kisa'i) Kisa'i, Muhammad ibn 'Abd Allah. *Tales of the Prophets.* Trans. Wheeler M. Thackston, Jr. Chicago: Great Books of the Islamic World, 1997.

(KJV) *Bible, The Holy (King James Version).* Cleveland: World Publishing Co., undated, but conforming to edition of 1611.

(Kramer-Myth) Kramer. Samuel Noah, ed. *Mythologies of the Ancient World.* Garden City: Doubleday & Co., 1961.

(Kramer-Sumer) Kramer, Samuel Noah. *History Begins at Sumer.* Garden City: Doubleday & Co., 1959.

(Laymon) Laymon, Charles M., ed. *The Interpreter's One-Volume Commentary on the Bible.* Nashville: Abingdon Press, 1971.

(LJ) Ginzberg, Louis. *The Legends of the Jews.* 7 volumes. Philadelphia: Jewish Publication Society of America, 1909-1938.

(LXX) *Bible: The Septuagint*, Greek &English Old Testament with the Apocrypha. Trans. Sir Launcelot Lee Brenton. London: Samuel Bagster & Sons, 1976.

(Mayhani) Mayhani, Muhammad bin Munawwar. *Asrar al-Tawhid* (Secrets of Divine Unity). Persian. Tehran: Amir Kabir, AHS1348.

(McEvedy) McEvedy and Richard Jones. *Atlas of World Population History.* Harmondsworth: Penguin Books, 1978.

(Nathan) Nathan, Rabbi. *The Fathers According to Rabbi Nathan.* Trans. Judah Goldin. New York: Shocken Books, 1974.

(OBA) May, Herbert G., ed. *Oxford Bible Atlas*, 2nd edition. London: Oxford Univ. Press, 1974.

(Olmstead) Olmstead, A.T. *History of the Persian Empire.* Chicago: Univ. of Chicago Press, 1948.

(OxBible) *Bible, The Oxford Annotated.* Revised Standard Version—College edition. H.G. May and B.M. Metzger, eds. New York: Oxford Univ. Press, 1962.

(Phipps) Phipps, William E. *Muhammad and Jesus.* New York: Continuum, 1996.

(PRE) Eliezer ben Hyrkanos, Rabbi. *Pirke de Rabbi Eliezer.* Trans. & ed. Gerald Friedlander. New York: Harmon Press, 1970; from London 1916 edition.

(Quran-Arberry) *Quran:* Arberry, Arthur J. The Koran Interpreted. London: Oxford Univ. Press, 1964.

(Quran-Dawood) *Quran:* The Koran. Trans. N.J. Dawood. Harmondsworth: Penguin Books, 1966.

(Quran-Farid) *Holy Quran, The.* Malik Ghulam Farid, ed. (and trans.?). Orig. publication by The Oriental and Religious Publishing Corp., Ltd., of Pakistan 1969. Present edition: Tilford: Islam International Publications, 1994.

(Quran-Maududi) *Quran:* Maududi, S. Abul A'la, commentator. The Meaning of the Quran. Trans. Muhammad Akbar Muradpuri. First 17 surahs in 6 vols. Lahore: Islamic Publications, 1971-73.

(Quran-MMA) *Quran:* The Holy Quran. Trans. & commentary by Maulana Muhammad Ali. 5th edition. Lahore: Ahmadiyyah Anjuman Isha'at Islam, 1963.

(Quran-Pickthall) *Quran:* The Meaning of the Glorious Koran. Trans. Mohammed Marmaduke Pickthall. New York: Mentor Books, 1953.

(Quran-Sale) The Koran. Trans. & annotated by George Sale. London: Frederick Warne and Co, undated.

(Quran-Yusuf Ali) *Quran:* The Holy Quran. Trans. & commentary by Abdullah Yusuf Ali, 2 vols., continuous pagination. Lahore: Sh. Muhammad Ashraf, 1969.

(RSV) *Bible, The Holy (Revised Standard Edition).* Revised 1952. London: Oxford Univ. Press, 1952.

(Saggs) Saggs, H.W.F. *The Greatness That was Babylon.* New York: The New American Library, 1968.

(Schauss) Schauss, Hayyim. *Guide to Jewish Holy Days: History and Observance.* New York: Schocken Books, 1962.

(SEI) Gibb, H.A.R. & Kramers, J.H., eds. *The Shorter Encyclopædia of Islam.* Leiden: E.J. Brill; London: Luzac & Co., 1961.

(Shinnie) Shinnie, P.L. *Meroe: A Civilization of the Sudan.* London: Thames and Hudson, 1967.

(Silver) Silver, Abba Hillel. *Moses and the Original Torah.* New York: Macmillan Co., 1961.

(Smith) Smith, W. Robertson. *The Religion of the Semites*. New York: Schocken Books, 1972 (1889)

(Surabadi) Surabadi, Abu Bakr 'Atiq Nayshaburi. *Stories From the Holy Quran*. Dr. Mahdavi, ed. Persian. No. 66 in Iranian Texts Series. Tehran: Tehran Univ., AHS1347.

(Tabari) Tabari, Muhammad bin Jarir. *Tarikh-i Tabari*. 16 vols. Persian trans. Abu al-Qasim Payandah. Tehran: Bunyad-i Farhang- Iran, AHS 1352-54.

(Tacitus) Tacitus, Cornelius. *The Annals of Imperial Rome*. Trans. Michael Grant. Harmondsworth: Penguin Books, 1959.

(Tisdall) Tisdall, Rev. Wm. St. Clair. *The Original Sources of the Quran*. London: 1905.

(Trawick-NT) Trawick, Buckner B. *The Bible as Literature: The New Testament*. Second edition. New York: Barnes & Noble, 1968.

(Weber) Weber, Max. *Ancient Judaism*. Trans. & ed. Hans H. Gerth & Don Martindale. New York: The Free Press, 1952.

(Webster) *Webster's Ninth New Collegiate Dictionary*, Springfield: Merriam-Webster, Inc., 1991.

(Wehr) Wehr, Hans. *Arabic-English Dictionary*. Trans. J.M. Cowan. Beirut: Librairie du Liban, 1980.

(Wolff) Wolff, Hans Walter. *The Old Testament: A Guide to Its Writings*. Trans. Keith R. Crim. London: SPCK, 1974.

(World Almanac) *The World Almanac and Book of Facts*. 2002 edition. New York: World Almanac Bks, 2002.

INDEX

This index is to the text and notes. *God* and *Moses* are not listed (except topically) as the words occur too frequently throughout the text to be indexed usefully. The reader should refer to the Table of Contents for the general location of broader topics. The Glossary also contains relevant information. References to the Quran and the 66 books of the Bible (see list on p. xiii) are not indexed.

A

Aaron, 2, 6, 7, 8, 14, 18, 20, 39, 46, 56, 72, 74, 83, 84, 88, 89-97, 99, 100, 105-7, 113, 116, 128, 129, 131, 134, 136-8, 140, 144, 145, 150-55, 158, 161-8, 173-5, 178, 179, 181, 182, 184, 195, 215-20, 223
Aaron exalted, 95
Aaron to be Moses' spokesman, 95
Aaronites, 73, 74, 159, 161, 164, 175, 180, 181, 218
Abarim, 220
Abida, 67
Abihu, son of Aaron, 140, 175, 216
Abiram, 56, 180, 181
Abkir Midrash, 87
Abraham, 4, 30, 42, 44, 58, 62, 66, 74, 75, 78, 79, 81, 87, 94, 103, 134, 136, 141, 162, 172, 175, 196, 208, 212, 222, 228
Abu Simbel, 28
Achilles, death of in Greek legend, 209
Ackroyd, Peter R., 172
Adam, 62, 71, 87
Adoniah, 195
Aegean Sea, 121
Afghanistan, 21, 63
Africanus, 79
Agade = Akkad, 50
Agagites, 32
Age of Pyramids, the, 27
Ahasuerus, 32, 33
Akhenaton, 11, 17, 19, 27, 36, 37, 108
Akkadians, 72, 197
Akki, a drawer of water, 51
Akrazaiel (angel), 223
Albright, W.F., x, 81, 108, 214
Alexander Romance, 200
Alexander the Great, 37, 119, 200, 204, 225
Ali, the son-in-law of the Prophet, 63
Al-Qantarah, 120
Amalekites, 7, 8, 14, 116, 144, 220
Amau ('Amau), a region about 50 miles NE of modern Aleppo, 214
Ambrosian rocks, the, 79
Amen-em-het, 69
Amil ('Amil), 183-6, 216
Amistris, 33
Amman, 208, 222
Ammon. *See* Amun
Ammonites, 206, 212
Amorites, 9, 141, 205, 206
Amram, father of Moses, 14
Amun (Egyptian deity), 17, 20, 26, 31, 35-8
Amun, High Priest of, 36-8
Amun, worship of, 17
Anab, 207
Anak, father of Og, 204, 207
Anakim, the, 207, 208
ancient populations and armies, 110
Angel of Death, the, 219, 223-5
Angel of the Face, the, 223
Anoqo, 43
Antalya, Gulf of, 119
Anthes, Rudolph, 23
Antioch (Syrian), 190
Antiquities of the Jews, 195
Antony and Cleopatra, 36
Aphaca, 79
Apiru ('Apiru), 28
Apis, Egyptian sacred bull, 160
Aqabah (city), 124
Aqabah depression, 10
Aqabah, Gulf of, 66-8, 76, 120, 123
Arab tradition, 196
Arabah (valley), 67, 68, 76, 132

Arabia, 4, 15, 26, 34, 35, 37, 38, 51, 56, 66, 67, 85, 109, 118, 129, 148, 168, 195, 196, 227
Arabian Gulf, the, 133
Arabian Peninsula, the, 196
Arabian Sea, the, 188
Arabic (language), x, xi, xiv, 4, 26, 46, 48, 49, 65, 69, 71, 81, 86, 98, 109, 133, 167, 168, 174, 176, 177, 189, 198, 199, 204
Arabs, 4, 26, 34, 38, 54, 66, 68, 82, 85, 148, 155, 181, 186, 189, 191, 195, 203
Arba, father of Anak, 207
Arberry, A.J., x, 98
Arce. *See* Petra
Arden, Harvey, 133
Argob, 205
Ark of the Covenant, 7, 8, 73, 171, 209
Arrian, 119
Artapanus, 56, 61, 121, 191, 193, 194, 195, 196, 203
Artaxerxes II, 34
Artaxerxes III, 33
Aryan religion, 34
Asher, Israelite tribe, 109
Ashkelon, 12
Ashtaroth (city), 206
Ashurbanipal, 33
Asia, 43
Asiatics, 69, 70
Asiyah, 44, 46, 48
Assumption of Moses, 2
Assyria, 33, 170, 176
Assyrians, 74, 82, 170, 171, 227
Astaboras (river, 192, 193
Astaboras (river), 192-4, 199
Astapus (river), 192, 193
Astarte, 34
astrologers, 38, 39, 41, 42
Astyages, king, 43
Aswan, 28, 195
Atbara. *See* Astaboras (river)
Atbara (city), 194
Aton (Egytian deity), 17, 19, 108
Awj ('Awj). *See* Og
Azov, Sea of, 120
Azupiranu, 50

B

Baal (Canaanite deity), 63, 112, 113, 120, 160, 211, 214
Baal-Hadad (Canaanite deity), 161
Baal-peor, 222
Baal-zephon, 112, 113, 120
Baba Batra, 224
Babylon, viii, 25, 34, 73, 227, 228
Babylonia, viii, 26, 33, 45, 72, 171, 191
Babylonians, 24, 33, 34, 35, 73, 170, 171, 198, 227, 228
Bahrain, 198, 199
Bahrain, meaning of, 198
Bakhtiar, Dr. Laleh, xii
Bal'ami, 4, 135, 136, 137, 144, 145, 148-50, 152-6, 162, 163, 166, 188-90, 198, 200
Balaam, 9, 10, 26, 30, 41, 93, 98, 156, 204, 209-15, 218
Balaam, origin and meaning of the name, 214
Balaam's ass speaks, 212
Balak, 210, 212, 213
Bamyan, 63
Bash Shawish, 130
Bashan, 205-7, 209
Bashanites, 212
Basrah, 197
Bathory, Countess Elizabeth, 31
Bathsheba, 162
Bedouins, 84, 132, 133
Beersheba, 10, 76, 170
Benjamin, Israelite tribe, 32, 109, 110, 174
Benjaminites, 32, 174
Beor, father of Balaam, 9, 204, 211, 212, 214
Berenice, 37
Bethaven. *See* Bethel
Bethel, 12, 160, 170, 176
Beth-peor, 222
Bibby, Geoffrey, 199
Bible, the, ix, x, xi, 1, 4, 5, 7, 9, 11-15, 17-19, 22-5, 27-30, 32, 33, 39, 40, 42-50, 52-4, 56-60, 62-8, 71-80, 82, 84-7, 89-93, 97-102, 104-12, 114-17, 119-23, 125, 127, 128, 133, 135-8, 141, 146-58, 161, 163-71, 174, 175, 179,-82, 186,-8, 191, 194,

195, 196, 204-7, 210-12, 214-23, 225, 227-9
Bietak, Manfred, 12
Bithiah, 48, 173
Bitter Lakes, the, 123, 124
Bjornard, Reidar B., 34
Blue Nile (river), 194
Blue Nile, the (river), 193
Book of Jubilees, 41, 61
Book of Law, viii
Book of the Covenant, the, 137, 145
Book of the Law, viii, 146
Book of Yashar, 43
Breasted, James H., 16, 17, 39
Breydenbach, 129
brides discovered at wells, 58
Broadman Bible Commentary (BC), xi, 101, 128
Brockington, L.H., 33
Buber, Martin, 11, 14
Buckingham Palace, 30
Bukhari, al- (Traditionist), 3
Bull of Heaven, the, 197
burning bush, the, 75, 77

C

Cairo, 12, 29, 37, 69, 117, 191
Caleb, 180, 207, 221, 223
Cambyses, 22, 37, 43, 192, 193
Campbell, Joseph, 85
Canaan, the land, 8, 10, 12-14, 20, 28, 29, 33, 46, 67, 72, 80, 82, 89, 94, 112, 122, 123, 126, 131, 133, 141, 145, 150, 157, 160, 171, 174, 196, 206, 207, 212, 220, 221, 228
Canaanite (language), 18
Canaanites, 18, 34, 73, 74, 82, 91, 141, 151, 160, 161, 206
Ch. *See* Chronicler (Ch)
Chaldeans, 33
Chanethothes, 56
Chenephres, 56, 191
Choga Zambil, 24
Chosen People, God's, 1, 71, 124, 141
Christ, 42, 76, 130, 131, 134
Christian literature, 167
Christian religious literature, 112
Christianity, 4, 99, 131
Christians, ix, x, 11, 15, 31, 32, 39, 43, 44, 63, 76, 123, 136, 145, 172, 210, 218, 225, 227, 228
Christians, non-Pauline, 3
Chronicler (Ch), ix, 38, 64
chronology, difficulties in, ix
clothing, miraculous provision of, 133
cloud, the miraculous, 134
Conquest, date of, 12
Conquest, Israelite, 12, 14, 84, 122, 157, 172, 207, 210, 220
Copts, 39
Cossaeans, 195
Creationism, ix
Crimea, 120
Croats, the, 15
Croesus, 182
Cush, 182, 193, 195, 203
Cushan, 182, 195
Cushanites, 182
Cushite woman, the, 182, 195, 196
Cushites, 8, 182, 195, 196
Cybele, 34
Cyrus the Great, 43, 171, 227
Cyrus the Great, birth story of, 43

D

D. *See* Deuteronomist (D)
Daedalus, 156
Dan, Israelite tribe, 43, 74, 109, 158, 159, 160, 170, 175, 222
Dan, tribe of, 55
Danites, 158-61
Dar‘a, 39
Darius the Great, 23
Darwin, ix
Dathan, 55, 56, 180, 181
David, vii, 8, 73, 83, 102, 108, 157, 162, 169, 170, 175, 180, 207, 225
Dead Sea, 8, 35, 67, 132, 152, 211, 222
Dead Sea Scrolls, ix
Deber. *See* Kiriath-sepher
Debir, 207
Decalogue. *See* Ten Commandments, the
Declaration of Faith, the (Shahadah), 117
Delilah, 157

Delta, the, 26, 27, 28, 40, 70, 100, 107, 121
Der'a, 205
Deuteronomist (D), viii, 5, 76, 80, 91, 99, 137, 146, 147, 165, 225
Deuteronomy Rabbah, 49, 223
Dhul-Qarnayn, 33, 204
Dibri, 55
Dictionary of the Bible (DB), xi
Dilmun, 197, 198, 199
Diodorus, 108, 193
Documentary Theory, ix, 1
Downing Street, 30
Duncan, George B., x

E

E. *See* Elohist Document (E)
Eber, 65
Eden, 62, 197
Edom, 38, 68, 76, 77, 124, 216
Edomites, 8, 9, 38, 175
Edrei, 205
Eglon, 12
Egypt, ix, 2, 5-10, 12, 13, 16-8, 20-23, 25-30, 33, 35-40, 42, 44, 46, 51, 61, 62-4, 66, 69-72, 77, 79-81, 83, 84, 86, 89-91, 93-101, 103-13, 116, 119, 121-4, 126-8, 130, 132, 133, 141, 146, 147, 150-52, 155-7, 160, 163, 172, 175, 188, 191, 192, 195-7, 199, 212, 222
Egypt, gods of, 84
Egypt, population of, 39, 108
Egypt, temple lands of, 36
Egyptian Empire, 28
Egyptian Museum, the, 117
Egyptian officer, the, 54
Egyptian Recension, ix
Egyptian use of stone in buildings, 26
Egyptians, 5, 11, 12, 13, 15-20, 22, 23, 25-9, 31, 34-6, 39, 40-42, 46, 48-56, 60, 66, 68, 70, 77, 80, 83-7, 89, 91, 93, 94, 96-100, 104-14, 116-19, 121, 123, 124, 136, 137, 144, 151, 153-57, 173, 174, 176, 188, 192, 193, 195, 196, 214
Eichrodt, Walter, 72
Eilat, 84
El (Canaanite deity), 15, 73, 160, 161
El Shaddai (Canaanite deity), 82
El-'Elyon (Canaanite deity), 73
Elam, 33
Elamites, 32, 34, 35
Eldaah, 67
Eleazar, son of Aaron, 140, 174, 184, 215-18, 221, 223, 225
Eli, 15
Eliezer, 219
Eliezer, second son of Moses, 64
Elijah, 76, 200, 201, 202, 203
Elim, 7, 127, 129
elohim (God), viii, 71, 72
elohim, meaning and use of, 71
Elohist Document (E), viii, 5, 10, 13, 40, 41, 47, 57, 64, 65, 70-76, 80-83, 86, 95, 99, 101, 102, 104, 106, 108, 112, 113, 127, 128, 137-42, 144-47, 150, 151, 154, 161, 163, 165, 175, 210, 212, 213, 222, 225, 227
Emim, the, 207
Encyclopædia Britannica (EB), xi
Encyclopædia Judaica, 46
Encyclopædia Judaica (EJ), xi
Encyclopædia of Islam (EI), xi
Enki, 197, 198
Enoch, 62
Ephah, 67
Epher, 67
ephod, the, 159
Ephraim, Israelite (Josephic) tribe, 10, 109, 122, 169, 170, 172, 174, 176, 220-22
Ephraimites, 158, 175, 221
Epic of Gilgamesh, 133, 197-200
Erech (Uruk, Warka), 197, 199
Essenes, the, 35
Essley, Philip L. Jr., 33
Esther, 31, 32, 33, 34, 35
Esther, her story discussed, 32
Esther, historicity of, 33
Esther, meaninng of name, 34
Etham, 111, 120
Ethiopia, 56, 182, 191-5, 203, 225
Ethiopians, 191-3, 195, 196
Euphrates (river), 15, 50, 197, 199, 212, 228, 229
Europeanization, 15
Eustathius, 79
Evolution, theory of, ix
Exile, the, 3, 73, 108, 169, 171, 175, 227

Exodus Rabbah, 30, 31, 76, 92, 98, 134
Exodus, size of, 109
Exodus, size of vastly exaggerated, 107
Exodus, the, 2, 6, 7, 8, 10-15, 17, 28-30, 40, 41, 63, 74, 77, 80, 83-5, 97, 102, 105, 107, 109, 110, 112, 120-23, 125, 137, 145, 146, 161, 165, 166, 174, 188, 197, 228
extra-Biblical, 42
Ezra, 73, 166, 171

F

Fairservis, Walter A., 23
Falashas, the, 225
Fars, 22
Fathers According to Rabbi Nathan, The, 115, 218
Faylakah (island), 199
Fertile Crescent, the, 19, 50, 121, 227, 228
fish of Moses' journey, the, 200
Flood, the, ix, 98, 197, 204, 208, 209
Freud, Sigmund, 17, 19

G

Gabriel (angel), 88, 92, 113, 114, 116-18, 153, 154, 156, 179, 205, 219, 224
Gad, Israelite tribe, 12, 109
Gadites, Israelite tribe, 9
Galilee, Sea of, 206
Ganon (Jair), 175
Gaster, Theodor H., 51
Geneva, Lake, 120
Gerizim, Mount, 172
Gershom, firstborn of Moses, 64, 159, 219
Gezer, 12
Ghillany, F.W., 82
Gibeah, 174
Gideon, 67
Gilead, 68, 222
Gilgamesh, 197, 198, 199, 200, 203
Ginzberg, Louis, 202, 224
God angered, 140
God permits Moses to see Himself, 141
Goedicke, Dr. Hans, 121
Goelet, Ogden, 17
Golden Calf, the, 7, 135, 137, 138, 140, 144, 146-8, 150-54, 156-61, 163, 166-8, 175, 176, 179
Goliath, 207
Golziher, I., 173
Goshen, 28, 55, 70, 124
graven image, 155, 158, 159
Gray, John, 141
Great Rift Valley, 68
Greece, 24, 33, 110, 148
Greek (language), ix
Greek mythology, 63, 156
Greenberg, Moshe, 3

H

Hadassah. *See* Esther
Hagar, 66, 136
Halpern, Baruch, 84
Hamadan, 33
Haman, 4, 21, 22, 23, 25, 31, 32, 33, 34, 35, 36, 37, 38, 44, 45, 46, 47, 48, 93, 116, 117, 178
Haman, etymology of, 34
Hammon. *See* Amun
Hammurabi, 15
Hanoch, 67
haoma (sacred drink), 34
Haran, the region, 58
Harpagus, 43
Hatshepsut, 121
Heber, 65
Hebrew (language), 14, 72, 80, 91, 103, 109, 119, 227, 229
Hebrews, 5-11, 13, 14, 16-18, 20, 27, 28, 32, 37, 40, 41, 47, 48, 50, 52-6, 64, 65, 71, 72, 81, 85, 94, 97, 98, 100, 101, 105, 107, 108, 110-12, 116, 121, 133, 137, 145, 146, 166, 174-6, 179, 192, 207, 212
Hebron, viii, 170, 207, 208
Hejaz, 26, 35, 37, 67, 85, 124, 148, 153, 174, 200
Hejazi Jews, 35, 196
Hellenistic literature, 191
Hellenization, 16, 227
Heman, 38
Hemanites, 38
henotheism, 84
Herat, 21

Hermon, Mount, 68, 158
Herod, 42, 229
Herodotus, 22, 43, 110
Heshbon (city), 205
Hezekiah, 64, 171
Hibbur Yafeh, 203
High Dam, the, 28
higher criticism, vii
History of Bukhara, 136
Hittites, 141, 206
Hivites, 141, 206
Hobab, 65
Holiness Code, viii
Holofernes, 33
Holy Mountain, the, 71, 77, 80, 95, 123-5, 137, 152, 166, 179
Holy Name, the, 155
Homan. *See* Heman
Honeycutt, Roy Jr., 101
Hophni, son of Eli, 15
Hor, Mount, 8, 216, 220
Horeb, Mount, 6, 7, 10, 75-8, 82, 123, 127-9, 157, 160, 161
Horites, 38
Horn of Africa, the, 195
Hosea. *See* Joshua
Hoshea. *See* Joshua
House of David, the, 21
Hud, 177
Human (Elamite deity), 34
Hur, 144, 155
Hurru, 12
Hyksos, the, 22, 27, 206

I

Iblis (the devil), 183
Icarus, 156
Inanna (Sumerian goddess), 100
India, gods of, 26
Interpreter's Bible (IB), xi
Interpreter's Bible Dictionary (IBD), xi
Iraq, 118, 197, 227-9
Isaac, 58, 62, 78, 79, 81, 85, 87, 94, 141, 148, 162, 222
Isaiah (prophet), 92
Ishmaelites, 67, 85
Ishtar, 33, 34, 51, 197
Isis, 34
Isiyah, 45-8, 88
Islam, vii, x, xi, 1- 4, 11, 15, 18, 24, 29, 31, 35, 39, 41, 45, 46, 54, 55, 65, 71, 75, 80, 87, 88, 92, 93, 97, 115, 119, 124, 129, 137, 148, 150, 157, 172, 177, 182, 188, 196, 199, 200, 203, 206, 209, 214, 215, 221, 225
Islamic religious literature, 112
Islamic tradition, 2, 18, 29, 35, 46, 55, 65, 87, 88, 148, 182, 188, 203, 215, 221
Israel, the nation, ix, 1, 2
Israel, the Northern kingdom, vii, viii, 159, 169-72
Israel, the people, x, 1-3, 7, 8, 11, 12, 13, 21, 27-30, 36, 39-41, 44, 46, 55, 62-4, 71, 72, 74, 80-85, 87, 90, 93-5, 97, 98, 104-8, 111-14, 117, 118, 122, 124, 127-9, 131, 133, 134, 136, 139-44, 146, 147, 149, 150, 152, 155, 156, 159-63, 166, 167, 170-72, 176, 178, 180, 181, 184-6, 206-8, 210-13, 215, 216, 218, 219, 220-22, 225, 228
Israel, the twelve tribes of, 122
Israelites, viii, x, 1, 3, 7-10, 12-14, 16-18, 26, 27, 29-31, 38-42, 45, 46, 54, 55, 61, 63, 64, 67, 71-3, 76, 79-86, 89, 91, 93-5, 97, 99, 104-11, 113, 115, 116, 119-24, 126, 128, 130-37, 141, 146-8, 150, 152-7, 160-63, 165-7, 169, 170, 174, 178, 180, 183, 185, 186, 190, 197, 205, 207-9, 211, 212, 215, 221, 228
Israelites complain at the crossing of the sea, 113
Israelites frightened by the size of the Egyptian army, 113
Israelitish. *See* Israelites
Issachar, Israelite tribe, 109
Ithamar, son of Aaron, 140, 216

J

J. See Yahwist Document (J)
J1 (First Yahwist), viii, 137, 229
J2 (Second Yahwist), viii, 75, 79, 137, 229
Jabal al-Lawz, 77
Jabal al-Naba, 222
Jabal Halal, 123
Jabal Harun, 216

Jabal Katerina, 123
Jabal Musa, 76, 123
Jabal Serbal, 123
Jabal Sinn Bishr, 124
Jabal Ya'allaq, 124
Jacob, vii, 2, 5, 20, 28, 30, 39, 58-62, 78, 79, 81, 85, 87, 94, 103, 114, 136, 141, 162, 174, 222, 228
Jair. *See* Ganon
Jalalayn, 187
Jambres, 156, 167
James, Greek form of Jacob, 20
Jannes, 156, 167
Jarvis, Maj. C.S., 130
JB. *See Jerusalem Bible*
Jebusites, 141, 206
Jephunneh, father of Caleb, 207, 221
Jericho, 9, 39, 133, 204, 209, 210, 212, 220, 222, 223
Jerichoans, 209
Jeroboam I, 159-61, 172, 175, 176
Jerusalem, vii-ix, 7, 8, 14, 32, 33, 39, 42, 73, 74, 83, 100, 140, 148, 158-61, 169-73, 223, 227, 228, 229
Jerusalem Bible (JB), xi
Jesus, 42, 43, 44, 76, 99, 131, 173, 179, 187, 210, 218
Jesus, Greek form of Joshua, 20
Jethro, 6, 17, 30, 41, 55, 60-62, 64,-6, 68, 75, 82, 83, 85, 87, 91, 92, 147, 196
Jewish commentators, 53, 179
Jewish law, 74, 158
Jewish literature, 112, 157, 167, 177, 200, 202, 209, 214, 223
Jewish scholars, 10, 11, 31, 210, 215
Jewish tradition, 2, 20, 25, 30, 32, 38, 41, 44, 45, 48, 49, 53, 55, 56, 61-3, 66, 76, 78, 87, 89, 91, 92, 97, 101, 107, 111, 112, 114, 130, 133, 134, 136, 137, 147, 148, 150, 154, 155-7, 160, 161, 163, 167, 168, 174-6, 180-82, 185, 196, 208, 209, 211, 214, 218, 223, 224
Jewish writers, 103
Jews, ix, x, 3, 18, 32-5, 38, 42, 73, 78, 80, 91, 105, 107, 108, 115, 122, 136, 156, 159, 162, 165, 172, 173, 176, 203, 206, 209, 214, 225, 227-9
Job, 30, 41, 173
Jochebed, mother of Moses, 14, 46
John Hyrcanus, 172
John of Patmos, author of *Revelation*, 210
Jonah, 118
Jonathan. son of Gershom, 159
Jones, Richard, 40, 108
Jordan (modern kingdom), 38, 222
Jordan (river), 9, 12, 15, 39, 67, 108, 133, 188, 204, 206-8, 210, 211, 216, 223
Joseph, ix, 5, 15, 21, 22, 27, 30, 39, 40, 42, 44, 62, 81, 111, 158, 172, 174, 179, 180, 188
Josephic tribes, 10, 12, 71, 81, 122, 169-72, 174, 176, 221
Josephites, 122
Josephus, 17, 19, 42, 44, 48, 49, 50, 90, 92, 107, 115, 119, 133, 179, 192-7, 203, 216, 217, 225
Joshua, 9, 12, 20, 29, 113, 116, 122, 126, 144, 145, 163, 188-90, 198, 204, 207, 209, 210, 214, 219-21, 223, 225, 227
Josiah, 171
Judaea, 42, 169, 170, 228
Judaeo-Christian tradition, 122, 191
Judah (tribe), vii
Judah, Israelite tribe, x, 48, 109, 110, 155, 161, 169, 171, 180, 207, 222
Judah, kingdom of, 33, 160
Judah, son of Jacob, 15, 162
Judah, the Southern kingdom, vii, viii, 169, 170, 171, 228
Judahites, 82, 122, 169-71
Judaism, 1, 3, 4, 19, 21, 24, 35, 73, 169, 175, 229

K

Kadesh, 6, 8, 10, 14, 17, 20, 77, 110, 124, 126, 128, 216
Kadesh-Barnea, 6, 8, 14, 77, 123
Kapelrud, A.S., 161
Karbala, 199
Karbala (in Iraq), 199
Karnak, Temple of, 28, 36
Kassites, 195
Kem-wer (island), 69
Kenite hypothesis, the, 11, 82, 84
Kenites, 10, 11, 65, 67, 68, 81-5

Keturah, 66
Kharbil, 55
Khazars,the, 3
Khidr, 189, 190, 199, 202, 203
Khirbat al-Shaykh, 222
Khorasan, 22, 116, 136
Khuzestan, 24
King James Version (KJV), xi
Kiriath-arba. *See* Hebron
Kiriath-sepher, 12
Korah, 8, 32, 36, 56, 174, 175, 177-82, 188, 211
Korah known as *Qarun* in Islam, 177
Korahites, 174, 175, 181
Krahmalkov, Charles, 121
Kremlin, the, 30
Kuwait, 199

L

Laban, 58
Lachish, 12
Laish (city), 158, 159
Lake. Manzalah, Lake
Laqitah, 45, 48, 49
Law of Moses, the, 1, 4, 7, 9, 19, 21, 74, 89, 135-7, 144, 145, 149-52, 163, 165, 166, 171, 179, 197, 205, 206, 219, 228
Leah, 14, 59
Legends of the Jews, 63, 118, 202
Lekah, 156
leprosy, 8, 30, 48, 55, 89, 90, 101, 173, 182, 195
leprosy and Moses, 173
Levi, son of Jacob, 15, 162
Levi, tribe of, 9, 13-15, 47, 140, 178, 186
Levite priesthood, 14
Levites, 14, 15, 20, 73, 74, 91, 109, 138, 141, 147, 158-61, 163, 164, 166, 175, 176, 180, 181
Levites slaughter 3,000 Israelite men, 140
Luxor, 27, 36
LXX. *See Septuagint* (LXX)
Lydia, 34

M

Ma'an, 68
Ma'asiyot, 203
Maccabeans, 172
Macedonia, 119
Madinah, 61, 139, 148, 206
Magi, the, 43
Mahdavi, Dr. Yahya, x, 4
Makkah, 38, 61, 130, 139, 143
Manasseh (king), 45
Manasseh, Israelite (Josephic) tribe, 10, 109, 122, 170, 188, 206, 222
Mandal bin Khaland al-Azdi, 190
Mandane, daughter of Astyages, 43
Manetho, 19
manna, 7, 8, 126, 127, 131-3, 137
manna, nature of, 132
Manzalah (lake), 120, 123
Manzaleh, Lake. *See* Manzalah, Lake
Marah, 127
Marah identified with 'Ayn Hawarah, 127
Marduk, 26, 33, 34, 63
Mari, 15
Mari archives, the, 15
Mashti, 34
Massah, 7, 127, 129
Matthew (disciple), xi
Maududi, Sayyid Abul A'la, x
McEvedy, Colin, 40, 108, 110
McNeile, A.H., 65
Medes, 43
Medians, 43
Mediterranean (sea), 12, 84, 112, 120, 123, 132, 133, 192, 222
Meek, T.J., 81
Mekilta Beshallah, 110, 111
Melchizedek, 74
Memphis, 56, 191, 192
Meribah, 7, 8, 127, 129, 216, 220
Merneptah, the Pharaoh, 28
Merneptah, the stele of, 12, 28, 29
Meroe, 192, 193
Mesopotamia, ix, 24, 25, 50, 51, 148, 196, 197, 228
Mesopotamian mythology, 63
Mesopotamians, 13, 25, 34, 197, 198, 229
Messiah, the, 185
Messianic era heralded, 43

Micah, 157-60, 167, 228
Michael (angel), 56, 156, 224
Michelangelo, 140
Midian, 2, 5, 16-18, 20, 28, 37, 38, 51, 57-9, 61, 63-70, 75-8, 82, 84-6, 91, 112, 124, 148, 182, 188, 191, 192, 195, 196, 199, 211
Midianites, 9, 18, 20, 26, 57, 61, 65-7, 81-5, 87, 91, 182, 211, 213
Migdol, 112, 120
Minaeans, 14, 15
miracle of the water duplicated in modern times, 130
Miriam, 8, 14, 20, 45, 49, 50, 72, 130, 134, 173, 179, 180, 182, 195
Miriam, death of, 8
Miriam, name of, 20
Mitradates, 43
mixed multitude, the, 108
Moab, 9, 68, 210-12, 220, 222
Moabites, 162, 207, 211-13
molten image, 155, 157-9
Mordecai, 32-5
Moriah, Mount, 148, 172
Mormons, 121
Moses, viii, ix
Moses accused of murdering Aaron, 217
Moses asserted to have spoken with God, 1
Moses commissioned as a messenger, 79
Moses complains to God of the unwillingness of the Israelites, 94
Moses contests with the Egyptian sorcerers, 96
Moses contests with the Egyptian sorcerers (Biblical version), 97
Moses flees to Midian, 57
Moses kills a dragon, 63
Moses kills an Egyptian, 5, 52, 90
Moses makes Israelites drink the dust of the Golden Calf, 165
Moses marries a Midianite, 60
Moses mentioned more times in the Quran than any other Biblical figure, 4
Moses orders massacre of Midianite prisoners, 9
Moses orders the slaughter of the Midianite captives, 211
Moses placed in a basket, 46
Moses provokes the wrath of God, 128
Moses put in a basket, 47
Moses raised as an Egyptian, 5
Moses raises objections to his mission, 87
Moses rejects wet nurses, 45
Moses the supreme hero of the Pentateuch, 1
Moses, age of at commission, 92
Moses, age of at death, 61
Moses, ascension of, 92
Moses, etymology of his name, 16
Moses, supposed speech defect of, 18, 88, 90, 91, 95
Moses' mother, name of, 46
Mosul, 118
Mount Esau. *See* Seir, Mount
Mountain of God, the, 76, 77, 83, 93, 127, 136, 139, 144, 148, 153, 162, 167
Mountain of Moses, 76
Muhammad Ali, x, 54, 61, 98, 151, 154, 186, 187
Muhammad, the Prophet, x, 1-4, 31, 61, 63, 66, 71, 92, 117, 129, 130, 153, 166, 176-8, 180, 199, 200, 226, 229
mummies, Pharaonic, 117
Muqanna', 136
Muslim (Traditionist), 3
Muslim commentators, 35, 42, 65, 135, 165, 178, 184
Muslim qiblah, the, 209
Muslim ritual, 143
Muslims, ix-xi, 4, 11, 15, 64, 67, 82, 136, 143, 206, 225, 226

N

Nabi Musa, shrine of, 223
Nadab, son of Aaron, 140, 175, 216
name of God, importance of its disclosure, 71
Name of God, the, viii
Naphtali, Israelite tribe, 109, 222
Nazirite vows, 162
Near Eastern art, 160
Nebo, Mount, 211, 220, 222
Nebuchadnezzar, 32, 43, 73, 227, 228
necktie, possible origin of, 15

Nefertiti, 19
Nefru, 69
Negeb, the, 222
Nehemiah, 73
Nephilim, the, 207, 208
New Empire (Egyptian), 13, 36, 40, 196
New Testament, ix
New Testament, the, 1, 16, 33, 35, 37, 43, 99, 130, 173, 210, 227
Night Journey, 92
Nile called a "sea" in Arabic, 46
Nile, the (river), 27, 28, 37, 40, 46, 56, 66, 89, 99-101, 107, 127, 191-5, 199
Nimrod, 25, 42
Nineveh, 50, 118
nisbah, *y* of, 168
Noah, 62, 98, 162, 197
non-Jews, 195
non-Levites, 158
non-Semites, 3, 51
Nubia, 193, 195
Nubians, 192, 196
Nun, father of Joshua, 144, 188, 219-21

O

Oak of Mamre, the, 79
Oak of Shechem, the, 79
Odyssey, The, 198
Og, 9, 204-9, 212
Og's bedstead, 206
Og's gigantic stature, 206
Og's gigantic stature in Jewish tradition, 208
Old Testament, vii
Old Testament, the, vii, ix, 1, 3, 4, 7, 32, 33, 35, 80, 121, 156, 169, 172, 227-9
Oman, Gulf of, 188
Omri, 170

P

P. *See* Priestly Document (P)
Palestine, vii, viii, 7, 29, 35, 39, 51, 67, 73, 74, 80, 108, 141, 158, 169-72, 176, 195, 204, 207, 222, 227, 228
Palm of Deborah, the, 79
Pamphylian Sea, the, 119
Paradise, scent of, 219
Parah, 185
parasang, defined, 205
Paschal Feast. *See* Passover, the
Passover, the, 105, 107, 108, 147
Paul, 130, 134, 228
Pentateuch, vii, viii, ix, 1, 2, 3, 5, 9, 10, 14, 19, 21, 84, 108, 122, 172, 175, 179, 195, 220, 225, 227, 228
people of the thicket, 66, 68
Peor, 211
Peor, the matter of, 211
Perekop, Isthmus of, 120
Perga, 119
Perizzites, 141, 206
Per-Ramses, 27, 28
Persia, 43
Persian (language), xi, xiv, 4, 6, 34, 72
Persian Gulf, the, 196
Persians, x, 22, 33, 34, 37, 43, 79, 110, 133, 171, 192, 198
Pethor, 212, 214
Petirat Aharon, 217
Petra, 68, 130, 216
Pharaoh, 4, 5, 6, 12, 13, 16-18, 21-3, 25-31, 36-50, 52, 54-7, 62, 63, 66, 69, 70, 80, 83, 86-9, 92-100, 104-7, 110-12, 116-18, 121, 134, 156, 173, 178, 179, 192, 212, 222
pharaoh, meaning of, 29
Pharaoh's daugher, name of, 48
Pharaohs, divinity of, 23
Phaselis, 119
Philistines, 111, 112, 158
Philo, 115
Phinehas, son of Eli, 15, 174
Phrygia, 34
Pickthall, M.M., x, 98
Pi-hahiroth, 112, 113, 120
Pilgrimage, the (Hajj), 137, 143
pillar of cloud, the, 111, 113, 134, 144, 145
pillar of light, the, 126
Pirke de Rabbi Eliezer, 30, 41, 46, 62, 92, 118, 155
Pisgah, 222
Pithom, 27
plagues, the last (death), 104, 106
plant of immortality, 197
Plataea, battle of, 33
pre-Islamic Haggadah, 203

Priestly Document (P), viii, 5, 9, 10, 13, 14, 40, 65, 67, 70-72, 74, 80, 82, 84, 95, 97, 99, 101, 103, 107, 109, 112, 119, 120, 123, 126, 127, 131, 136-8, 145, 147, 149, 181, 184, 197, 210, 211, 214, 216, 220, 225
Prince of the Sea, 63
Promised Land, the, 9, 129, 220, 223
Protevangelium, 44
Proverbs Midrash, 93
Puah, Hebrew midwife, 40
Purim, feast of, 32, 33
Pushanj (a town in Khorasan), 21, 116
Pyramids, Age of, 26

Q

Qa-nefru, 69
quails, 7, 8, 126, 127, 131-3, 137, 147
Qumran, 35
Quqanos, 195
Quran, the, ix, x, 4, 9, 10, 11, 18, 19, 22-6, 28-32, 34-9, 41, 44-54, 56-64, 66, 68, 75-9, 82, 85-90, 92, 93, 95-103, 105-7, 109, 113, 116-19, 122, 124, 126, 127, 129, 130, 133-7, 145-54, 157, 162-8, 172-82, 185-90, 192, 194-204, 213, 215, 219, 221, 228, 229
Quranic signs (nine) given to Moses, 98
Qurayzah, treatment of, 206

R

Ra (Egyptian sun god), 17, 36
Raamses (city), 27, 28
Rabbah, 92, 206, 208
Rabbi Jehudah, 156
Rabbi Joshua ben Levi, 200-203
Rabbi Levi, 62
Rabbi Nisin, 185
Rachel, 58, 59, 174
Rameses (city), 107, 120
Rameses II, 12, 21, 26,-30, 36, 37, 40, 50, 108, 110, 117
Rameses III, 36
Rameses XII, 36
Rameses, meaning of name, 17
Ramses. *See* Rameses II
Ras Shamra, 160
Rayyan bin Walid, 21
Rebekah, 58
red heifer, the, 184, 185
Red Mountain, 69
Red Sea, 37, 105, 111, 115-19, 121, 132, 133, 152, 188
Rehoboam, 160-72
Rendsburg, Gary A., 101
Rephaim, the, 206, 207, 208
Rephidim, 127
Return, the, 170
Reuben, 67
Reuben, Israelite tribe, 12, 109, 180, 222
Reuben, son of Jacob, 15, 162
Reubenites, Israelite tribe, 9, 67
Reuel. *See* Jethro
revelation of the divine name, the, 80
Revised Standard Version, xi
Revised Standard Version (RSV), x, 34, 100, 101, 128
Rhone (river), 120
Richardson, H. Neil, 35
Riqa, 54, 56
rod of Moses. *See* staff of Moses
Roman Catholic Church, 1
Rome, 24
RSV. *See Revised Standard Version*
Russians, 120

S

Sa‘d bin Mu‘adh, 206
Saba, royal city of the Ethiopians, 192
Salamis, battle of, 33
Sale, George, 129
Salecah. *See* Salkhad
Salem. *See* Jerusalem
Salkhad, 206
Samael. *See* Sammael
Samaria (city), 170
Samaria (region), 170-74, 176
Samaritan schism, 168
Samaritans, vii, 137, 168-70, 172-6
Samir. *See* Samiri, al-
Samiri, al-, 137, 151-4, 156, 162, 167, 168, 173-7
Samiri, al-, meaning of, 167, 174, 176

Sammael (the devil), 156, 168, 173, 174, 176, 177, 224
Samson, 157, 162
Sand-crossers, 69
Sanhedrin, 149
Sargon of Akkad, 50, 51, 170
Satan, 52, 168, 176, 189, 204, 217
Saudi Arabia, 67, 68, 77, 198
Saul, 169
Second Theophany a different version of the first, 95
Seir, Mount, 15, 38, 66, 68, 76-8, 123, 124, 128, 216
Sellin, Ernst, 17
Semites, 17-19, 20, 22, 25, 30, 34, 38, 40, 50, 65, 70, 71, 85, 91, 108, 160, 197, 214, 227
Sen-Usert, 69
Septuagint (LXX), ix, 100, 146, 228, 233
Seraphim, the, 224, 228
serpent, bronze or copper, 8, 10, 64, 84
servant of God explains his actions to Moses, 190
servant of God found by Moses, 189
servant of God holes the boat, 189
servant of God slays the boy, 190
servant of God stops to repair a wall, 190
Seth (Egyptian deity), 51
Seti I, 12, 29
seven plagues, the, 102
seventy elders, the, 137, 138, 140, 145-9, 153, 217
Shahidi, Dr. Sayyid Ja'far, xi
Shakespeare, W., 36
Sheba, 15
Shechem, 170-2
Shekinah, the, 49
Shelomith, 55, 56
Shemer, 170, 174
Shifa, 68
Shinar, land of, 24
Shiprah, Hebrew midwife, 40
Shittim (place), 211
Shobek, 68
Shu'ayb, 57, 59, 61-6, 68, 74, 77, 85, 177
Sicard, 129
Sihon, 9, 205, 209, 212
Simeon, Israelite tribe, 109, 110
Simeon, son of Jacob, 15
Sinai, 2, 6, 7, 69, 77, 82, 109, 122, 123, 130, 132, 133, 136, 137
Sinai Camel Corps, the, 130
Sinai, Mount, viii, 10, 76, 83, 123, 124, 127, 135, 136, 138, 139, 148, 149, 167, 175, 223
Sinuhe, 68, 69, 70
Sirbonis (lake), 123
slaughter of the infants, the, 41
Snow White and the Seven Dwarfs, 43
Solomon, vii, 38, 73, 83, 108, 148, 157, 160, 169, 170-72, 175
Song of Songs Rabbah, 156
Sotah, 41, 44
Spring of Youth, the, 133
St. George, 63
staff of Aaron, the, 178, 181
staff of Moses, the, 6-8, 61-4, 77, 78, 86-8, 91, 93, 96-100, 102, 103, 105, 113-16, 126-8, 178, 205, 219
Story of Sinuhe, 68
Styx (river), 209
Sublime Porte, the, 30
Succoth, 107, 111, 120, 123
Sudan (modern country), 195
Suez Canal, the, 120
Suez, Gulf of, 123, 124
Suez, Isthmus of, 37, 69, 76, 120
Sumeria, 22, 51, 229
Sumerians, 15, 51, 100, 197, 198, 203, 229
Surabadi, x, 4, 10, 21, 22, 30-32, 37-9, 41-9, 52-9, 61-5, 74, 77-9, 86, 88, 92, 93, 96, 98, 104-8, 110-13, 115-17, 122, 124, 126, 133, 135, 178-81, 183, 185-8, 202, 204, 205, 207-9, 212, 214-20, 223, 224
Susa, 32, 33
Syria, 15, 28, 29, 38, 39, 70, 78, 108, 110, 123, 130, 190, 199, 205, 206, 227, 229
Syrians, 34

T

Tabari, 4
Taberah, 148
Tabernacle, 7, 134, 145
Tabernacle, the, as the residence of God, 7

Table of Nations, the, 195
Tables of Law, the, 149, 163
Tables of the Law, the, 146, 149-51, 165, 171, 219
Tablets. *See* Tablets of the Law
Tablets of the Law, 5, 7
Tacitus, 37, 38
Talmud, the, 41, 44, 48, 56, 115, 149, 167, 179, 182, 185, 195, 208, 222, 224, 225, 227-9
Tanhuma, 91, 97
Tanis, 16, 27, 107, 111
Targum Yerushalmi, 114, 195
Tarikh-i Bal'ami, 4
Tehran University, x
Tell Defneh, 120
Tell el-Mashkatah, 120
Temple (Jerusalem), the, ix, 7, 8, 36, 73, 148, 158, 160, 161, 165, 170, 171, 181, 185, 216, 229
Ten Commandments, the, 103, 137, 139, 144-6, 149, 153
Ten Commandments, the (common version), 145
ten plagues as battles between YHWH and the Egyptian gods, 99
Tennyson, Alfred Lord, 188
teraphim, 159
Tharbis, 193
the staff of Aaron, the, 178
Thebes, 27, 28, 36
Thera, volcanic eruption of, 121
Thermuthis, 48, 49, 192
Thetis, 209
Thiele, E.R., x
Thutmose III, 11
Tigris (river), 228, 229
Timsah (lake), 120
Tisisthene, 19
Tohorot, 185
Toombs, Lawrence E., 102
Torah, the, 1, 9, 10, 19, 148, 149, 166, 167, 172, 210, 228
Tower of Babel, ix, 24, 25, 26
Traditions (Islamic), 3, 196, 229
Turkey, 30, 119
Turks, the, 15, 120
Tuwa, valley of, 78
Tuwa, wilderness of, 78
Tyre, 79

U

Ugartic mythology, 63
Ulysses, 188
Umayyads, 4
Universal History (Tabari), 4
Unuq ('Unuq). *See* Anak
Ur, 196
Utah, 121
Utnapishtim, the Mesopotamian Noah, 133, 197, 199, 203

V

Vashti, 32-4

W

Wa Yosha', 114, 116
Wadi Musa (Valley of Moses), 68, 124
Wadi Tumilat, 120
Wady Hesa, 68
Walid bin Rayyan. *See* Rayyan bin Walid
Wall of the Ruler, the, 69
Wandering, the, 126, 129, 130, 147, 160, 174
Watts, Alan W., 11
Way of the Land of the Philistines, 123
Weber, Max, 14, 15
Wensinck, A.J., 202
Western Sea, the. *See* Mediterranean (sea)
white hand of Moses, the, 6, 89, 93, 99, 102, 103, 173
White House, the, 30
White Nile (river), 194
wife of Balaam, the, 209
Wilderness of Tih, the, 124
Wilderness, the, 7, 122

X

Xerxes, 32-4

Y

Yahweh, viii, 2, 3, 6-8, 10, 11, 14, 19, 20, 26, 64, 70-74, 77, 80-85, 87, 89, 94, 97, 99, 100, 106-8, 112, 137,

142, 151, 160, 161, 163, 169, 170, 171, 175, 181, 197, 216, 218, 229
Yahweh (YHWH), meaning discussed, 81
Yahwist Document (J), viii, 5, 10, 13, 24, 40, 41, 47, 57, 65, 67, 70-72, 74, 75, 79, 80-83, 87, 89, 95, 99, 101, 102, 104, 106-8, 112, 113, 119, 120, 123, 127, 128, 136, 138-42, 144-7, 165, 175, 197, 210, 212, 213, 222, 225, 229
Yalkut, 87
Yanbu', 37
Yanoam, 12
Yemen, 15
YHWH, pronunciation and meaning of, 80
Yinoam. *See* Yanoam
Youngblood, Robert, 145
Yusuf Ali, A., x, 54, 98, 99, 130, 154, 174

Z

Zadok, 73, 74
Zadokites, 73, 74, 156, 161, 181
Zagzagel (angel), 224
Zaphenath-paneah. *See* Joseph
Zebulon, Israelite tribe, 109
Zeus-Jupiter, 140
ziggurats, 25
Zin, wilderness of, 220
Zipporah, 6, 10, 60, 62-4, 78, 182, 196
Zoar, 222
Zohar, 110